FIRE FORCE

09

ATSUSHI OHKUBO

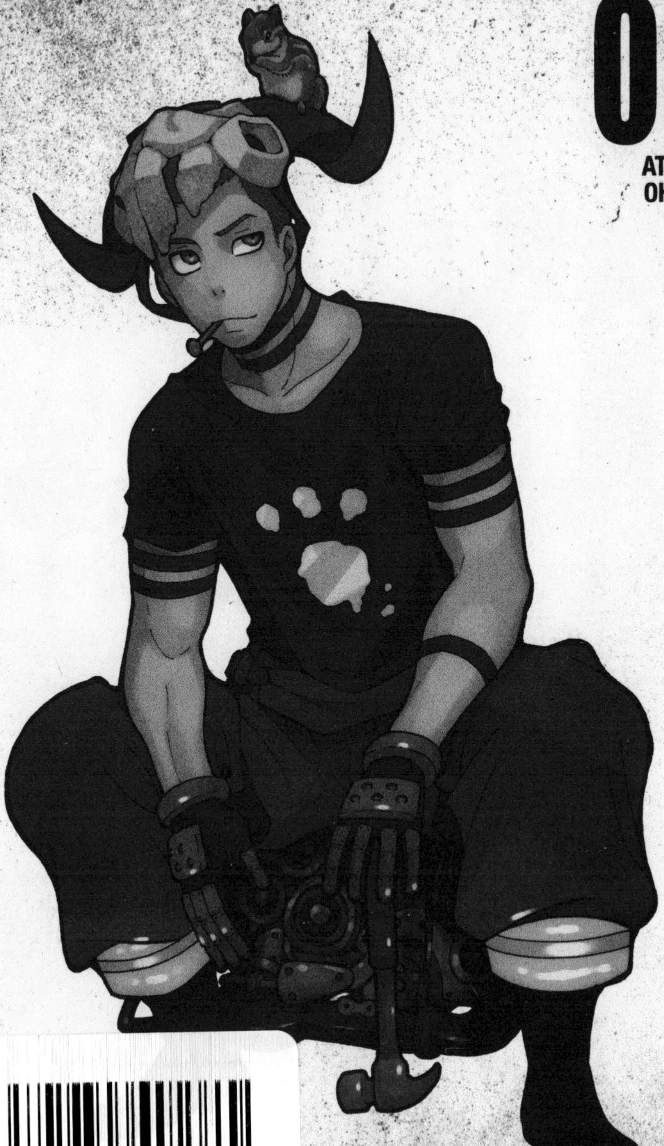

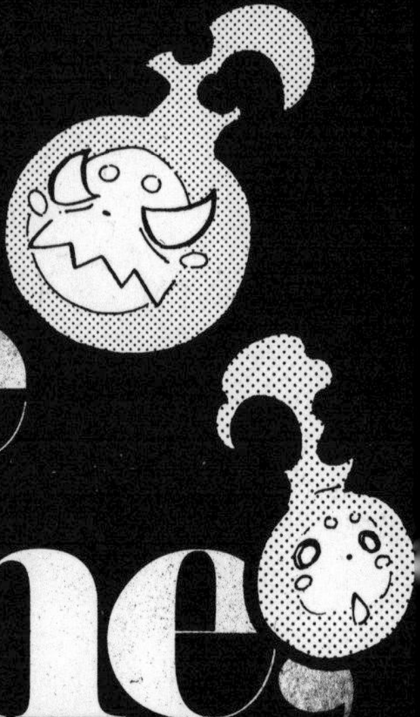

of the flame, the light.

VOL.9

ATSUSHI OHKUBO

Into the heart unholy seeking

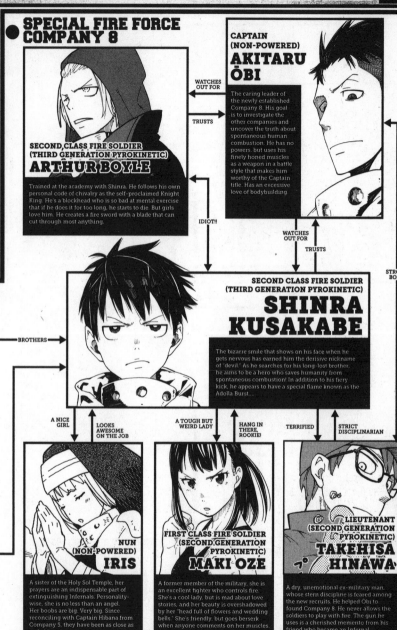

SPECIAL FIRE FORCE COMPANY 8

SECOND CLASS FIRE SOLDIER (THIRD GENERATION PYROKINETIC)

ARTHUR BOYLE

Trained at the academy with Shinra. He follows his own personal code of chivalry as the self-proclaimed Knight King. He's a blockhead who is so bad at mental exercise that if he does it for too long, he starts to die. But girls love him. He creates a fire sword with a blade that can cut through most anything.

WATCHES OUT FOR

TRUSTS

CAPTAIN (NON-POWERED)

AKITARU ŌBI

The caring leader of the newly established Company 8. His goal is to investigate the other companies and uncover the truth about spontaneous human combustion. He has no powers, but uses his finely honed muscles as a weapon in a battle style that makes him worthy of the Captain title. Has an excessive love of bodybuilding.

IDIOT!!

WATCHES OUT FOR

TRUSTS

STRONG BOND

SECOND CLASS FIRE SOLDIER (THIRD GENERATION PYROKINETIC)

SHINRA KUSAKABE

The bizarre smile that shows on his face when he gets nervous has earned him the derisive nickname of "devil." As he searches for his long-lost brother, he aims to be a hero who saves humanity from spontaneous combustion! In addition to his fiery kick, he appears to have a special flame known as the Adolla Burst....

BROTHERS

A NICE GIRL

LOOKS AWESOME ON THE JOB

A TOUGH BUT WEIRD LADY

HANG IN THERE, ROOKIE!

TERRIFIED

STRICT DISCIPLINARIAN

NUN (NON-POWERED)

IRIS

A sister of the Holy Sol Temple, her prayers are an indispensable part of extinguishing Infernals. Personality-wise, she is no less than an angel. Her boobs are big. Very big. Since reconciling with Captain Hibana from Company 5, they have been as close as real sisters.

FIRST CLASS FIRE SOLDIER (SECOND GENERATION PYROKINETIC)

MAKI OZE

A former member of the military, she is an excellent fighter who controls fire. She's a cool lady, but is mad about love stories, and her beauty is overshadowed by her "head full of flowers and wedding bells." She's friendly, but goes berserk when anyone comments on her muscles. Apparently she used to be slender.

LIEUTENANT (SECOND GENERATION PYROKINETIC)

TAKEHISA HINAWA

A dry, unemotional ex-military man, whose stern discipline is feared among the new recruits. He helped Obi to found Company 8. He never allows the soldiers to play with fire. The gun he uses is a cherished memento from his friend who became an Infernal.

THE GIRLS' CLUB

RESPECTS

FOLLOWERS OF THE EVANGELIST

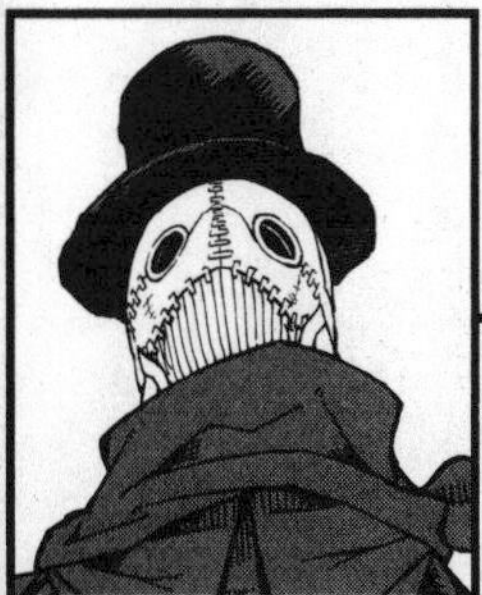

CAPTAIN OF SPECIAL FIRE FORCE COMPANY 3 (SECOND GENERATION PYROKINETIC?)

DR. GIOVANNI

A traitor who started working for the Evangelist despite being a captain in the Special Fire Force. He fights by using fire to control mechanical limbs. It is his policy to knock on a stone bridge multiple times before crossing it.

SUB-ORDINATE

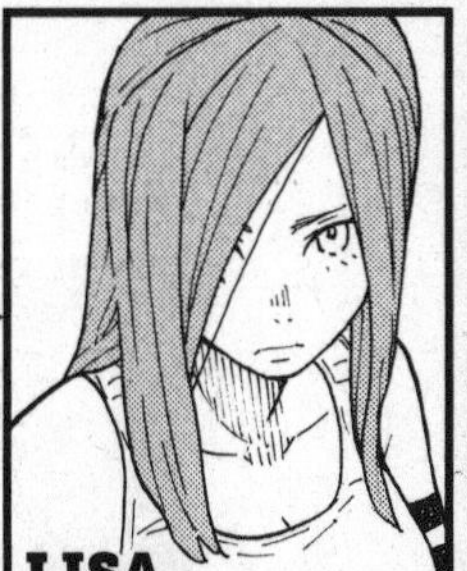

LISA

(THIRD GENERATION PYROKINETIC)

Had been living in Vulcan's home after he took her in, but was actually a spy sent by Dr. Giovanni. Controls tentacles of flame.

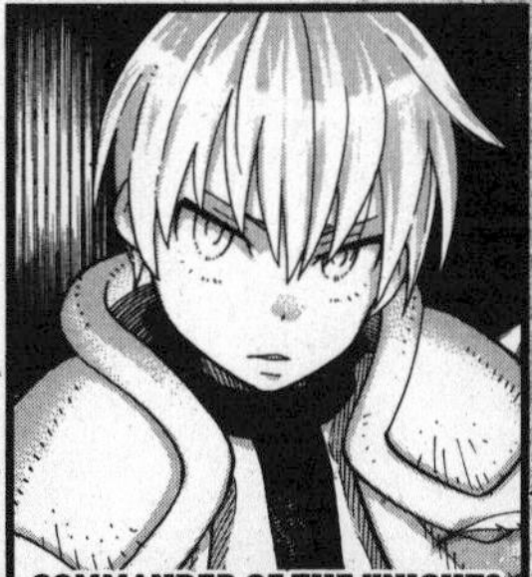

COMMANDER OF THE KNIGHTS OF THE ASHEN FLAME

SHŌ KUSAKABE

Shinra's long-lost brother, the commander of an order of knights that works for the Evangelist. His powers are still shrouded in mystery, but anyway, he's ridiculously strong!!

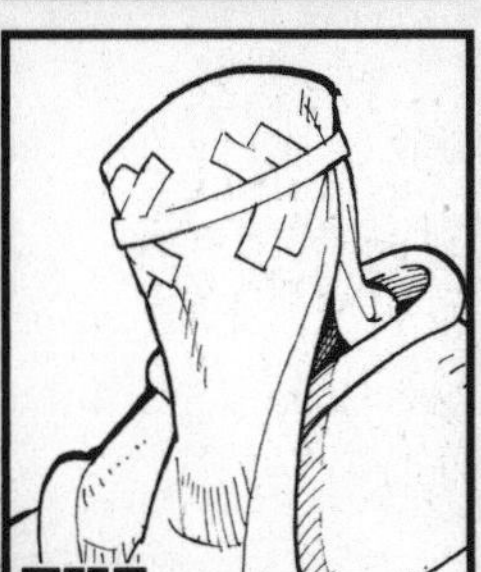

THE WHITE-CLAD

An esoteric group possessing fighting skills equal to or better than those of the Special Fire Force. They can be identified by the white clothing they wear over their entire bodies.

WE'RE FAMILY!

YOU GULLIBLE BLEEDING HEART!

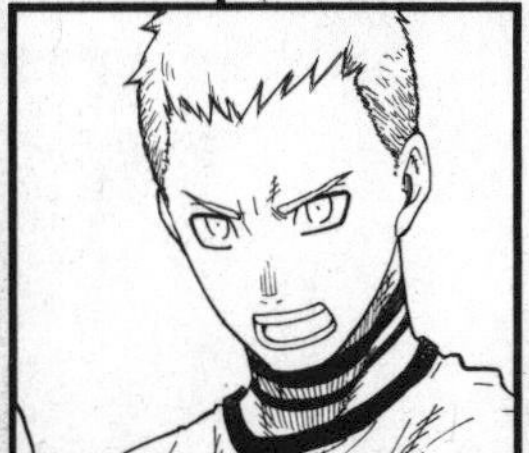

ENGINEER

VULCAN

The greatest engineer of the day, renowned as the God of Fire and the Forge. He originally hated the Fire Force, but he sympathized with Obi's and Shinra's ideals and agreed to join Company 8 as their engineer. His dream is to revive the world's extinct animals!

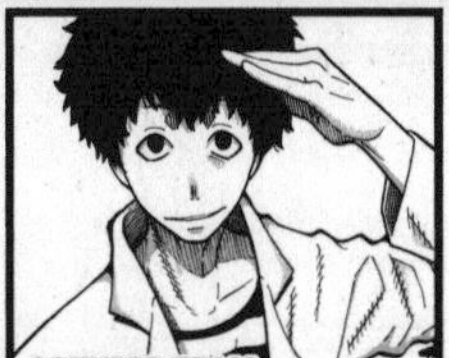

SCIENCE TEAM

VIKTOR LICHT

A morally ambiguous man deployed from Haijima Industries to fill the vacancy in Company 8's science department. Apparently a genius.

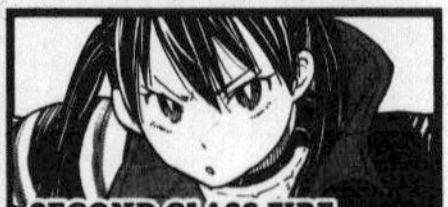

SECOND CLASS FIRE SOLDIER (THIRD GENERATION PYROKINETIC)

TAMAKI KOTATSU

Originally a rookie member of Company 1, she was caught up in the treasonous plot of her superior officer Hoshimiya, and is currently being disciplined under Company 8's watch. A tough girl with an unfortunate "lucky lecher lure" condition, she nevertheless has a pure heart.

HAS HIM ON HER MIND

SUMMARY...

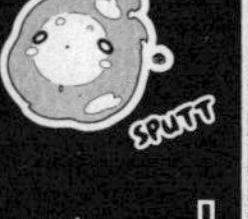
SPUTT
SPUTT

After deducing that the White-Clad are hiding out in the Nether, Company 8 and their new engineer Vulcan decide to launch an attack. However, the enemy uses their powers to separate the team, and each member of the company is forced to confront the White-Clad soldiers alone! Now, Ōbi and Vulcan find their path blocked by Dr. Giovanni and Lisa!!

FIRE FORCE 09
CONTENTS

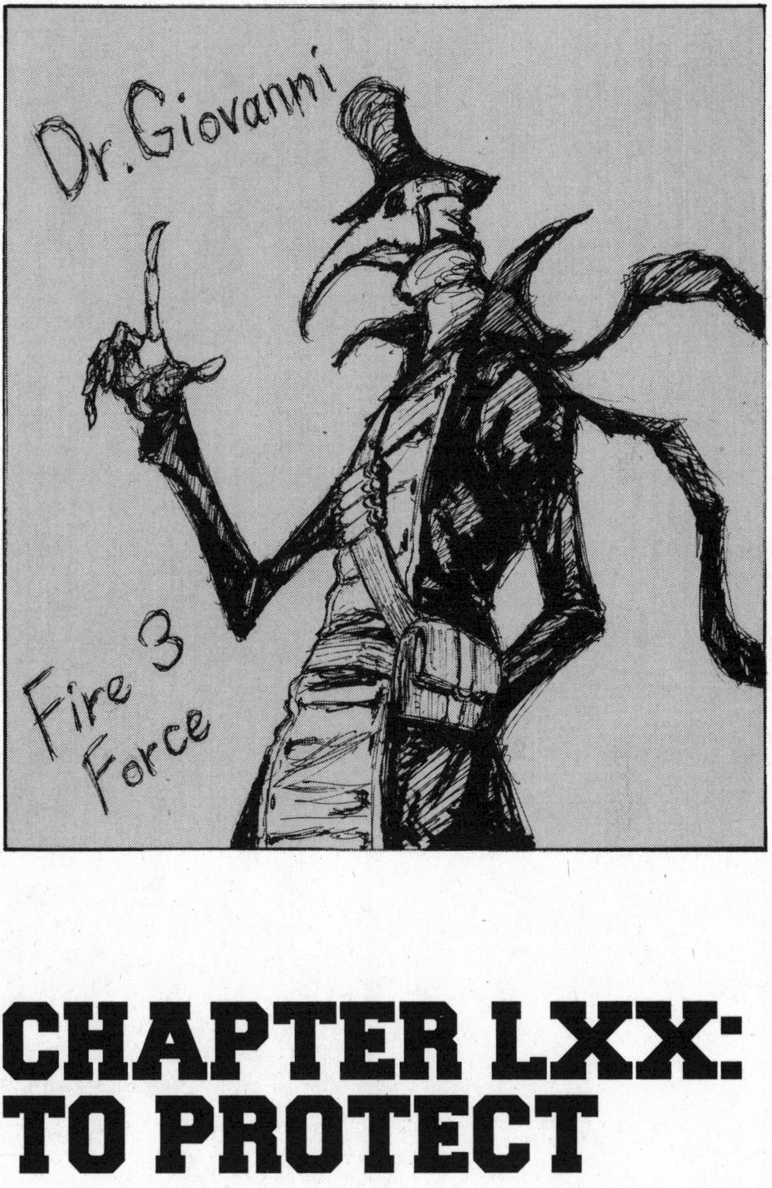
Dr. Giovanni
Fire Force 3

CHAPTER LXX: TO PROTECT

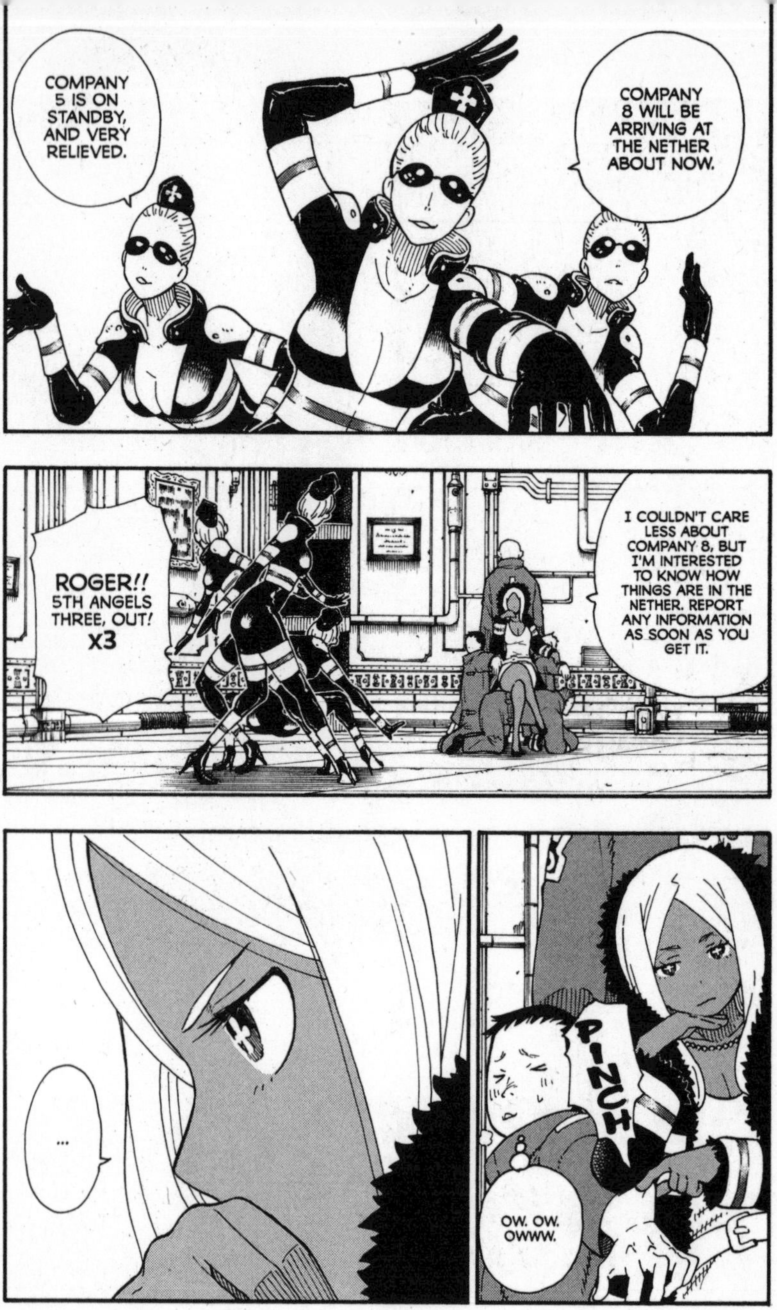
COMPANY 8 WILL BE ARRIVING AT THE NETHER ABOUT NOW.
COMPANY 5 IS ON STANDBY, AND VERY RELIEVED.
I COULDN'T CARE LESS ABOUT COMPANY 8, BUT I'M INTERESTED TO KNOW HOW THINGS ARE IN THE NETHER. REPORT ANY INFORMATION AS SOON AS YOU GET IT.
ROGER!! 5TH ANGELS THREE, OUT! x3
PINCH
OW. OW. OWWW.
...

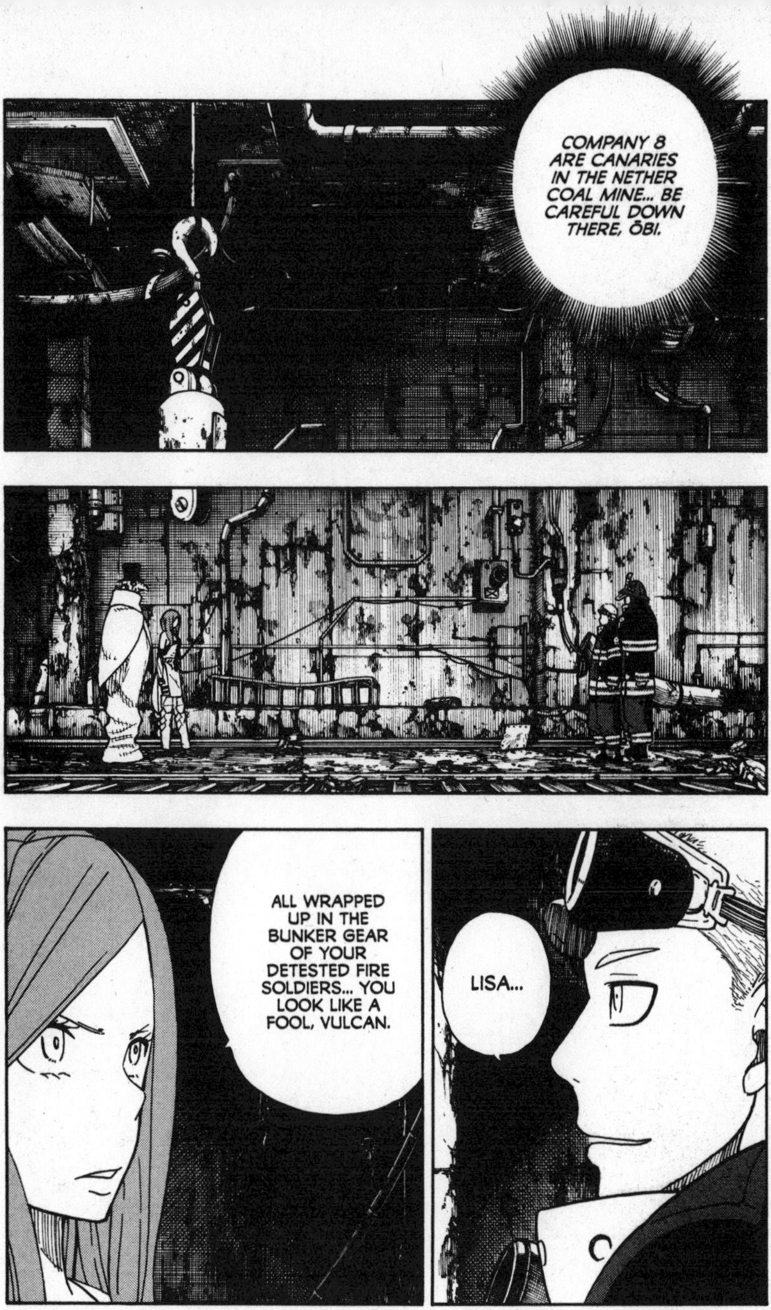
COMPANY 8 ARE CANARIES IN THE NETHER COAL MINE... BE CAREFUL DOWN THERE, ŌBI.
LISA...
ALL WRAPPED UP IN THE BUNKER GEAR OF YOUR DETESTED FIRE SOLDIERS... YOU LOOK LIKE A FOOL, VULCAN.

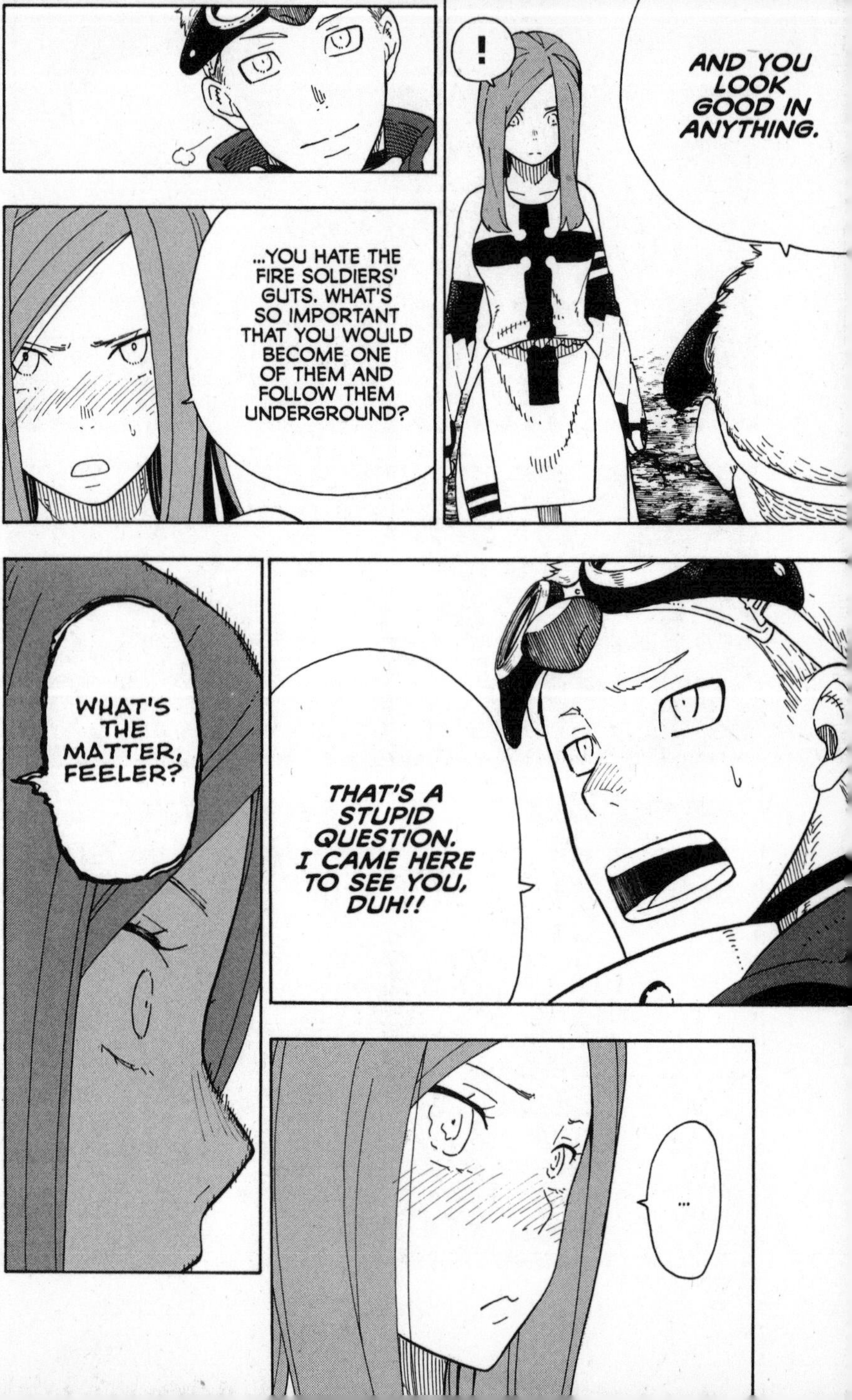
AND YOU LOOK GOOD IN ANYTHING.
!
...YOU HATE THE FIRE SOLDIERS' GUTS. WHAT'S SO IMPORTANT THAT YOU WOULD BECOME ONE OF THEM AND FOLLOW THEM UNDERGROUND?
THAT'S A STUPID QUESTION. I CAME HERE TO SEE YOU, DUH!!
...
WHAT'S THE MATTER, FEELER?

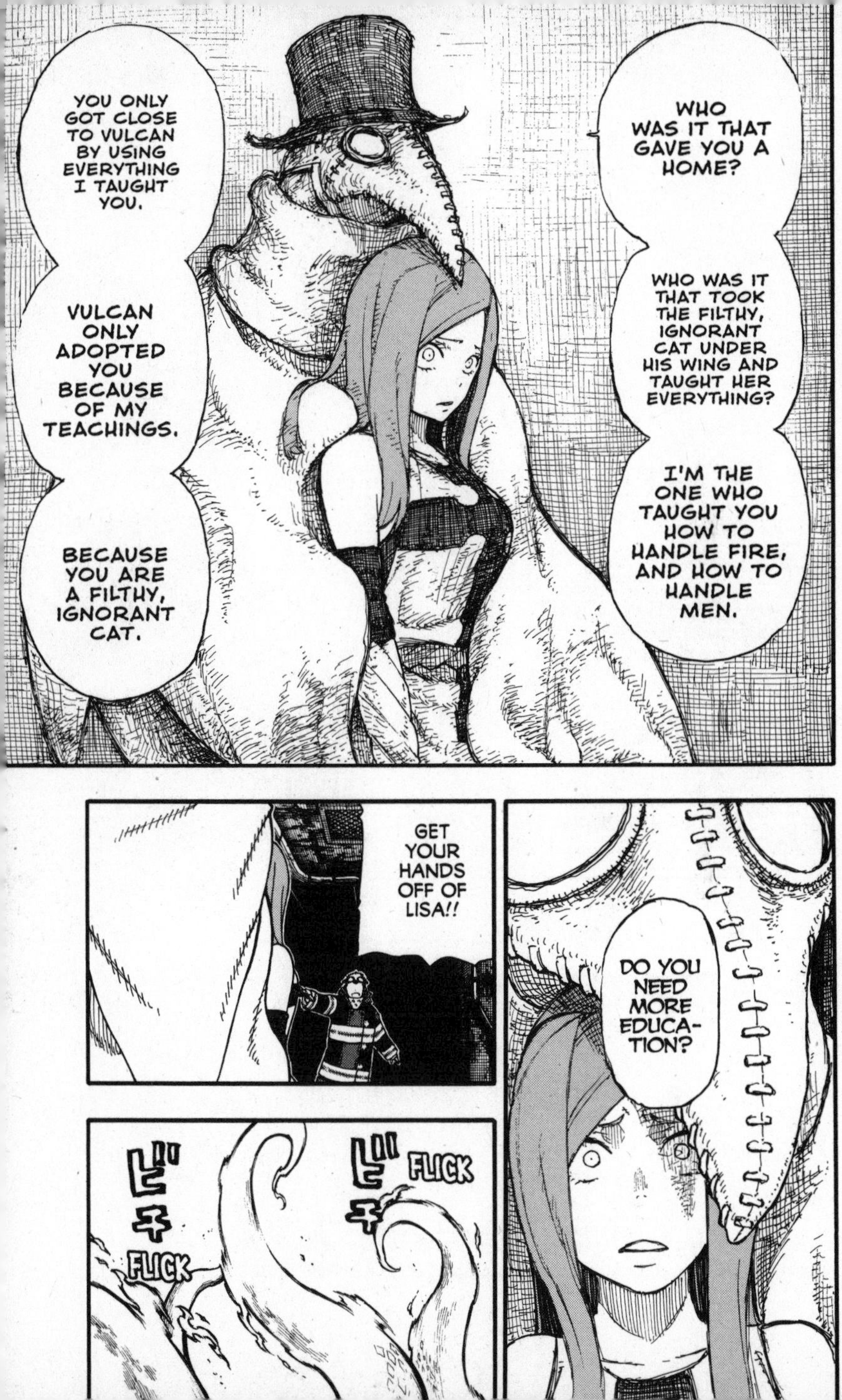
WHO WAS IT THAT GAVE YOU A HOME?
WHO WAS IT THAT TOOK THE FILTHY, IGNORANT CAT UNDER HIS WING AND TAUGHT HER EVERYTHING?
I'M THE ONE WHO TAUGHT YOU HOW TO HANDLE FIRE, AND HOW TO HANDLE MEN.
YOU ONLY GOT CLOSE TO VULCAN BY USING EVERYTHING I TAUGHT YOU.
VULCAN ONLY ADOPTED YOU BECAUSE OF MY TEACHINGS.
BECAUSE YOU ARE A FILTHY, IGNORANT CAT.
DO YOU NEED MORE EDUCATION?
GET YOUR HANDS OFF OF LISA!!
FLICK
FLICK

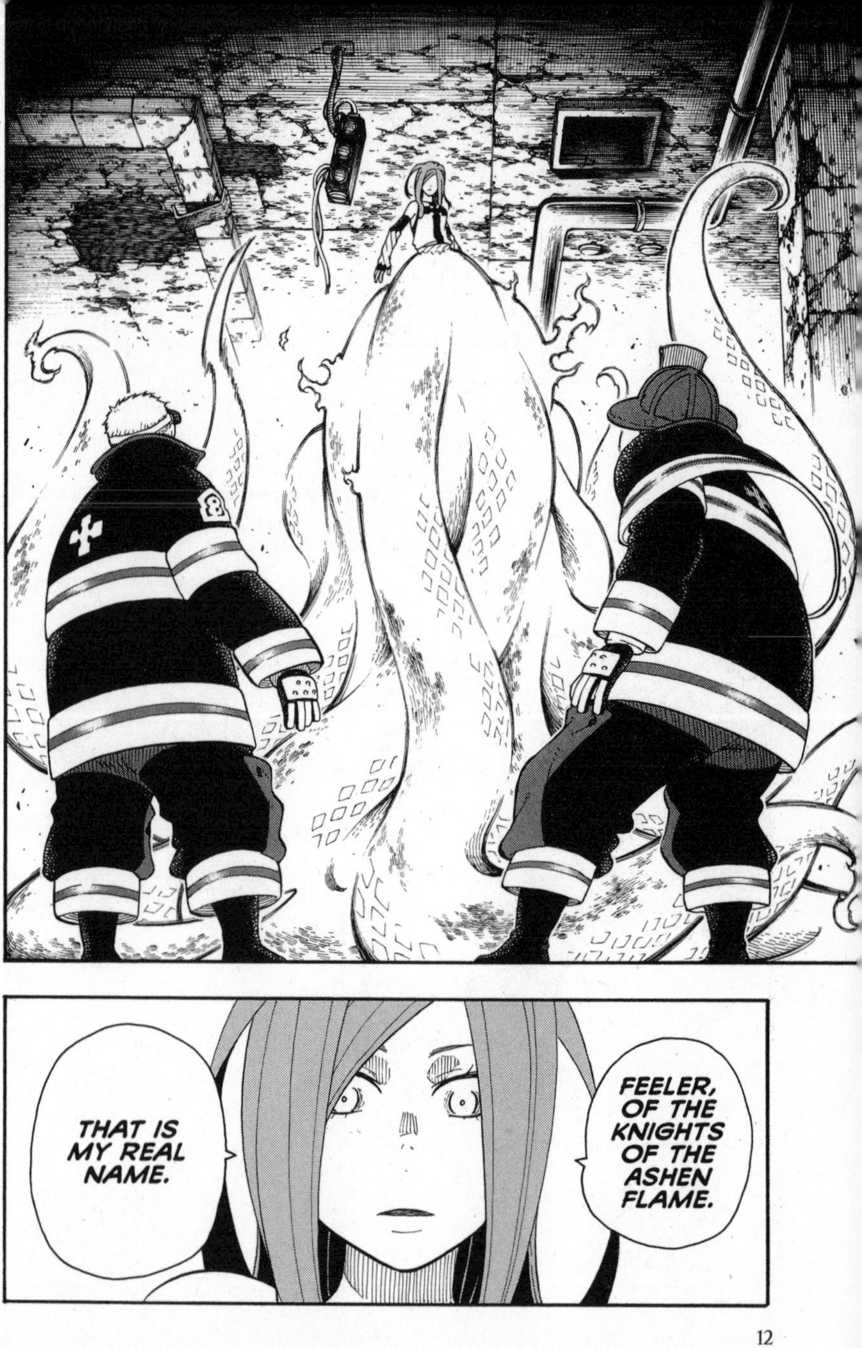
FEELER, OF THE KNIGHTS OF THE ASHEN FLAME.
THAT IS MY REAL NAME.

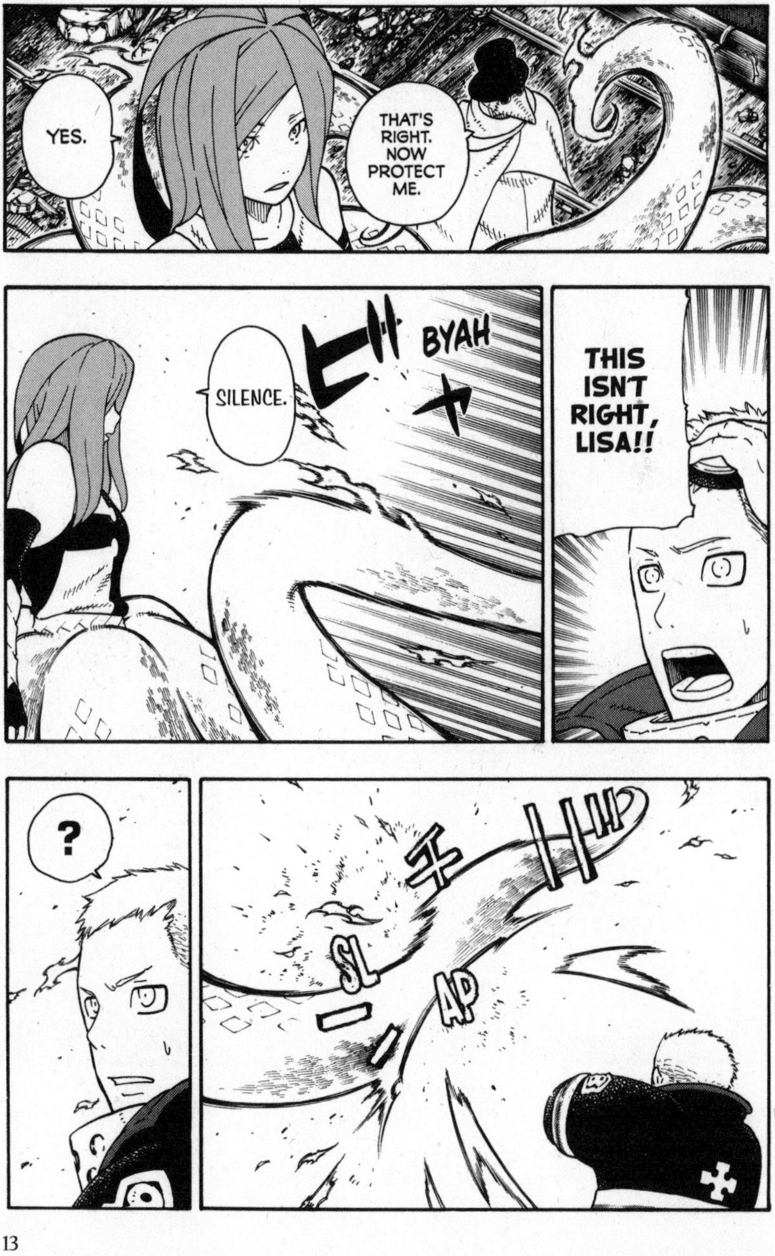
THAT'S RIGHT. NOW PROTECT ME.
YES.
THIS ISN'T RIGHT, LISA!!
BYAH
SILENCE.
SLAP
?

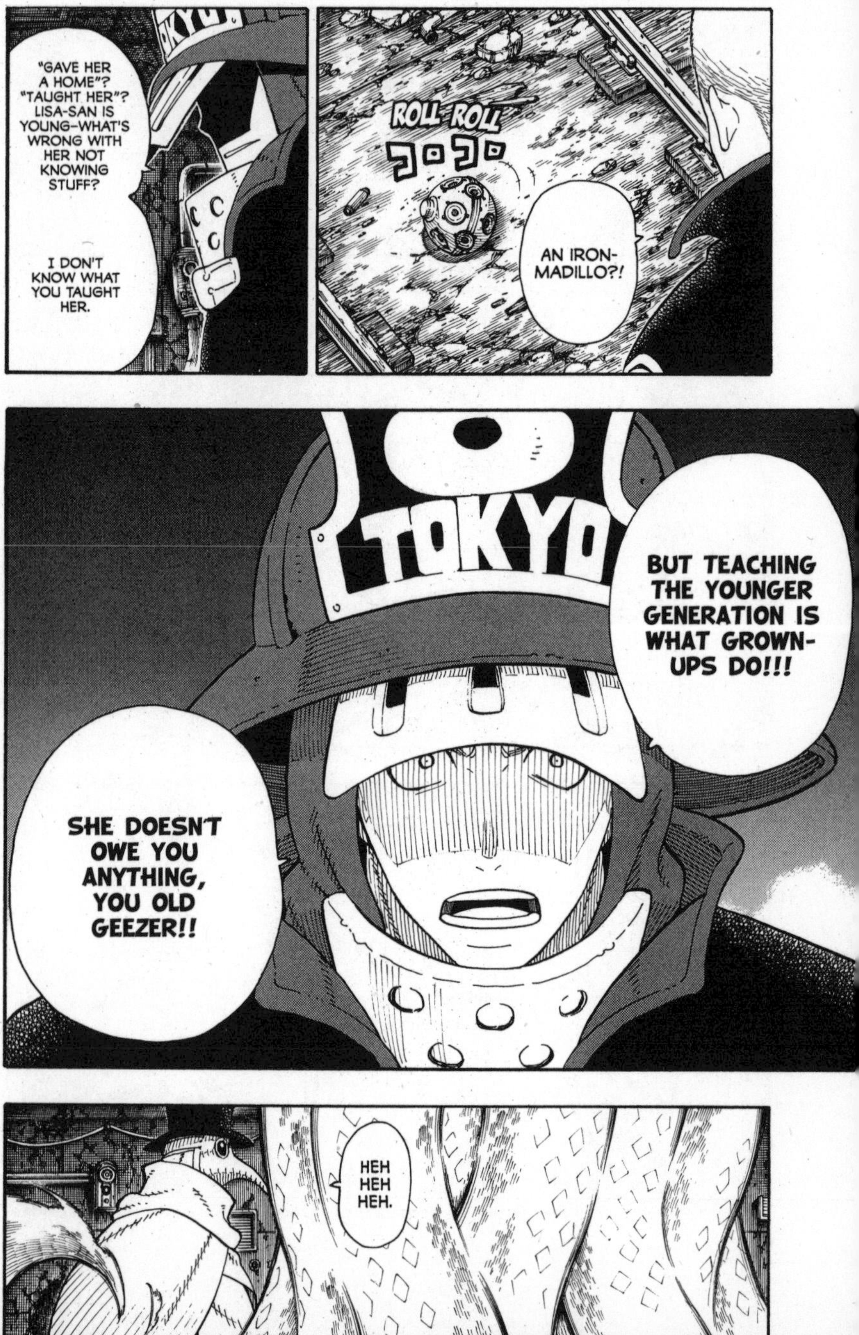
ROLL ROLL
コロコロ
AN IRON-MADILLO?!
"GAVE HER A HOME"? "TAUGHT HER"? LISA-SAN IS YOUNG–WHAT'S WRONG WITH HER NOT KNOWING STUFF?
I DON'T KNOW WHAT YOU TAUGHT HER.
TOKYO
BUT TEACHING THE YOUNGER GENERATION IS WHAT GROWN-UPS DO!!!
SHE DOESN'T OWE YOU ANYTHING, YOU OLD GEEZER!!
HEH HEH HEH.

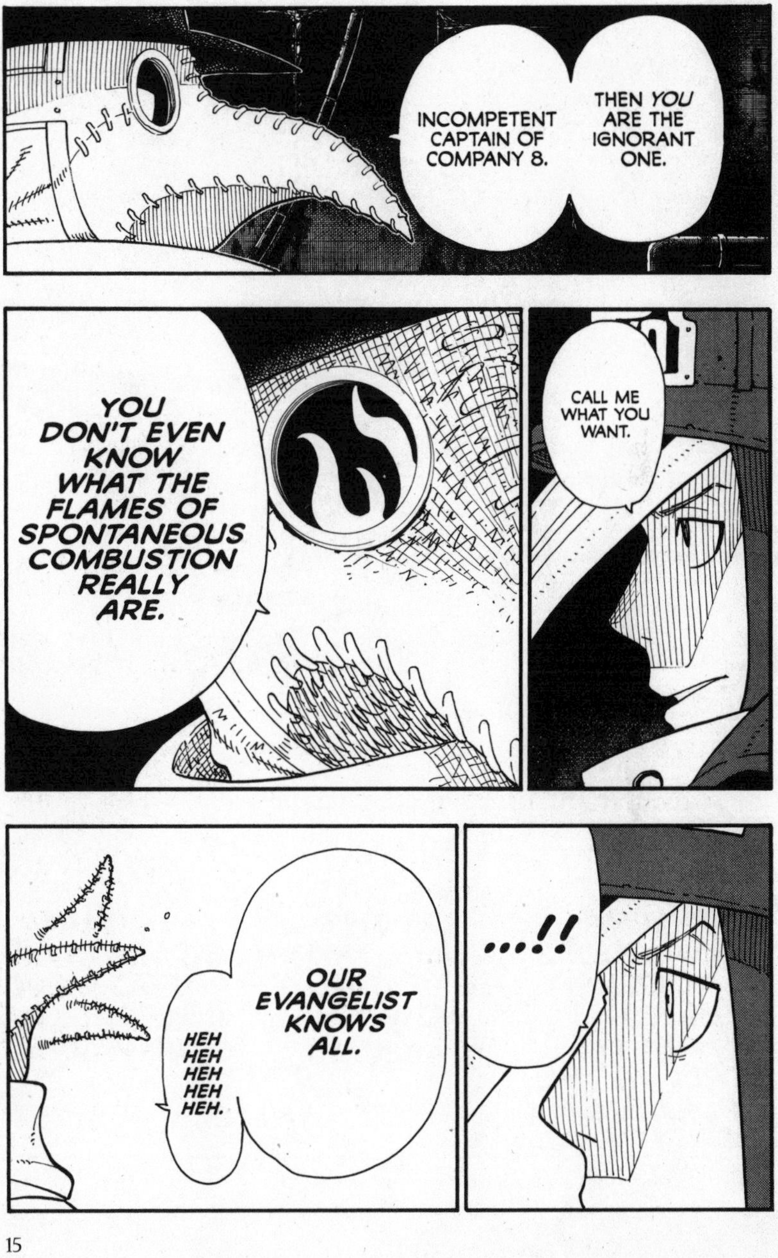
THEN *YOU* ARE THE IGNORANT ONE.
INCOMPETENT CAPTAIN OF COMPANY 8.
CALL ME WHAT YOU WANT.
YOU DON'T EVEN KNOW WHAT THE FLAMES OF SPONTANEOUS COMBUSTION REALLY ARE.
...!!
OUR EVANGELIST KNOWS ALL.
HEH HEH HEH HEH HEH.

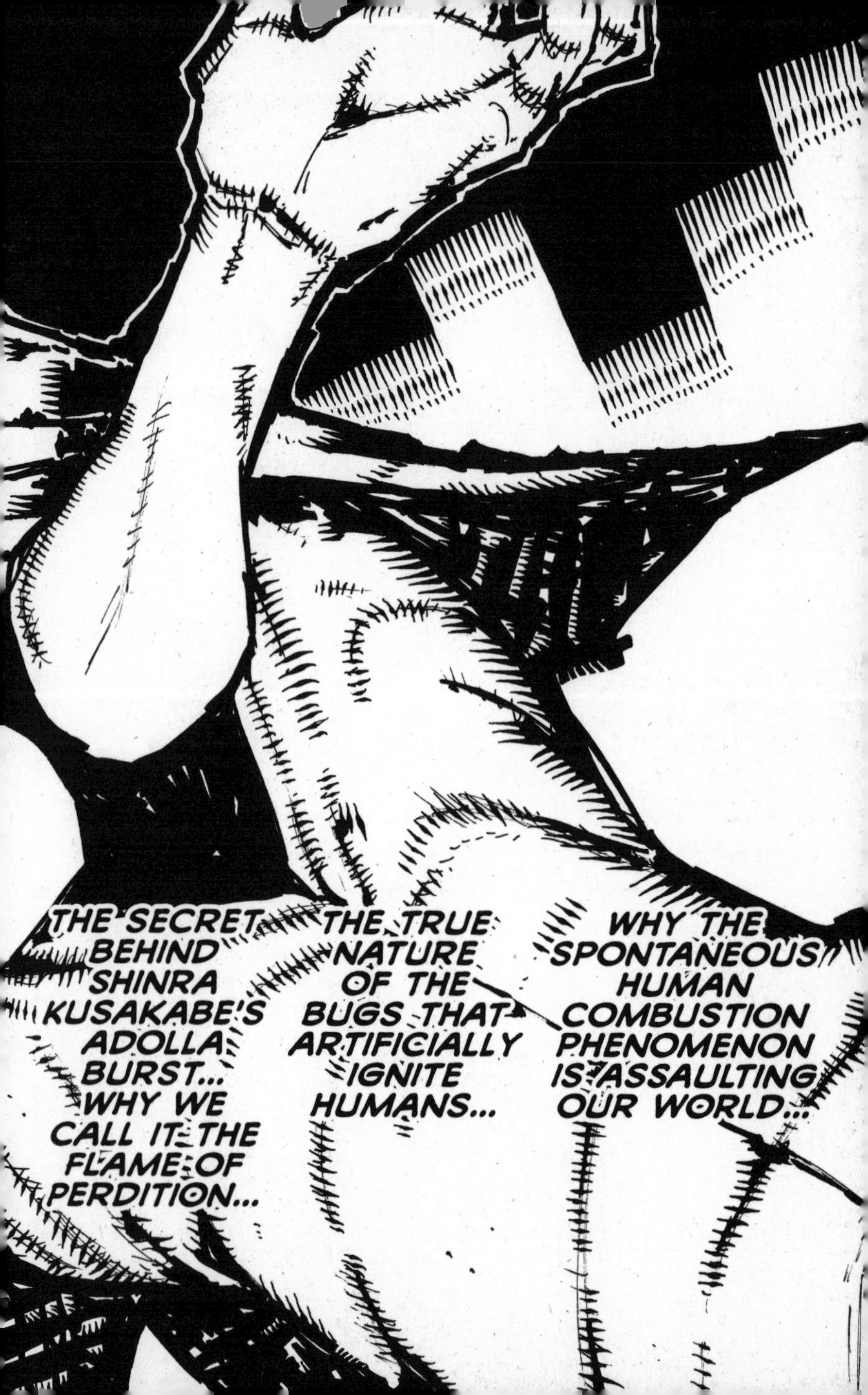
WHY THE SPONTANEOUS HUMAN COMBUSTION PHENOMENON IS ASSAULTING OUR WORLD...
THE TRUE NATURE OF THE BUGS THAT ARTIFICIALLY IGNITE HUMANS...
THE SECRET BEHIND SHINRA KUSAKABE'S ADOLLA BURST... WHY WE CALL IT THE FLAME OF PERDITION...

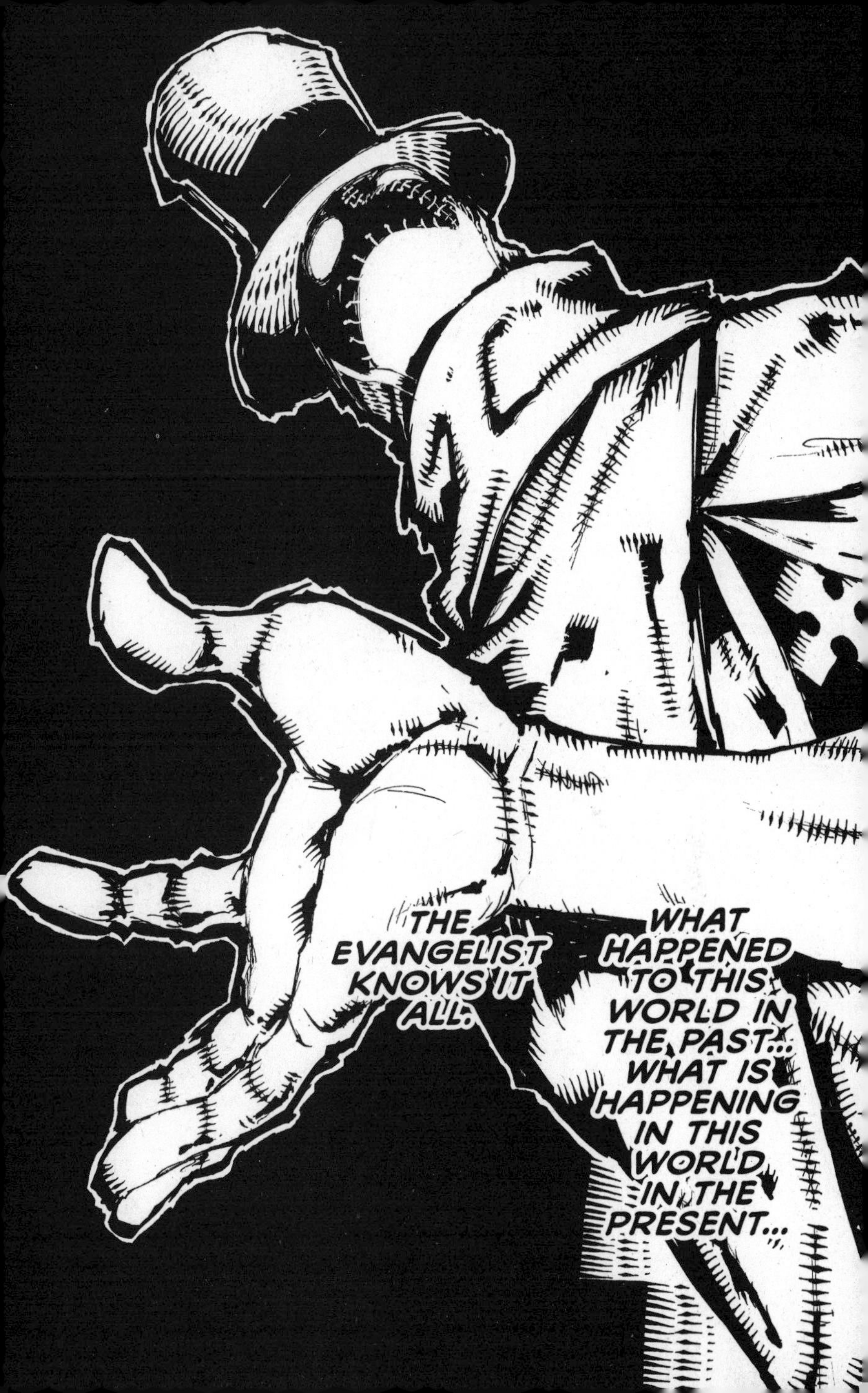
WHAT HAPPENED TO THIS WORLD IN THE PAST... WHAT IS HAPPENING IN THIS WORLD IN THE PRESENT...
THE EVANGELIST KNOWS IT ALL.

CLANK

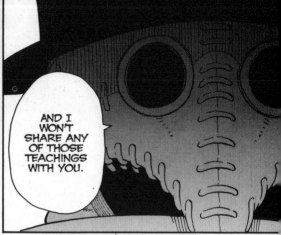

AND I WON'T SHARE ANY OF THOSE TEACHINGS WITH YOU.

WOW. TURNS OUT YOU ACTUALLY *ARE* A BAD TEACHER.

HEH HEH HEH. YOU ARE AN INTERESTING MAN.

STAY AWAY FROM US!!

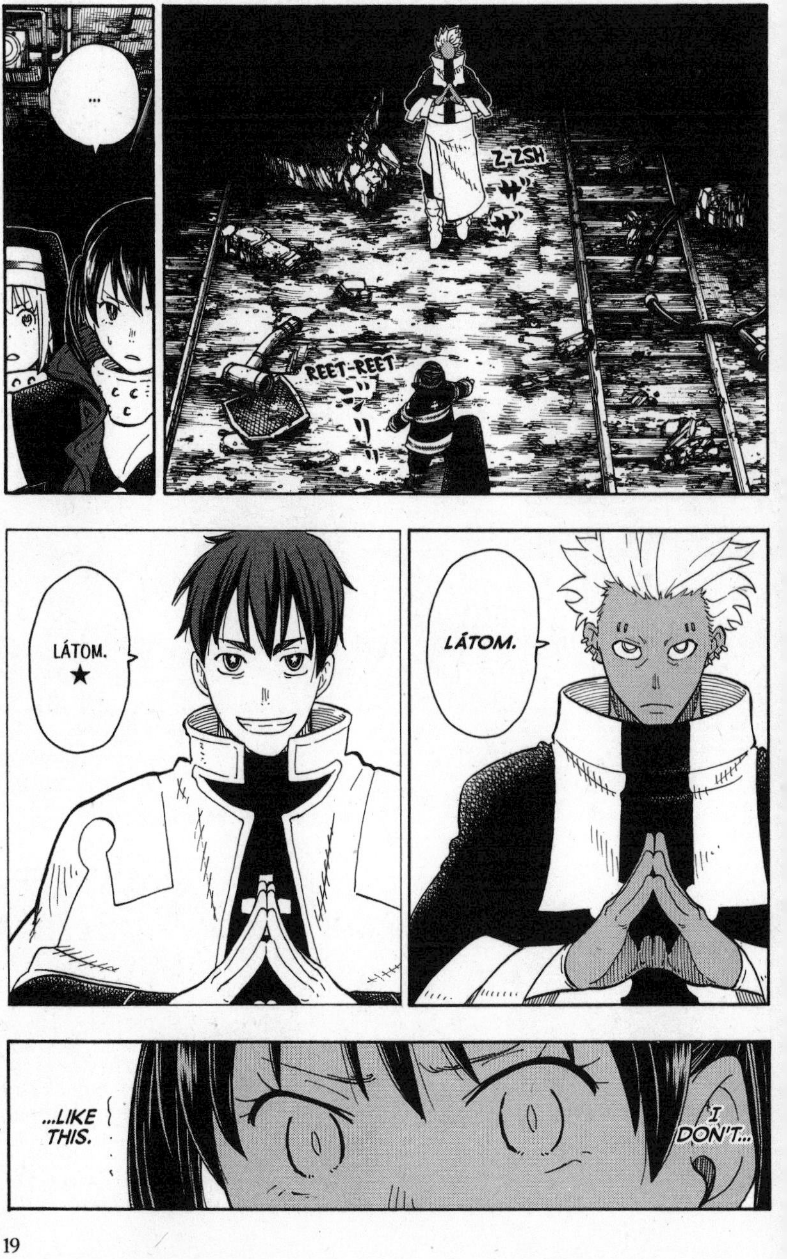
Z-ZSH
REET-REET
...
LÁTOM.
LÁTOM. ★
I DON'T...
...LIKE THIS.

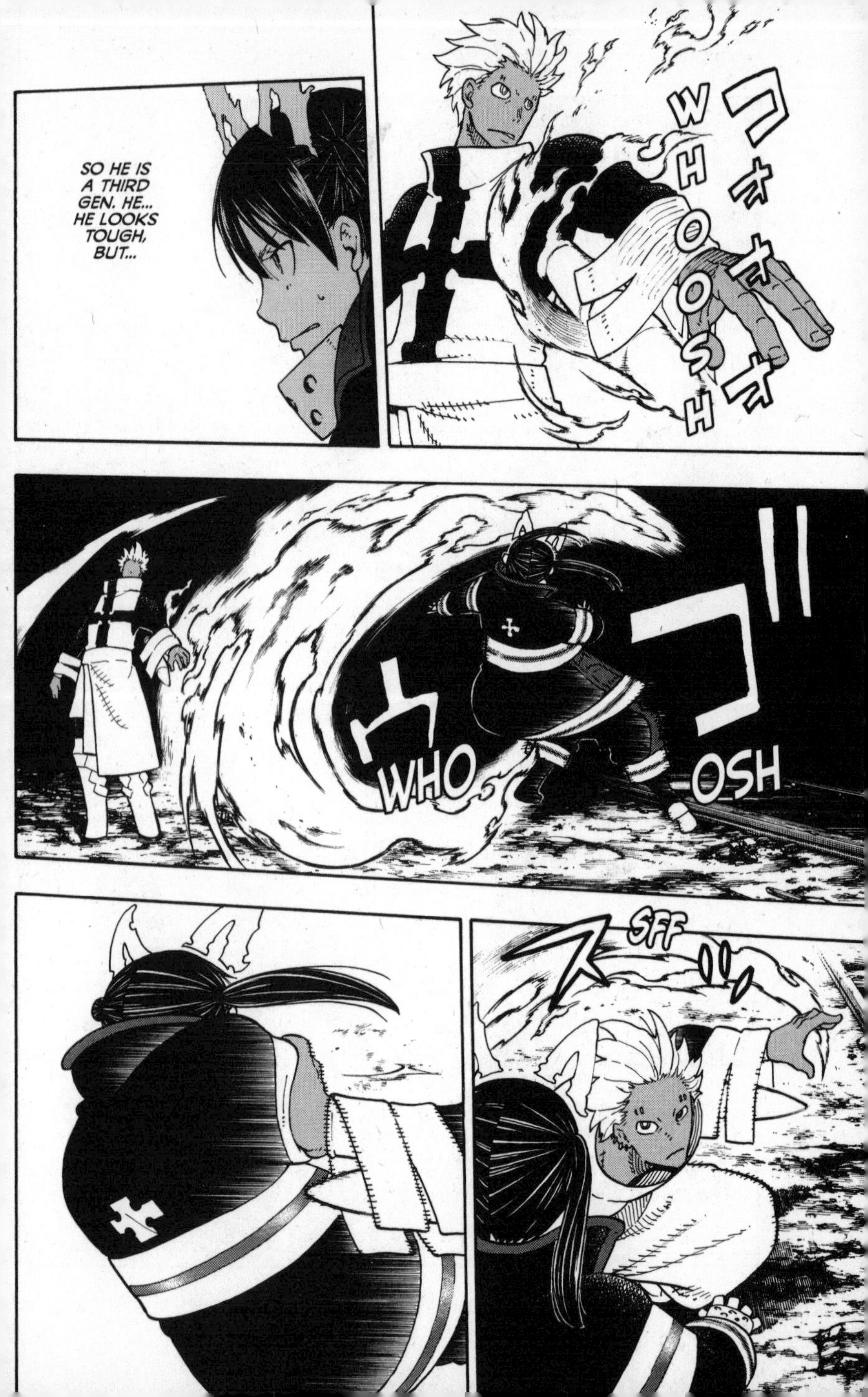
WHOOSH
SO HE IS A THIRD GEN. HE... HE LOOKS TOUGH, BUT...
WHOOSH
SFF

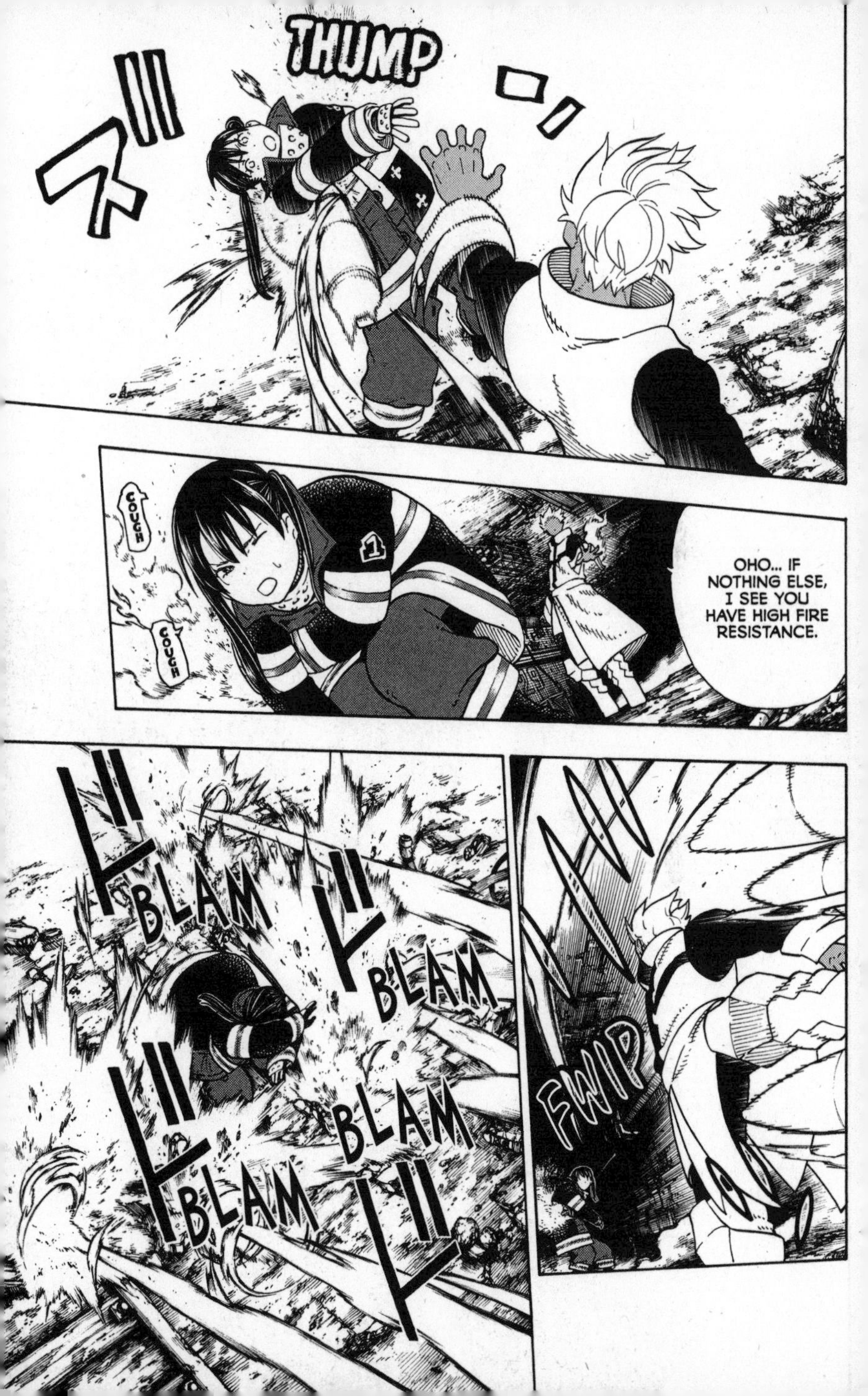
THUMP
OHO... IF NOTHING ELSE, I SEE YOU HAVE HIGH FIRE RESISTANCE.
COUGH
COUGH
FWIP
BLAM
BLAM
BLAM
BLAM

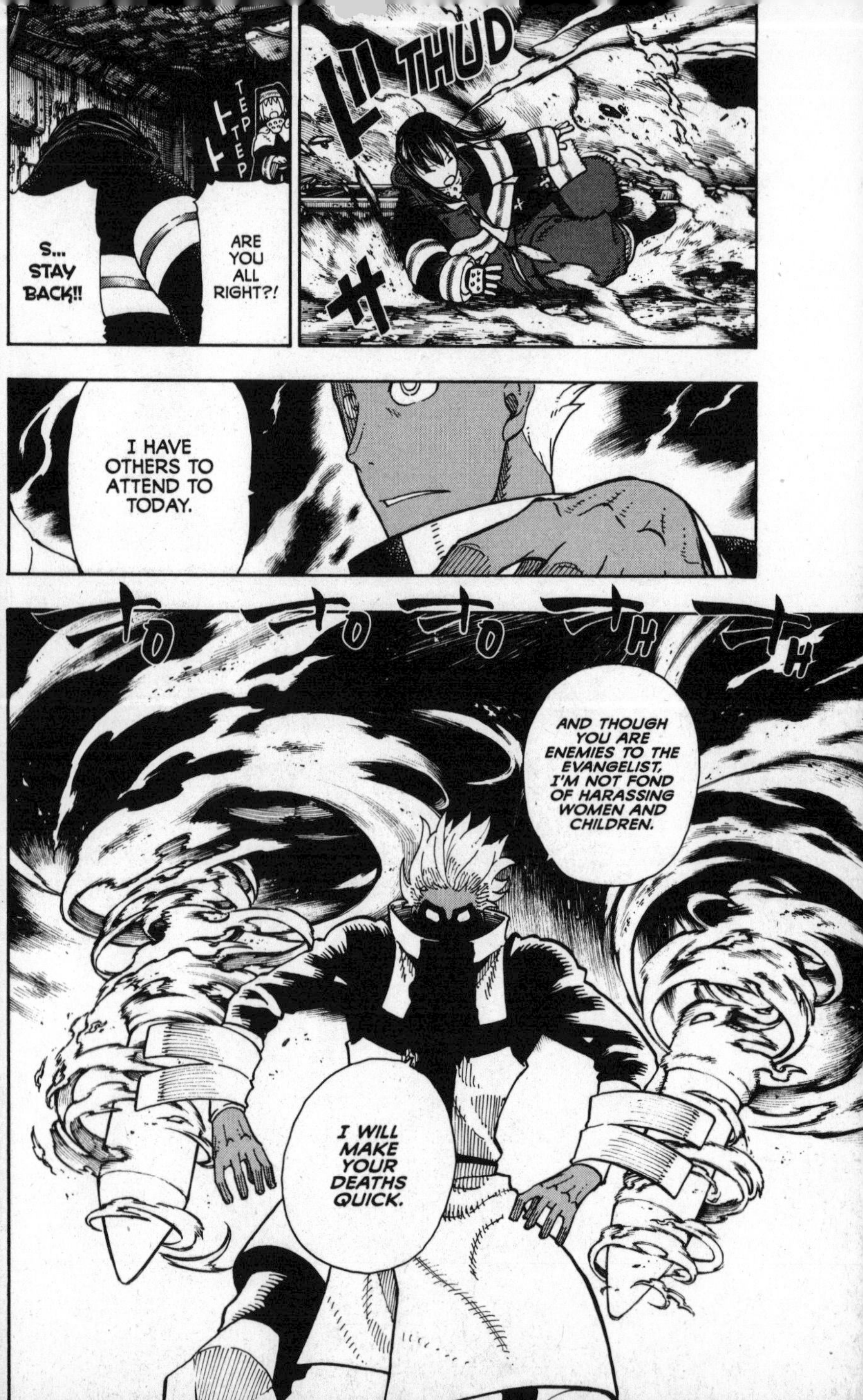
THUD
TEP TEP
ARE YOU ALL RIGHT?!
S... STAY BACK!!
I HAVE OTHERS TO ATTEND TO TODAY.
AND THOUGH YOU ARE ENEMIES TO THE EVANGELIST, I'M NOT FOND OF HARASSING WOMEN AND CHILDREN.
I WILL MAKE YOUR DEATHS QUICK.

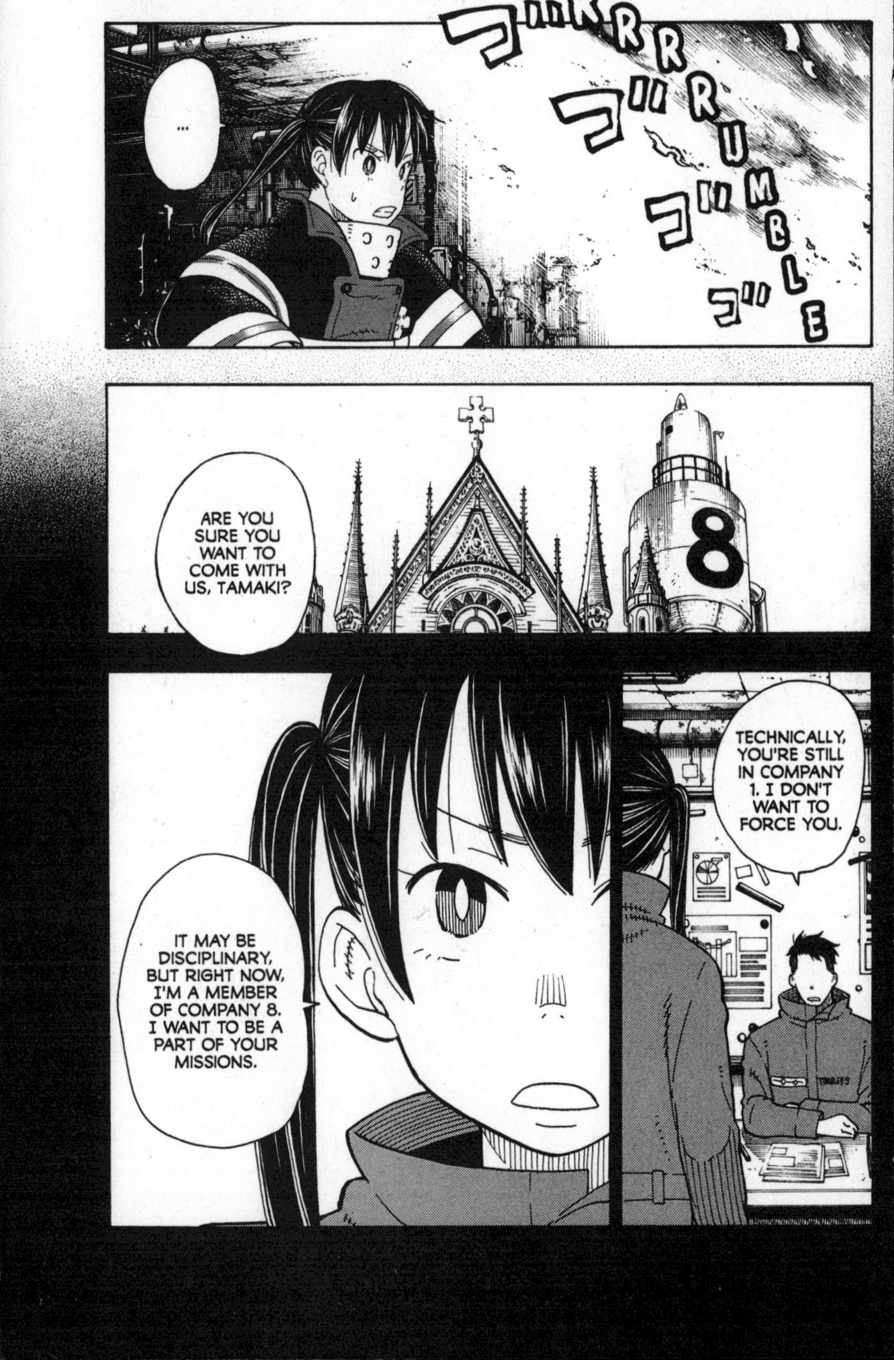
RRRRUMBLE
...
ARE YOU SURE YOU WANT TO COME WITH US, TAMAKI?
TECHNICALLY, YOU'RE STILL IN COMPANY 1. I DON'T WANT TO FORCE YOU.
IT MAY BE DISCIPLINARY, BUT RIGHT NOW, I'M A MEMBER OF COMPANY 8. I WANT TO BE A PART OF YOUR MISSIONS.

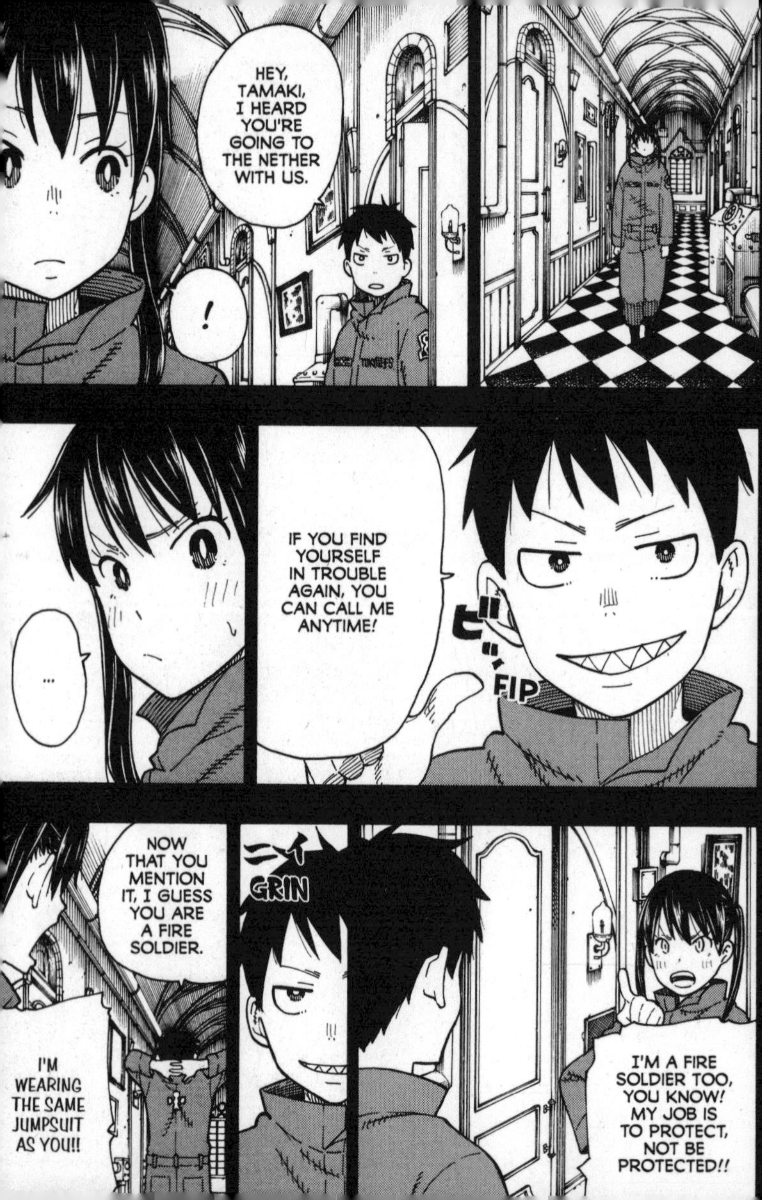

HEY, TAMAKI, I HEARD YOU'RE GOING TO THE NETHER WITH US.
!
IF YOU FIND YOURSELF IN TROUBLE AGAIN, YOU CAN CALL ME ANYTIME!
ピッ
FIP
...
I'M A FIRE SOLDIER TOO, YOU KNOW! MY JOB IS TO PROTECT, NOT BE PROTECTED!!
ニィ
GRIN
NOW THAT YOU MENTION IT, I GUESS YOU ARE A FIRE SOLDIER.
I'M WEARING THE SAME JUMPSUIT AS YOU!!

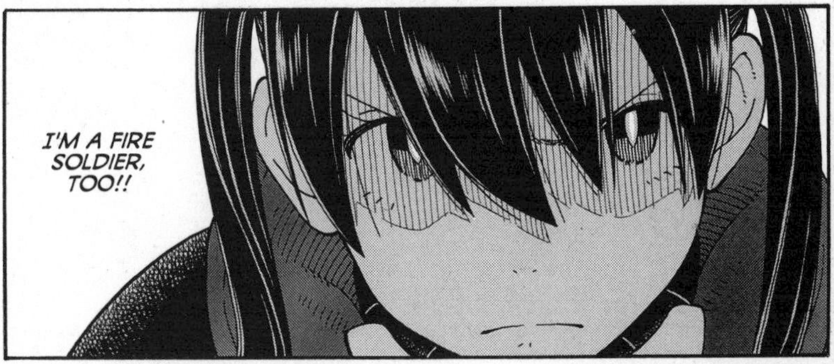
I'M A FIRE SOLDIER, TOO!!

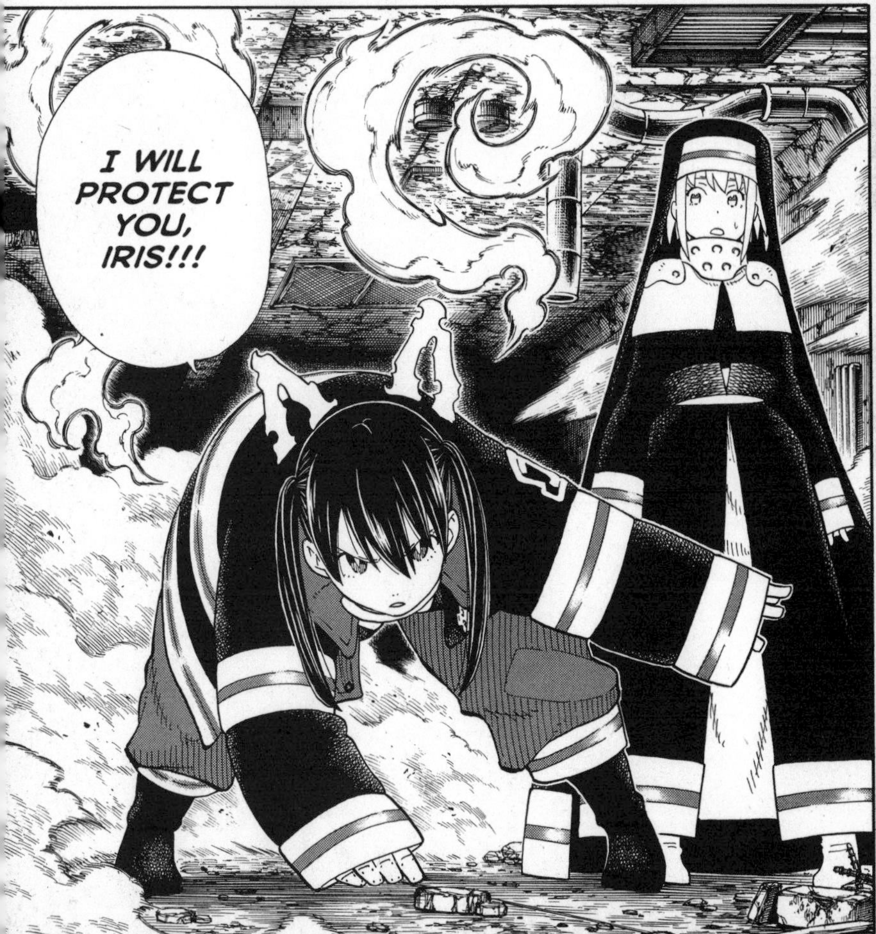
I WILL PROTECT YOU, IRIS!!!

FIRE FORCE

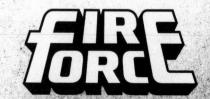

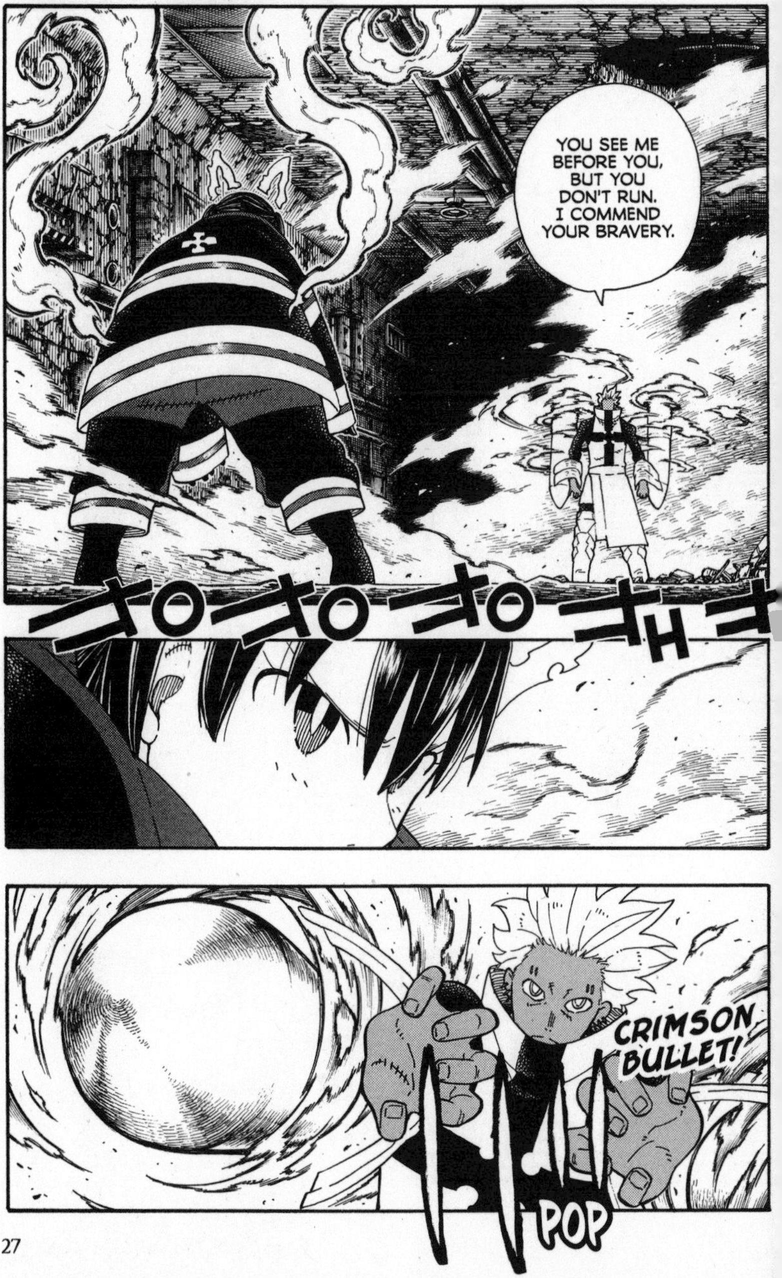
YOU SEE ME BEFORE YOU, BUT YOU DON'T RUN. I COMMEND YOUR BRAVERY.
CRIMSON BULLET!
POP

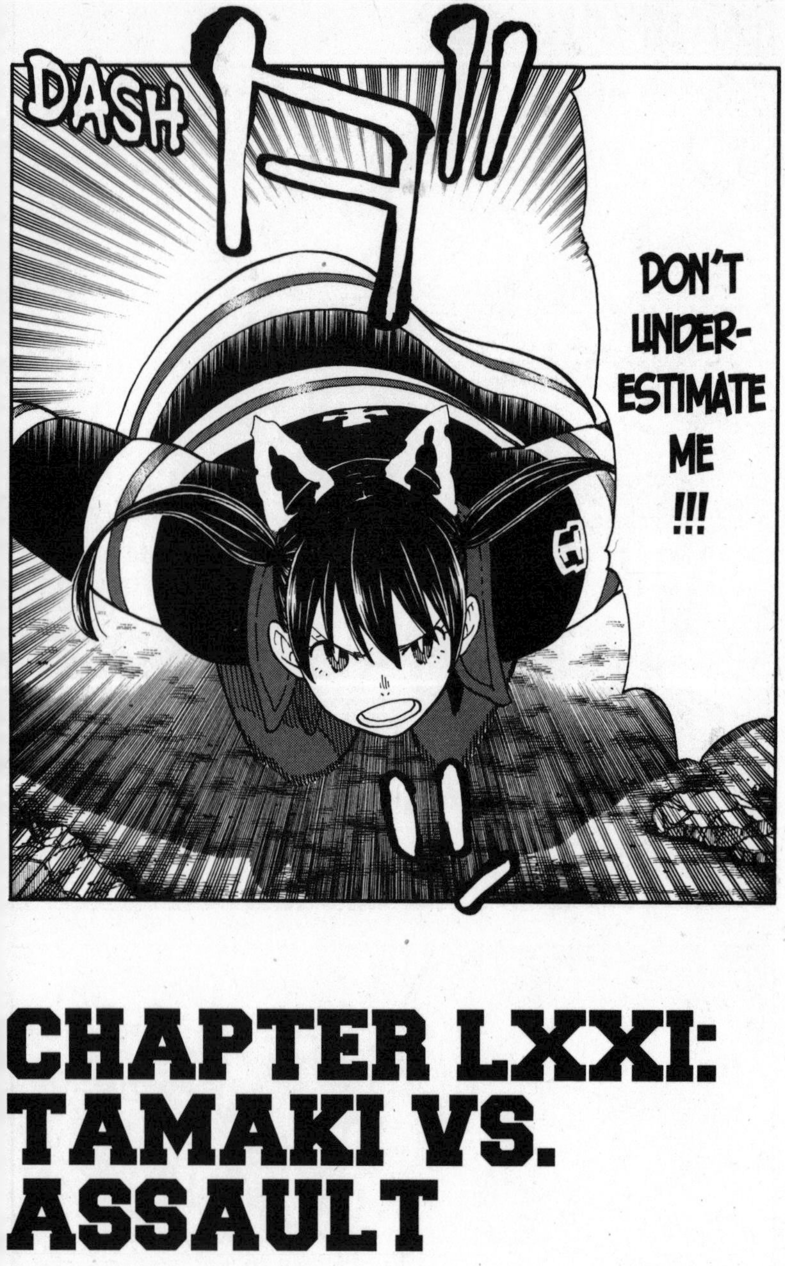
DASH
DON'T UNDER-ESTIMATE ME !!!

CHAPTER LXXI: TAMAKI VS. ASSAULT

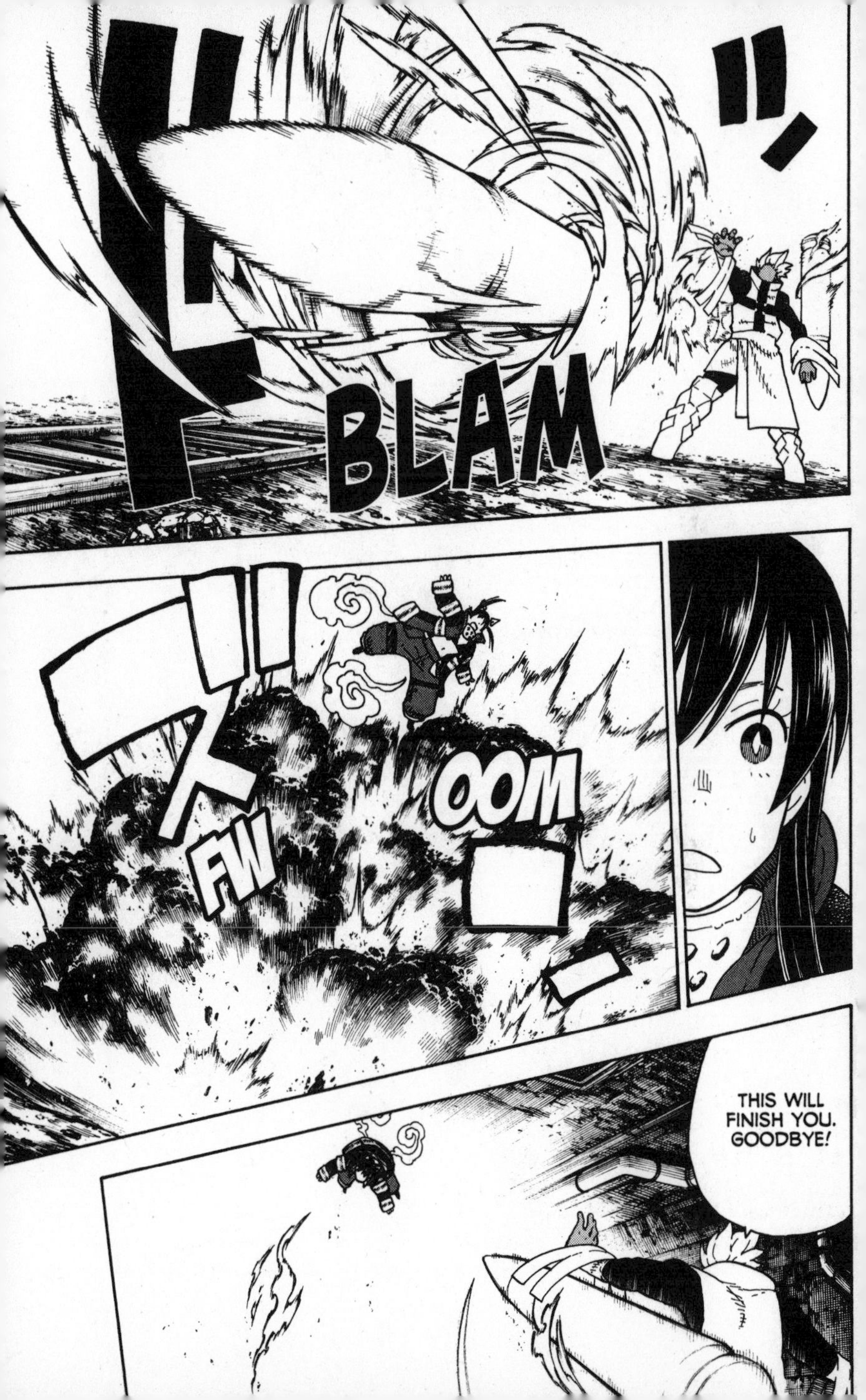
BLAM
FWOOM
THIS WILL FINISH YOU. GOODBYE!

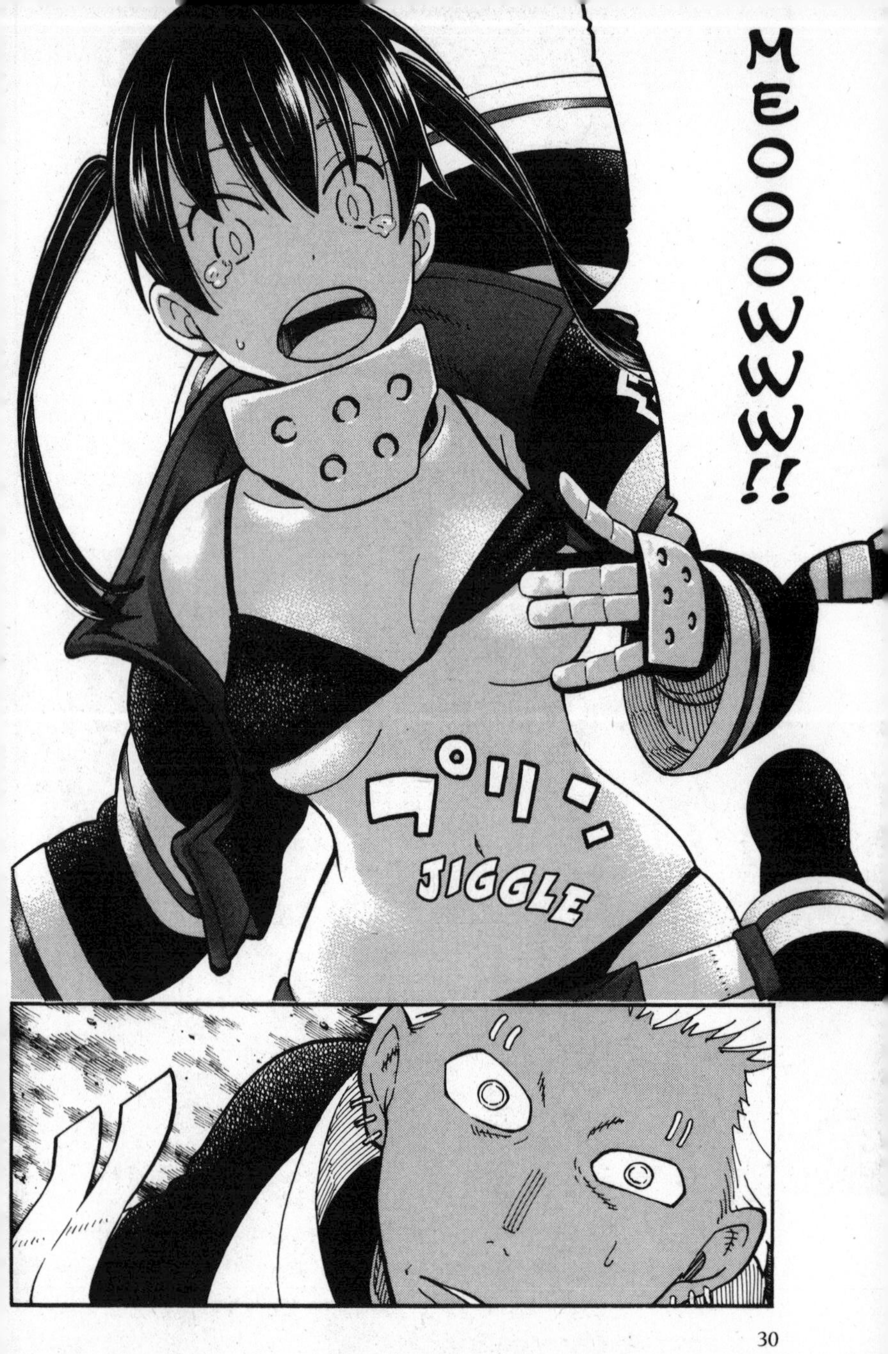
MEOOOWWW!!
JIGGLE

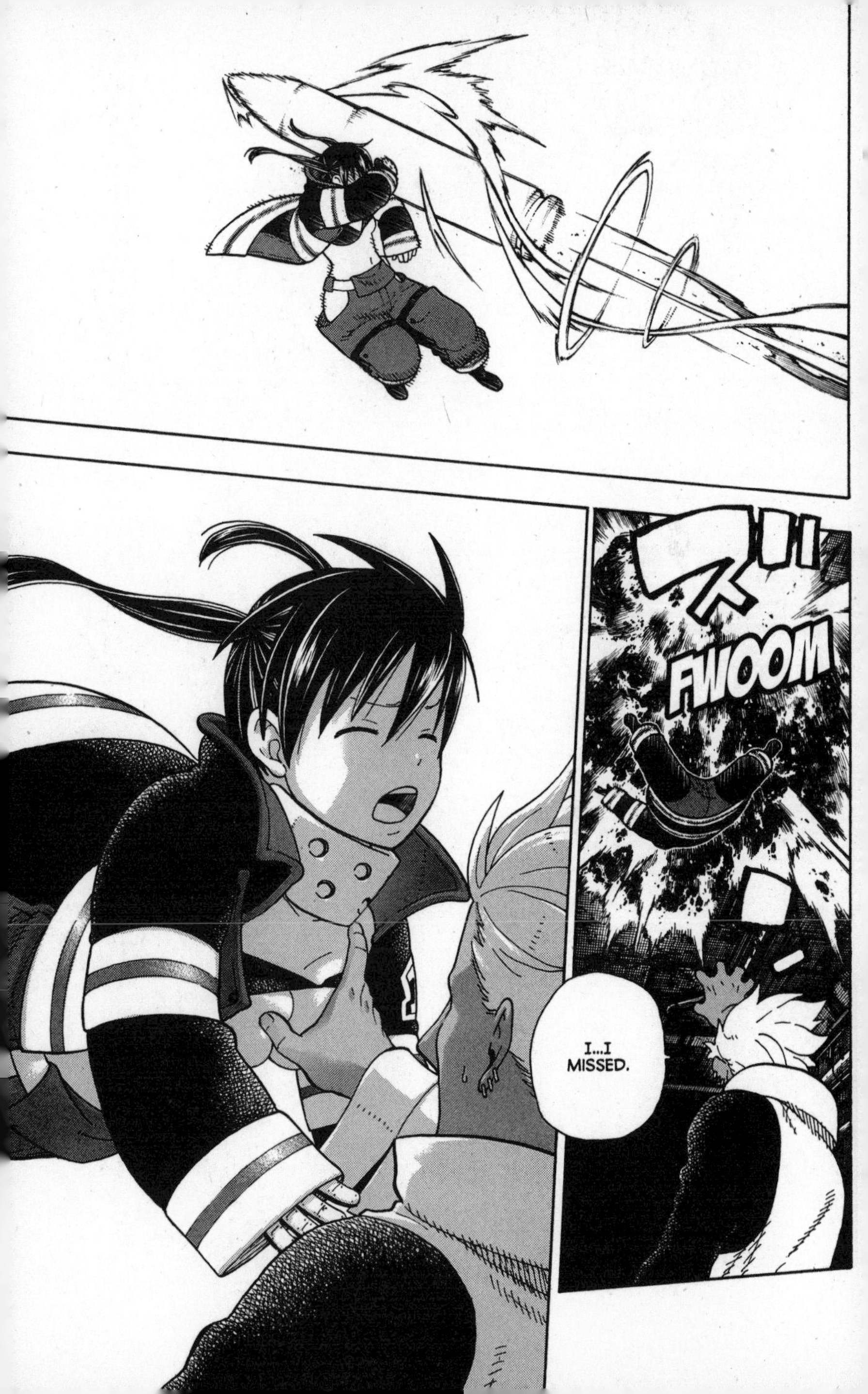
FWOOM
I...I MISSED.

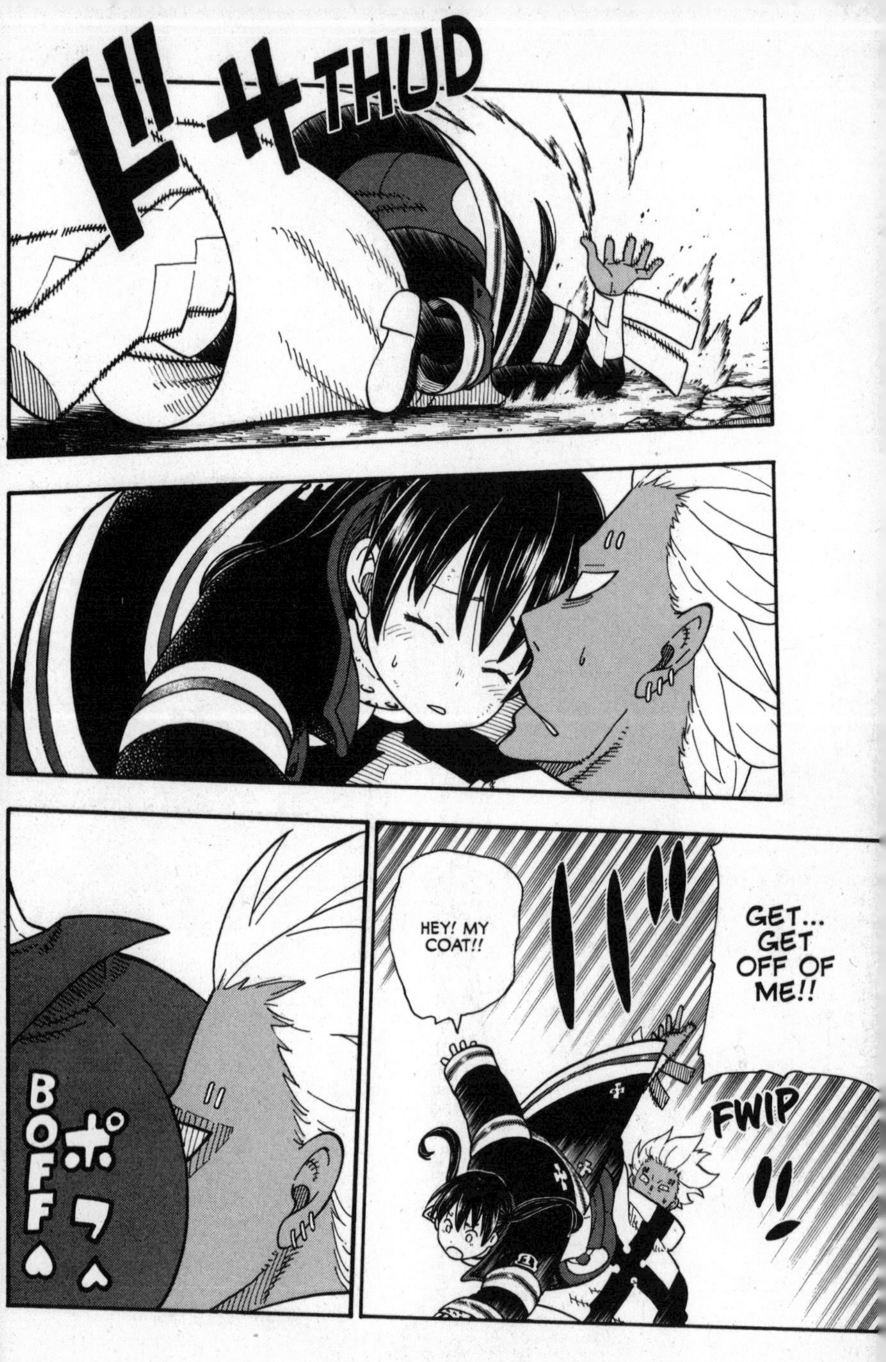
THUD
GET... GET OFF OF ME!!
HEY! MY COAT!!
FWIP
BOFF♥

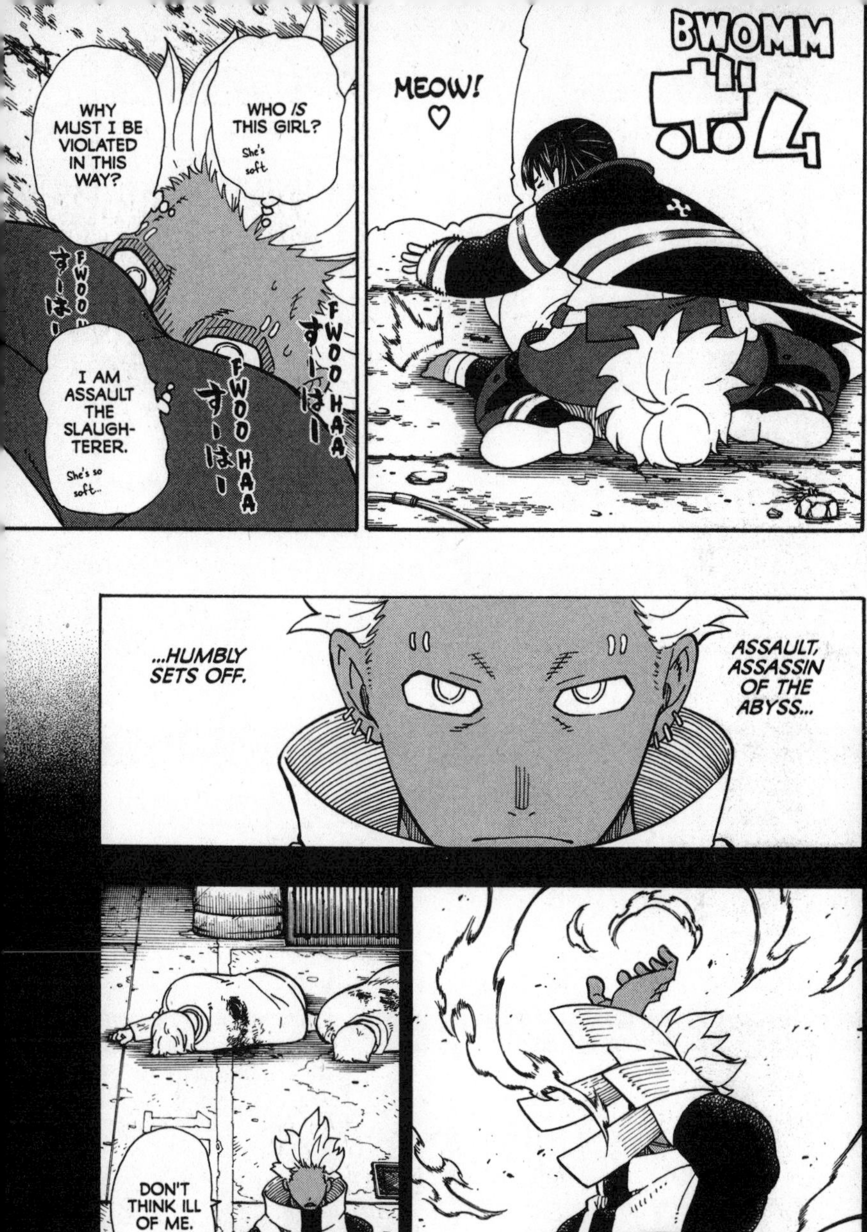
BWOMM
MEOW! ♡
WHO *IS* THIS GIRL?
She's soft.
WHY MUST I BE VIOLATED IN THIS WAY?
FWOO HAA
すーはー
FWOO HAA
すーはー
I AM ASSAULT THE SLAUGHTERER.
She's so soft...
ASSAULT, ASSASSIN OF THE ABYSS...
...HUMBLY SETS OFF.
DON'T THINK ILL OF ME.

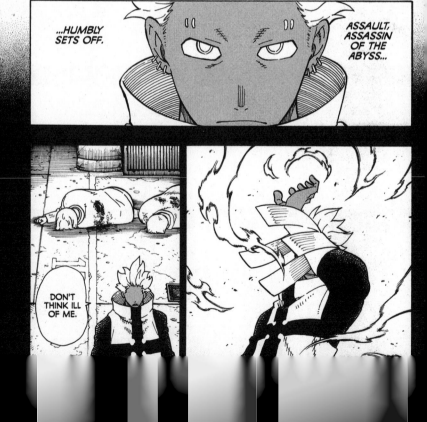

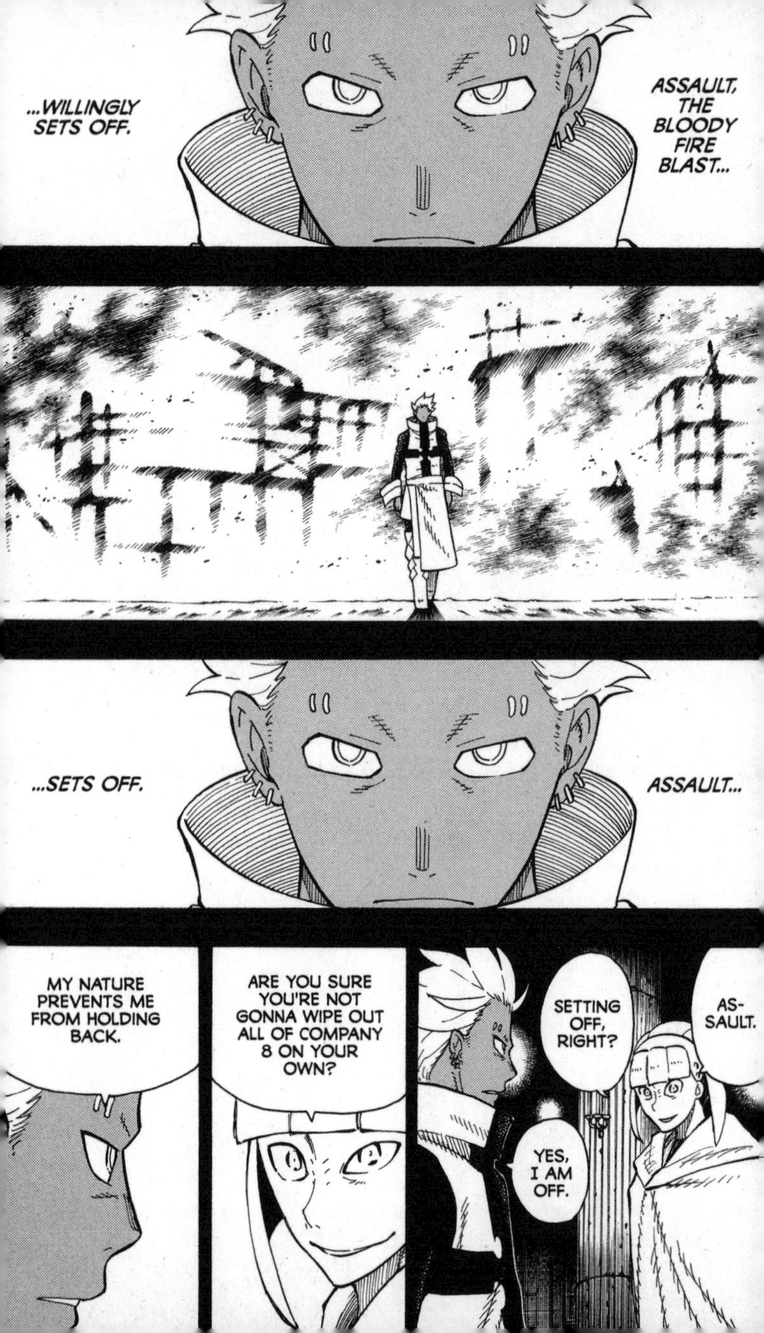
ASSAULT, THE BLOODY FIRE BLAST...
...WILLINGLY SETS OFF.
ASSAULT...
...SETS OFF.
AS-SAULT.
SETTING OFF, RIGHT?
YES, I AM OFF.
ARE YOU SURE YOU'RE NOT GONNA WIPE OUT ALL OF COMPANY 8 ON YOUR OWN?
MY NATURE PREVENTS ME FROM HOLDING BACK.

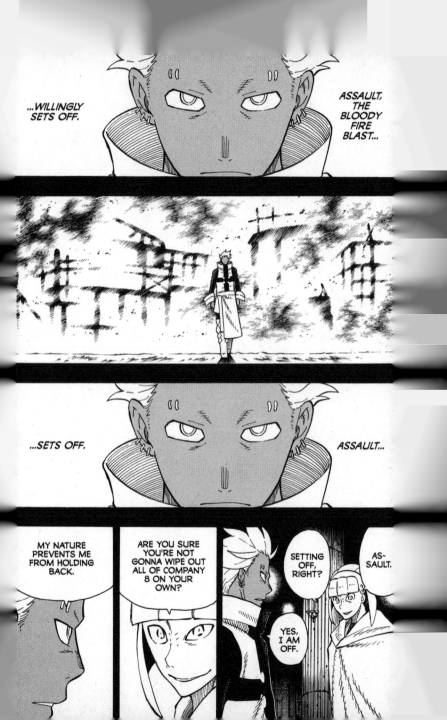

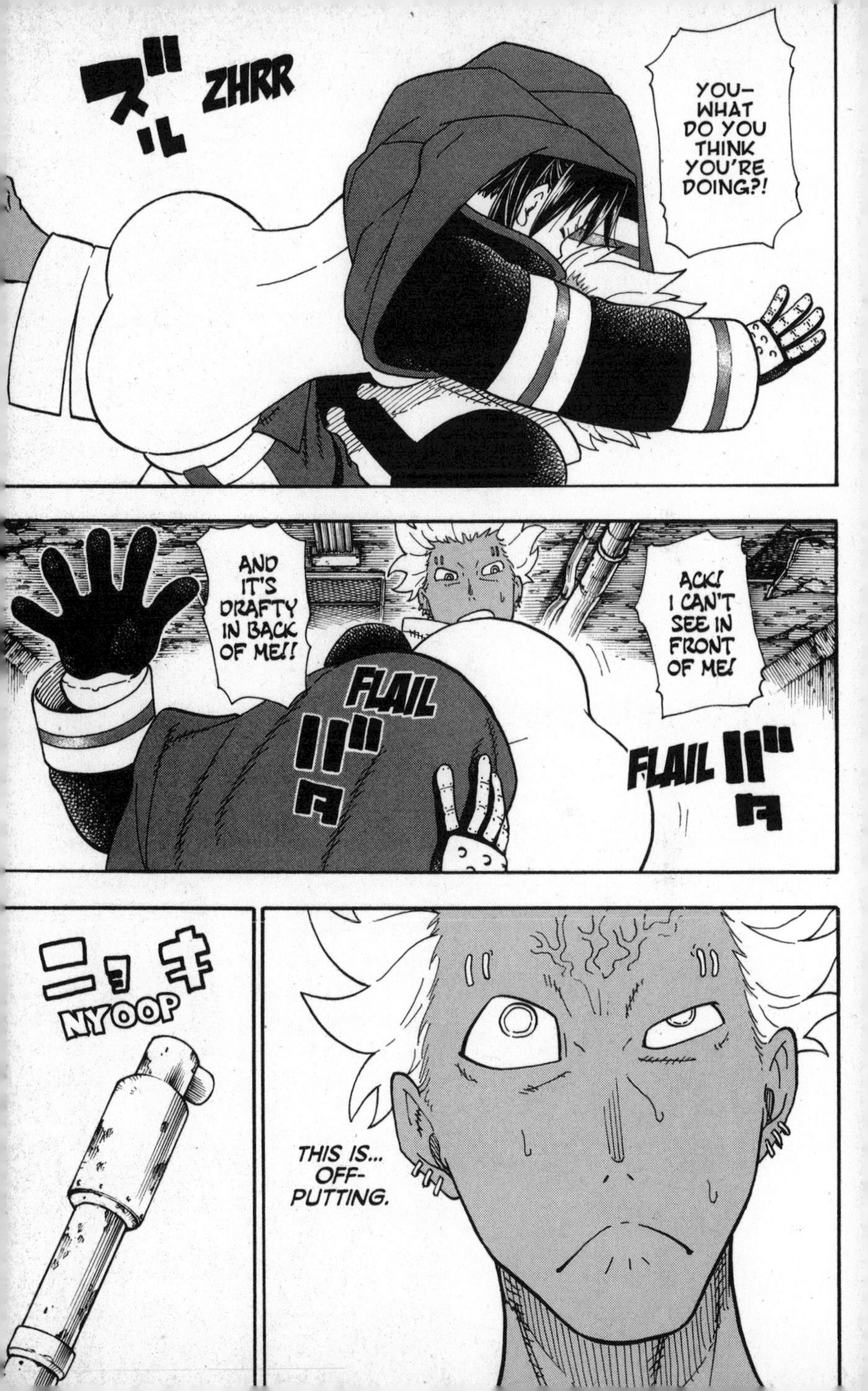
YOU— WHAT DO YOU THINK YOU'RE DOING?!
ズル
ZHRR
ACK! I CAN'T SEE IN FRONT OF ME!
バタ
FLAIL
バタ
FLAIL
AND IT'S DRAFTY IN BACK OF ME!!
THIS IS... OFF-PUTTING.
ニョキ
NYOOP

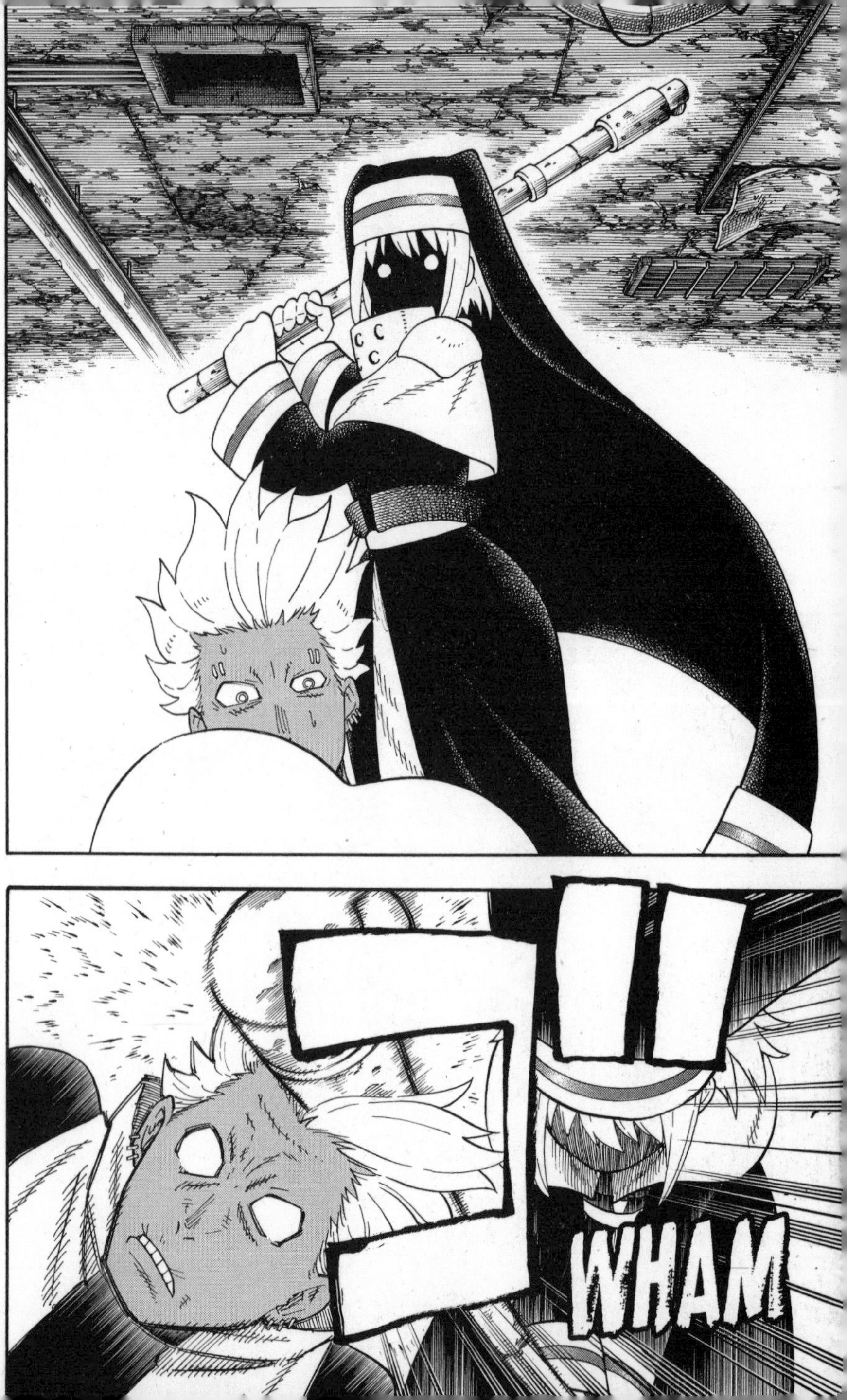
WHAM

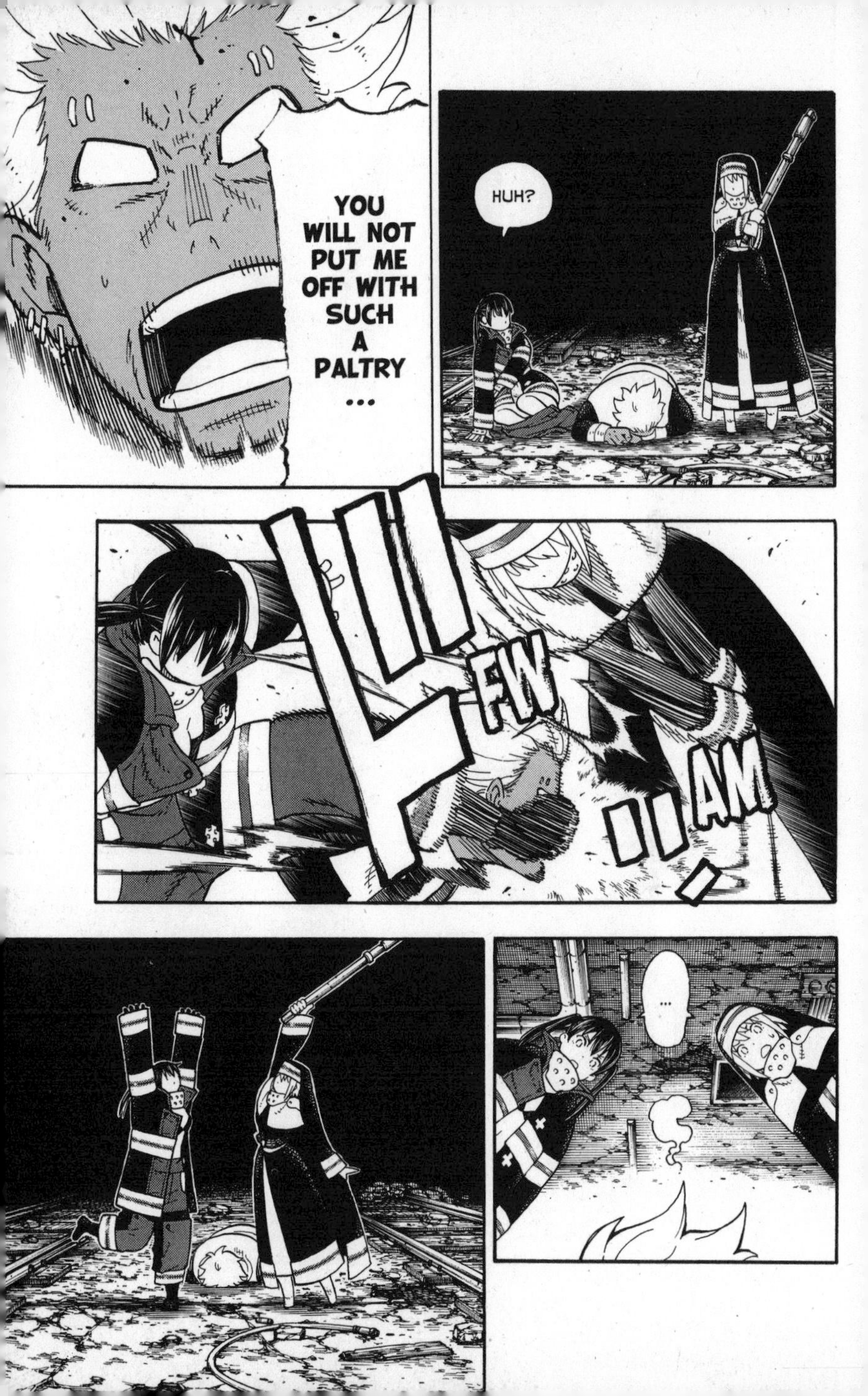
HUH?
YOU WILL NOT PUT ME OFF WITH SUCH A PALTRY ...
FW
AM
...

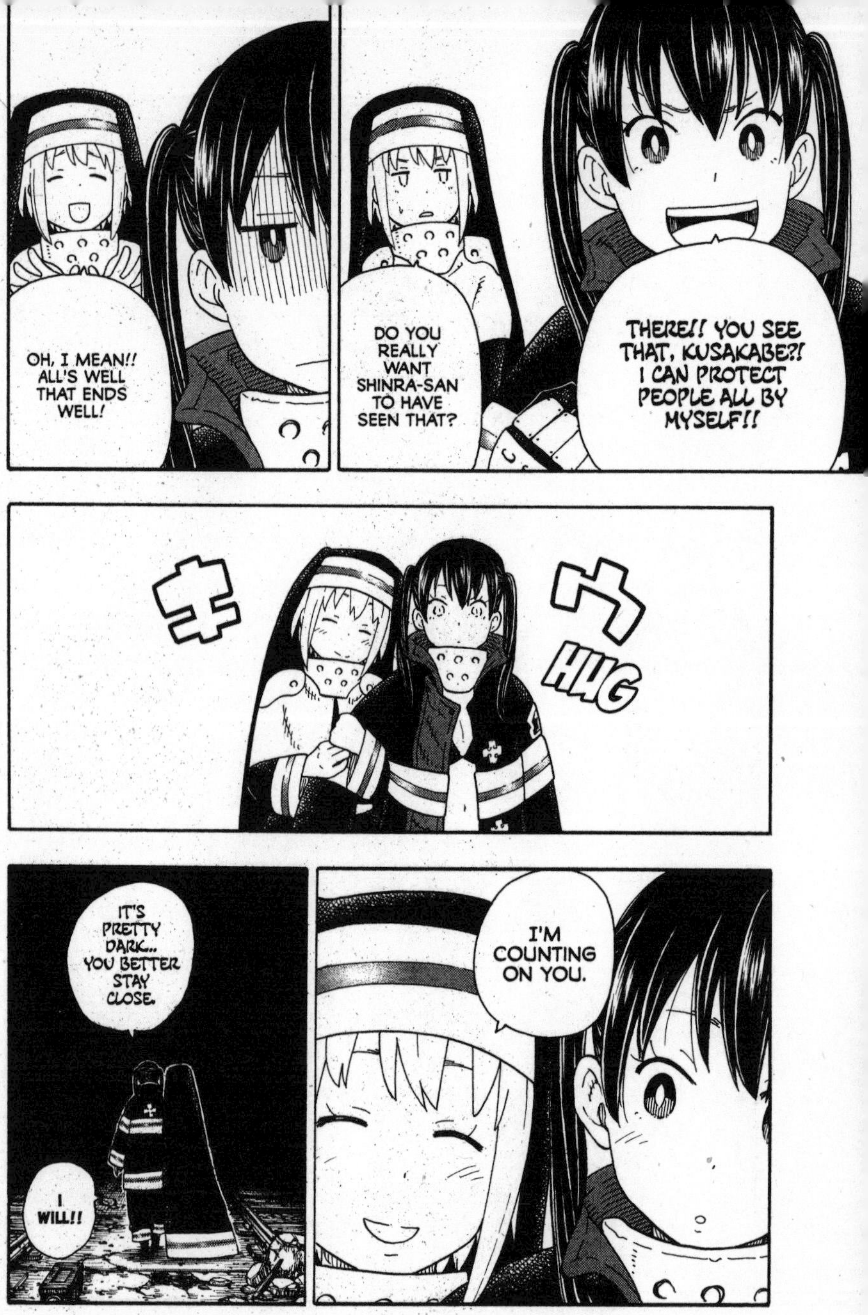
THERE!! YOU SEE THAT, KUSAKABE?! I CAN PROTECT PEOPLE ALL BY MYSELF!!
DO YOU REALLY WANT SHINRA-SAN TO HAVE SEEN THAT?
OH, I MEAN!! ALL'S WELL THAT ENDS WELL!
HUG
I'M COUNTING ON YOU.
IT'S PRETTY DARK... YOU BETTER STAY CLOSE.
I WILL!!

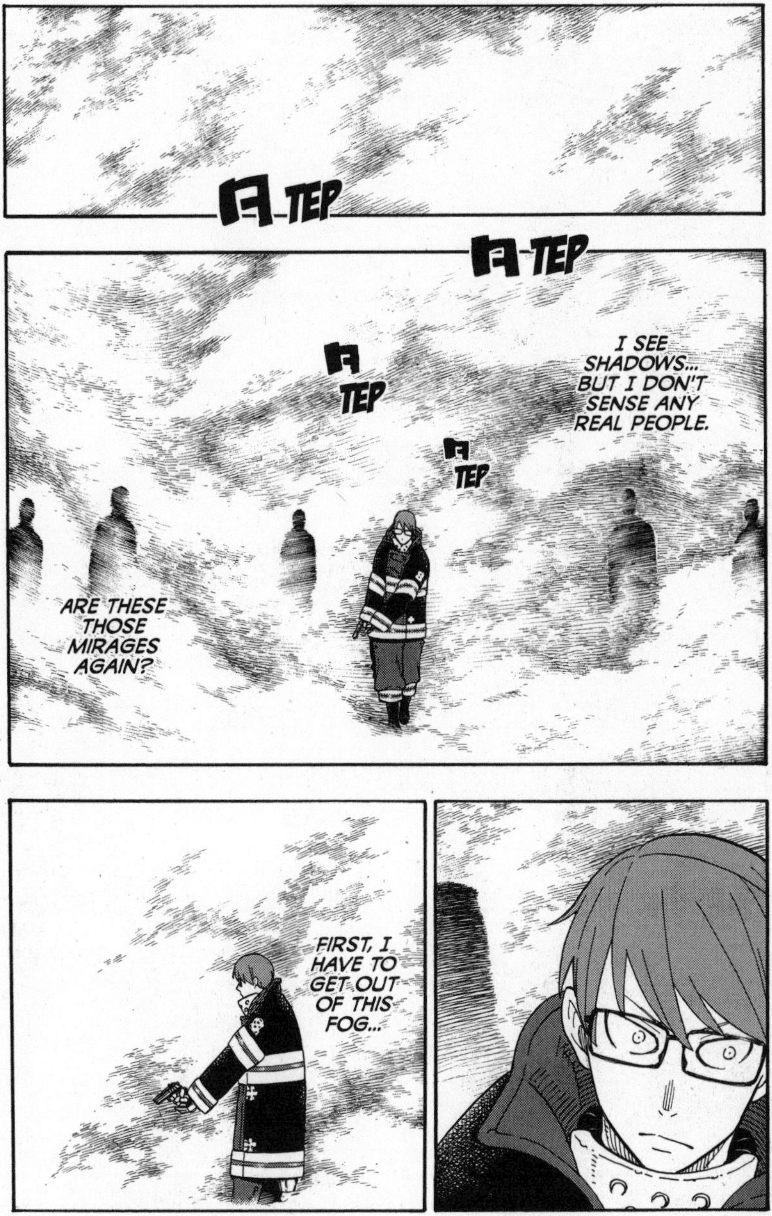
STEP
STEP
STEP
STEP
STEP
I SEE SHADOWS... BUT I DON'T SENSE ANY REAL PEOPLE.
ARE THESE THOSE MIRAGES AGAIN?
FIRST, I HAVE TO GET OUT OF THIS FOG...

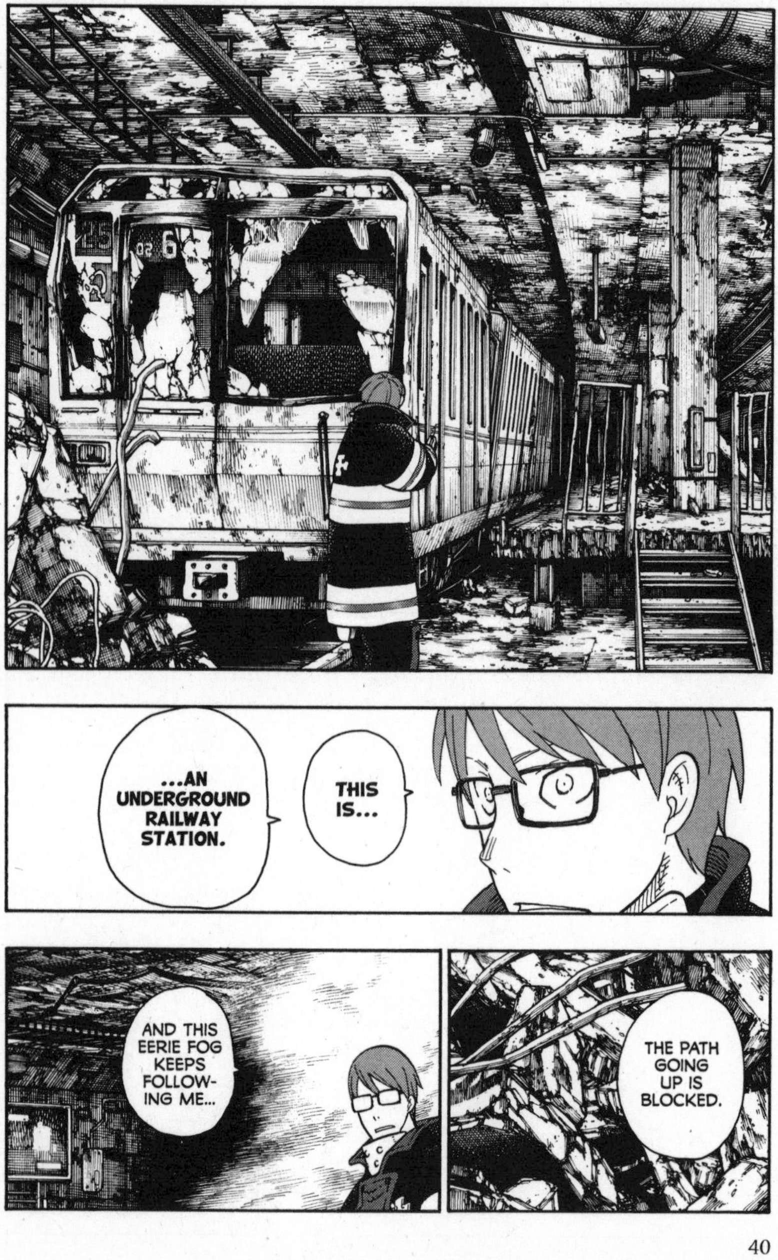
THIS IS...
...AN UNDERGROUND RAILWAY STATION.
THE PATH GOING UP IS BLOCKED.
AND THIS EERIE FOG KEEPS FOLLOW-ING ME...

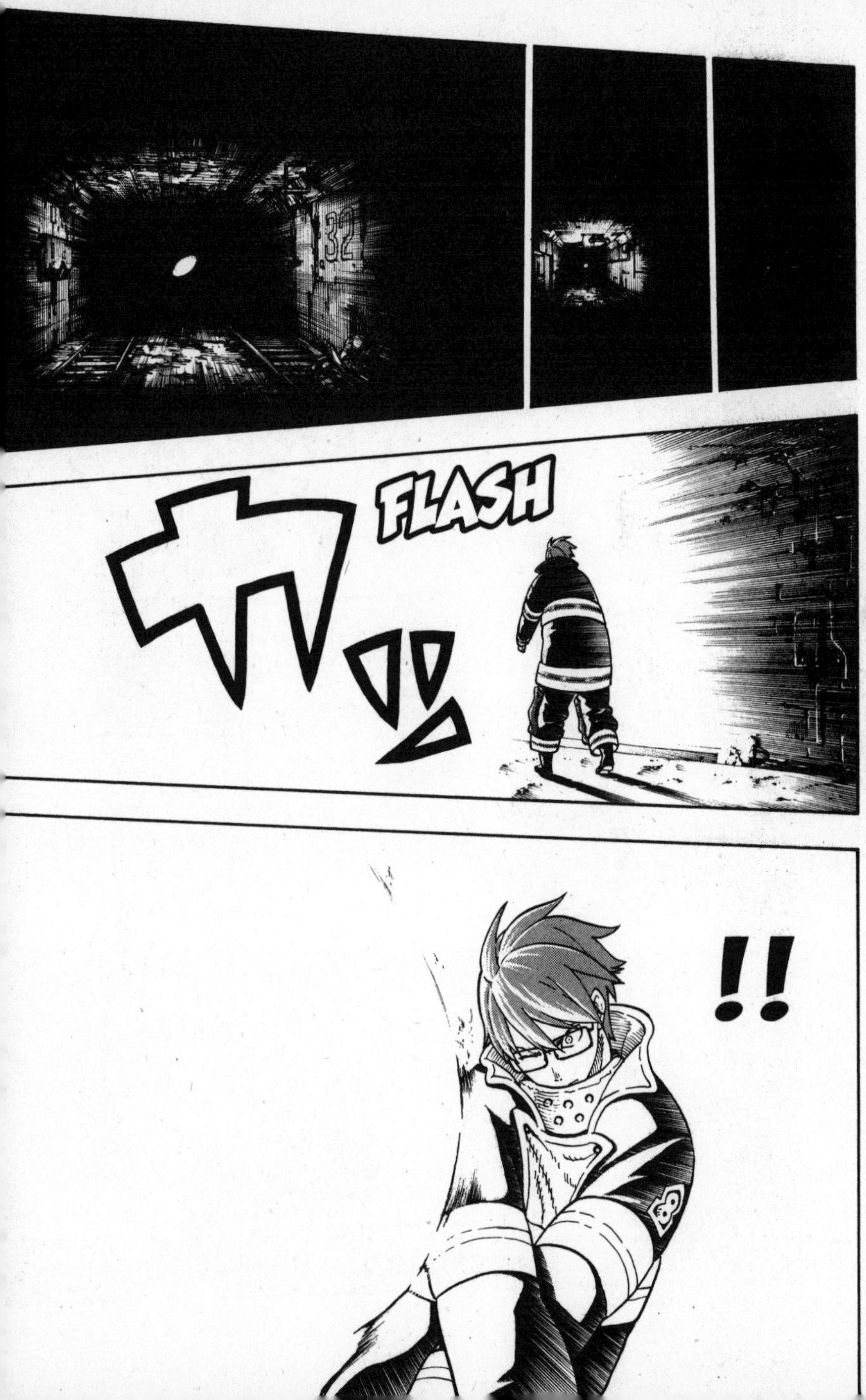

32
FLASH
!!

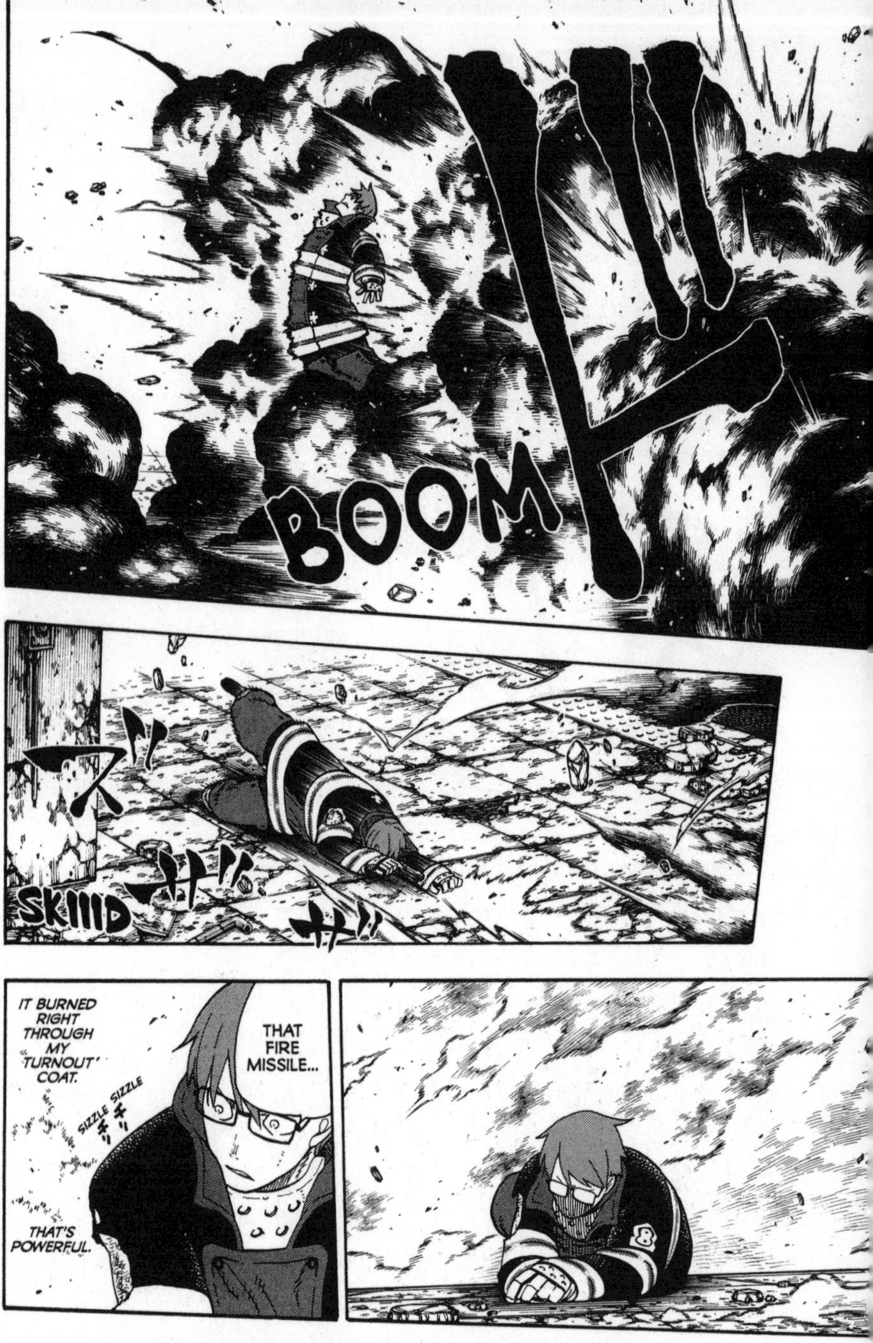
BOOM
SKIIID
THAT FIRE MISSILE...
IT BURNED RIGHT THROUGH MY 'TURNOUT' COAT.
SIZZLE SIZZLE
THAT'S POWERFUL.

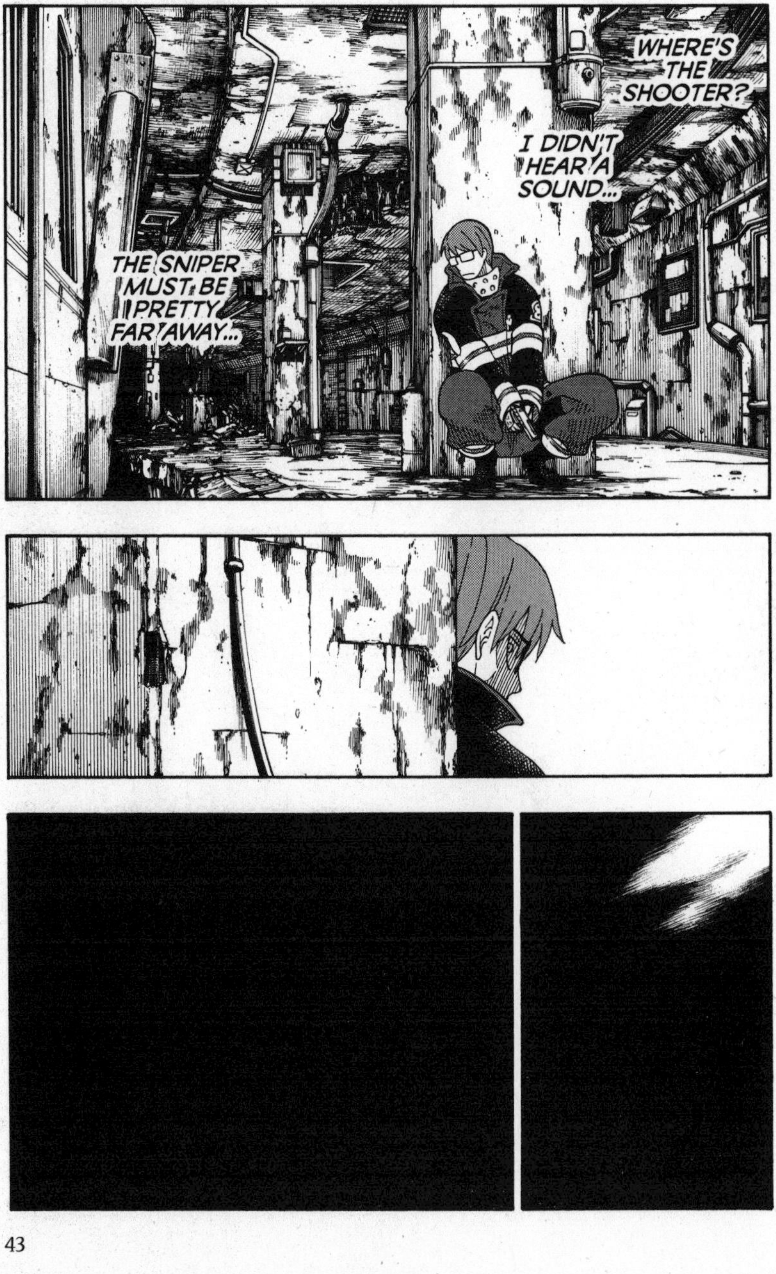
WHERE'S THE SHOOTER?
I DIDN'T HEAR A SOUND...
THE SNIPER MUST BE PRETTY FAR AWAY...

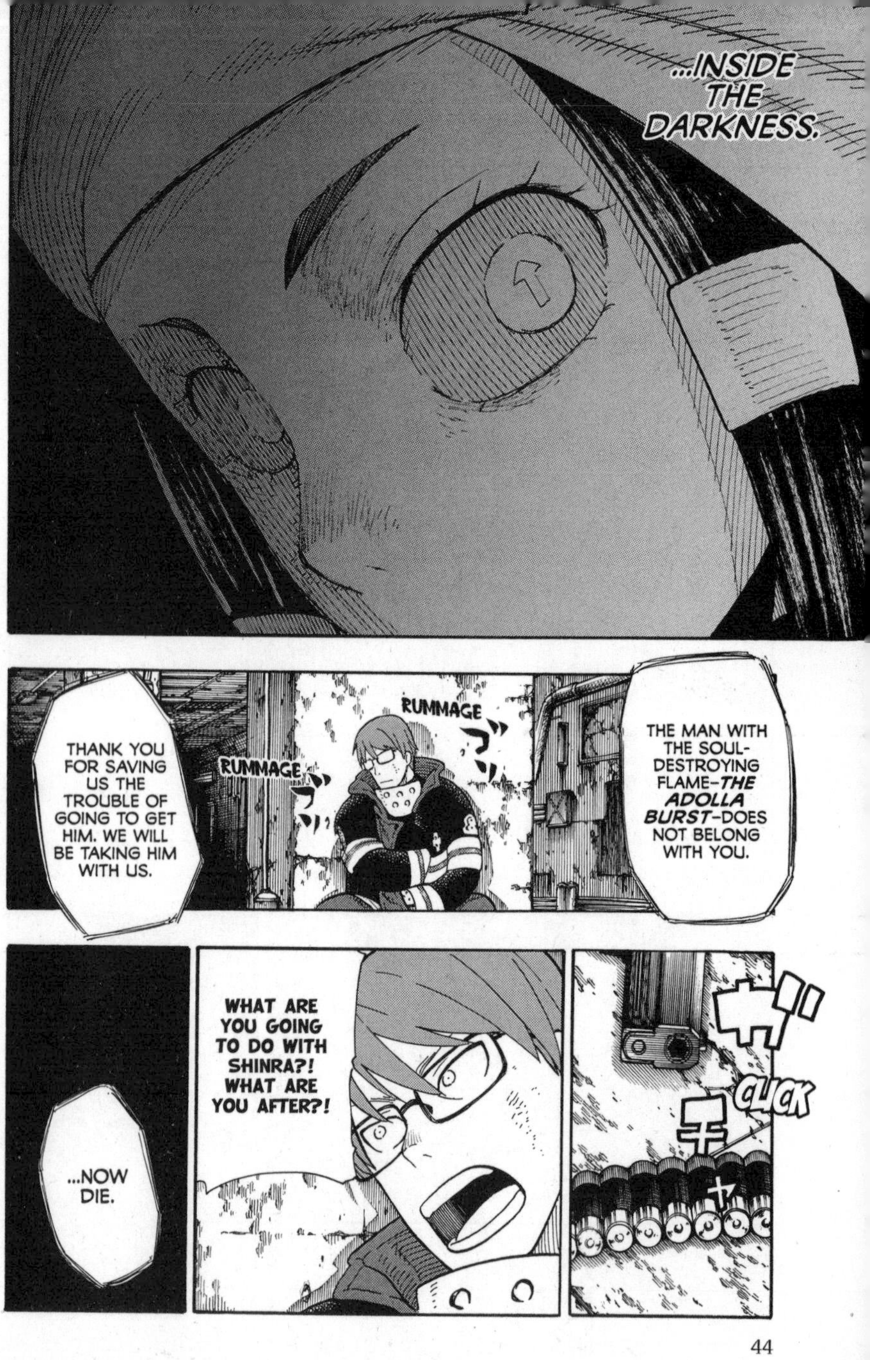
...INSIDE THE DARKNESS.
THE MAN WITH THE SOUL-DESTROYING FLAME—*THE ADOLLA BURST*—DOES NOT BELONG WITH YOU.
RUMMAGE
RUMMAGE
THANK YOU FOR SAVING US THE TROUBLE OF GOING TO GET HIM. WE WILL BE TAKING HIM WITH US.
CLICK
WHAT ARE YOU GOING TO DO WITH SHINRA?! WHAT ARE YOU AFTER?!
...NOW DIE.

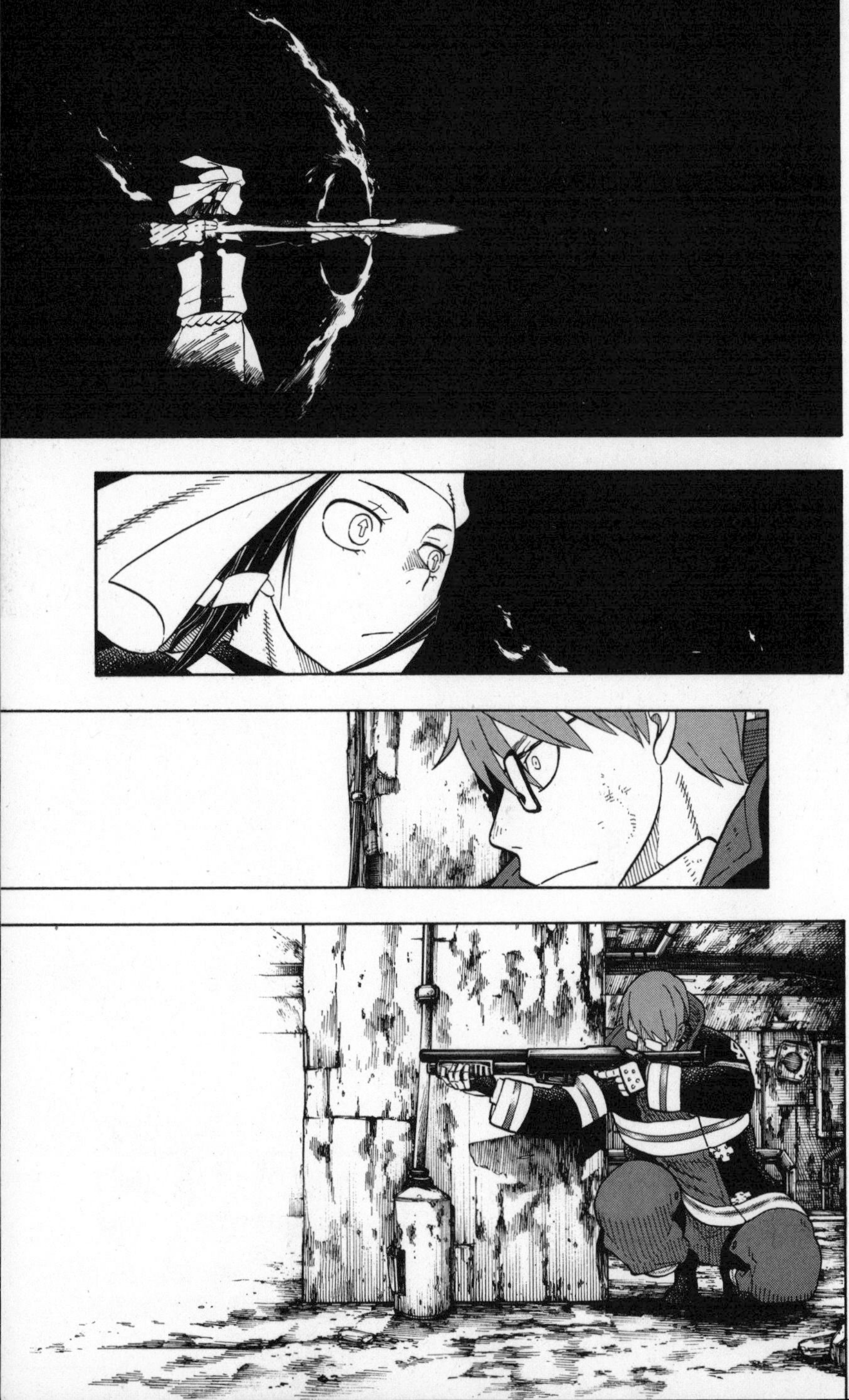

FIRE FORCE

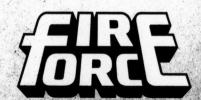

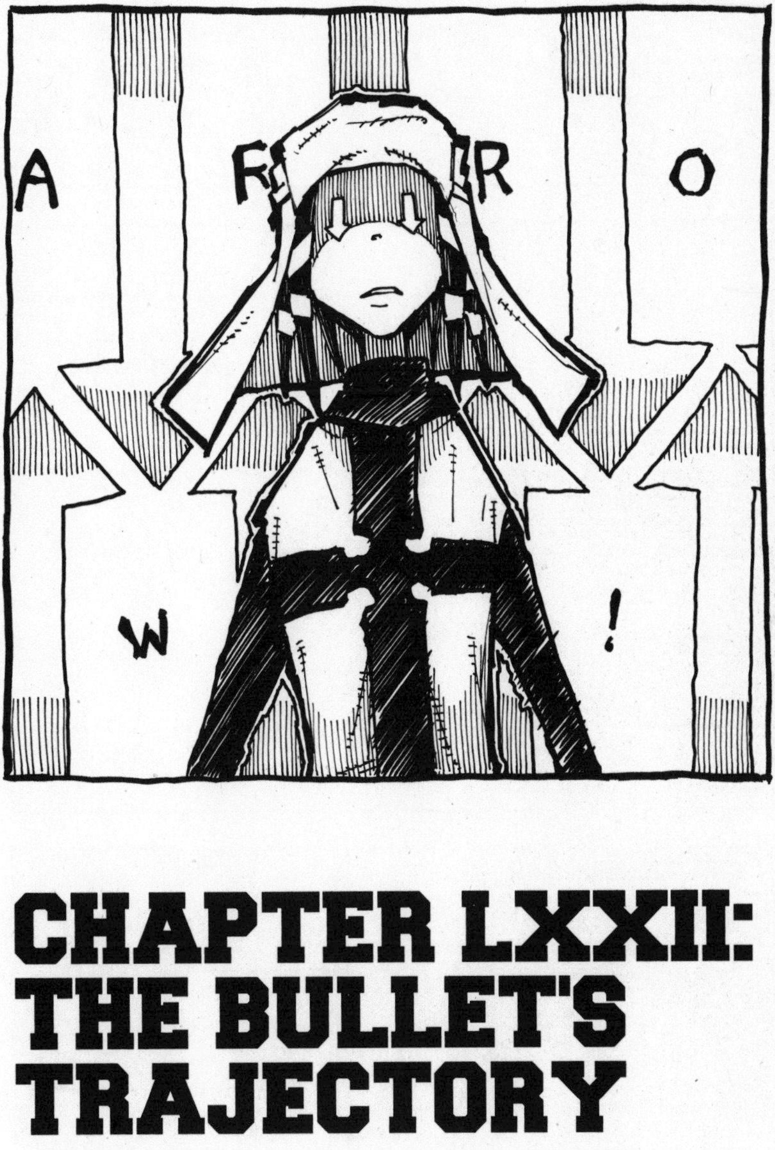
ARROW!

CHAPTER LXXII: THE BULLET'S TRAJECTORY

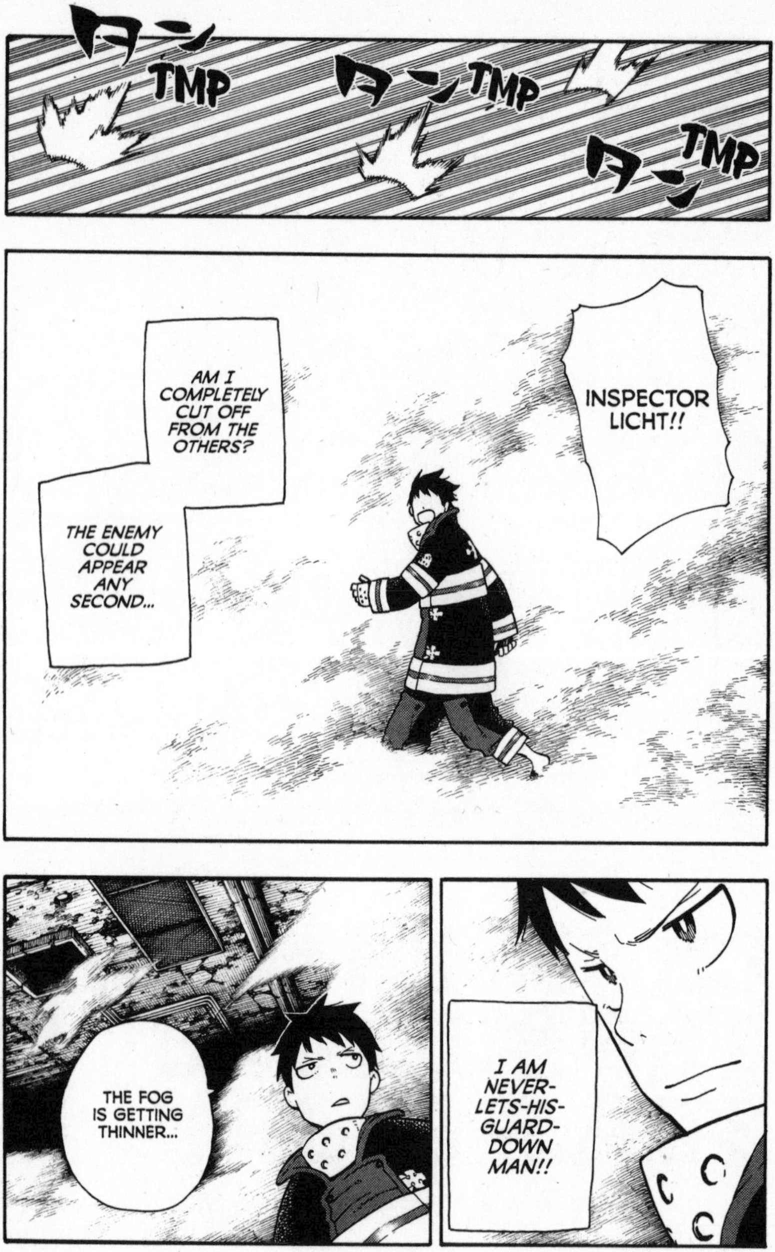
TMP
TMP
TMP
INSPECTOR LICHT!!
AM I COMPLETELY CUT OFF FROM THE OTHERS?
THE ENEMY COULD APPEAR ANY SECOND...
I AM NEVER-LETS-HIS-GUARD-DOWN MAN!!
THE FOG IS GETTING THINNER...

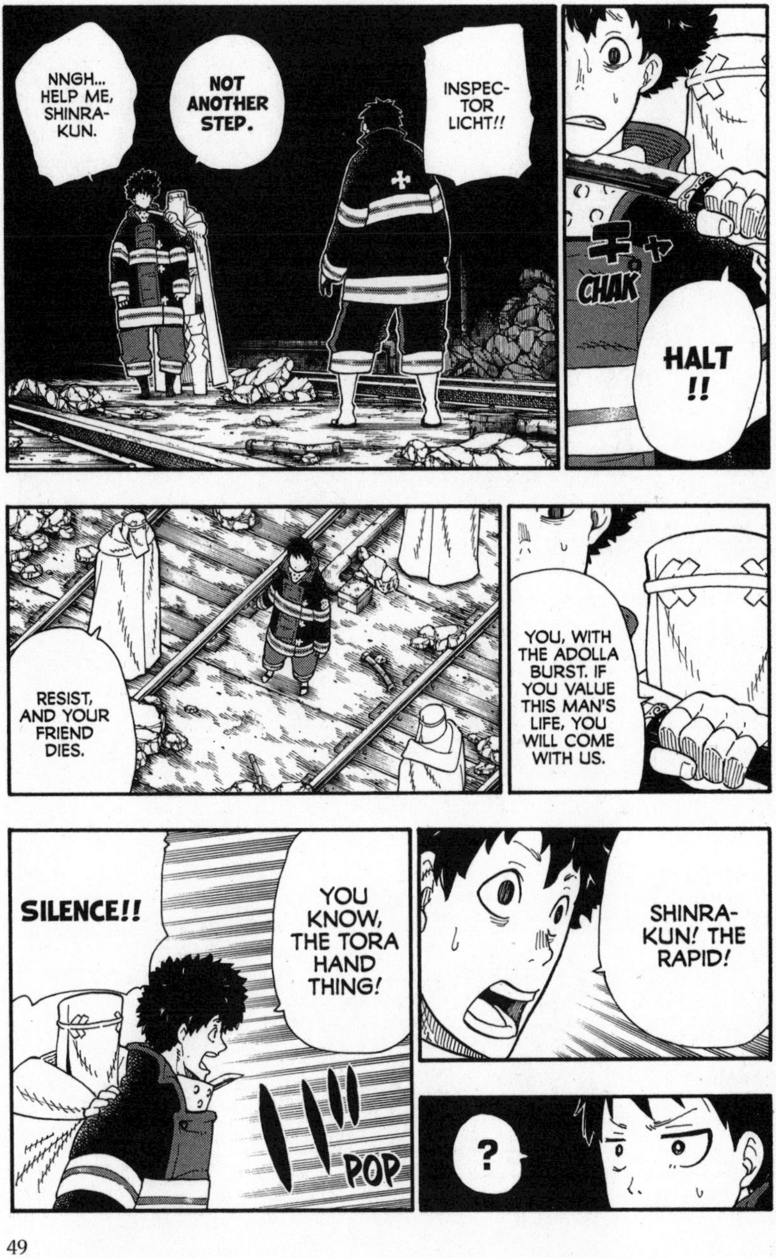
チャ
CHAK
HALT!!
INSPECTOR LICHT!!
NOT ANOTHER STEP.
NNGH... HELP ME, SHINRA-KUN.
YOU, WITH THE ADOLLA BURST. IF YOU VALUE THIS MAN'S LIFE, YOU WILL COME WITH US.
RESIST, AND YOUR FRIEND DIES.
SHINRA-KUN! THE RAPID!
?
YOU KNOW, THE TORA HAND THING!
SILENCE!!
POP

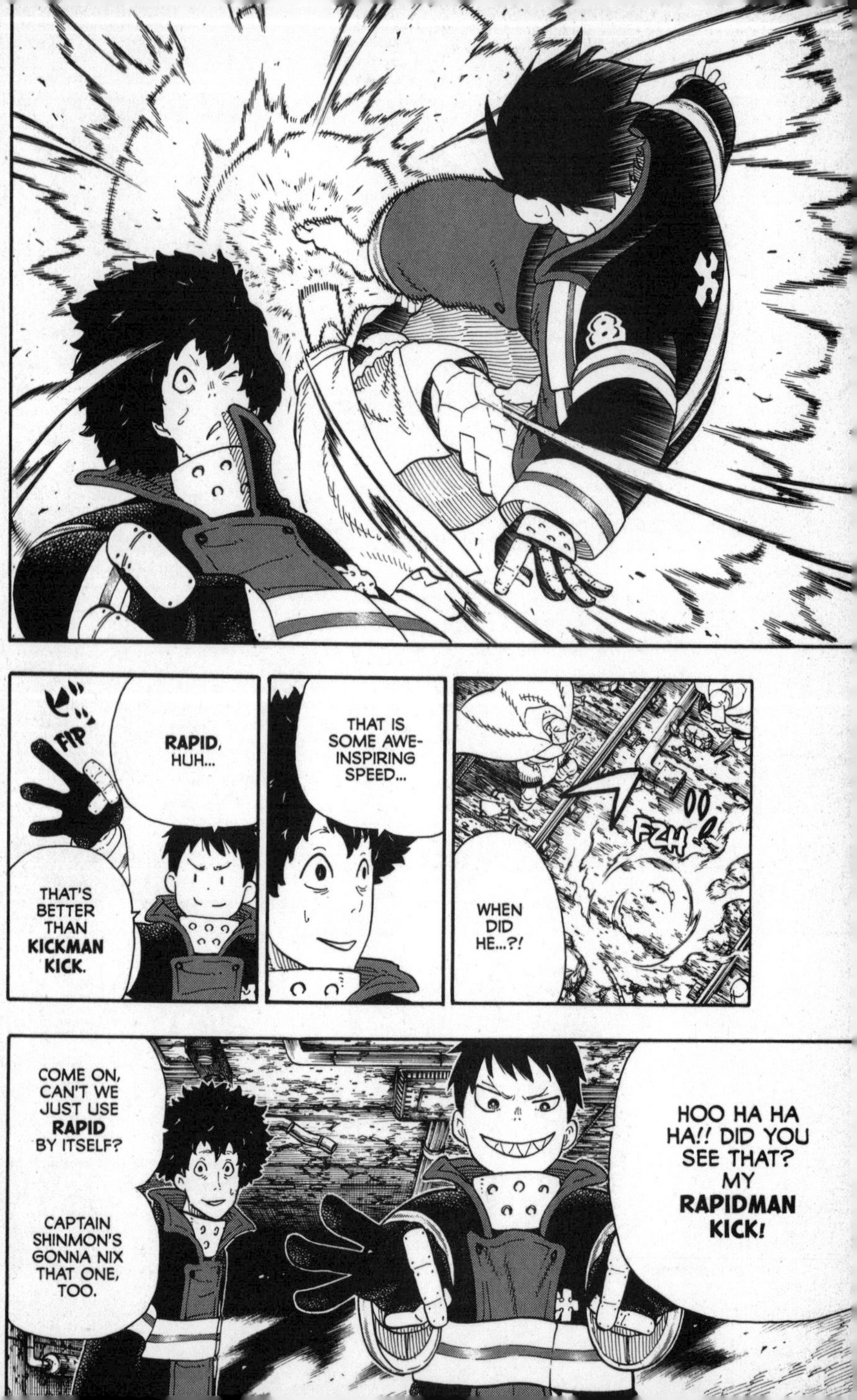
FZH
WHEN DID HE...?!
THAT IS SOME AWE-INSPIRING SPEED...
ピッ
FIP
RAPID, HUH...
THAT'S BETTER THAN KICKMAN KICK.
HOO HA HA HA!! DID YOU SEE THAT? MY RAPIDMAN KICK!
COME ON, CAN'T WE JUST USE RAPID BY ITSELF?
CAPTAIN SHINMON'S GONNA NIX THAT ONE, TOO.

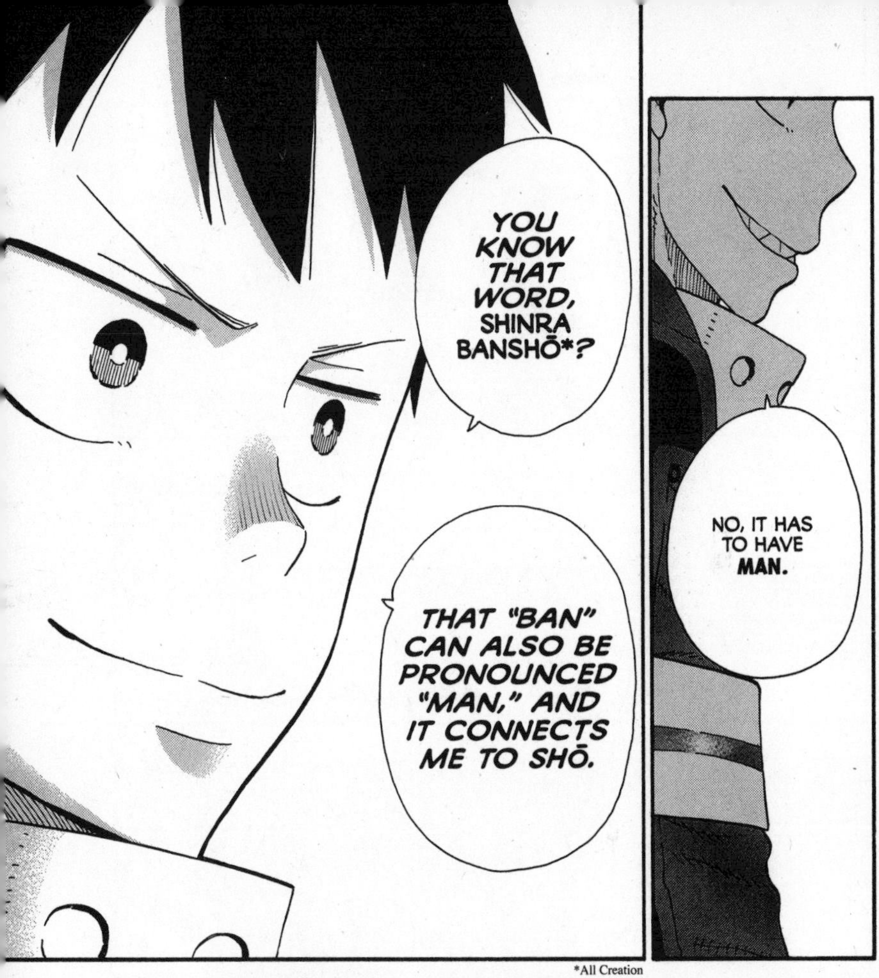
NO, IT HAS TO HAVE MAN.
YOU KNOW THAT WORD, SHINRA BANSHŌ*?
THAT "BAN" CAN ALSO BE PRONOUNCED "MAN," AND IT CONNECTS ME TO SHŌ.

*All Creation

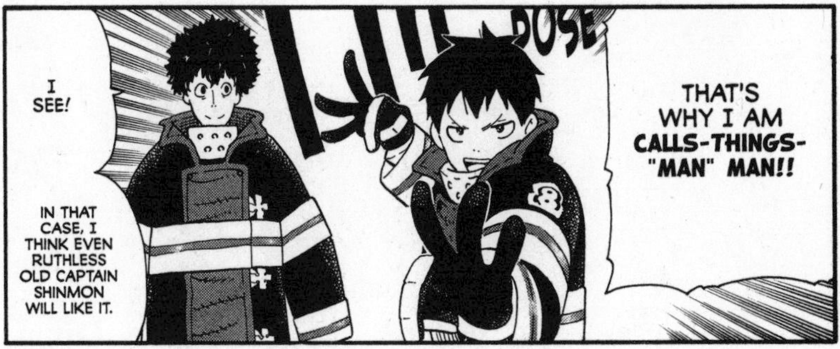
THAT'S WHY I AM CALLS-THINGS-"MAN" MAN!!
I SEE!
IN THAT CASE, I THINK EVEN RUTHLESS OLD CAPTAIN SHINMON WILL LIKE IT.

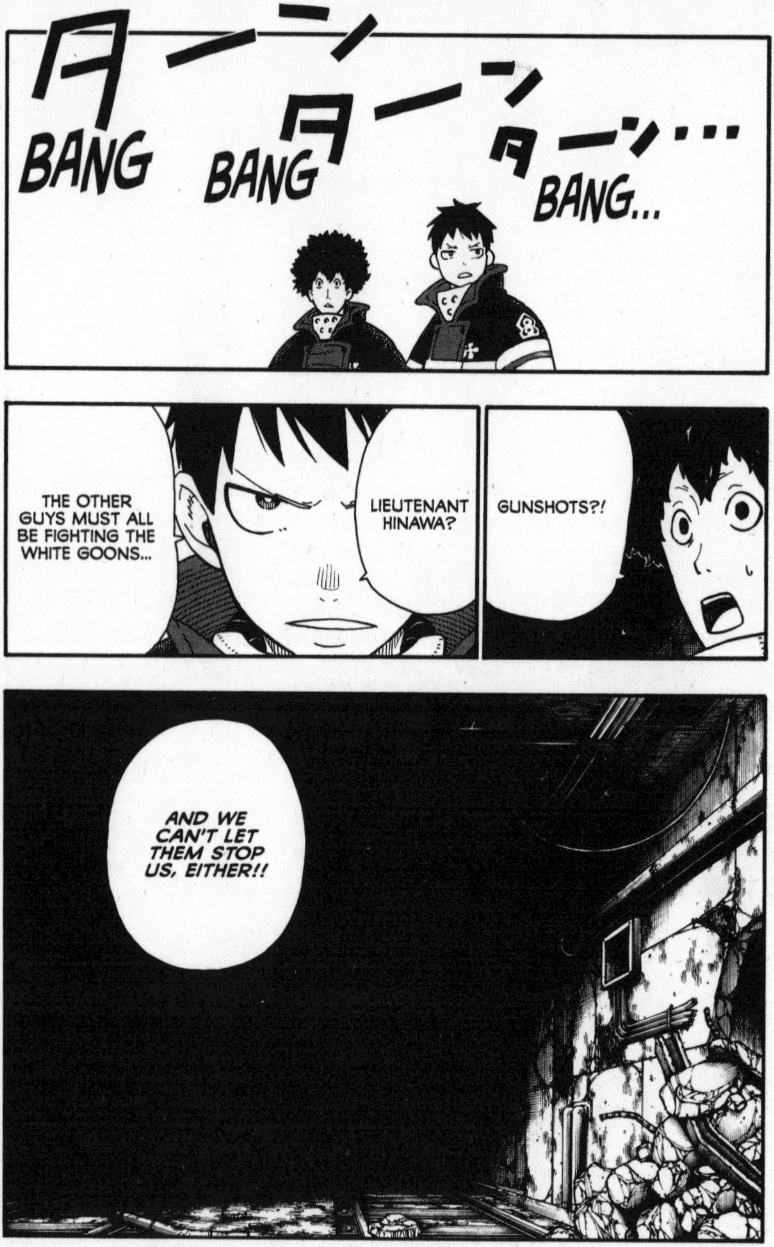
ターン
BANG
ターン
BANG
ターン…
BANG...
GUNSHOTS?!
LIEUTENANT HINAWA?
THE OTHER GUYS MUST ALL BE FIGHTING THE WHITE GOONS...
AND WE CAN'T LET THEM STOP US, EITHER!!

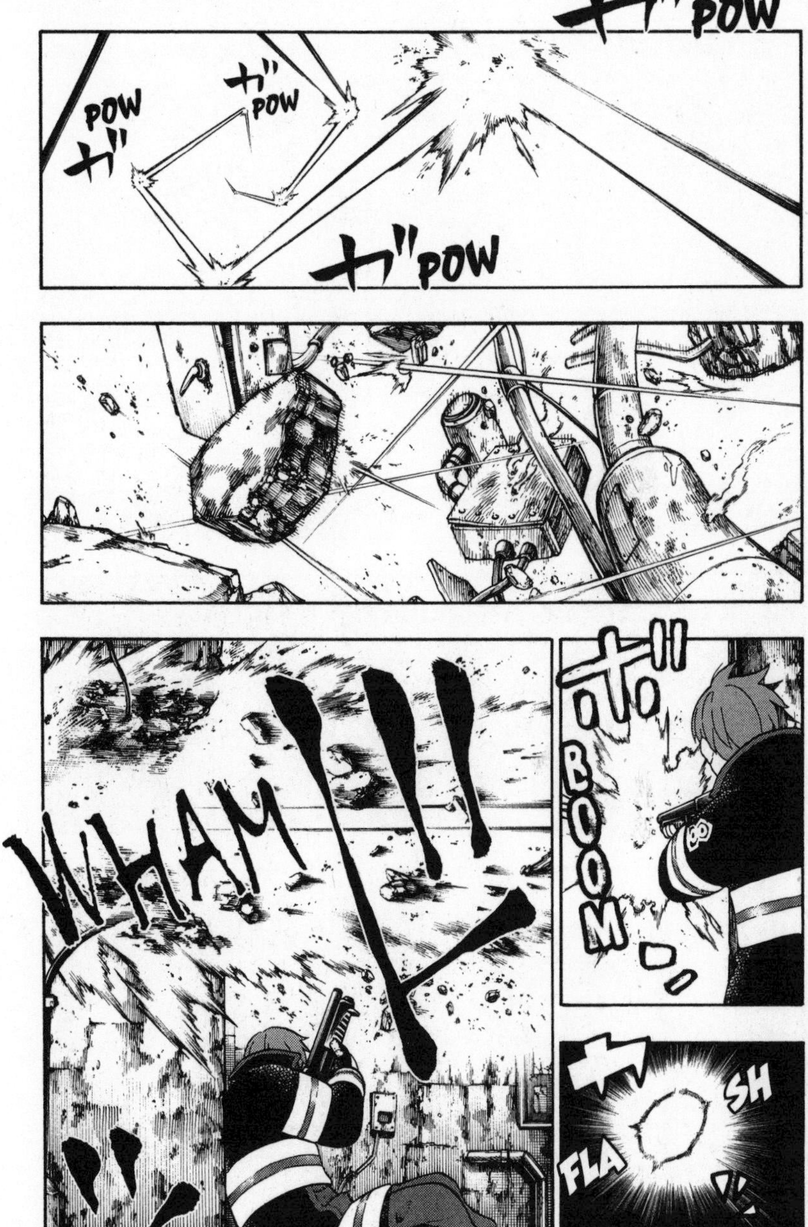

ガ POW
ガ POW
POW ガ
ガ POW
BOOM
FLASH
WHAM!!

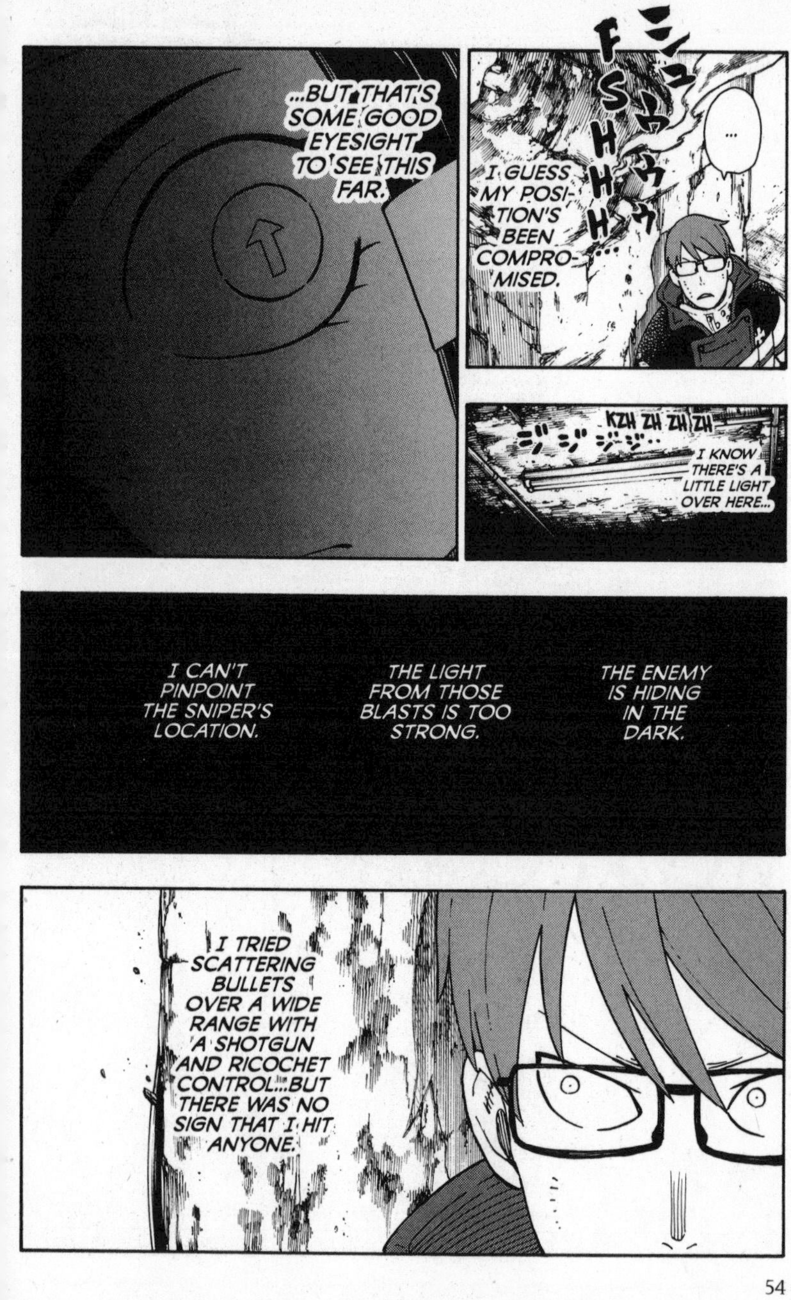
FSHHH
...
I GUESS MY POSITION'S BEEN COMPROMISED.
KZH ZH ZH ZH
I KNOW THERE'S A LITTLE LIGHT OVER HERE...
...BUT THAT'S SOME GOOD EYESIGHT TO SEE THIS FAR.
THE ENEMY IS HIDING IN THE DARK.
THE LIGHT FROM THOSE BLASTS IS TOO STRONG.
I CAN'T PINPOINT THE SNIPER'S LOCATION.
I TRIED SCATTERING BULLETS OVER A WIDE RANGE WITH A SHOTGUN AND RICOCHET CONTROL...BUT THERE WAS NO SIGN THAT I HIT ANYONE.

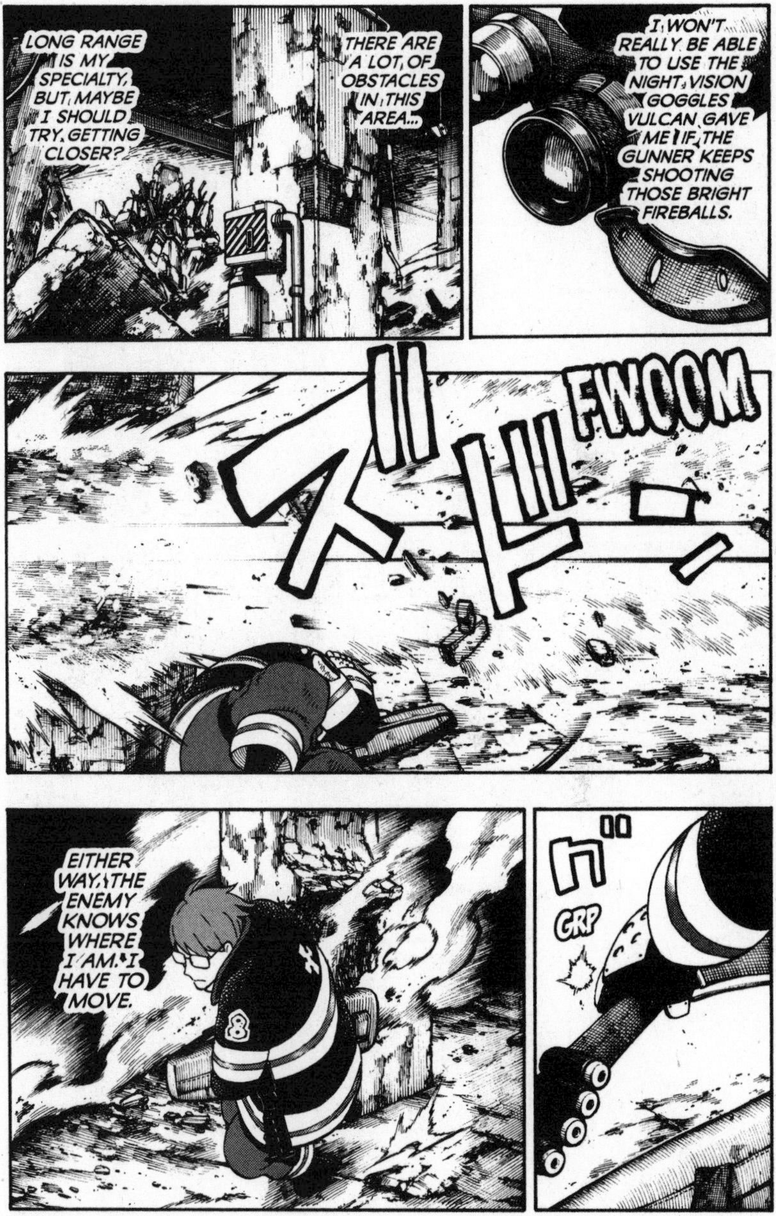
I WON'T REALLY BE ABLE TO USE THE NIGHT VISION GOGGLES VULCAN GAVE ME IF THE GUNNER KEEPS SHOOTING THOSE BRIGHT FIREBALLS.
LONG RANGE IS MY SPECIALTY, BUT MAYBE I SHOULD TRY GETTING CLOSER?
THERE ARE A LOT OF OBSTACLES IN THIS AREA...
FWOOM
GRP
EITHER WAY, THE ENEMY KNOWS WHERE I AM. I HAVE TO MOVE.

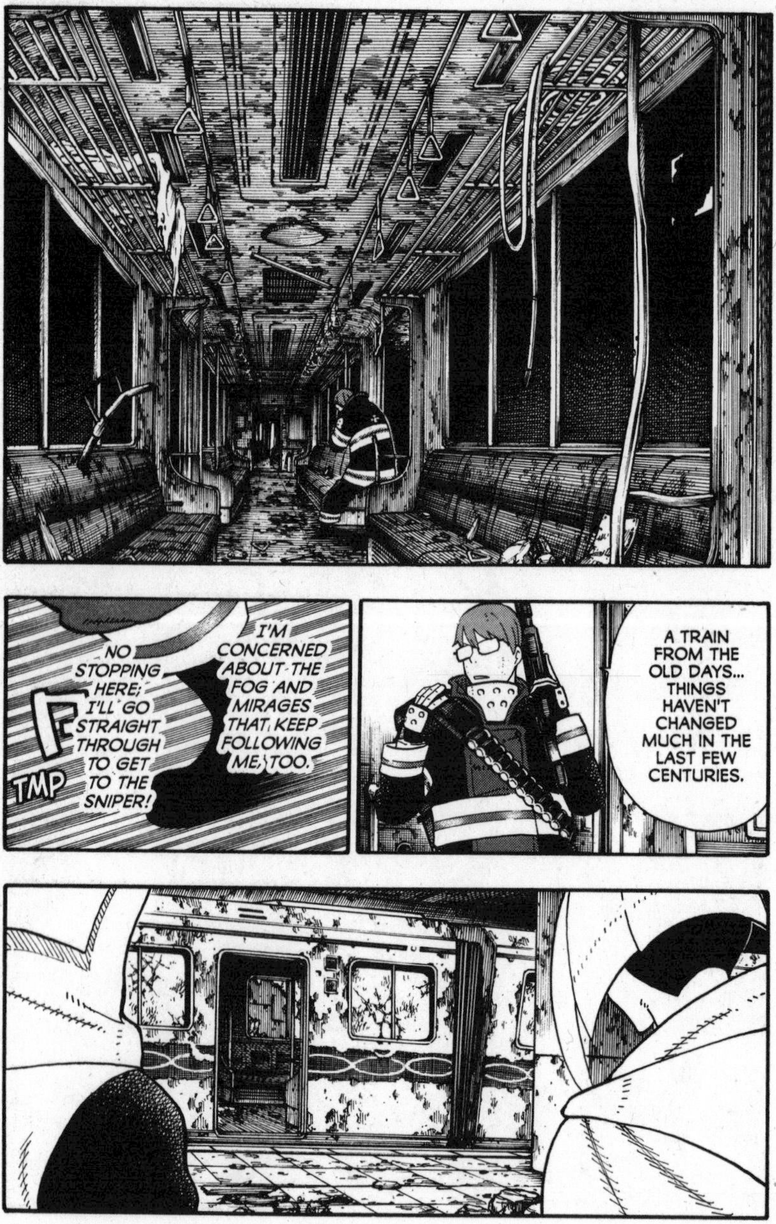
A TRAIN FROM THE OLD DAYS... THINGS HAVEN'T CHANGED MUCH IN THE LAST FEW CENTURIES.
I'M CONCERNED ABOUT THE FOG AND MIRAGES THAT KEEP FOLLOWING ME, TOO.
NO STOPPING HERE; I'LL GO STRAIGHT THROUGH TO GET TO THE SNIPER!
TMP

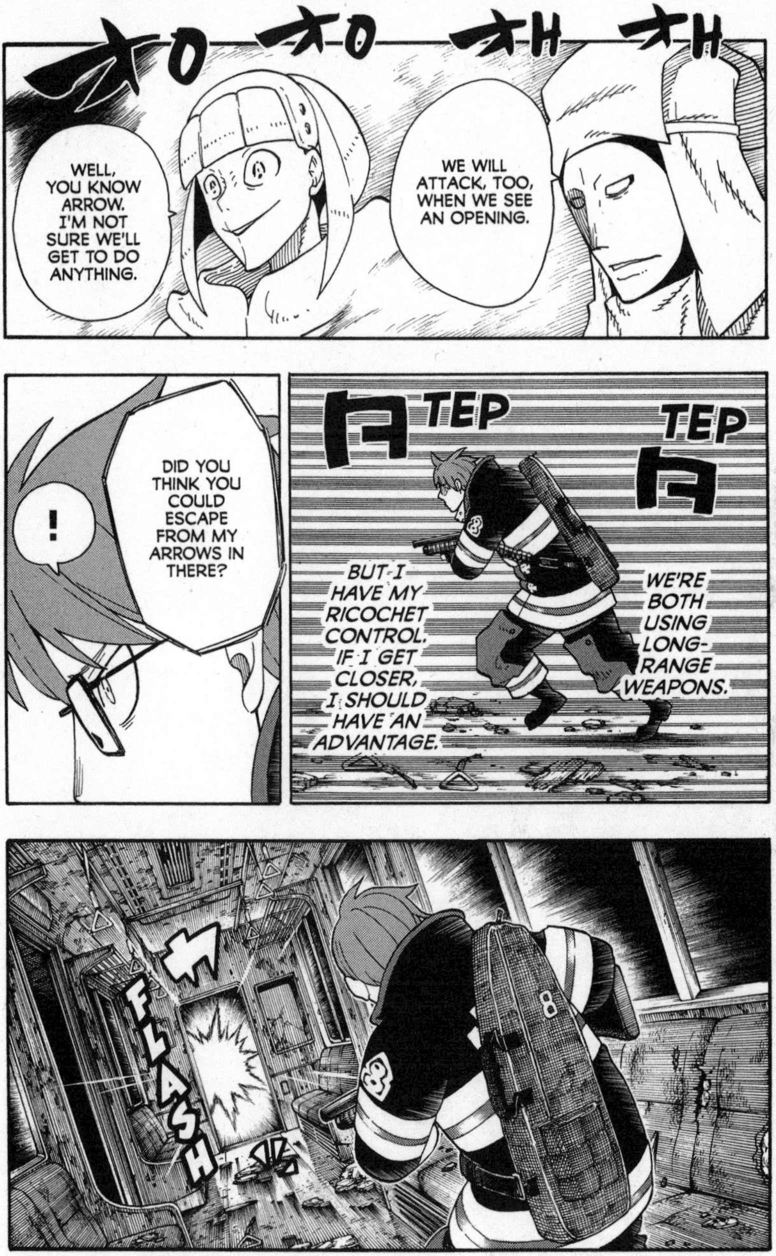
WE WILL ATTACK, TOO, WHEN WE SEE AN OPENING.
WELL, YOU KNOW ARROW. I'M NOT SURE WE'LL GET TO DO ANYTHING.
TEP
TEP
WE'RE BOTH USING LONG-RANGE WEAPONS.
BUT I HAVE MY RICOCHET CONTROL. IF I GET CLOSER, I SHOULD HAVE AN ADVANTAGE.
DID YOU THINK YOU COULD ESCAPE FROM MY ARROWS IN THERE?
!
FLASH

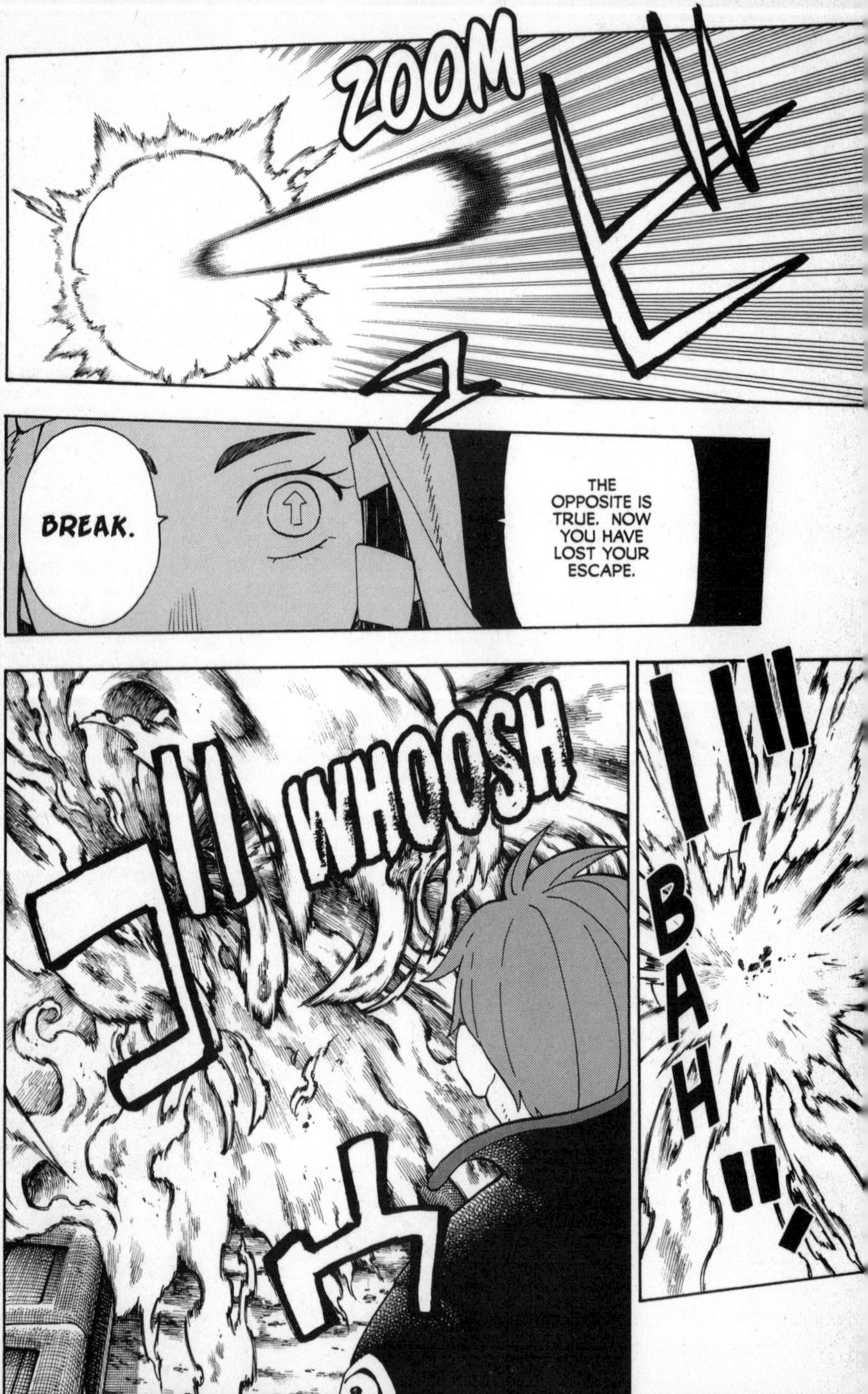
ZOOM
THE OPPOSITE IS TRUE. NOW YOU HAVE LOST YOUR ESCAPE.
BREAK.
BAH
WHOOSH

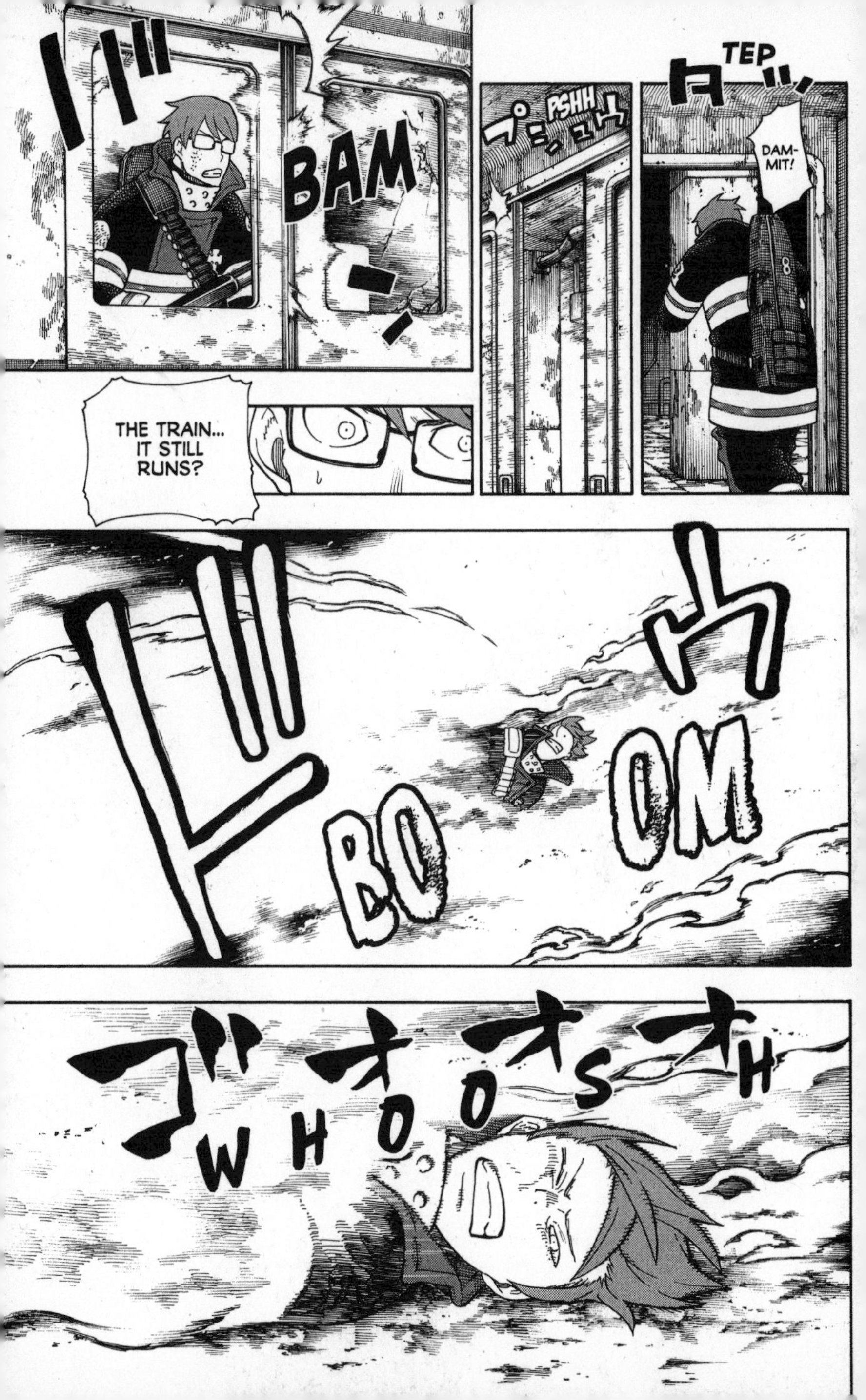
TEP
DAM-MIT!
PSHH
BAM
THE TRAIN... IT STILL RUNS?
BOOM
WHOOSH

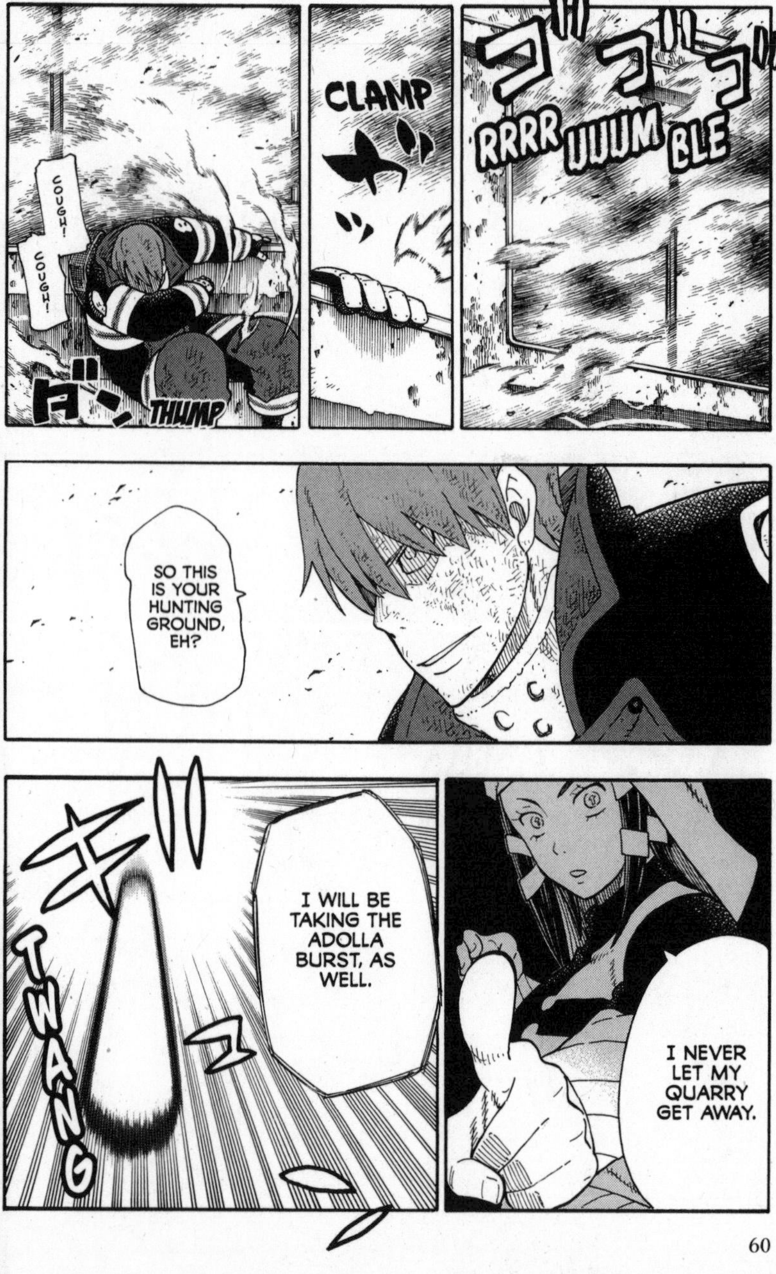
RRRRUUUMBLE
CLAMP
COUGH! COUGH!
THUMP
SO THIS IS YOUR HUNTING GROUND, EH?
I NEVER LET MY QUARRY GET AWAY.
I WILL BE TAKING THE ADOLLA BURST, AS WELL.
TWANG

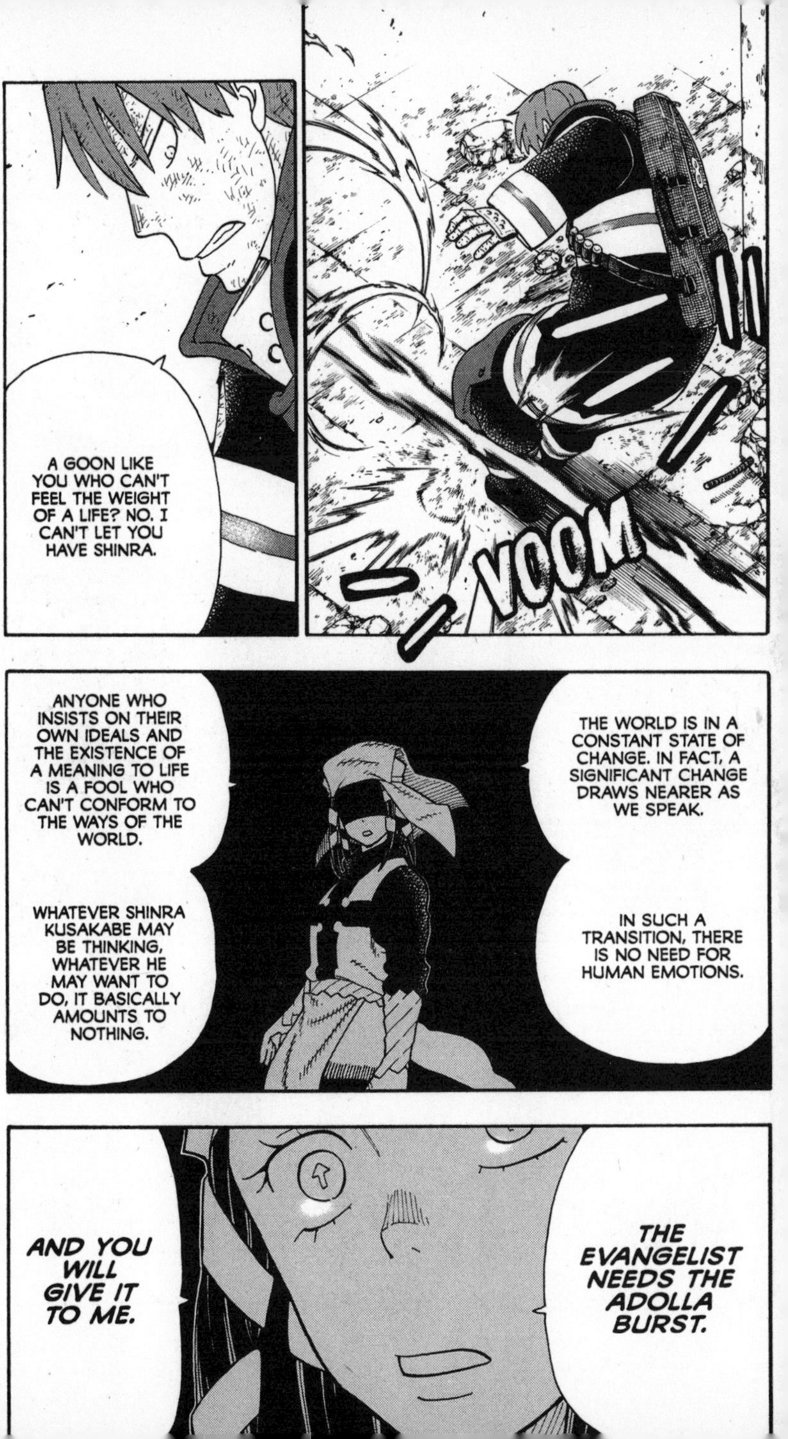
VOOM
A GOON LIKE YOU WHO CAN'T FEEL THE WEIGHT OF A LIFE? NO. I CAN'T LET YOU HAVE SHINRA.
THE WORLD IS IN A CONSTANT STATE OF CHANGE. IN FACT, A SIGNIFICANT CHANGE DRAWS NEARER AS WE SPEAK.
IN SUCH A TRANSITION, THERE IS NO NEED FOR HUMAN EMOTIONS.
ANYONE WHO INSISTS ON THEIR OWN IDEALS AND THE EXISTENCE OF A MEANING TO LIFE IS A FOOL WHO CAN'T CONFORM TO THE WAYS OF THE WORLD.
WHATEVER SHINRA KUSAKABE MAY BE THINKING, WHATEVER HE MAY WANT TO DO, IT BASICALLY AMOUNTS TO NOTHING.
THE EVANGELIST NEEDS THE ADOLLA BURST.
AND YOU WILL GIVE IT TO ME.

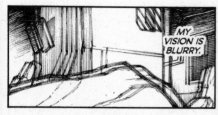

FSH
DAMMIT... MY GLASSES...
MY VISION IS BLURRY.
AND THIS OBNOXIOUS FOG...
WHEN YOU BELONG TO AN ORGANIZATION, YOUR INDIVIDUAL EMOTIONS ARE NO LONGER IMPORTANT.
EVEN MORE SO IF THAT ORGANIZATION IS A GOVERNMENT OR THE WHOLE WORLD.
FZHH
IN OUR WORLD, PEOPLE BURST INTO FLAMES...AND BURN TO NOTHING.
RATHER THAN GETTING STUCK WHERE YOU ARE, CONSTANTLY LOST AND CONFUSED,
IT'S PROBABLY BETTER FOR EVERYONE IF YOU STAY INDIFFERENT AND UNEMOTIONAL, JUST DOING YOUR DUTY AS ANOTHER COG IN THE MACHINE.
MORE THAN A FEW PEOPLE THINK THAT, MYSELF INCLUDED.

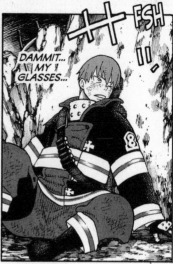

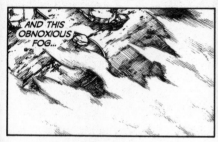

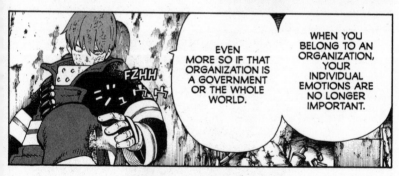

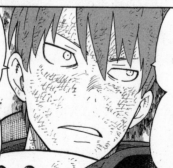

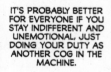

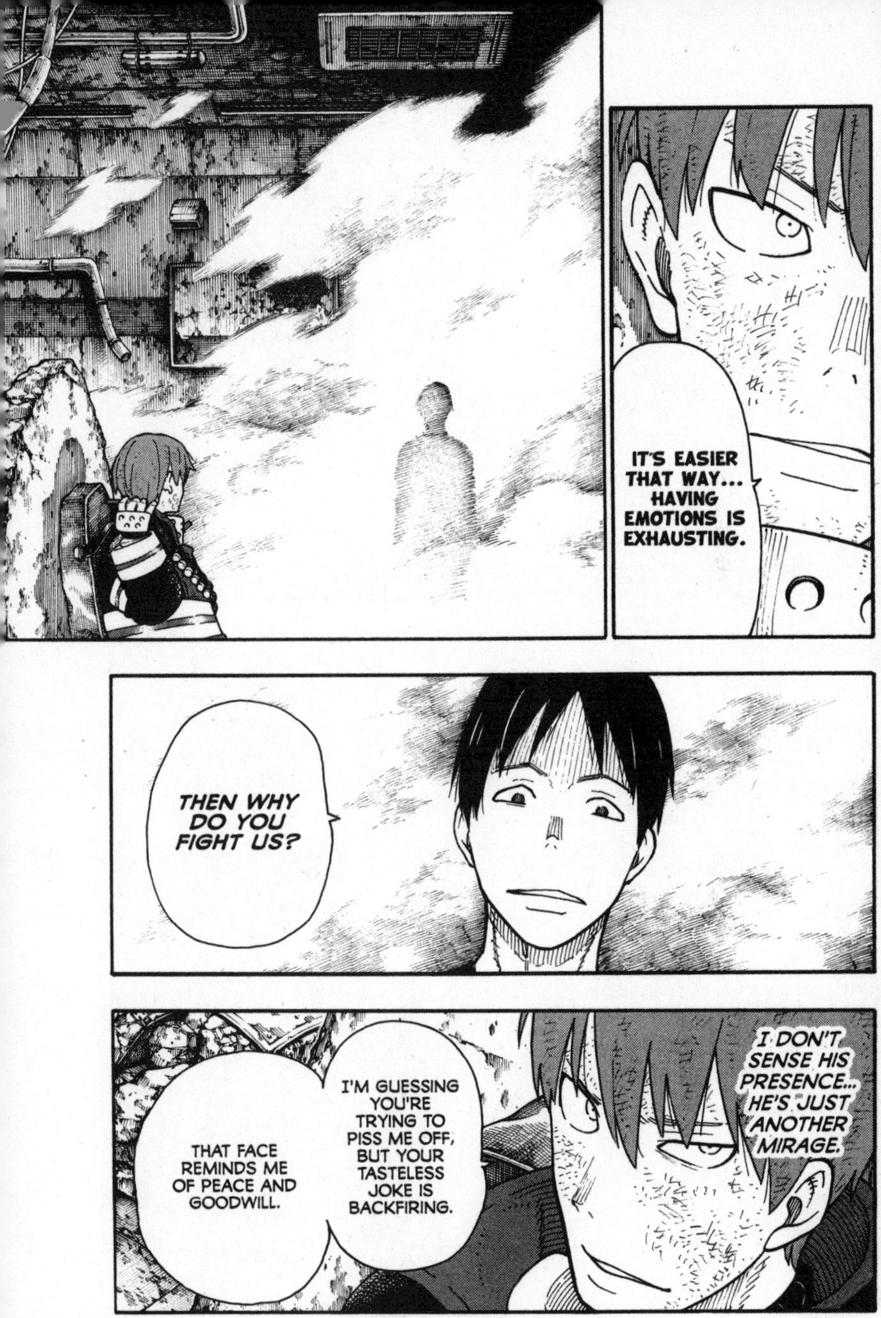
IT'S EASIER THAT WAY... HAVING EMOTIONS IS EXHAUSTING.
THEN WHY DO YOU FIGHT US?
I DON'T SENSE HIS PRESENCE... HE'S JUST ANOTHER MIRAGE.
I'M GUESSING YOU'RE TRYING TO PISS ME OFF, BUT YOUR TASTELESS JOKE IS BACKFIRING.
THAT FACE REMINDS ME OF PEACE AND GOODWILL.

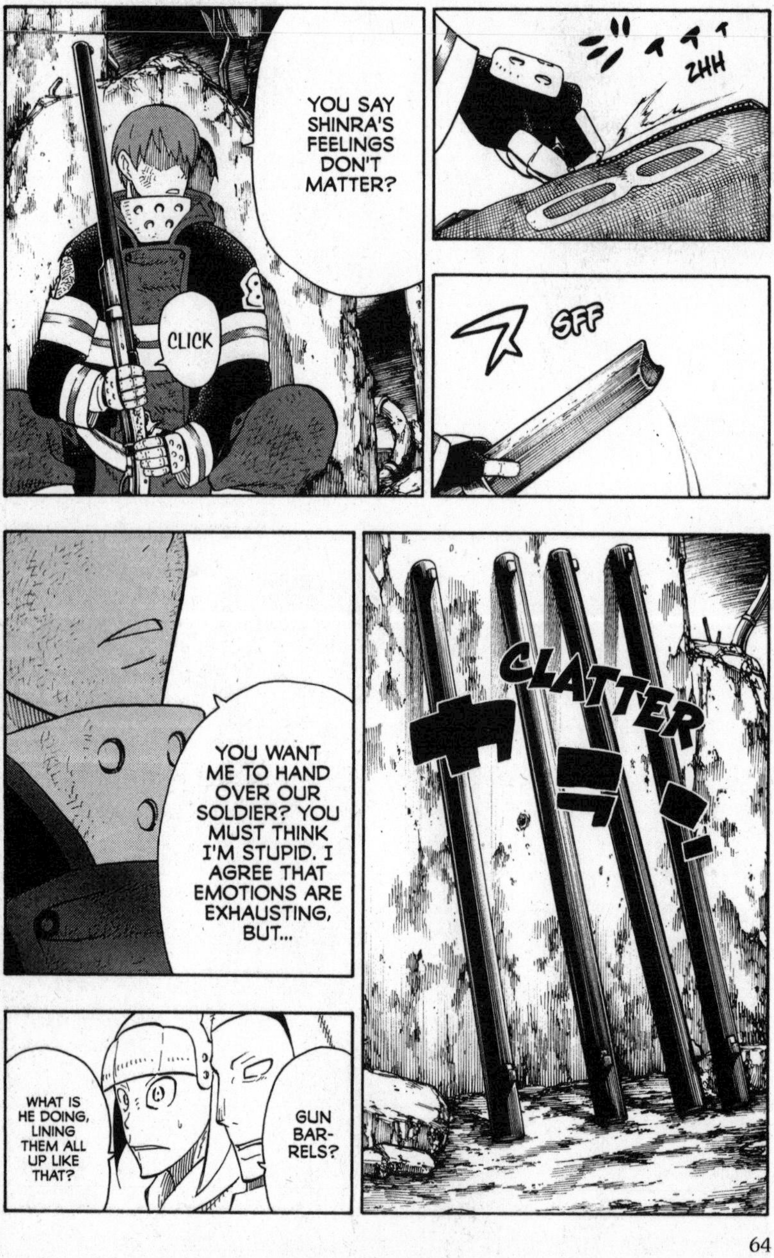
ZHH
SFF
YOU SAY SHINRA'S FEELINGS DON'T MATTER?
CLICK
CLATTER
YOU WANT ME TO HAND OVER OUR SOLDIER? YOU MUST THINK I'M STUPID. I AGREE THAT EMOTIONS ARE EXHAUSTING, BUT...
GUN BARRELS?
WHAT IS HE DOING, LINING THEM ALL UP LIKE THAT?

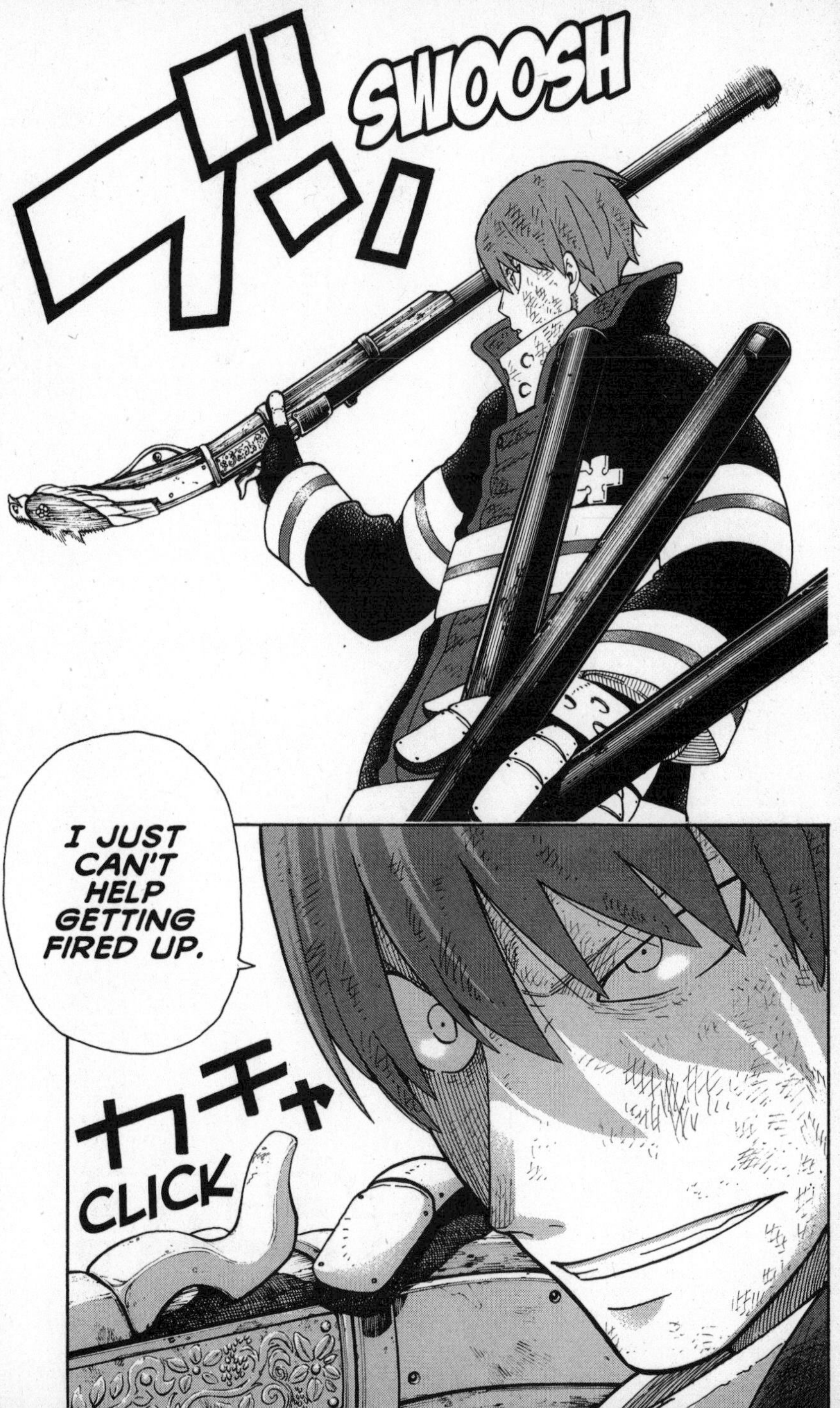
SWOOSH
I JUST CAN'T HELP GETTING FIRED UP.
カチャ
CLICK

FIRE FORCE

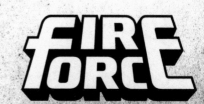

Broken glasses

CHAPTER LXXIII: WEARING HIS PRIDE

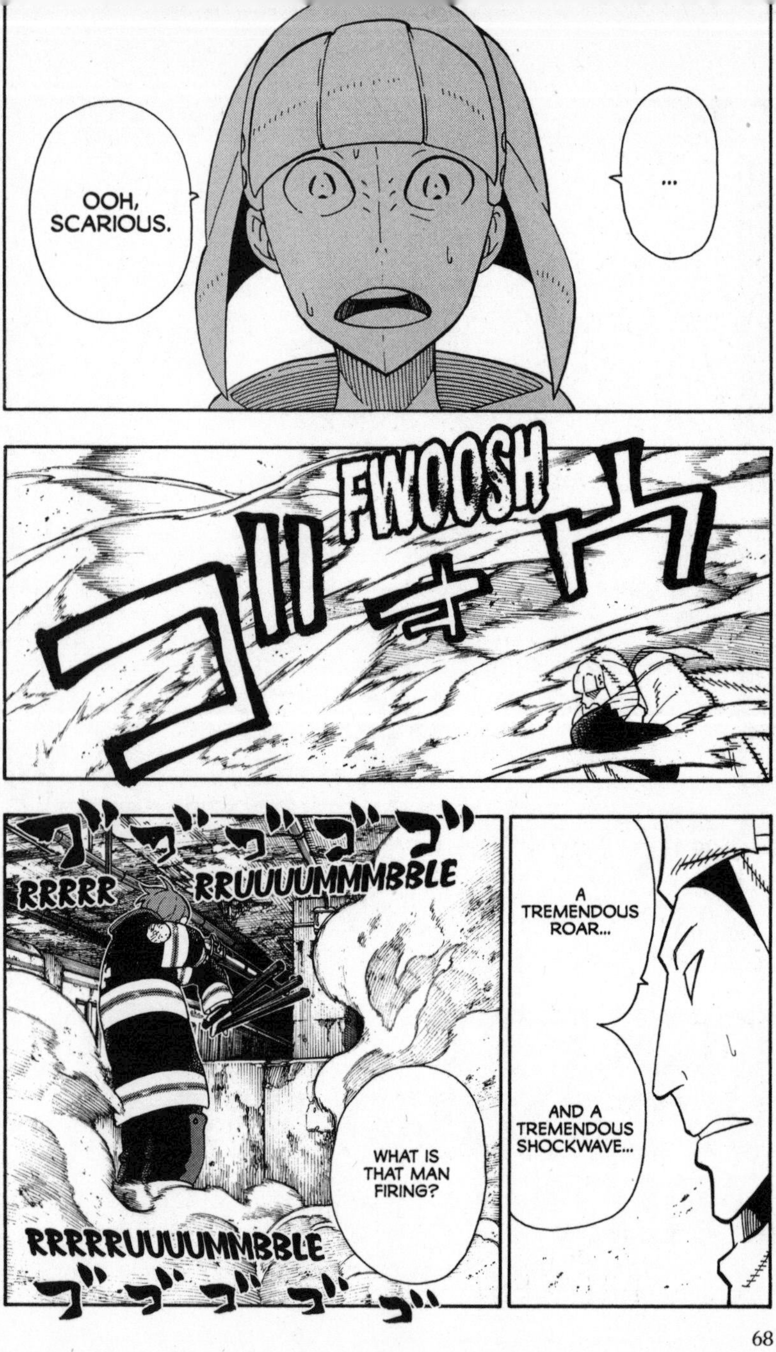
...
OOH, SCARIOUS.
FWOOSH
A TREMENDOUS ROAR...
AND A TREMENDOUS SHOCKWAVE...
RRUUUUMMMBBLE
RRRRR
WHAT IS THAT MAN FIRING?
RRRRRUUUUMMBBLE

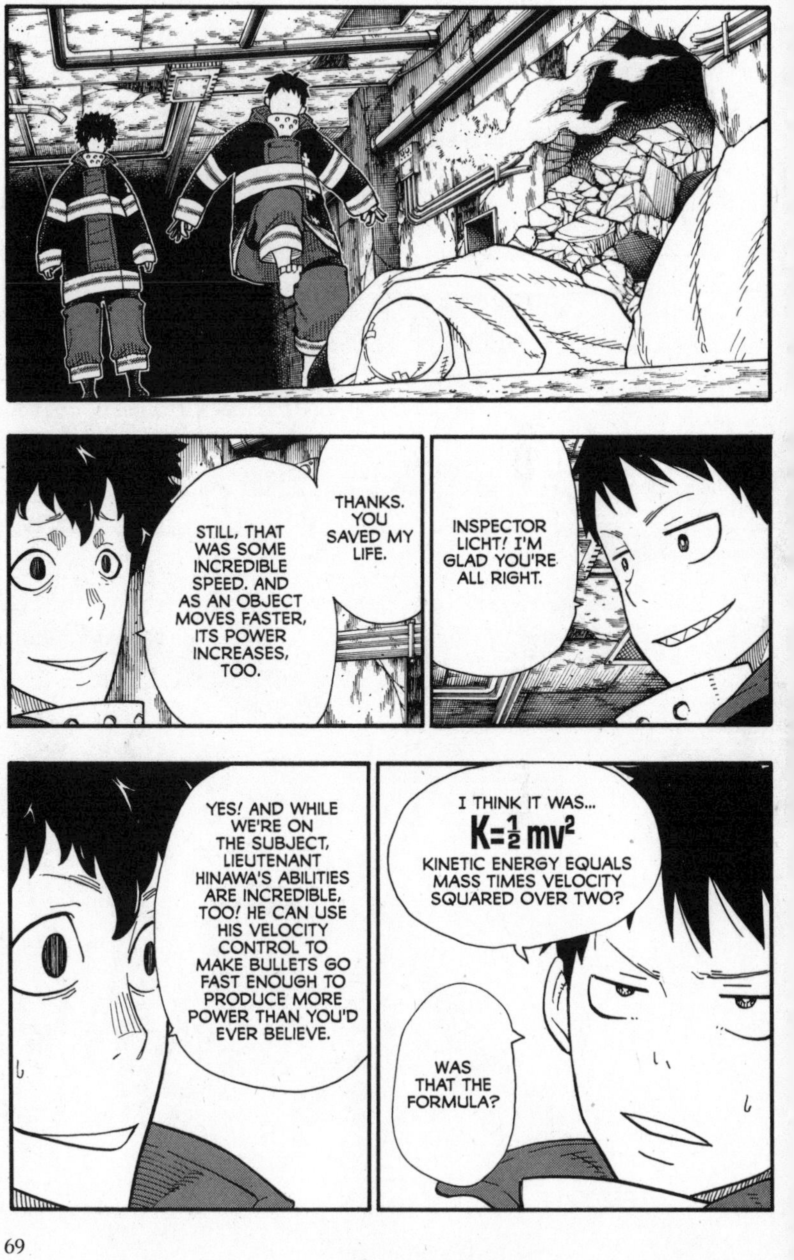
INSPECTOR LICHT! I'M GLAD YOU'RE ALL RIGHT.
THANKS. YOU SAVED MY LIFE.
STILL, THAT WAS SOME INCREDIBLE SPEED. AND AS AN OBJECT MOVES FASTER, ITS POWER INCREASES, TOO.
I THINK IT WAS... $K=\frac{1}{2}mv^2$ KINETIC ENERGY EQUALS MASS TIMES VELOCITY SQUARED OVER TWO?
WAS THAT THE FORMULA?
YES! AND WHILE WE'RE ON THE SUBJECT, LIEUTENANT HINAWA'S ABILITIES ARE INCREDIBLE, TOO! HE CAN USE HIS VELOCITY CONTROL TO MAKE BULLETS GO FAST ENOUGH TO PRODUCE MORE POWER THAN YOU'D EVER BELIEVE.

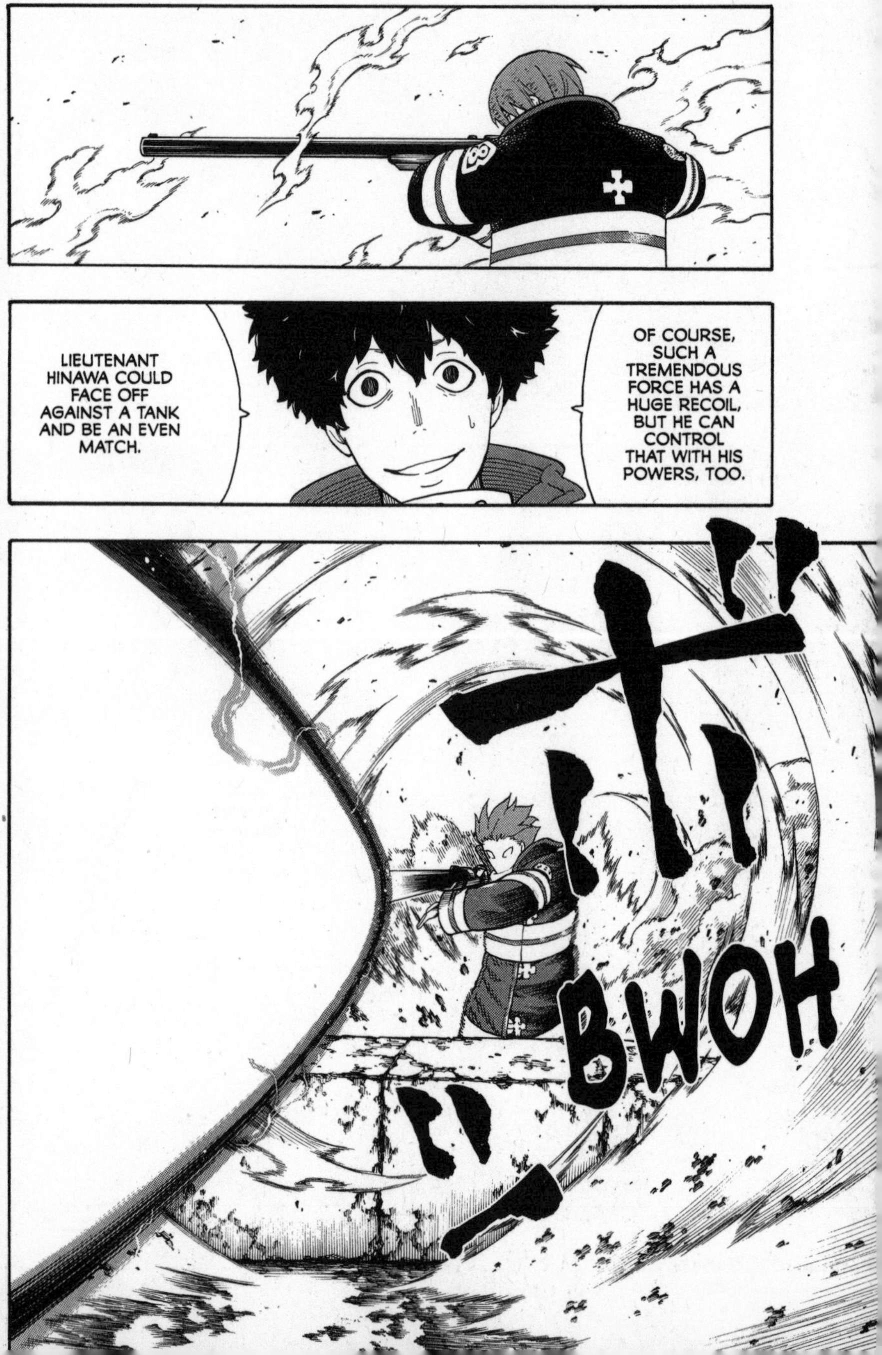
OF COURSE, SUCH A TREMENDOUS FORCE HAS A HUGE RECOIL, BUT HE CAN CONTROL THAT WITH HIS POWERS, TOO.
LIEUTENANT HINAWA COULD FACE OFF AGAINST A TANK AND BE AN EVEN MATCH.
BWOH

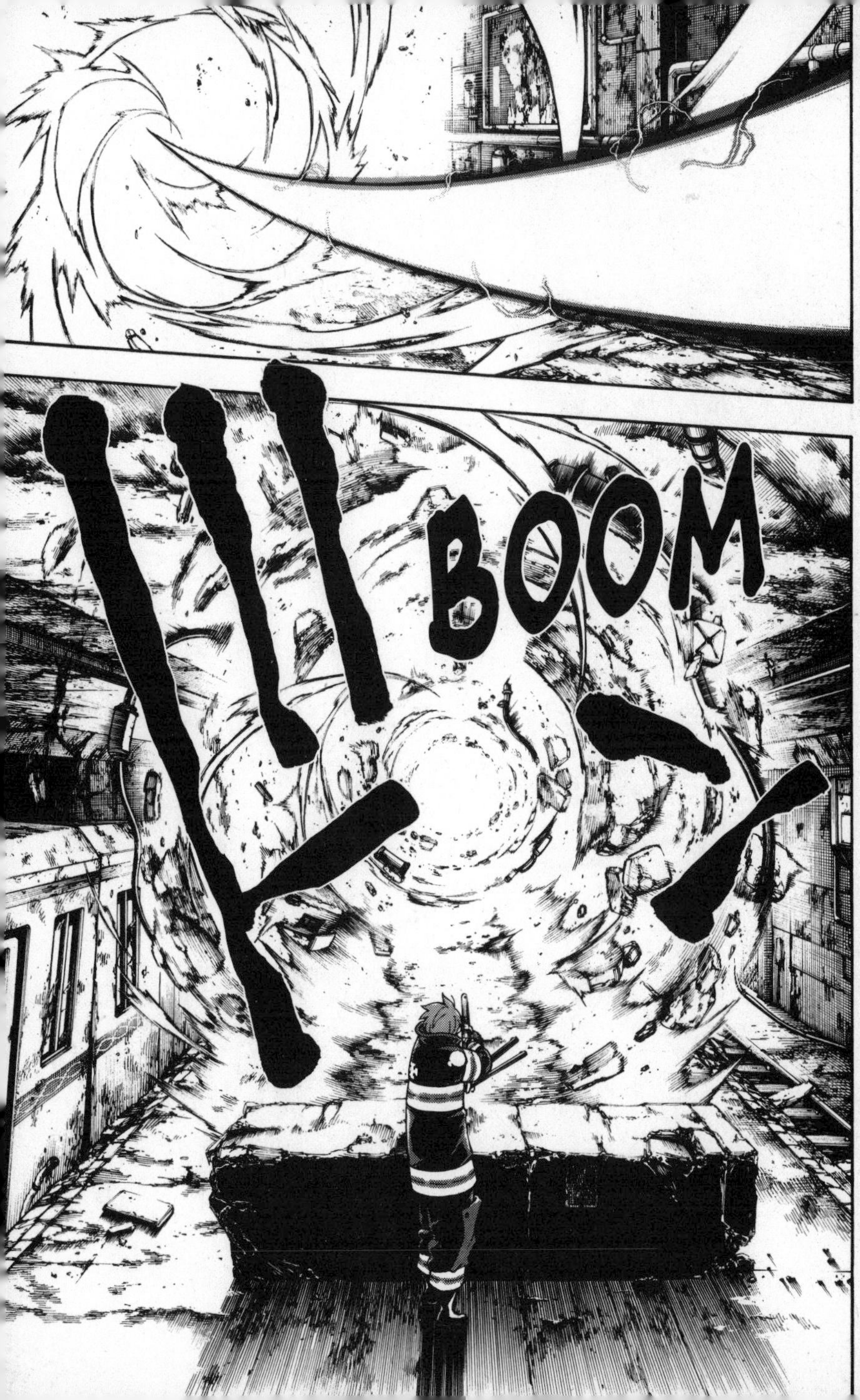
BOOM

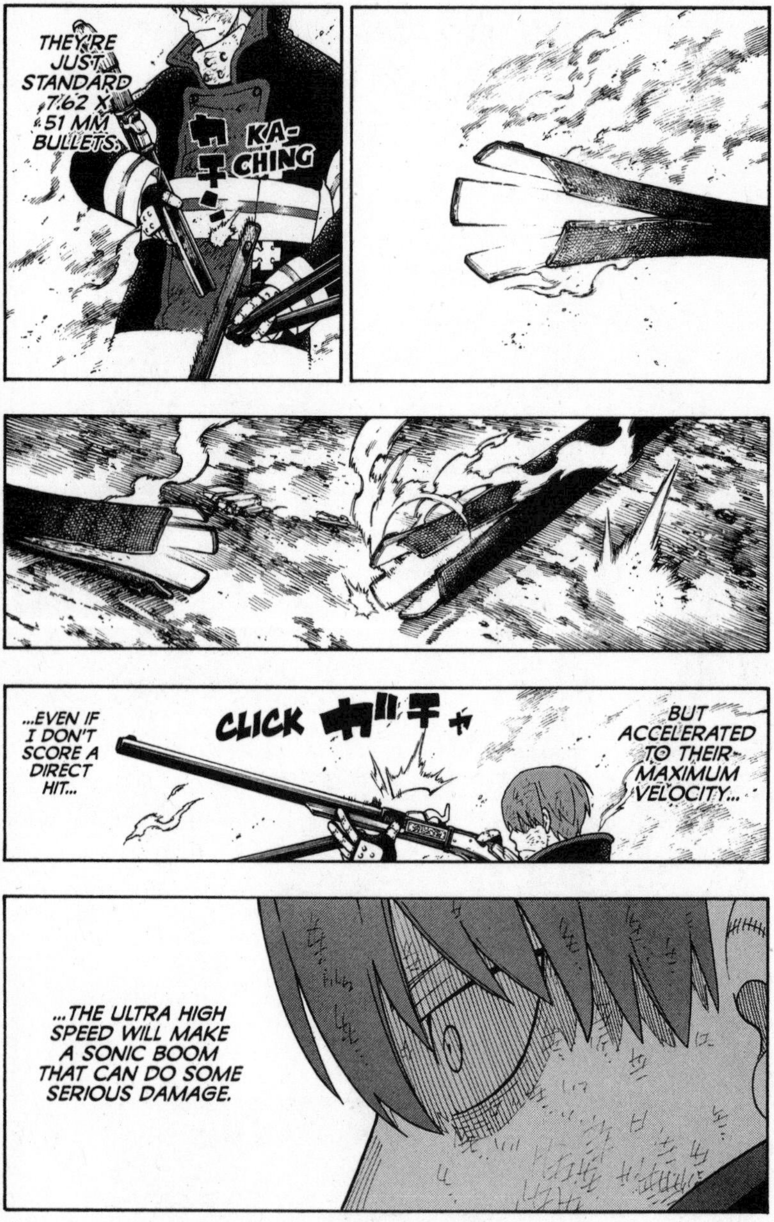
THEY'RE JUST STANDARD 7.62 X 51 MM BULLETS.
KA-CHING
BUT ACCELERATED TO THEIR MAXIMUM VELOCITY...
CLICK
...EVEN IF I DON'T SCORE A DIRECT HIT...
...THE ULTRA HIGH SPEED WILL MAKE A SONIC BOOM THAT CAN DO SOME SERIOUS DAMAGE.

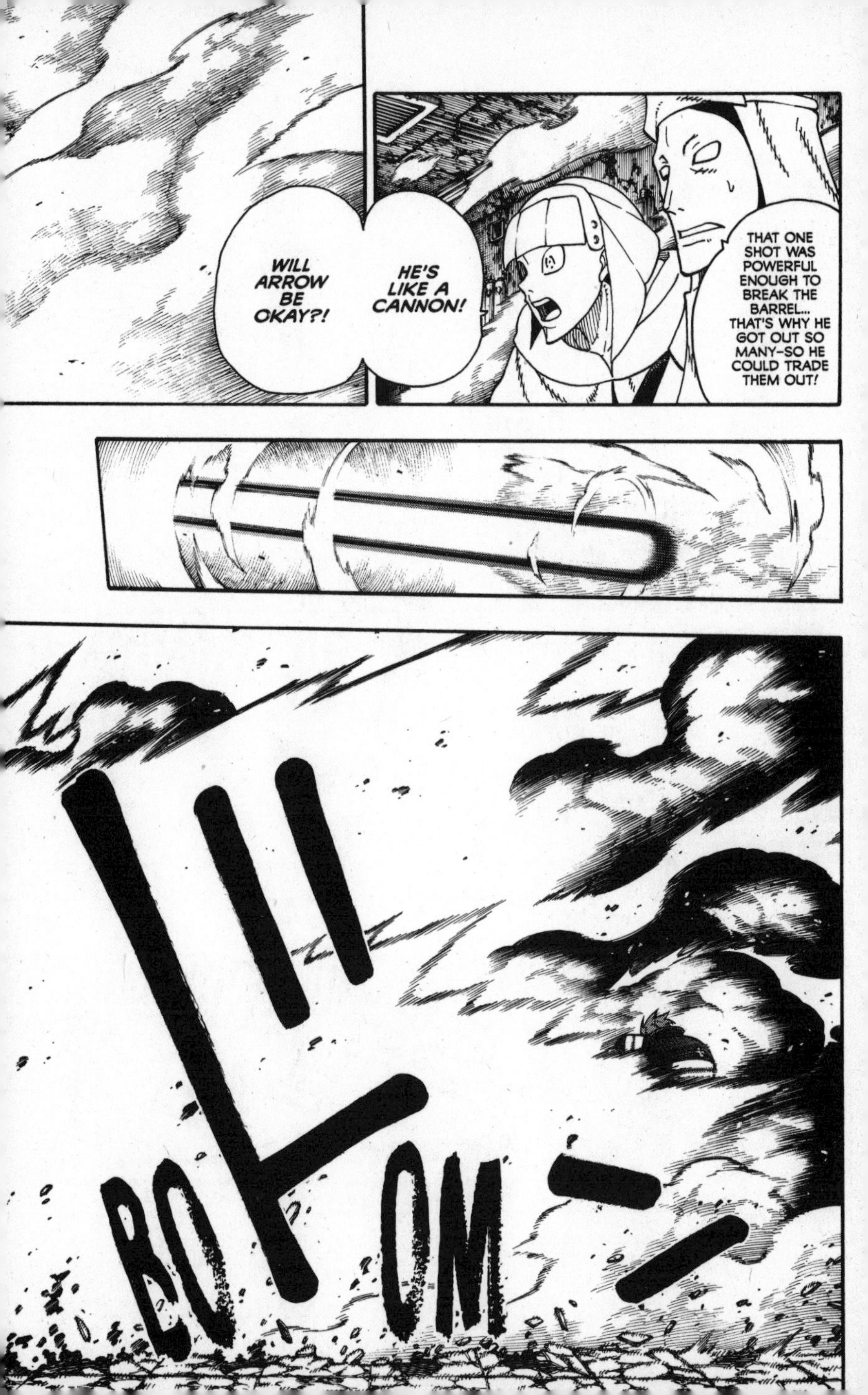
THAT ONE SHOT WAS POWERFUL ENOUGH TO BREAK THE BARREL... THAT'S WHY HE GOT OUT SO MANY–SO HE COULD TRADE THEM OUT!
HE'S LIKE A CANNON!
WILL ARROW BE OKAY?!
BOOM

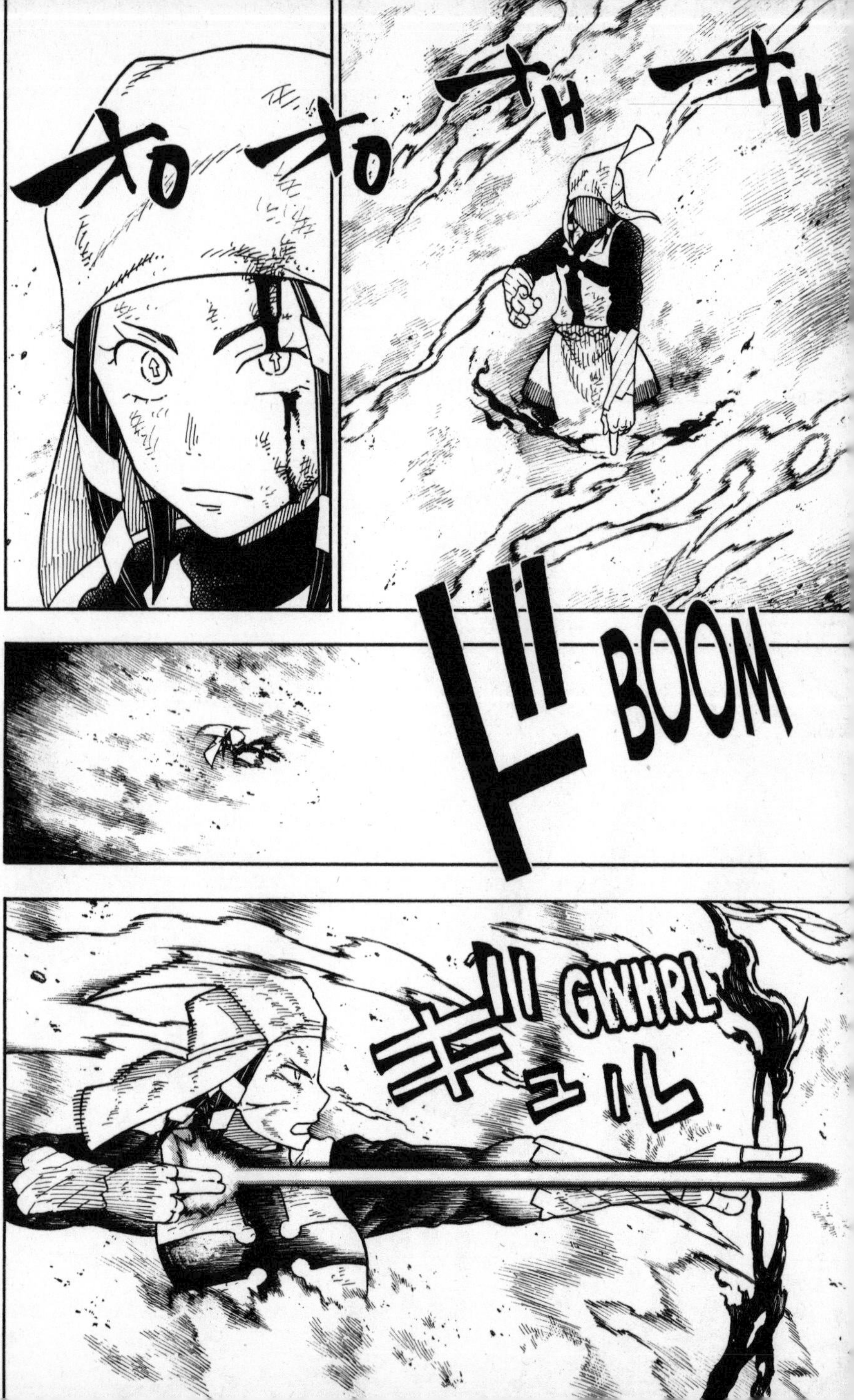

TH
TH
BOOM
GWHRL

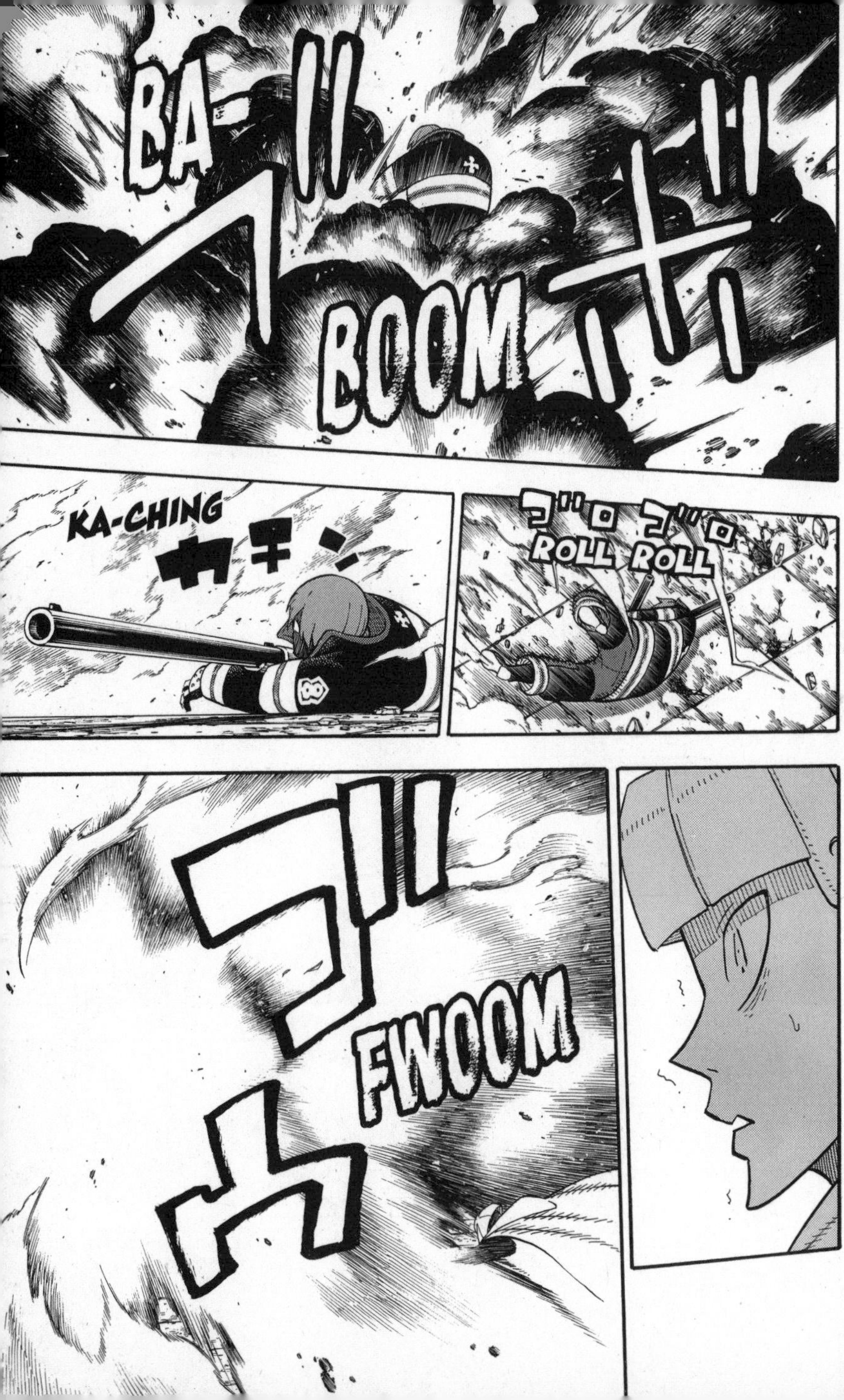
BA-
BOOM
ゴロゴロ
ROLL ROLL
KA-CHING
カチン
FWOOM

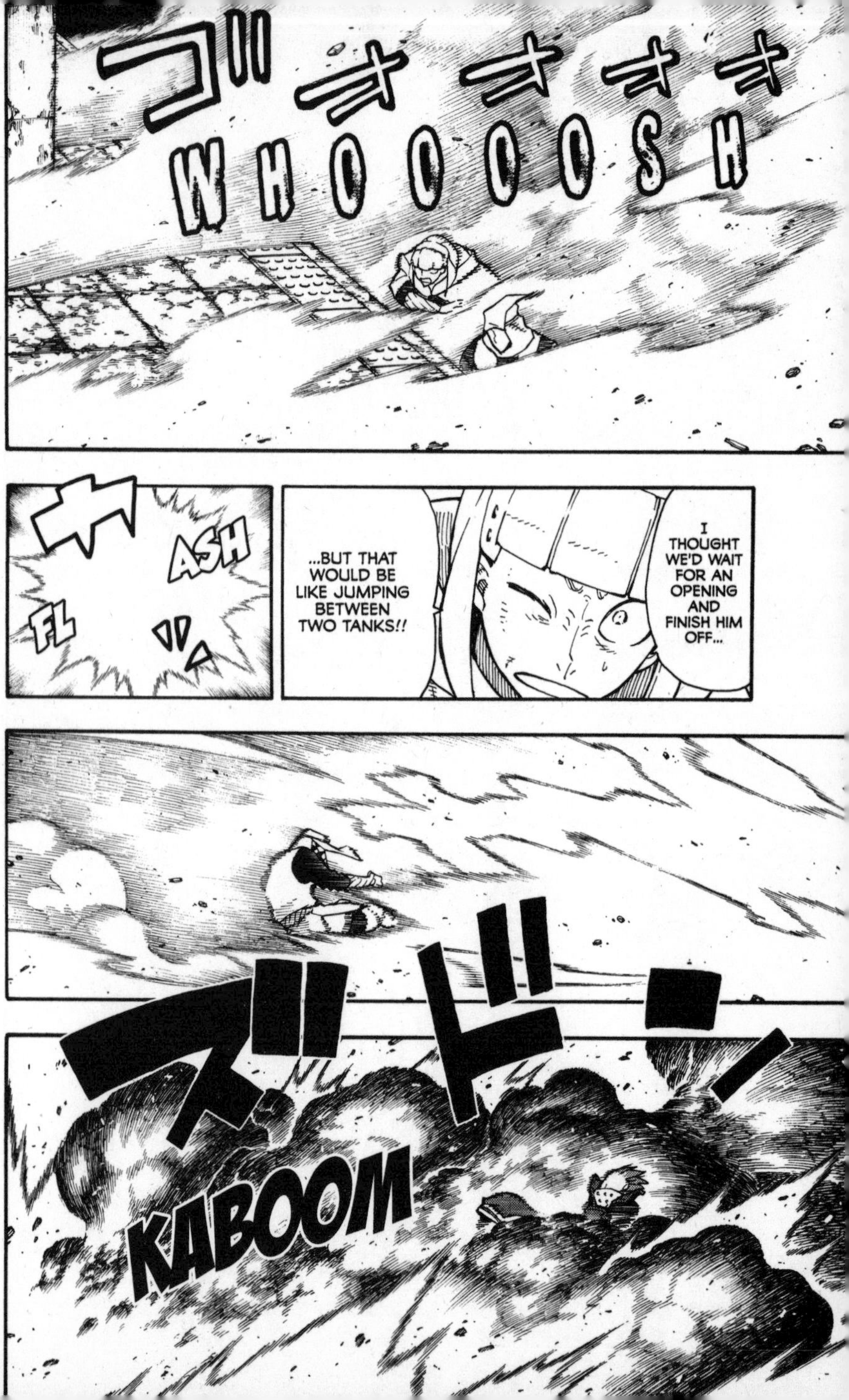
WHOOOOSH
I THOUGHT WE'D WAIT FOR AN OPENING AND FINISH HIM OFF...
...BUT THAT WOULD BE LIKE JUMPING BETWEEN TWO TANKS!!
FL
ASH
KABOOM

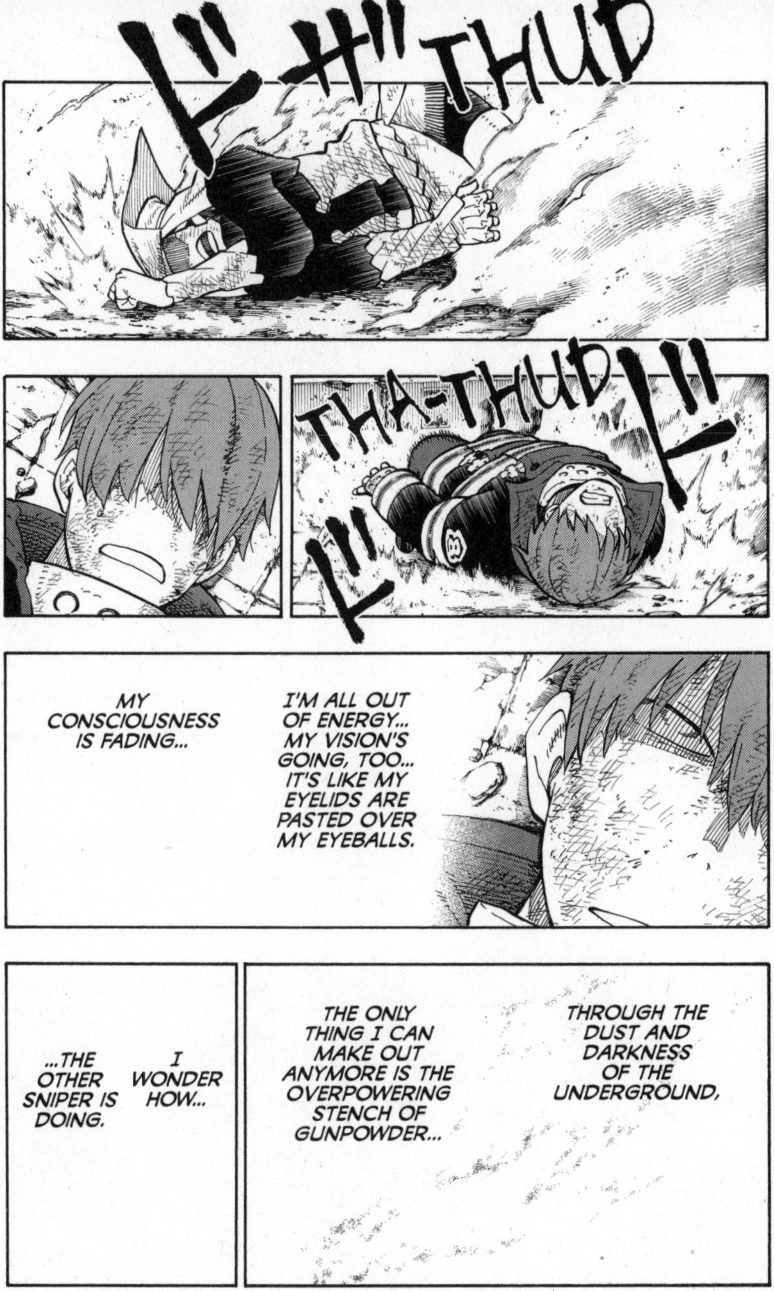

ドザ
THUD
THA-THUD
ド
ド
I'M ALL OUT OF ENERGY... MY VISION'S GOING, TOO... IT'S LIKE MY EYELIDS ARE PASTED OVER MY EYEBALLS.
MY CONSCIOUSNESS IS FADING...
THROUGH THE DUST AND DARKNESS OF THE UNDERGROUND,
THE ONLY THING I CAN MAKE OUT ANYMORE IS THE OVERPOWERING STENCH OF GUNPOWDER...
I WONDER HOW...
...THE OTHER SNIPER IS DOING.

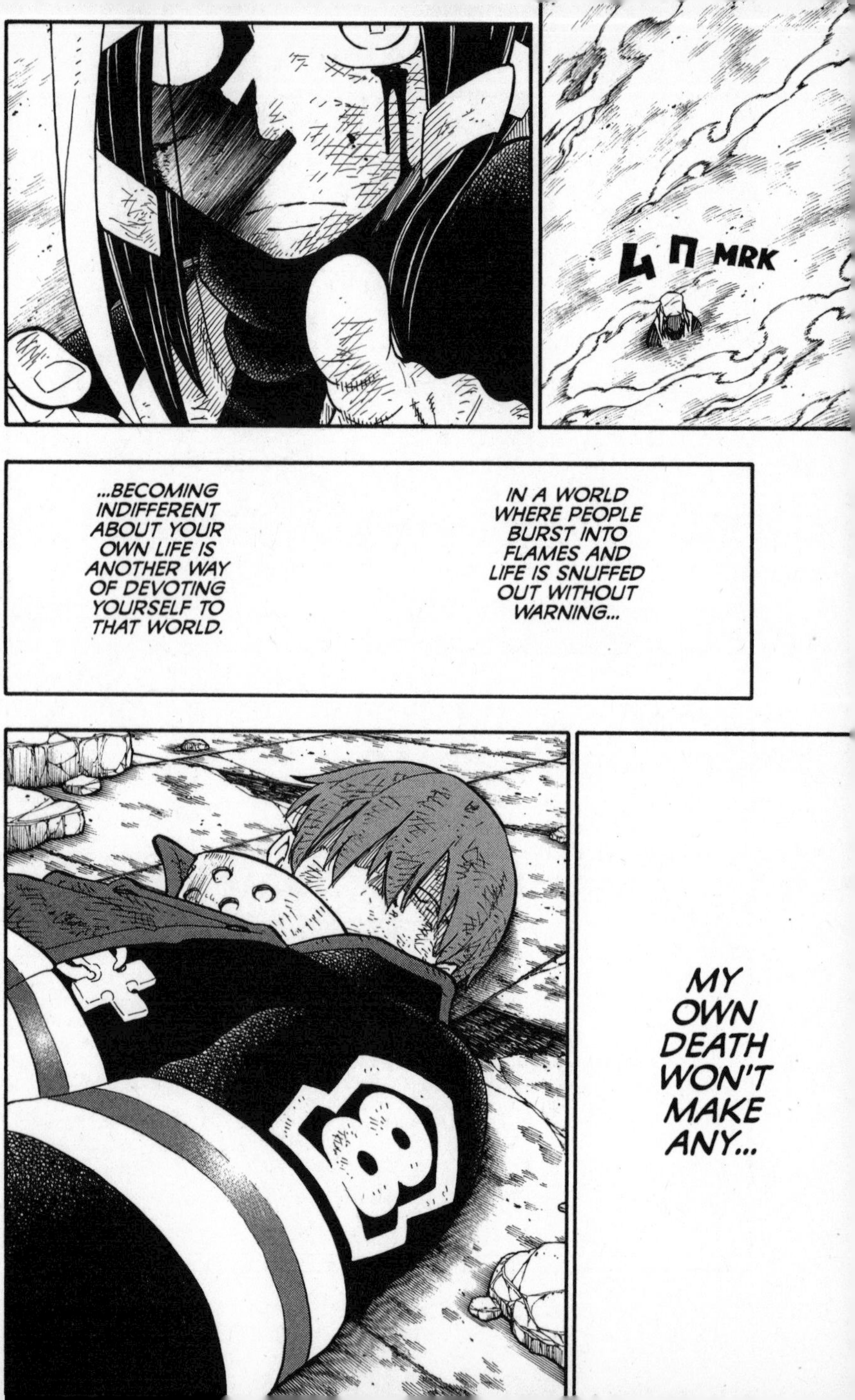
MRK
IN A WORLD WHERE PEOPLE BURST INTO FLAMES AND LIFE IS SNUFFED OUT WITHOUT WARNING...
...BECOMING INDIFFERENT ABOUT YOUR OWN LIFE IS ANOTHER WAY OF DEVOTING YOURSELF TO THAT WORLD.
MY OWN DEATH WON'T MAKE ANY...

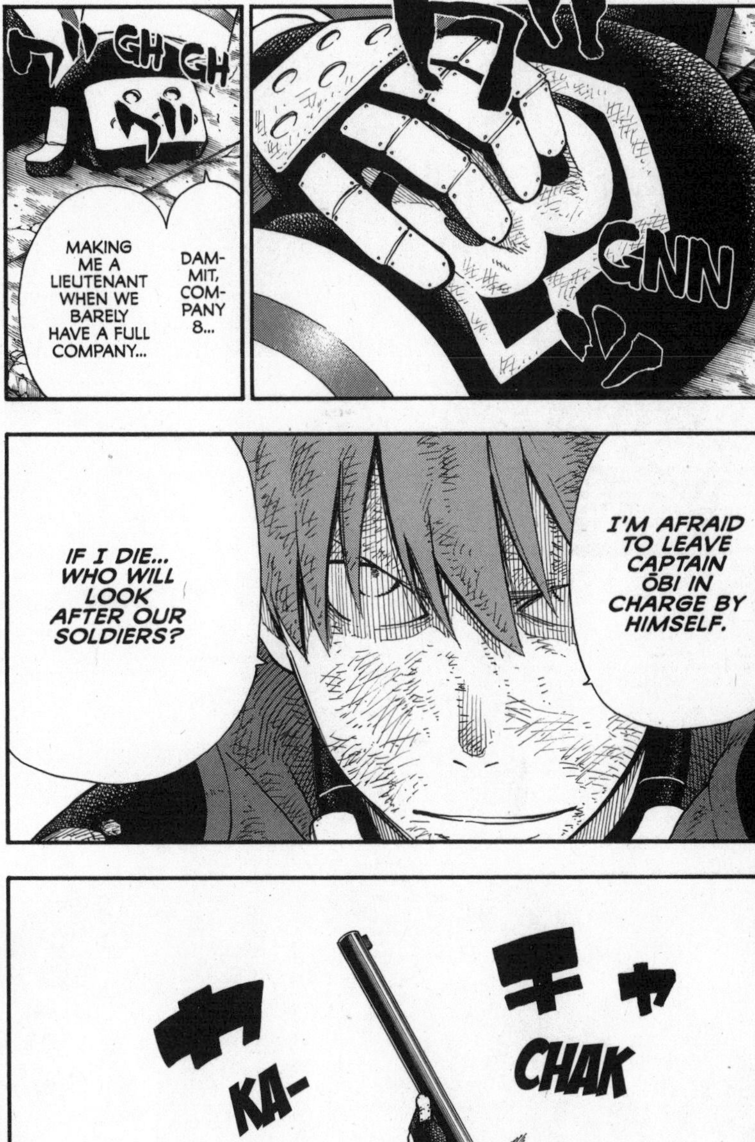
GNN
GH GH
DAM-MIT, COMPANY 8...
MAKING ME A LIEUTENANT WHEN WE BARELY HAVE A FULL COMPANY...
I'M AFRAID TO LEAVE CAPTAIN ŌBI IN CHARGE BY HIMSELF.
IF I DIE... WHO WILL LOOK AFTER OUR SOLDIERS?
KA-
CHAK

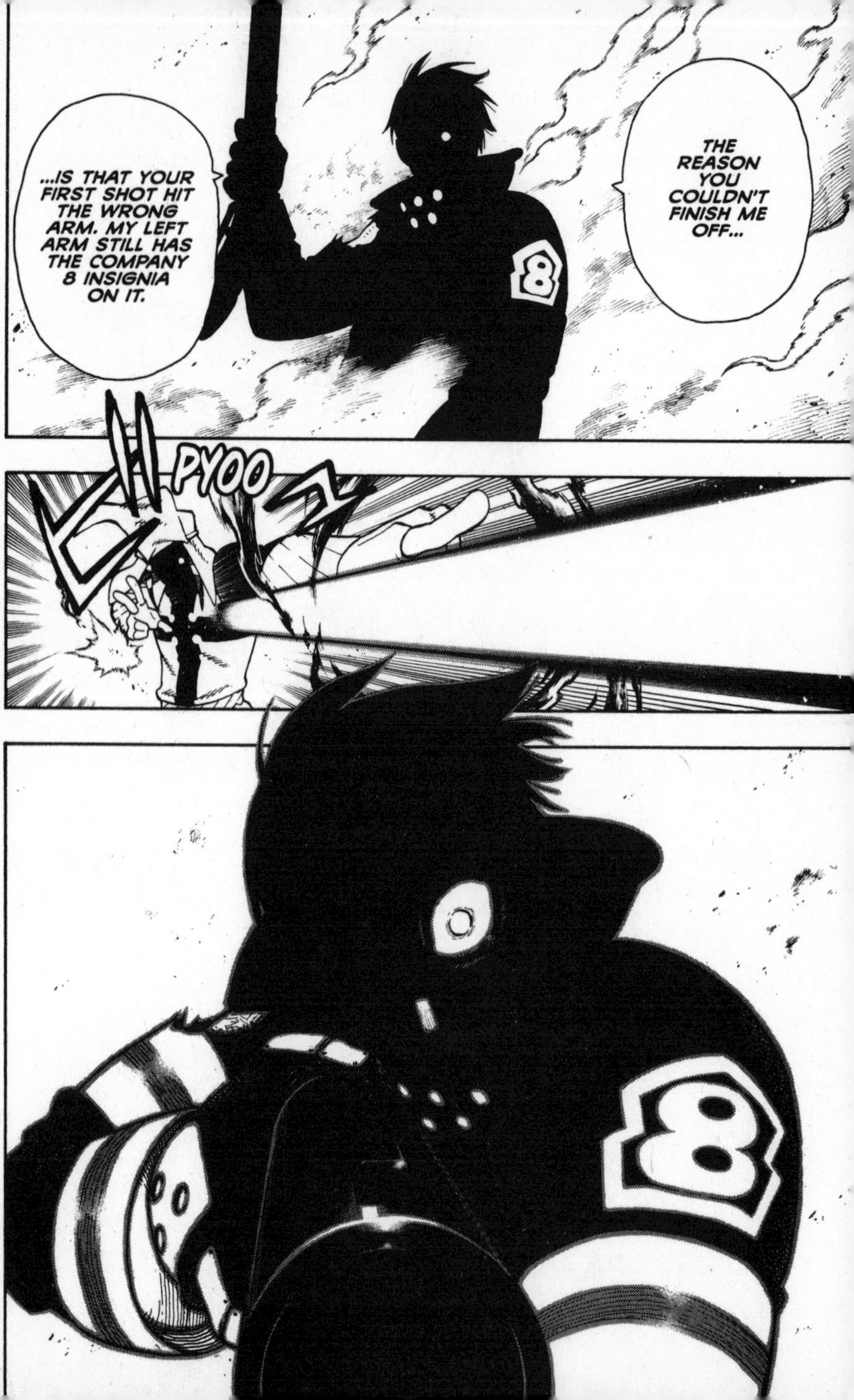
THE REASON YOU COULDN'T FINISH ME OFF...
...IS THAT YOUR FIRST SHOT HIT THE WRONG ARM. MY LEFT ARM STILL HAS THE COMPANY 8 INSIGNIA ON IT.
PYOO

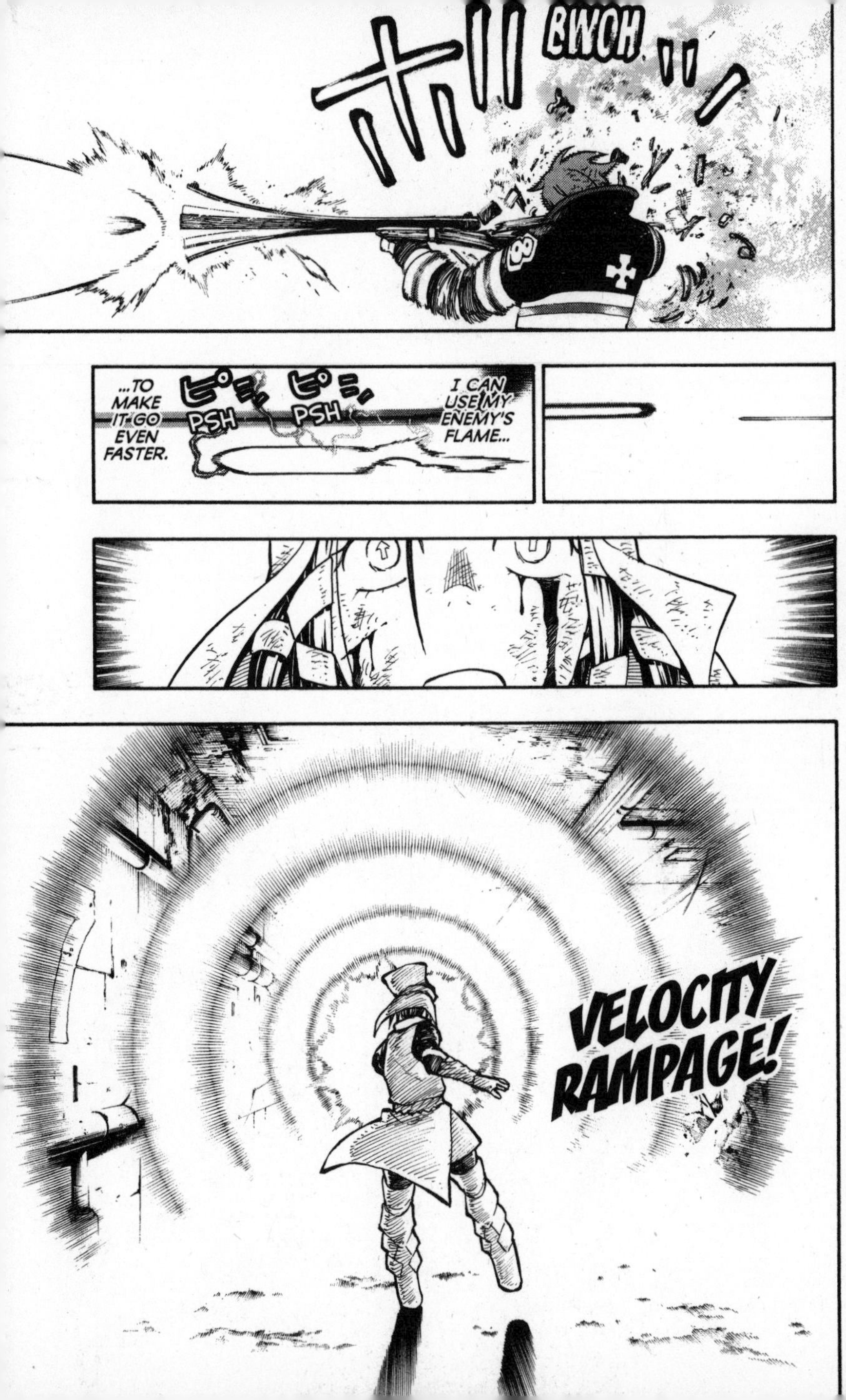
BWOH
I CAN USE MY ENEMY'S FLAME...
PSH
PSH
...TO MAKE IT GO EVEN FASTER.
VELOCITY RAMPAGE!

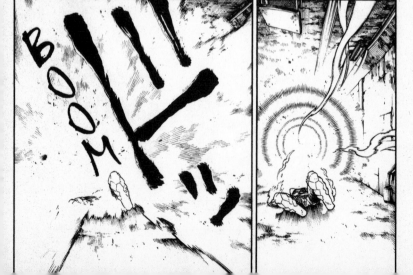

BOOOM

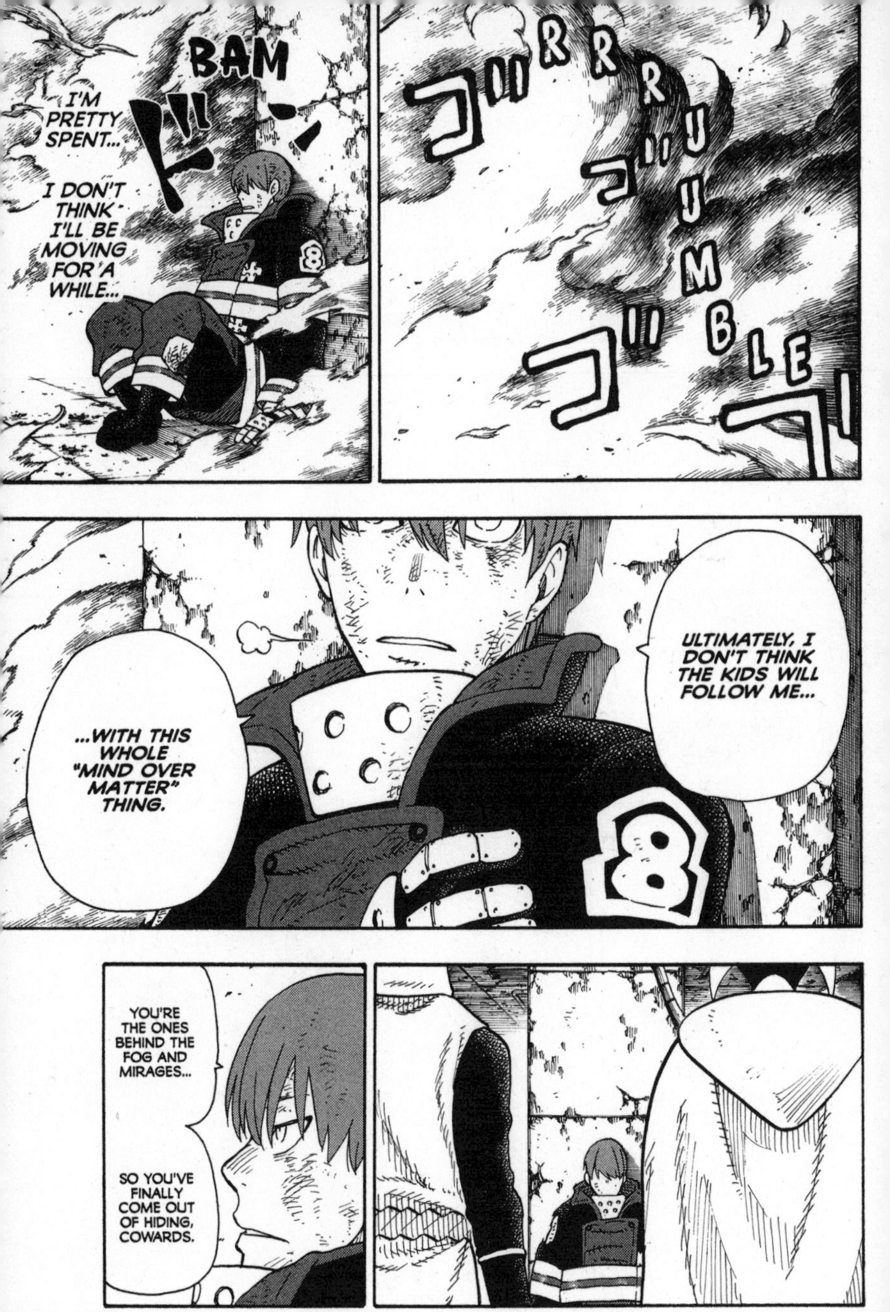
RRRUUMBLE
BAM
I'M PRETTY SPENT...
I DON'T THINK I'LL BE MOVING FOR A WHILE...
ULTIMATELY, I DON'T THINK THE KIDS WILL FOLLOW ME...
...WITH THIS WHOLE "MIND OVER MATTER" THING.
YOU'RE THE ONES BEHIND THE FOG AND MIRAGES...
SO YOU'VE FINALLY COME OUT OF HIDING, COWARDS.

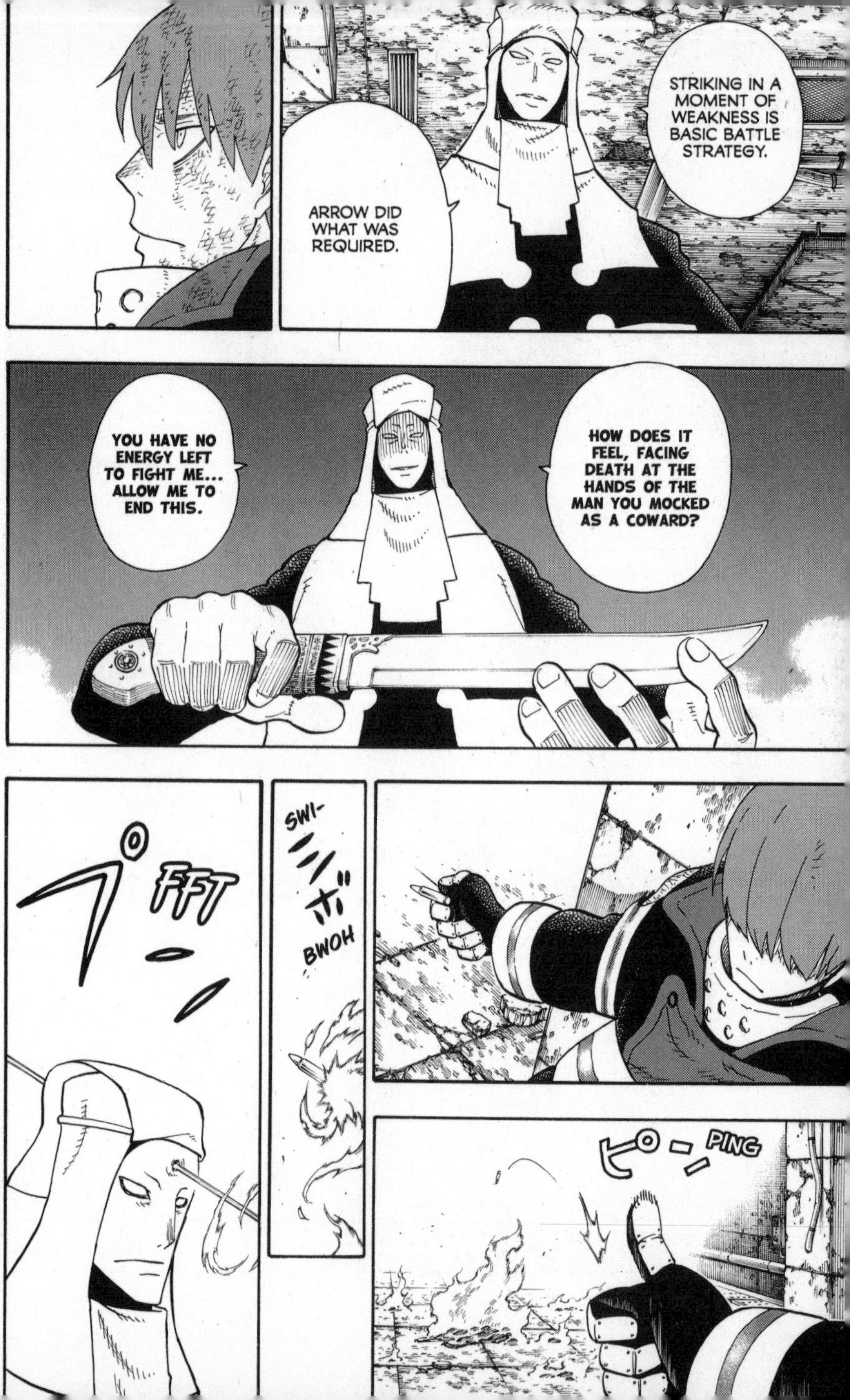

STRIKING IN A MOMENT OF WEAKNESS IS BASIC BATTLE STRATEGY.
ARROW DID WHAT WAS REQUIRED.
HOW DOES IT FEEL, FACING DEATH AT THE HANDS OF THE MAN YOU MOCKED AS A COWARD?
YOU HAVE NO ENERGY LEFT TO FIGHT ME... ALLOW ME TO END THIS.
PING
SWI-
BWOH
FFT

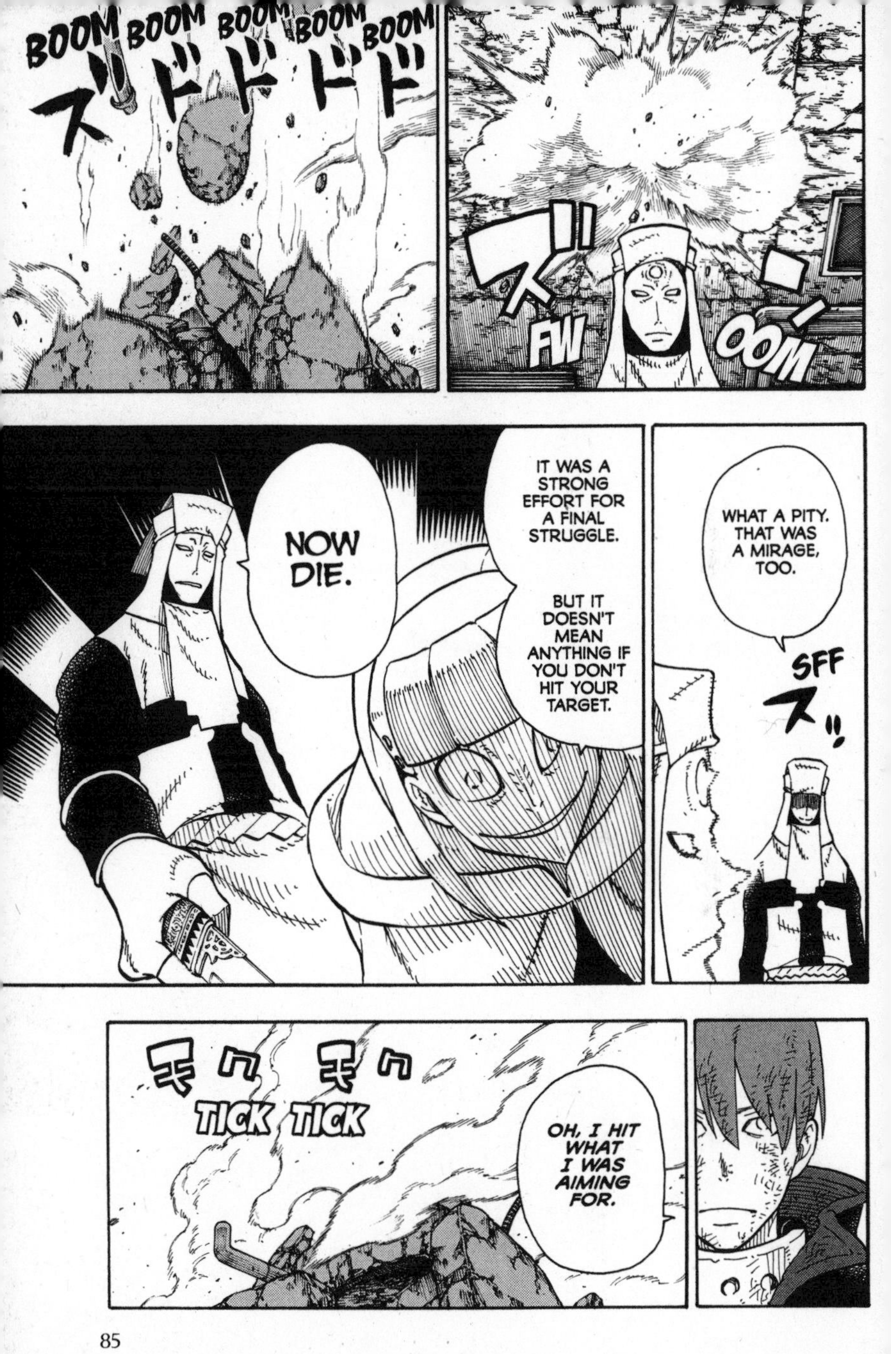
FW
OOM
BOOM BOOM BOOM BOOM BOOM
WHAT A PITY. THAT WAS A MIRAGE, TOO.
SFF
IT WAS A STRONG EFFORT FOR A FINAL STRUGGLE.
BUT IT DOESN'T MEAN ANYTHING IF YOU DON'T HIT YOUR TARGET.
NOW DIE.
TICK TICK
OH, I HIT WHAT I WAS AIMING FOR.

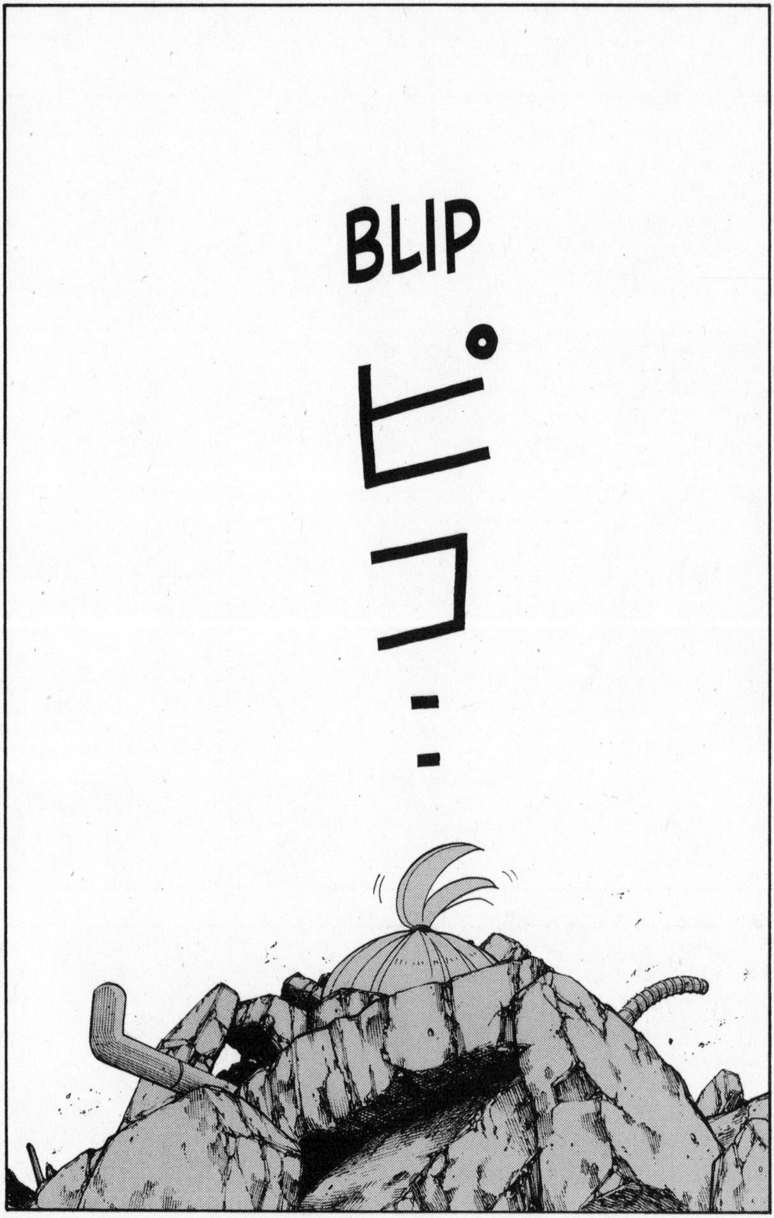
BLIP
ピコ‥

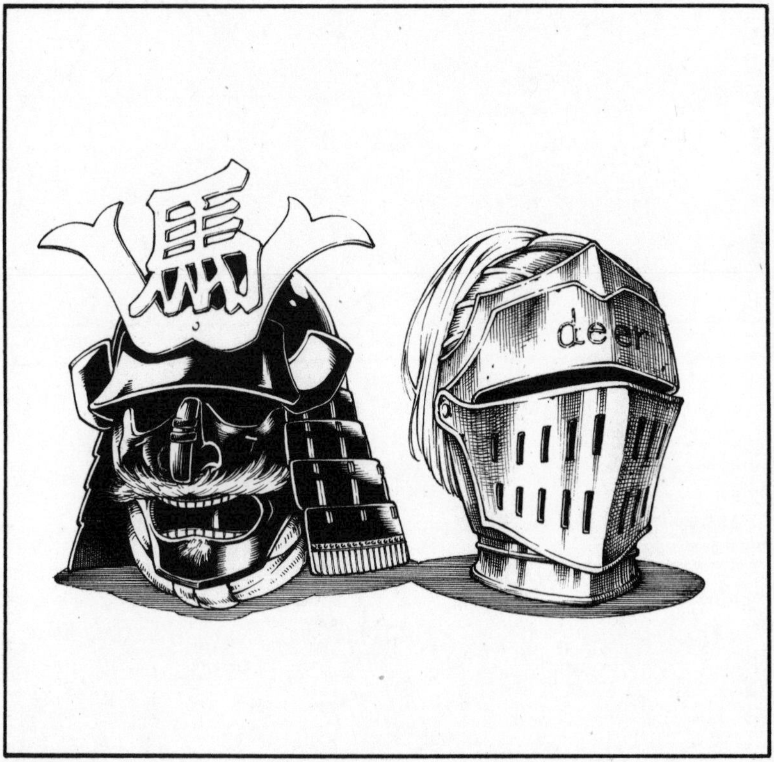
馬
deer
Helmet: Horse

CHAPTER LXXIV: THE FLASH OF A BLADE

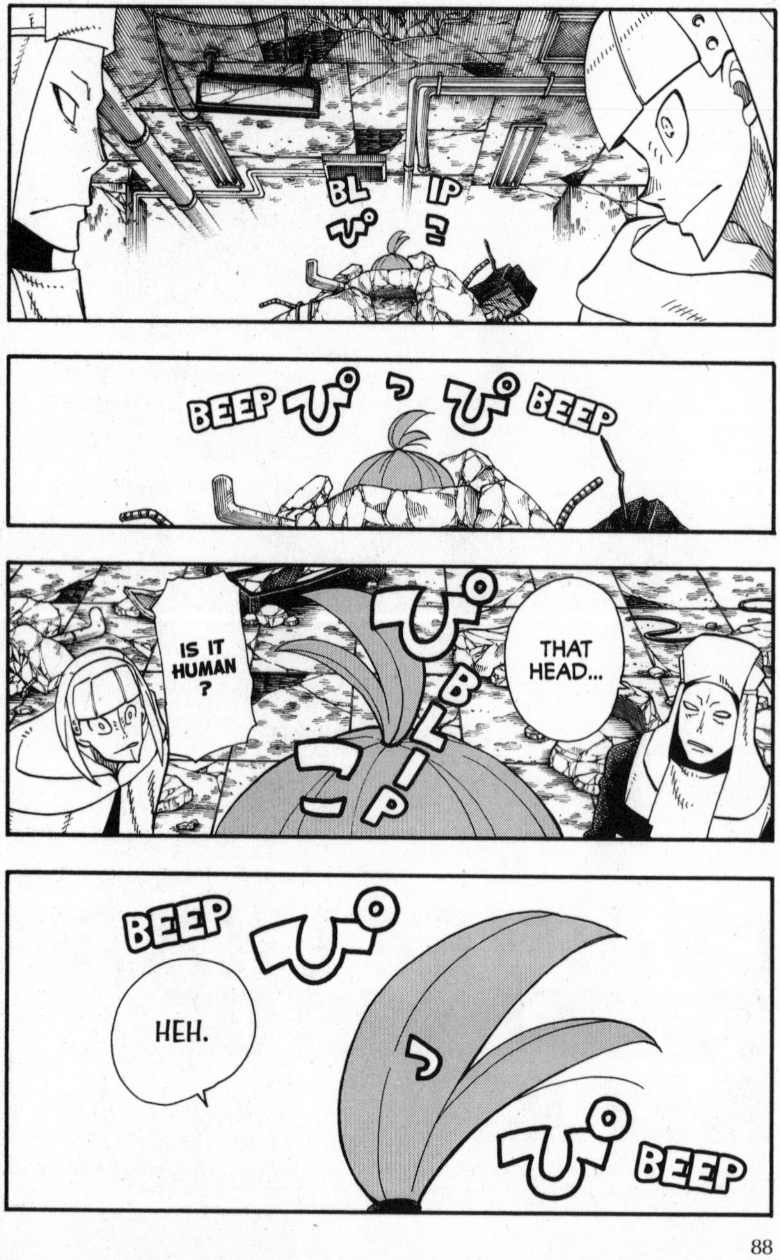

BL IP
BEEP
BEEP
THAT HEAD...
BLIP
IS IT HUMAN ?
BEEP
HEH.
BEEP

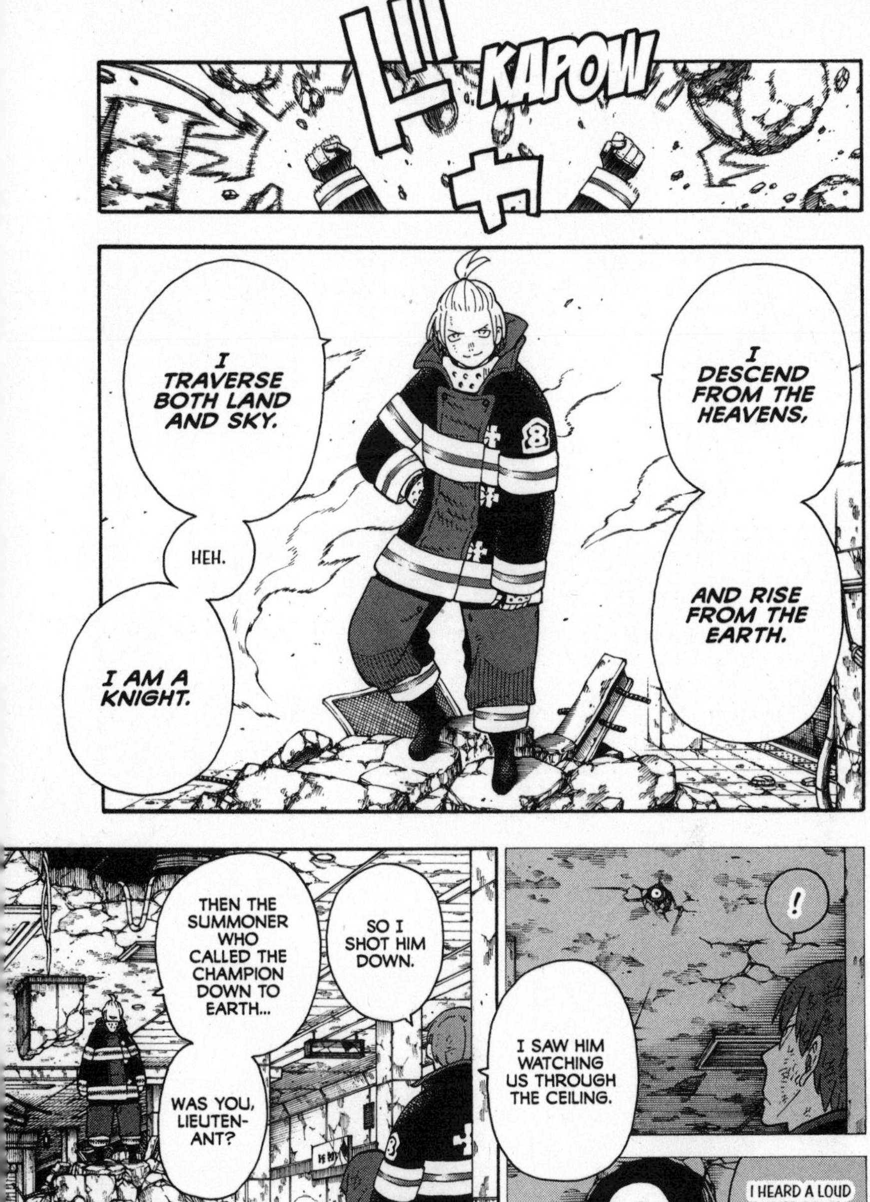
KAPOW
I DESCEND FROM THE HEAVENS,
AND RISE FROM THE EARTH.
I TRAVERSE BOTH LAND AND SKY.
HEH.
I AM A KNIGHT.
!
I HEARD A LOUD NOISE DOWN THERE... WHAT WAS IT?
I SAW HIM WATCHING US THROUGH THE CEILING.
SO I SHOT HIM DOWN.
THEN THE SUMMONER WHO CALLED THE CHAMPION DOWN TO EARTH...
WAS YOU, LIEUTENANT?

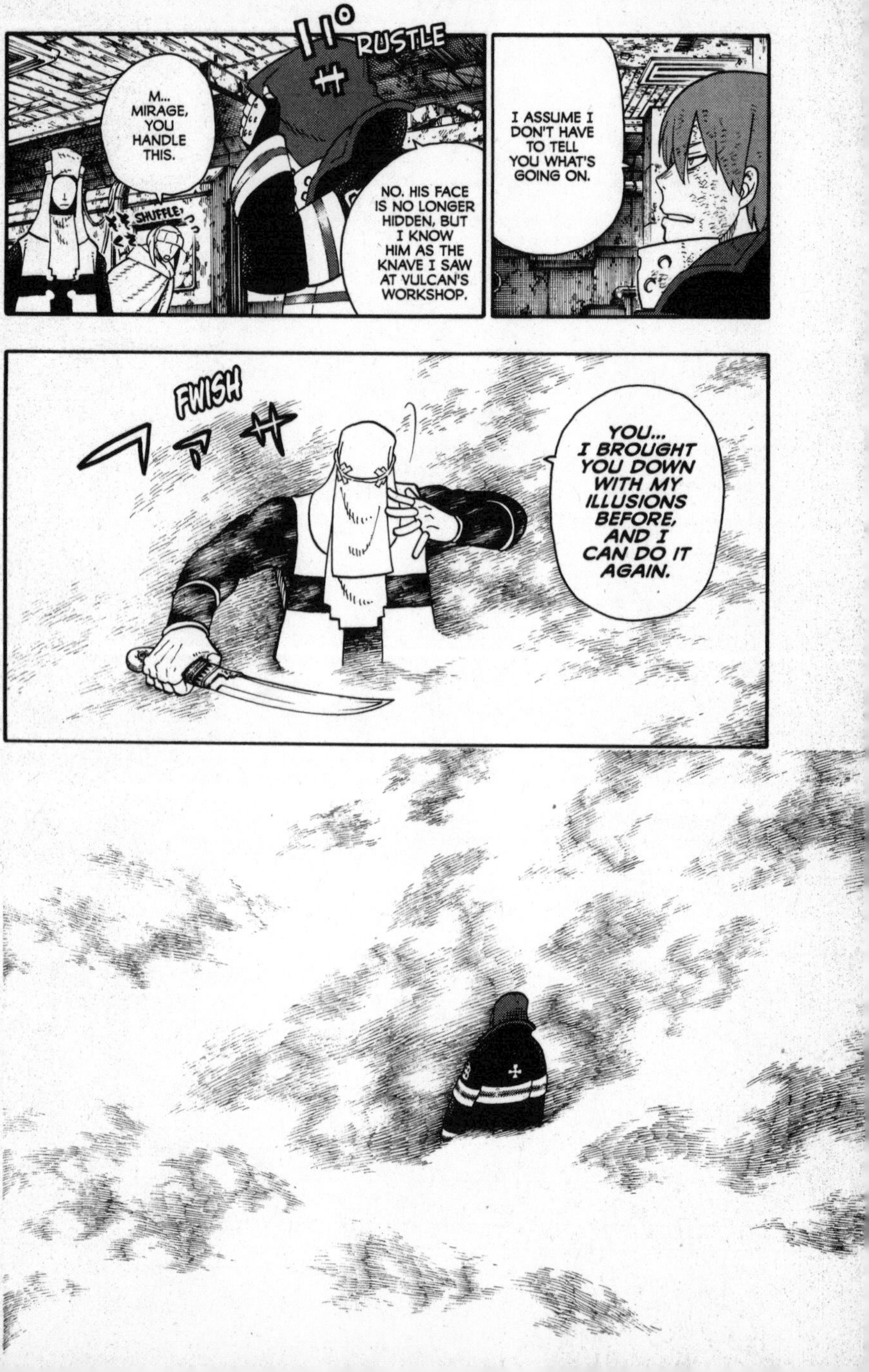
I ASSUME I DON'T HAVE TO TELL YOU WHAT'S GOING ON.
RUSTLE
NO. HIS FACE IS NO LONGER HIDDEN, BUT I KNOW HIM AS THE KNAVE I SAW AT VULCAN'S WORKSHOP.
M... MIRAGE, YOU HANDLE THIS.
SHUFFLE
YOU... I BROUGHT YOU DOWN WITH MY ILLUSIONS BEFORE, AND I CAN DO IT AGAIN.
FWISH

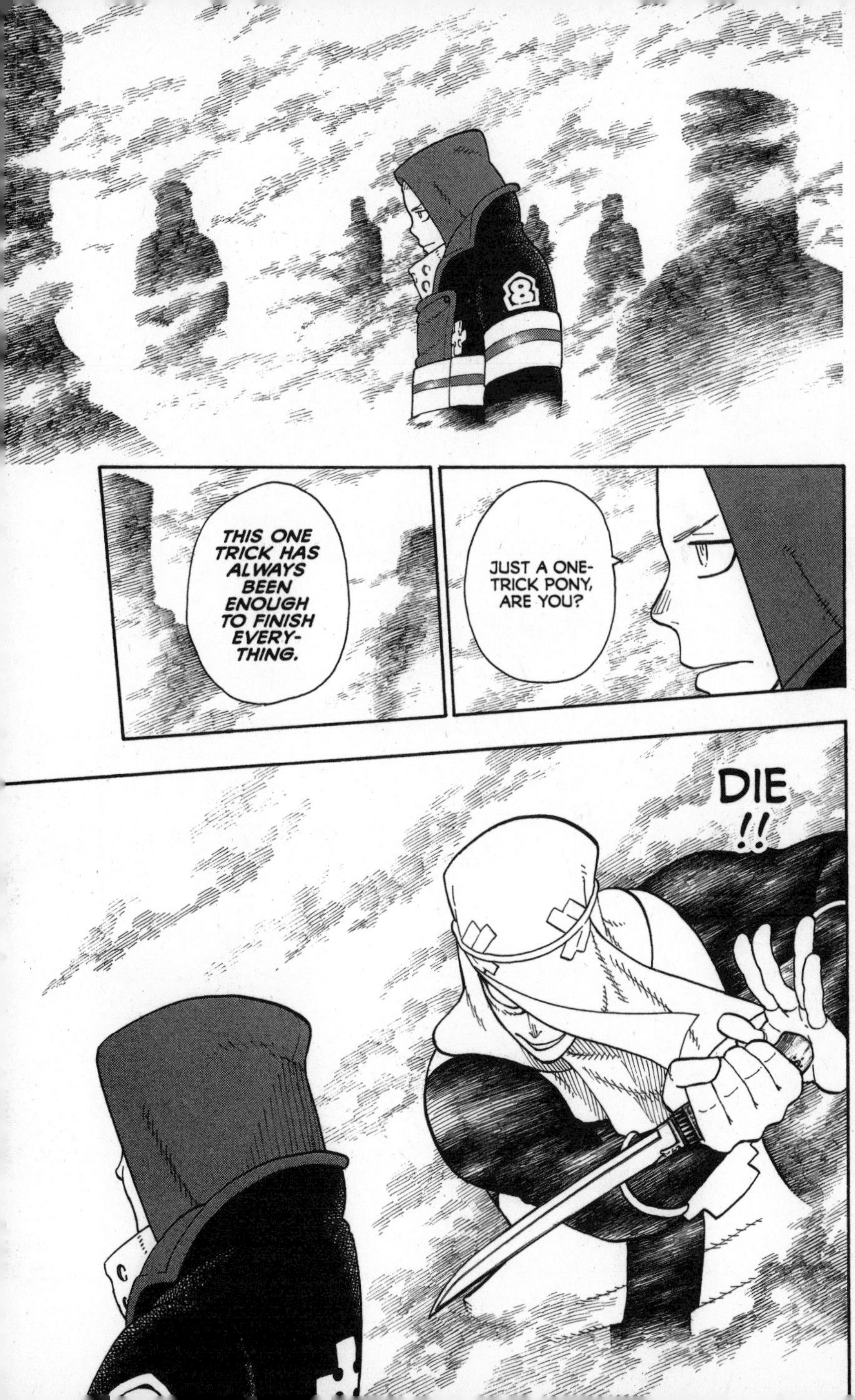
JUST A ONE-TRICK PONY, ARE YOU?
THIS ONE TRICK HAS ALWAYS BEEN ENOUGH TO FINISH EVERY-THING.
DIE!!

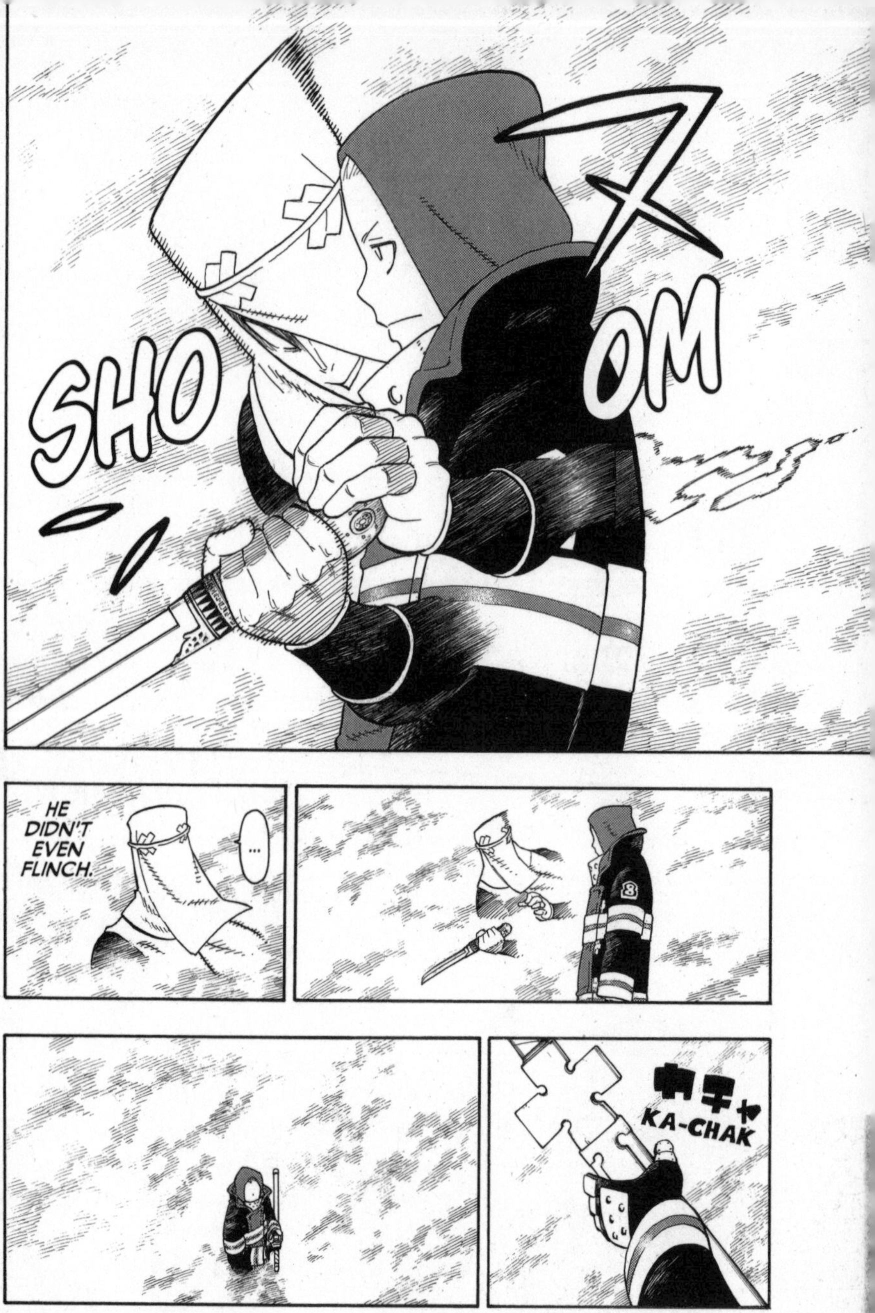
SHOOM
HE DIDN'T EVEN FLINCH.
...
カチャ
KA-CHAK

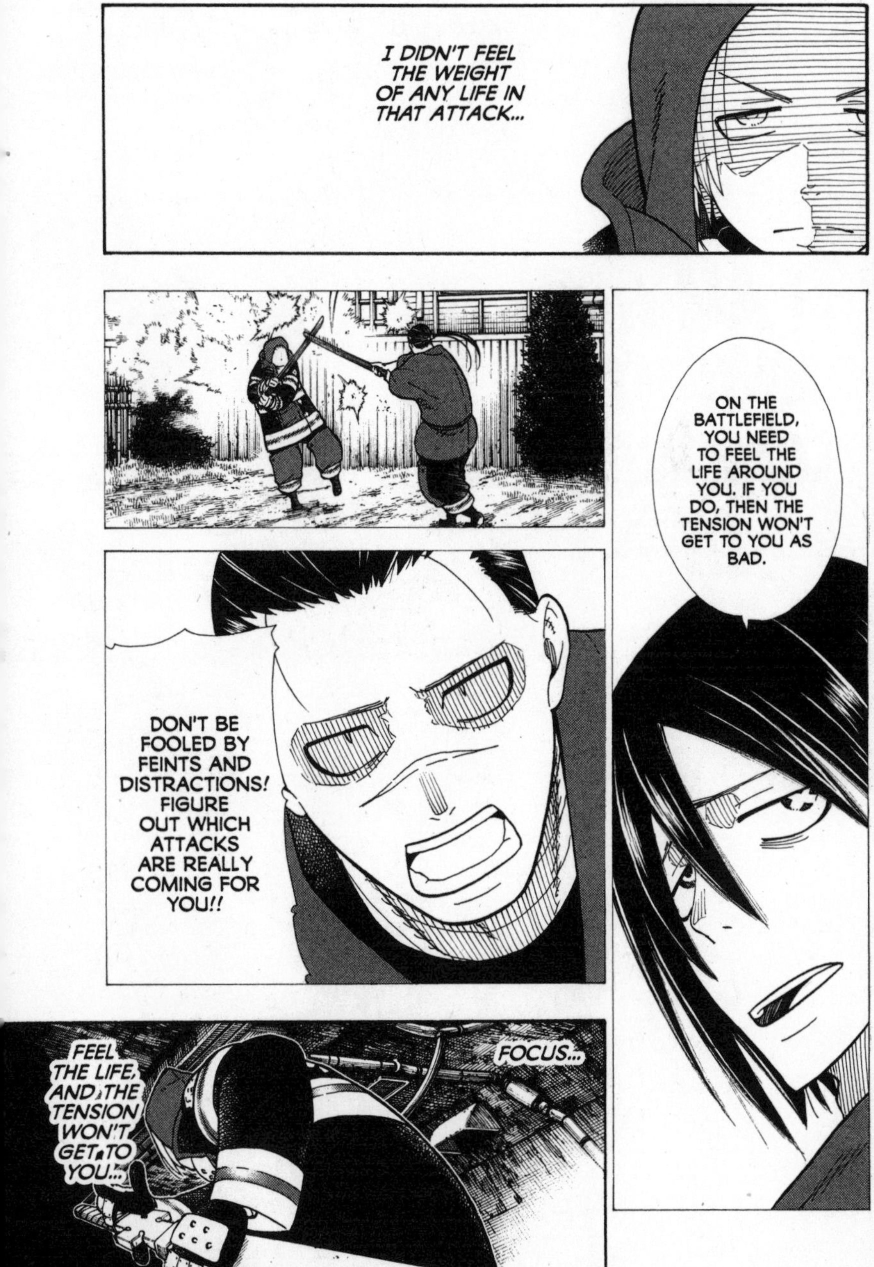
I DIDN'T FEEL THE WEIGHT OF ANY LIFE IN THAT ATTACK...
ON THE BATTLEFIELD, YOU NEED TO FEEL THE LIFE AROUND YOU. IF YOU DO, THEN THE TENSION WON'T GET TO YOU AS BAD.
DON'T BE FOOLED BY FEINTS AND DISTRACTIONS! FIGURE OUT WHICH ATTACKS ARE REALLY COMING FOR YOU!!
FOCUS...
FEEL THE LIFE, AND THE TENSION WON'T GET TO YOU...

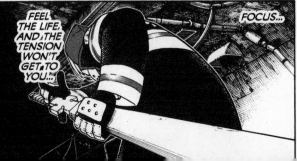

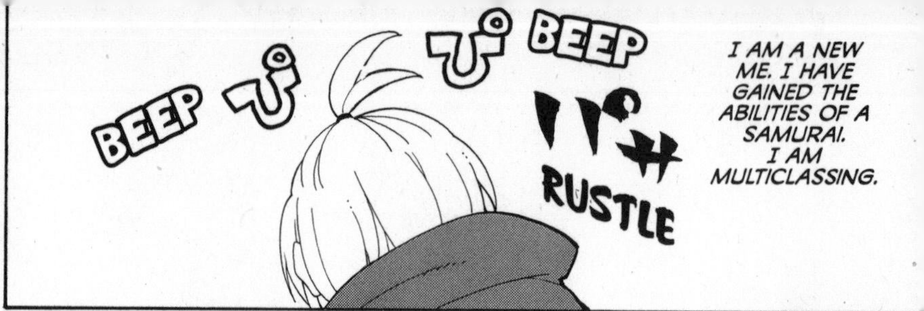
I AM A NEW ME. I HAVE GAINED THE ABILITIES OF A SAMURAI. I AM MULTICLASSING.
ぴ BEEP
ぴ BEEP
パサ
RUSTLE
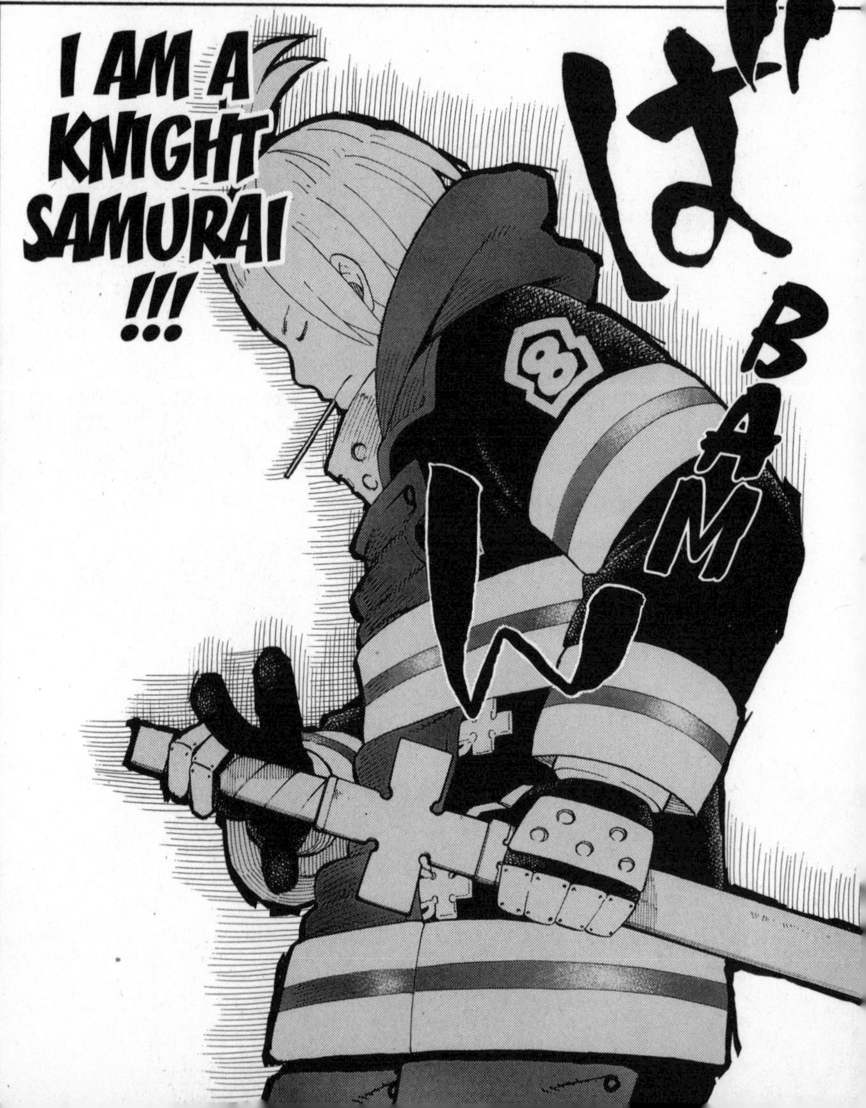
ば!!
ん
BAM
I AM A KNIGHT SAMURAI!!!

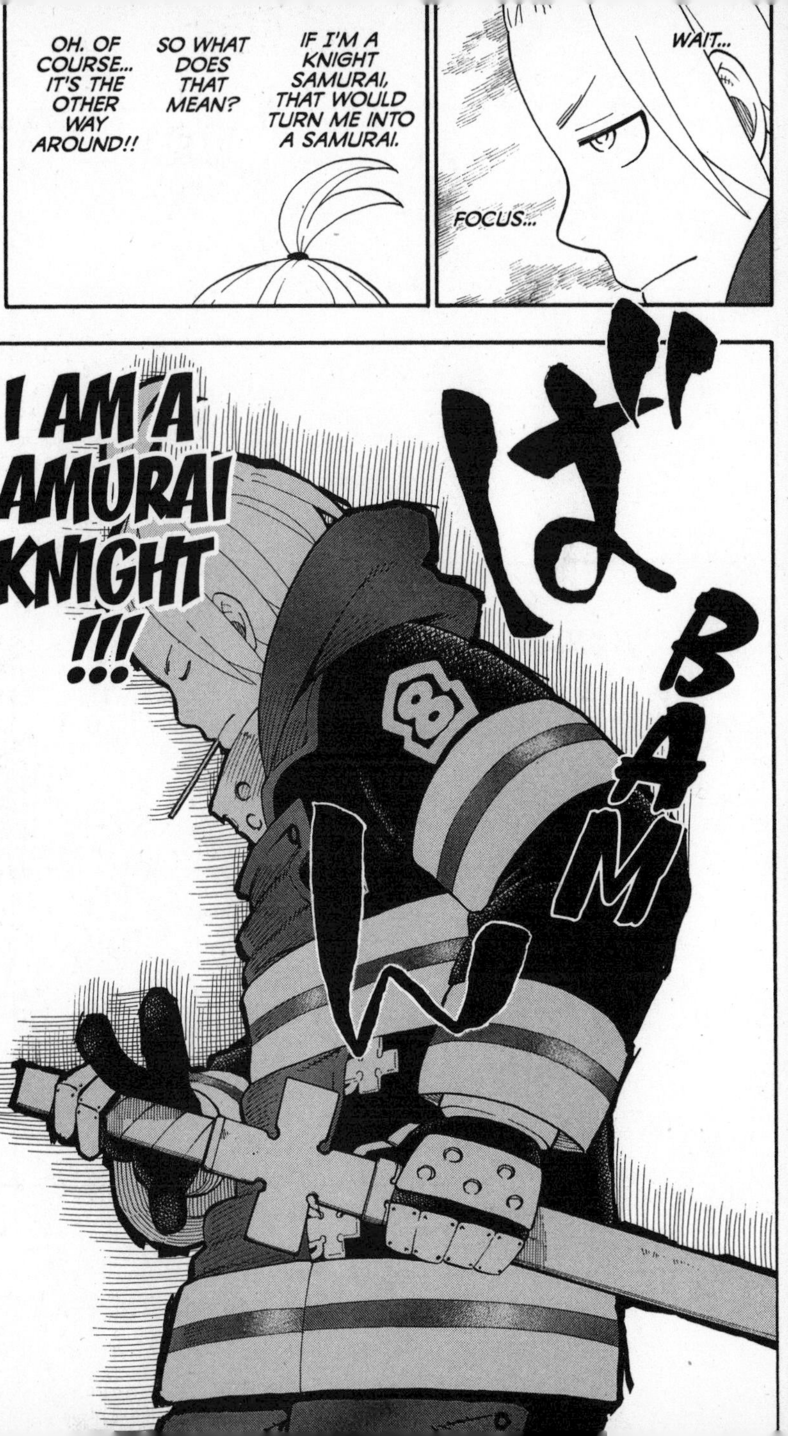
WAIT...
FOCUS...
IF I'M A KNIGHT SAMURAI, THAT WOULD TURN ME INTO A SAMURAI.
SO WHAT DOES THAT MEAN?
OH. OF COURSE... IT'S THE OTHER WAY AROUND!!
ばっ
BAM
I AM A SAMURAI KNIGHT!!!

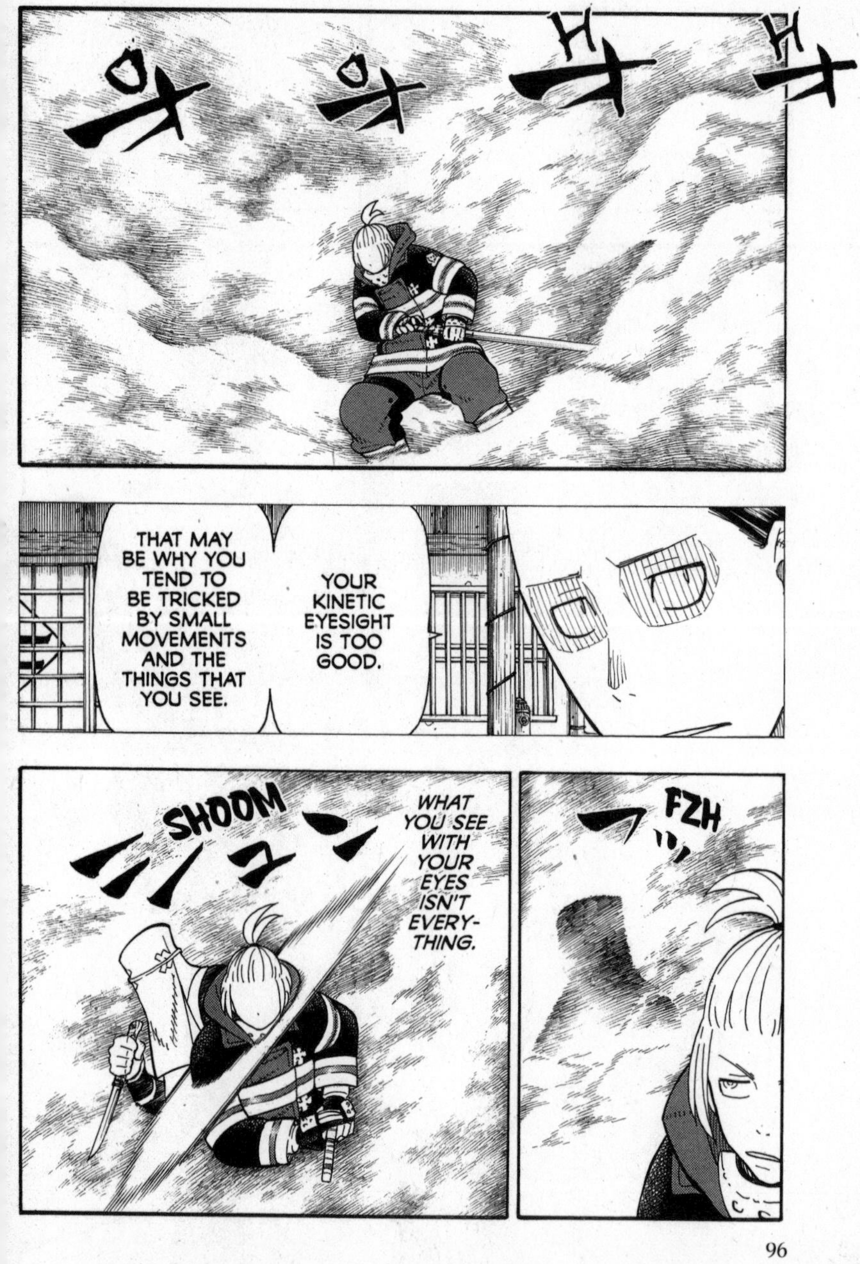
YOUR KINETIC EYESIGHT IS TOO GOOD.
THAT MAY BE WHY YOU TEND TO BE TRICKED BY SMALL MOVEMENTS AND THE THINGS THAT YOU SEE.
FZH
WHAT YOU SEE WITH YOUR EYES ISN'T EVERY-THING.
SHOOM

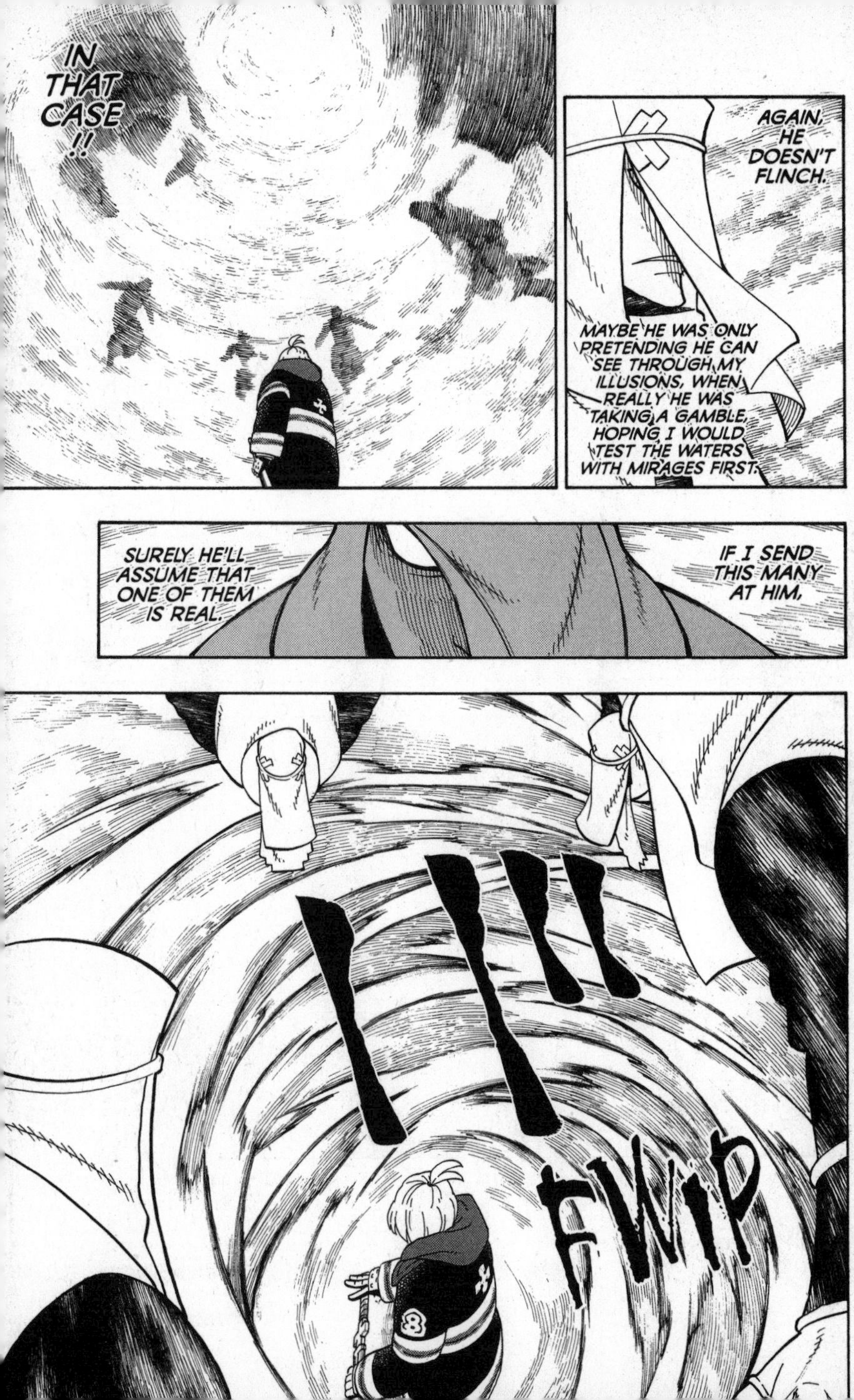
AGAIN, HE DOESN'T FLINCH.
MAYBE HE WAS ONLY PRETENDING HE CAN SEE THROUGH MY ILLUSIONS, WHEN REALLY HE WAS TAKING A GAMBLE, HOPING I WOULD TEST THE WATERS WITH MIRAGES FIRST.
IN THAT CASE!!
IF I SEND THIS MANY AT HIM,
SURELY HE'LL ASSUME THAT ONE OF THEM IS REAL.
FWIP

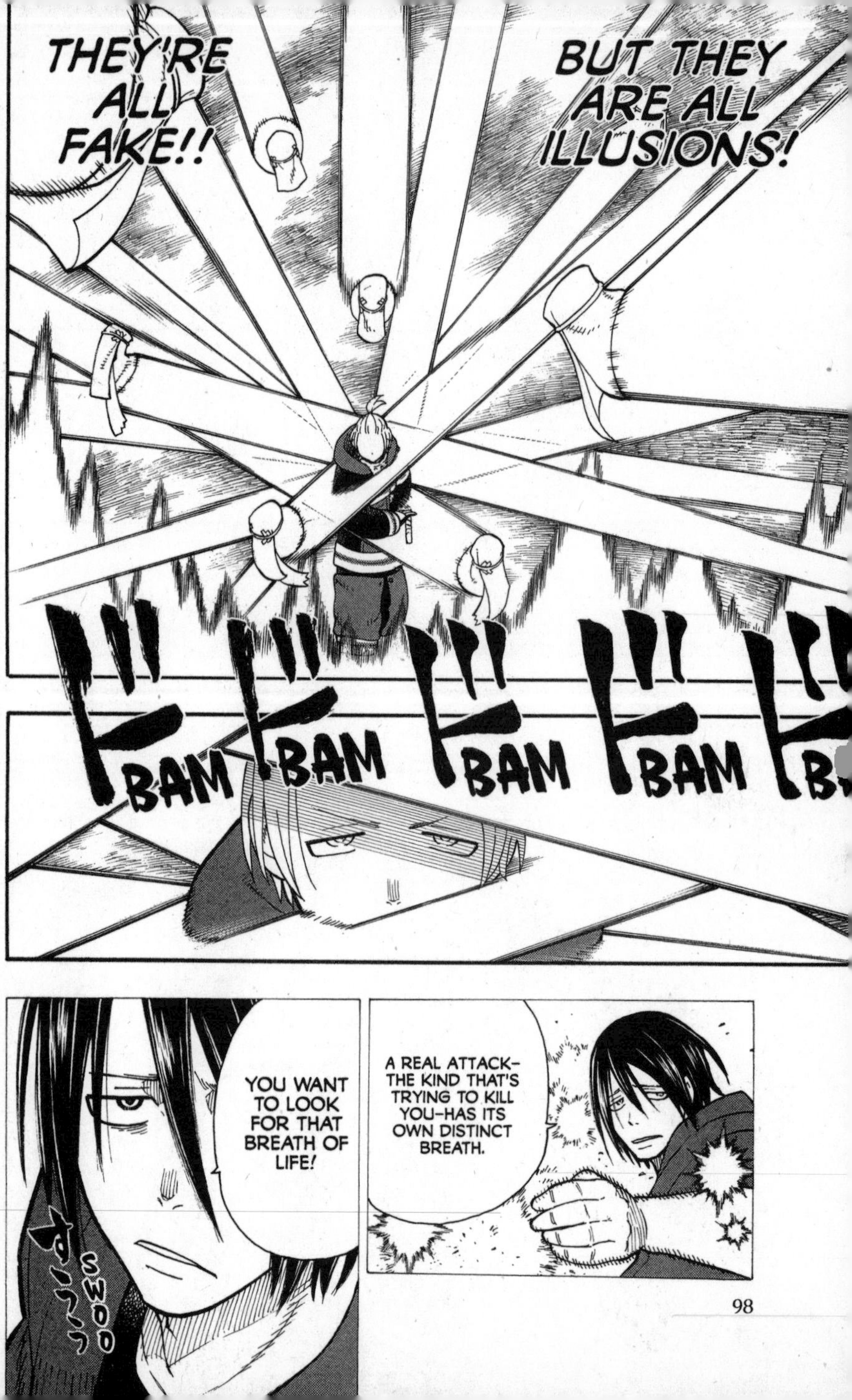
BUT THEY ARE ALL ILLUSIONS!
THEY'RE ALL FAKE!!
BAM BAM BAM BAM
A REAL ATTACK—THE KIND THAT'S TRYING TO KILL YOU—HAS ITS OWN DISTINCT BREATH.
YOU WANT TO LOOK FOR THAT BREATH OF LIFE!
SWOO

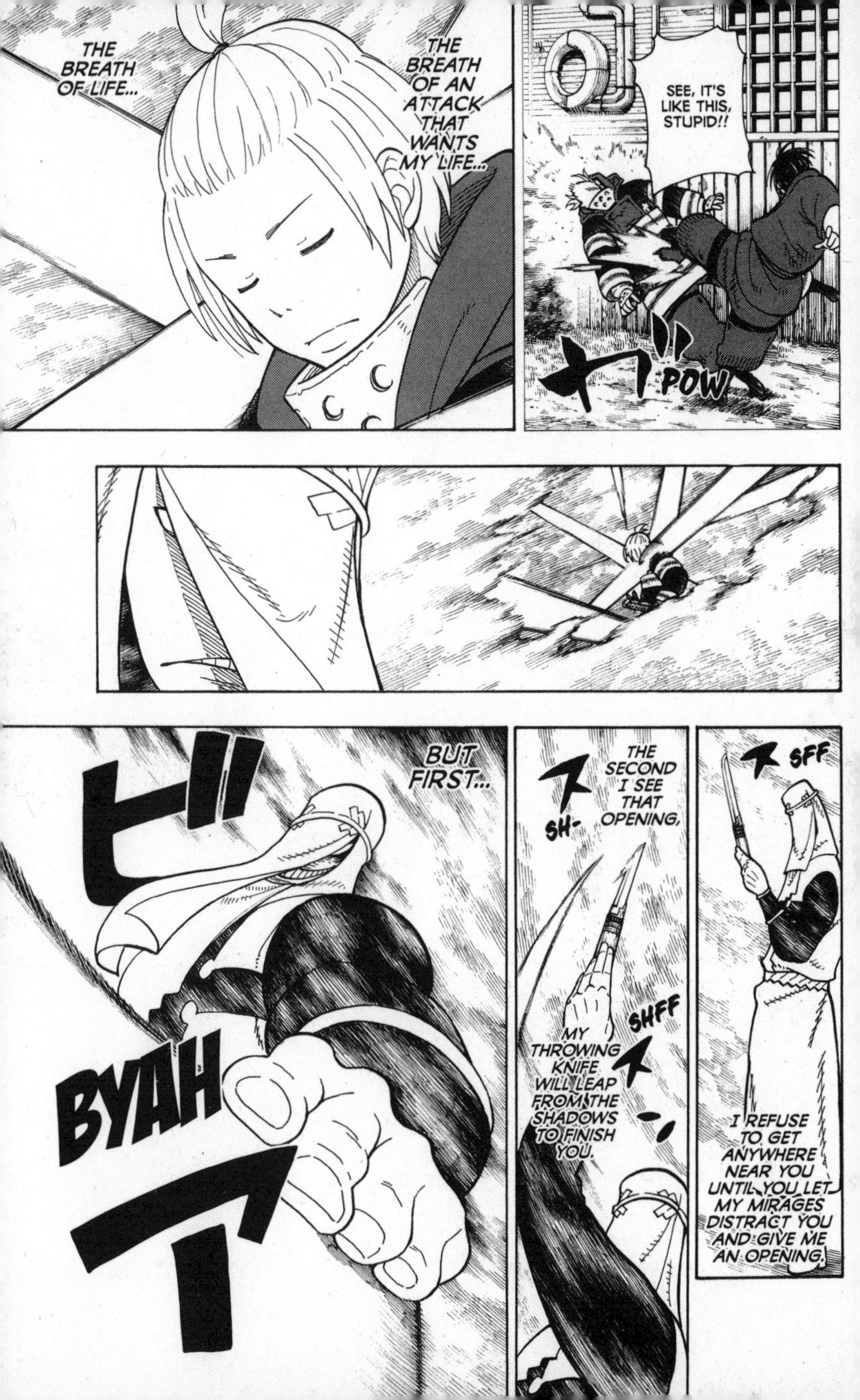
SEE, IT'S LIKE THIS, STUPID!!
POW
THE BREATH OF AN ATTACK THAT WANTS MY LIFE...
THE BREATH OF LIFE...
SFF
I REFUSE TO GET ANYWHERE NEAR YOU UNTIL YOU LET MY MIRAGES DISTRACT YOU AND GIVE ME AN OPENING.
THE SECOND I SEE THAT OPENING,
SH-
SHFF
MY THROWING KNIFE WILL LEAP FROM THE SHADOWS TO FINISH YOU.
BUT FIRST...
BYAH

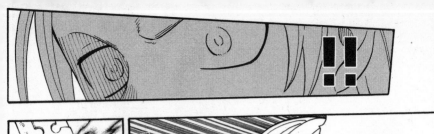

THE
BREATH
OF LIFE
!!

CHING

IAI-
CALIBUR
!!!

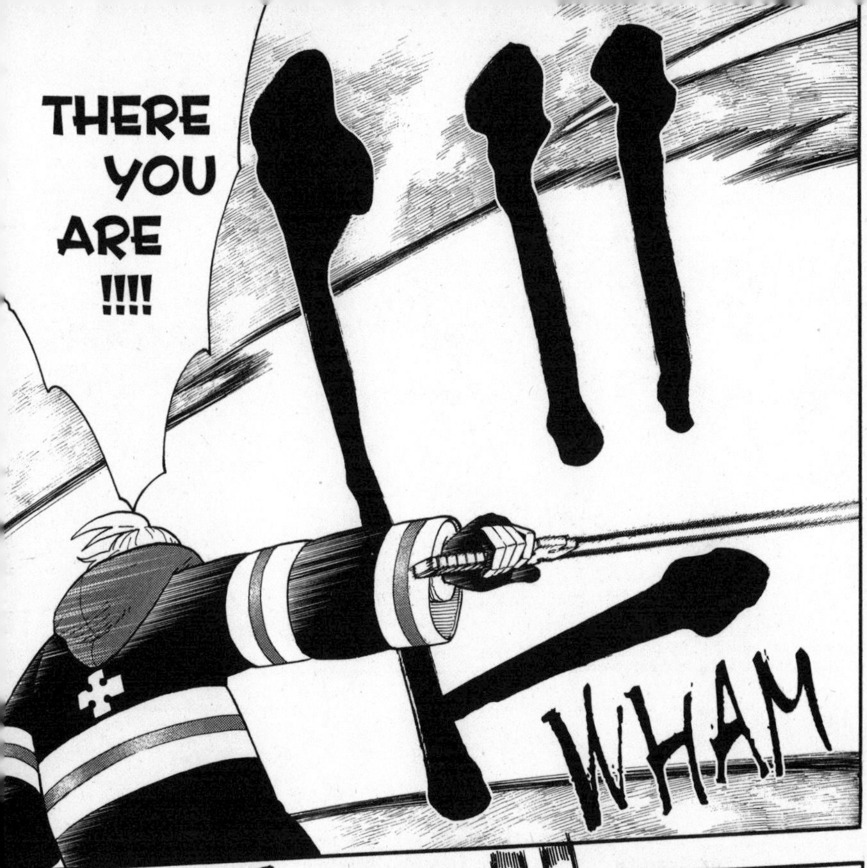
THERE YOU ARE !!!!
WHAM
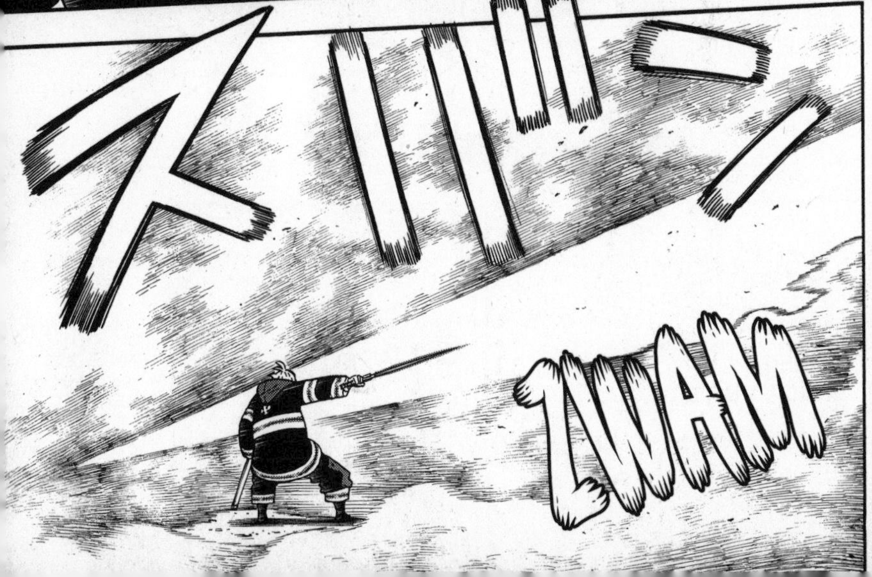
ZWAM

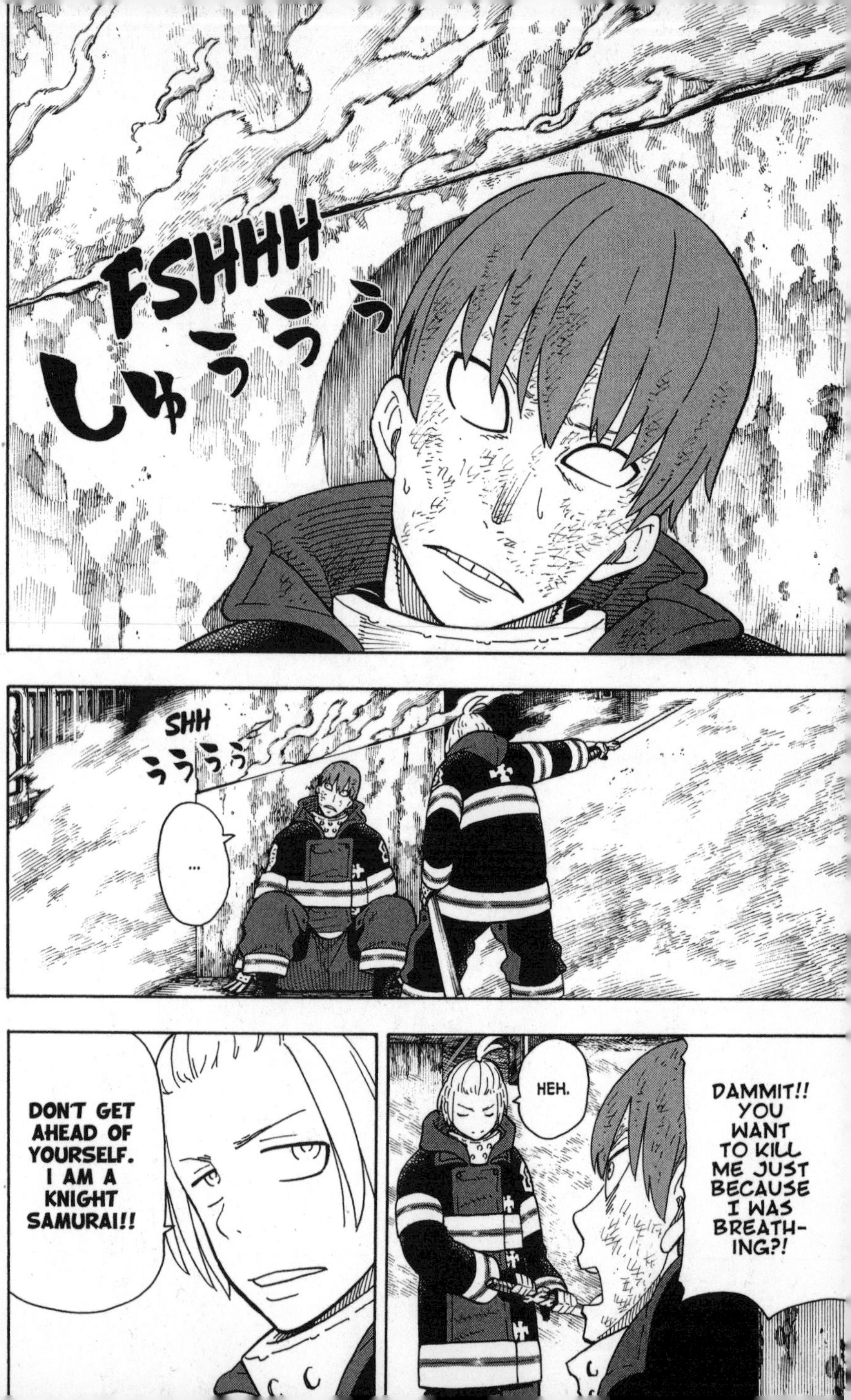
FSHHH
しゅううう
SHH
うううう
...
DAMMIT!! YOU WANT TO KILL ME JUST BECAUSE I WAS BREATH-ING?!
HEH.
DON'T GET AHEAD OF YOURSELF. I AM A KNIGHT SAMURAI!!

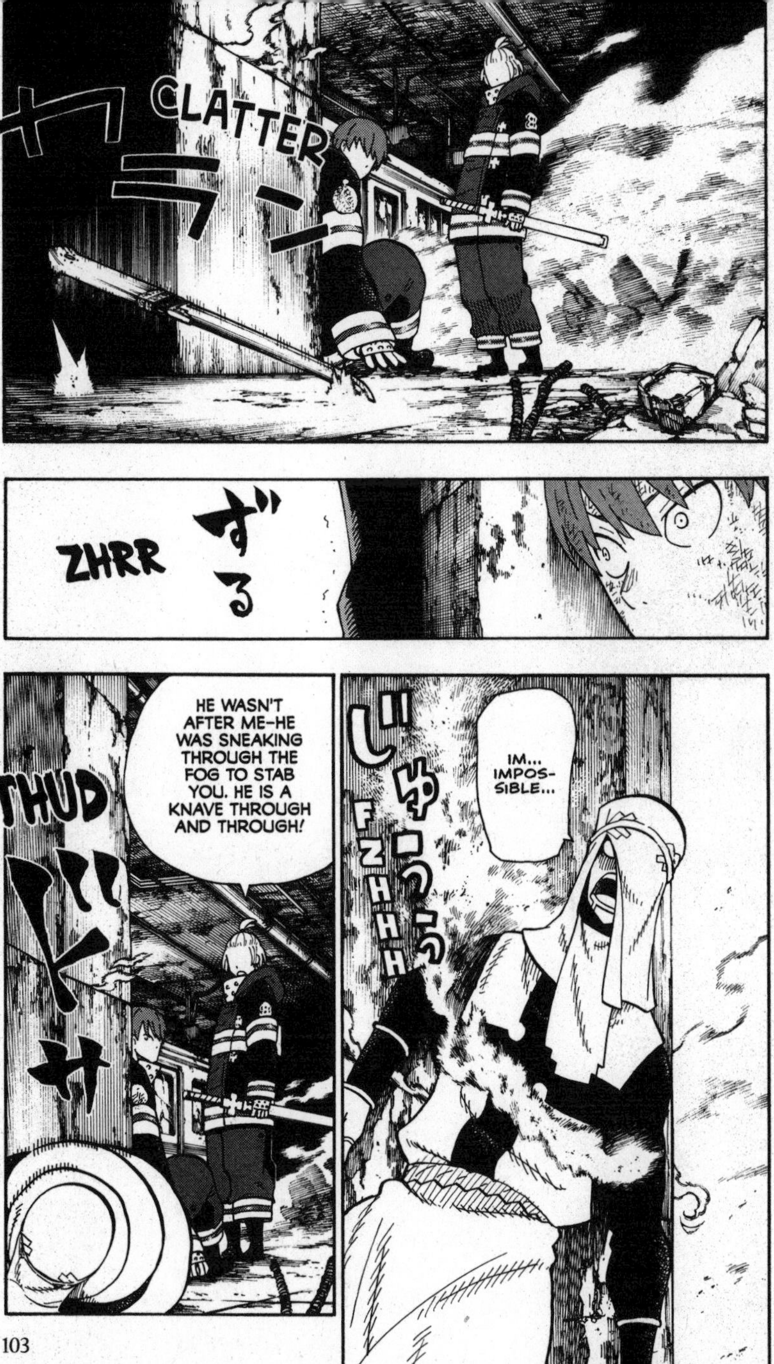
CLATTER
ZHRR
ずる
IM... IMPOSSIBLE...
FZHHHH
HE WASN'T AFTER ME—HE WAS SNEAKING THROUGH THE FOG TO STAB YOU. HE IS A KNAVE THROUGH AND THROUGH!
THUD

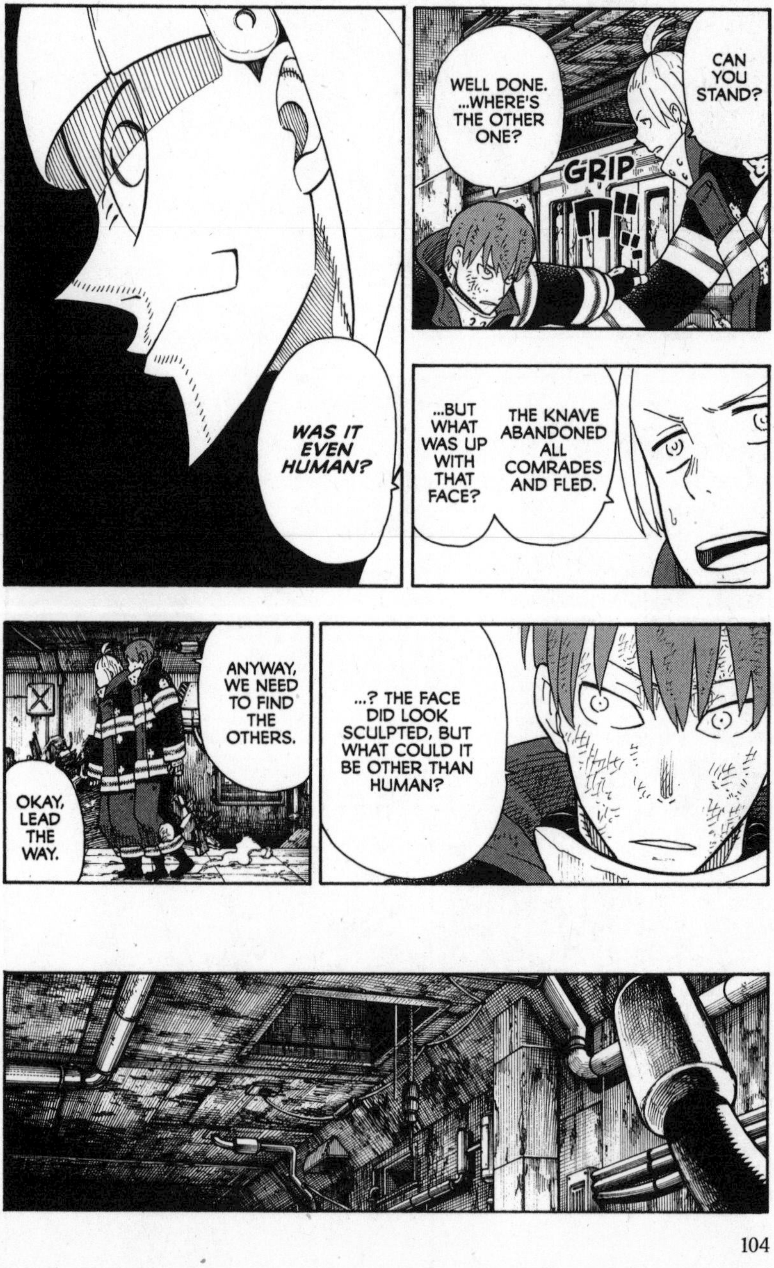
CAN YOU STAND?
WELL DONE. ...WHERE'S THE OTHER ONE?
GRIP
THE KNAVE ABANDONED ALL COMRADES AND FLED.
...BUT WHAT WAS UP WITH THAT FACE?
WAS IT EVEN HUMAN?
...? THE FACE DID LOOK SCULPTED, BUT WHAT COULD IT BE OTHER THAN HUMAN?
ANYWAY, WE NEED TO FIND THE OTHERS.
OKAY, LEAD THE WAY.

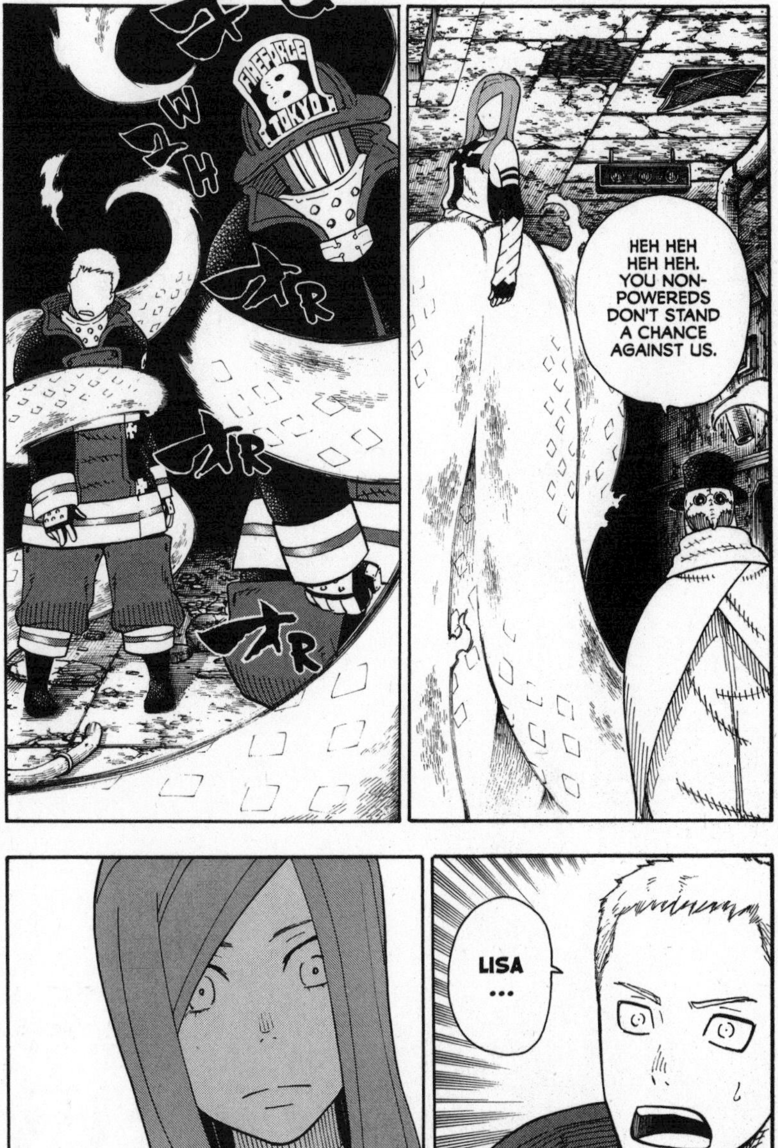
HEH HEH HEH HEH. YOU NON-POWEREDS DON'T STAND A CHANCE AGAINST US.
G
WH
R
R
R
LISA ...

FIRE FORCE

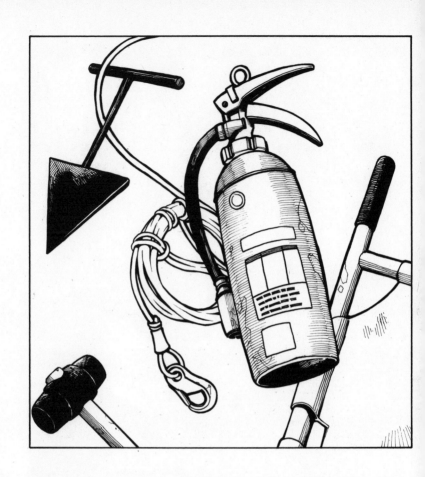

CHAPTER LXXV: THE PRIDE OF A FIRE SOLDIER

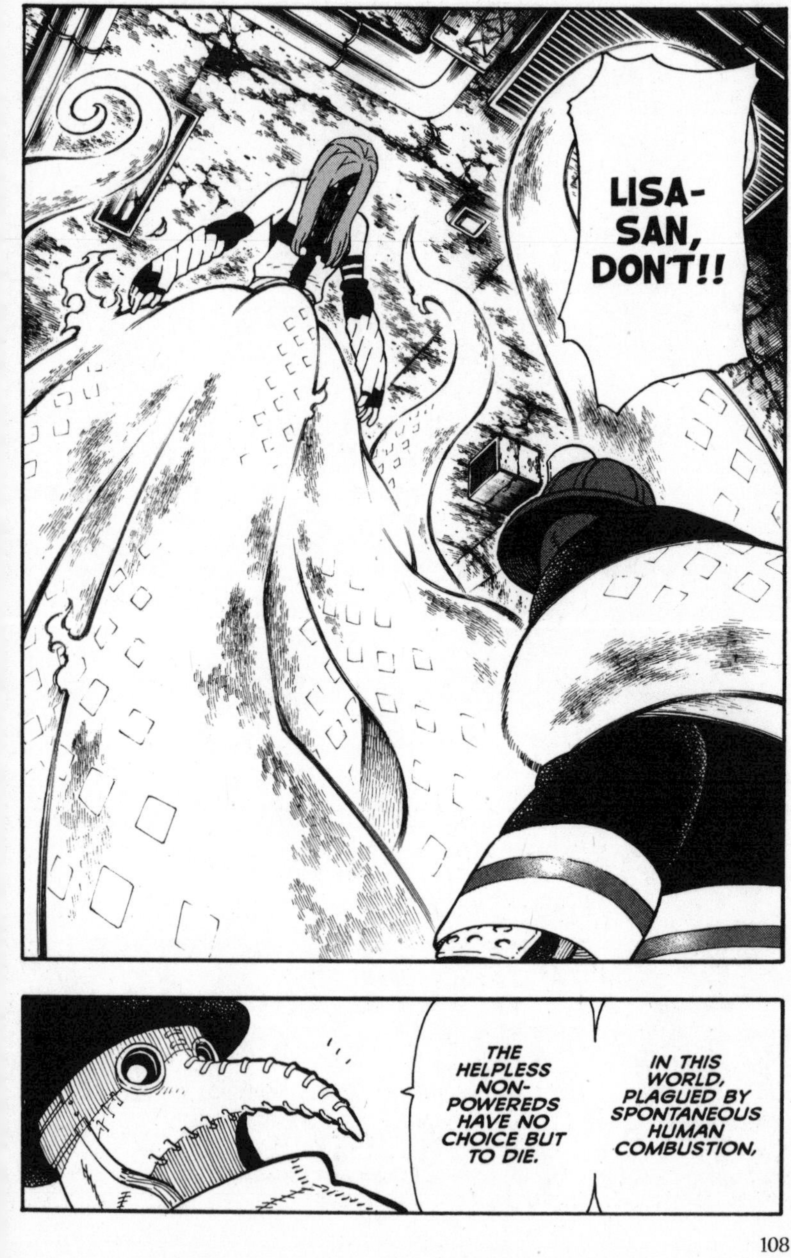
LISA-SAN, DON'T!!
IN THIS WORLD, PLAGUED BY SPONTANEOUS HUMAN COMBUSTION,
THE HELPLESS NON-POWEREDS HAVE NO CHOICE BUT TO DIE.

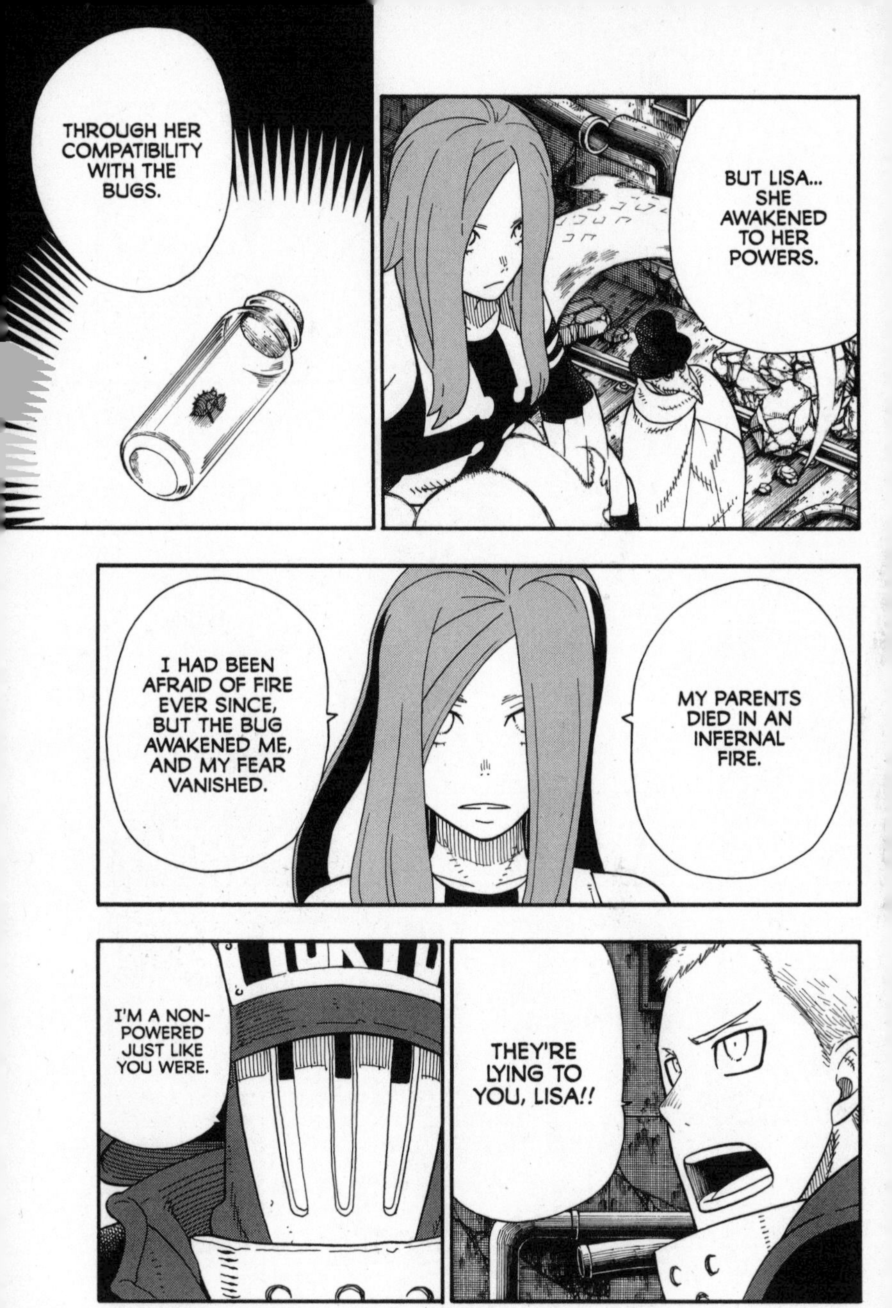
BUT LISA... SHE AWAKENED TO HER POWERS.
THROUGH HER COMPATIBILITY WITH THE BUGS.
MY PARENTS DIED IN AN INFERNAL FIRE.
I HAD BEEN AFRAID OF FIRE EVER SINCE, BUT THE BUG AWAKENED ME, AND MY FEAR VANISHED.
THEY'RE LYING TO YOU, LISA!!
I'M A NON-POWERED JUST LIKE YOU WERE.

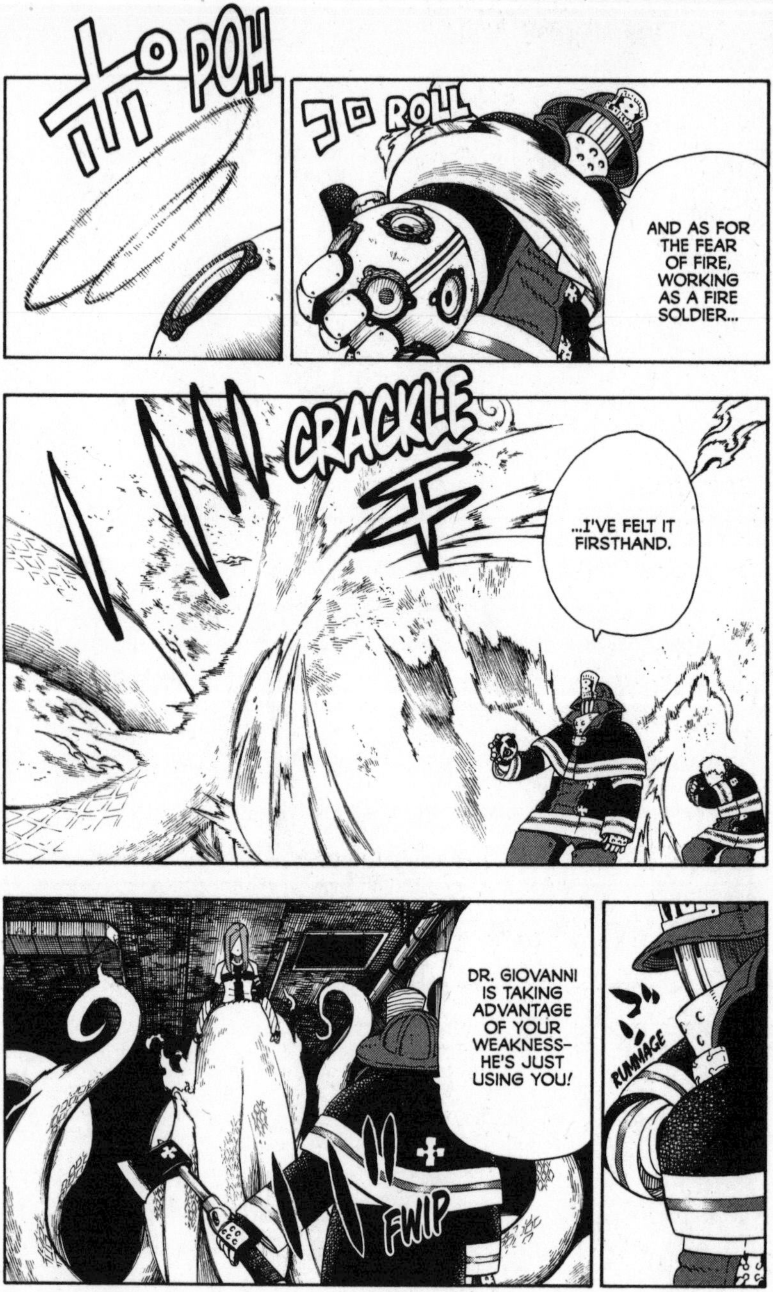
ROLL
AND AS FOR THE FEAR OF FIRE, WORKING AS A FIRE SOLDIER...
POH
CRACKLE
...I'VE FELT IT FIRSTHAND.
RUMMAGE
DR. GIOVANNI IS TAKING ADVANTAGE OF YOUR WEAKNESS– HE'S JUST USING YOU!
FWIP

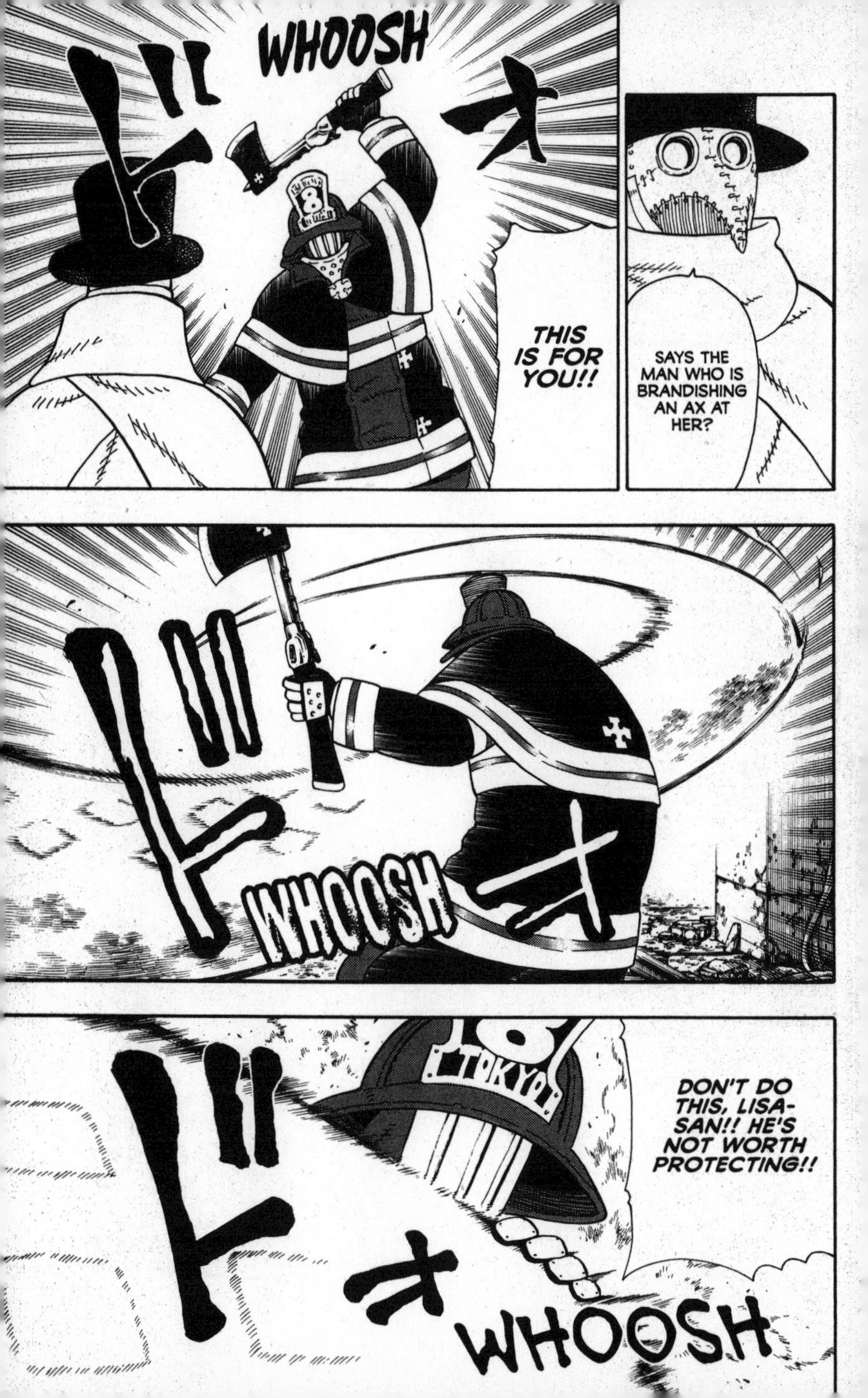
SAYS THE MAN WHO IS BRANDISHING AN AX AT HER?
THIS IS FOR YOU!!
WHOOSH
ドォ
WHOOSH
DON'T DO THIS, LISA-SAN!! HE'S NOT WORTH PROTECTING!!
ドォ
WHOOSH

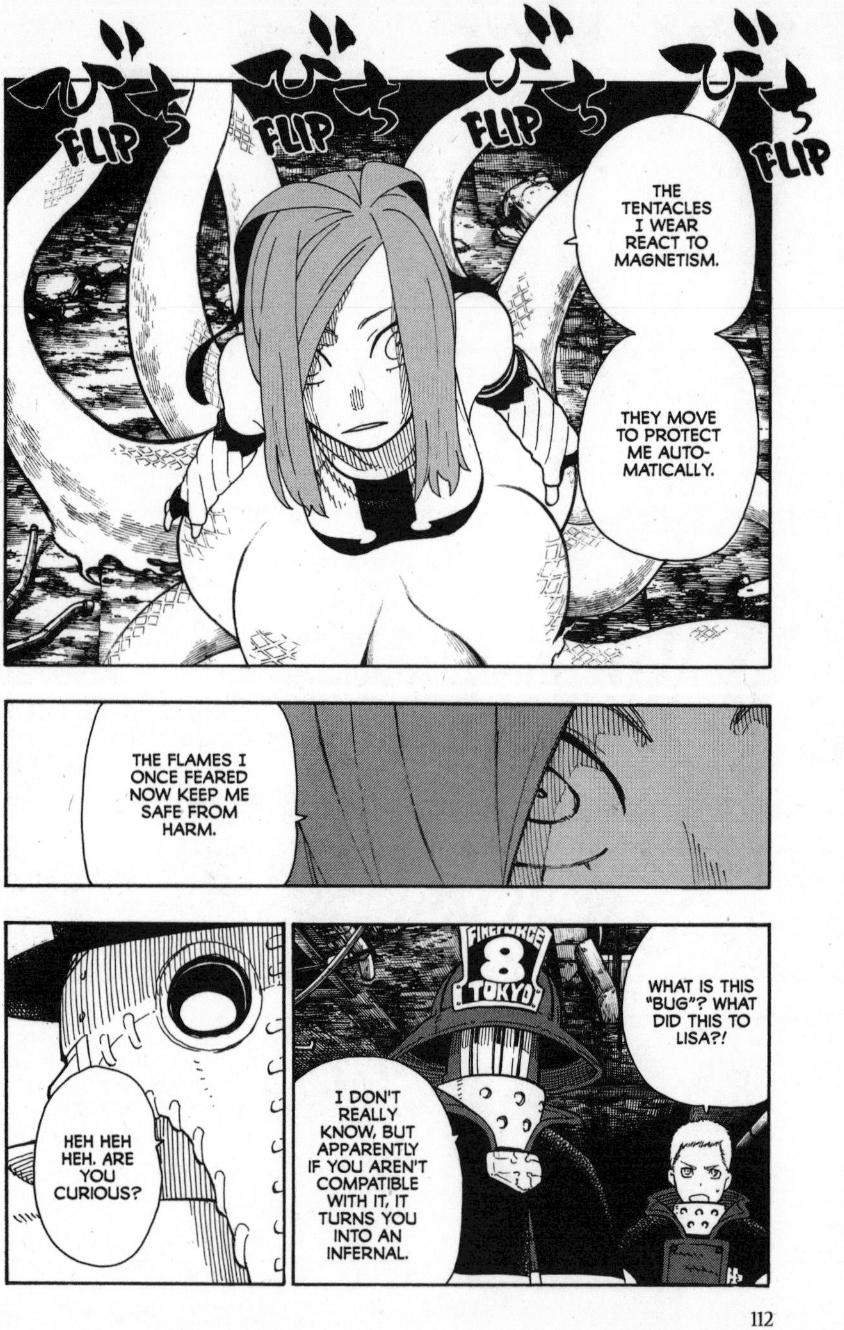
びち FLIP
びち FLIP
びち FLIP
びち FLIP
THE TENTACLES I WEAR REACT TO MAGNETISM.
THEY MOVE TO PROTECT ME AUTO-MATICALLY.
THE FLAMES I ONCE FEARED NOW KEEP ME SAFE FROM HARM.
WHAT IS THIS "BUG"? WHAT DID THIS TO LISA?!
8 TOKYO
I DON'T REALLY KNOW, BUT APPARENTLY IF YOU AREN'T COMPATIBLE WITH IT, IT TURNS YOU INTO AN INFERNAL.
HEH HEH HEH. ARE YOU CURIOUS?

YOU'VE HEARD THE SAYING, "LIKE A MOTH TO A FLAME," YES...? YOU KNOW THAT INSECTS WILLINGLY APPROACH A FLAME, EVEN THOUGH IT WILL KILL THEM.

THEY CALL THIS THE INSECTS' "TRUE PHOTOTAXIS." THIS PHENOMENON HAS YET TO BE SUFFICIENTLY EXPLAINED BY SCIENCE. THERE ARE MANY MYSTERIES SURROUNDING IT.

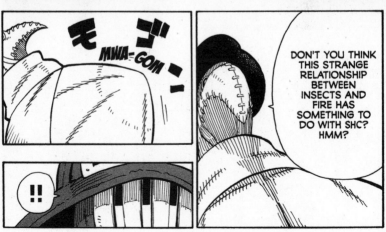

MWA-GOM

!!

DON'T YOU THINK THIS STRANGE RELATIONSHIP BETWEEN INSECTS AND FIRE HAS SOMETHING TO DO WITH SHC? HMM?

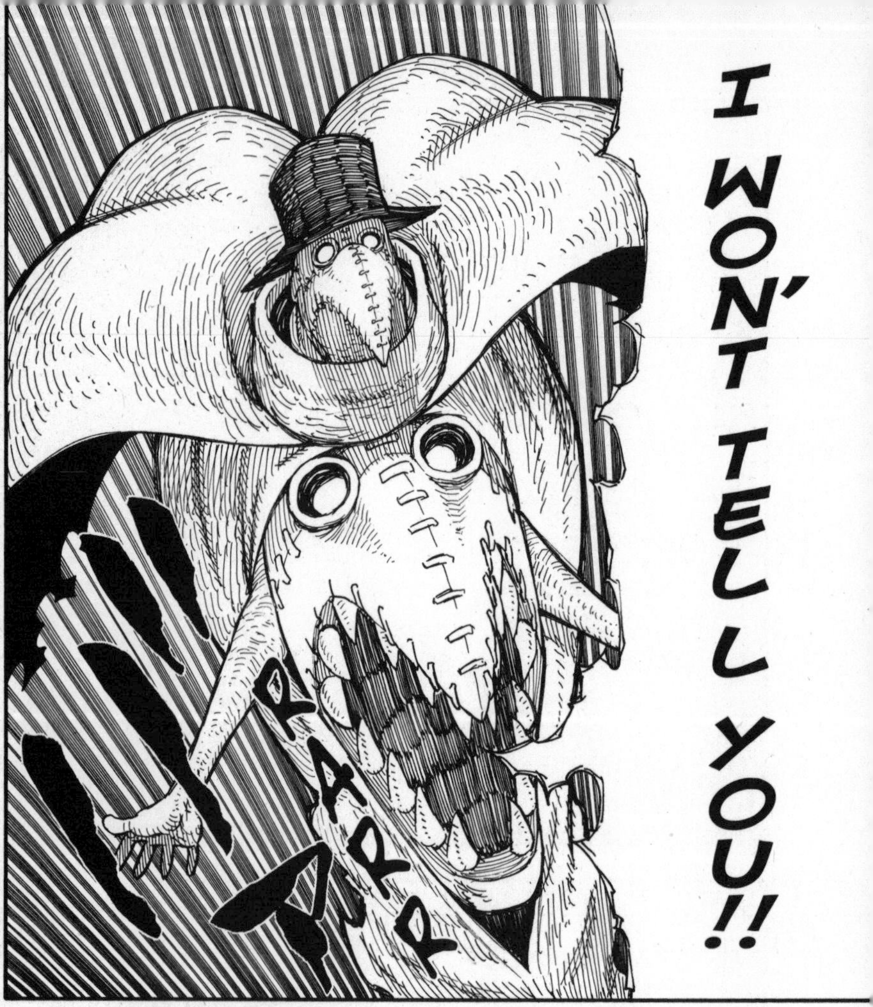
I WON'T TELL YOU!!
RARRR

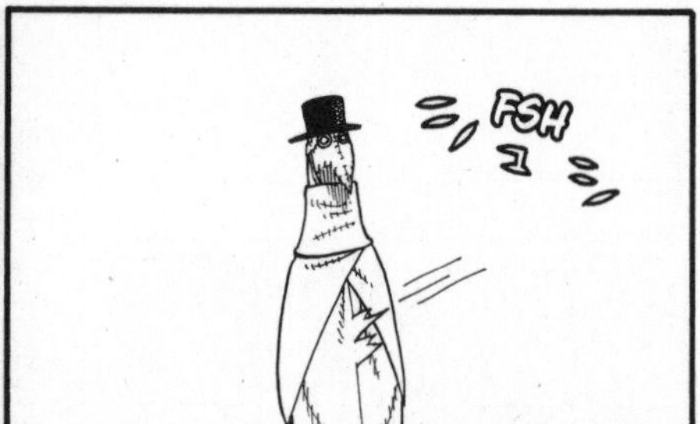
FSH

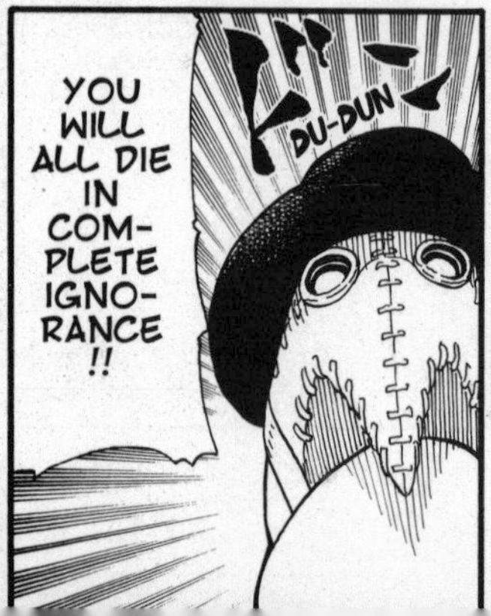
DU-DUN
YOU WILL ALL DIE IN COMPLETE IGNORANCE!!

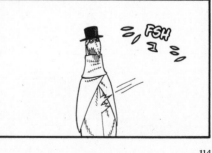

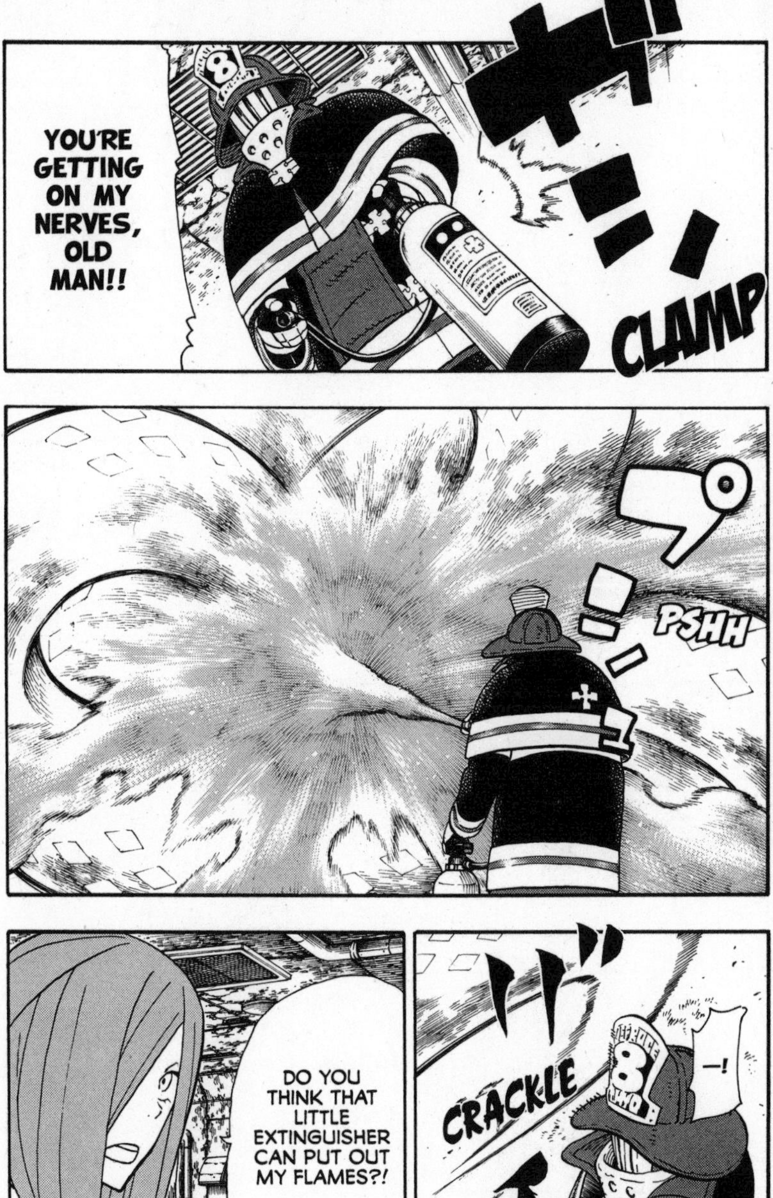
CLAMP
YOU'RE GETTING ON MY NERVES, OLD MAN!!
PSHH
CRACKLE
—!
DO YOU THINK THAT LITTLE EXTINGUISHER CAN PUT OUT MY FLAMES?!

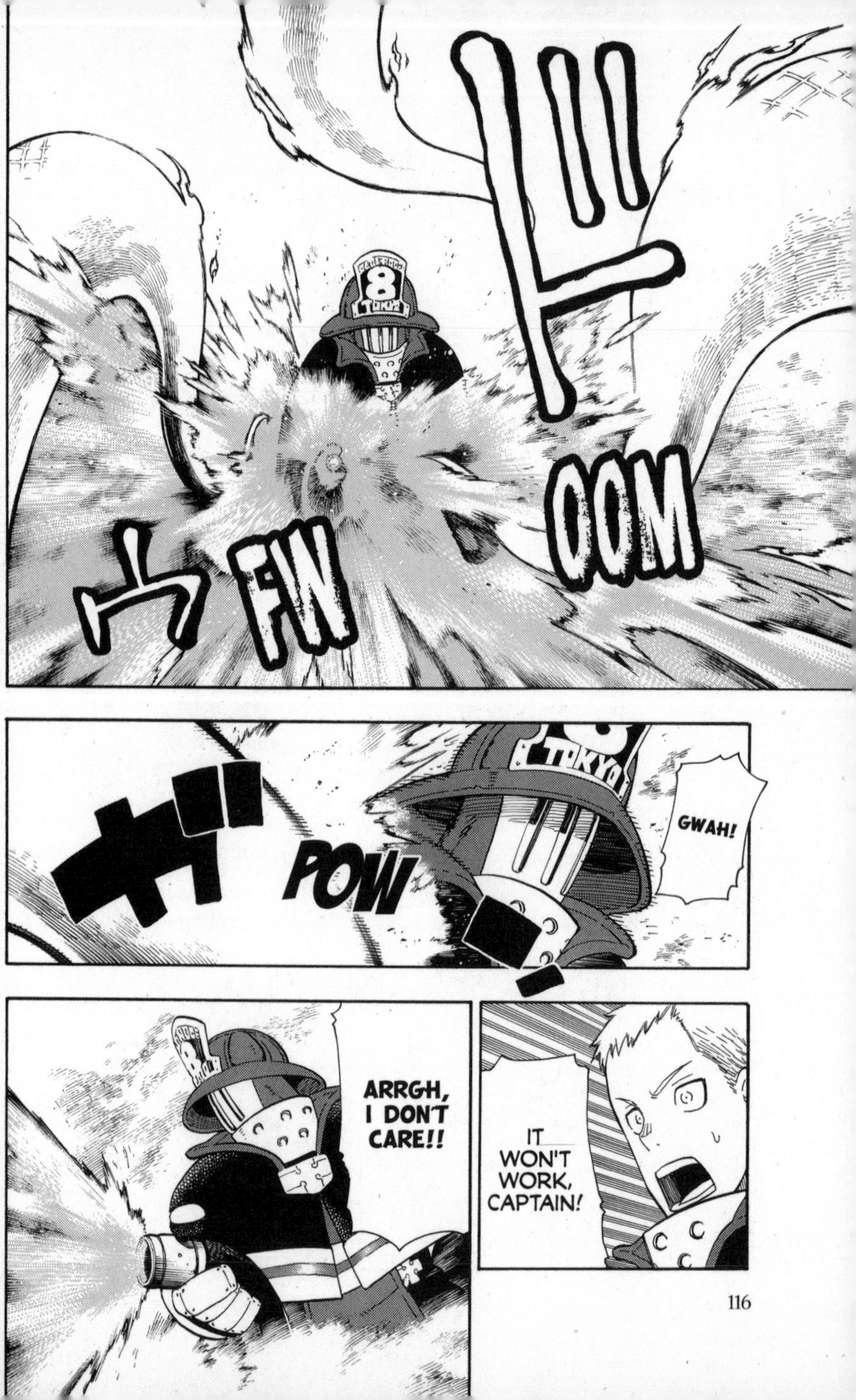
FW
OOM
GWAH!
POW
IT—— WON'T WORK, CAPTAIN!
ARRGH, I DON'T CARE!!

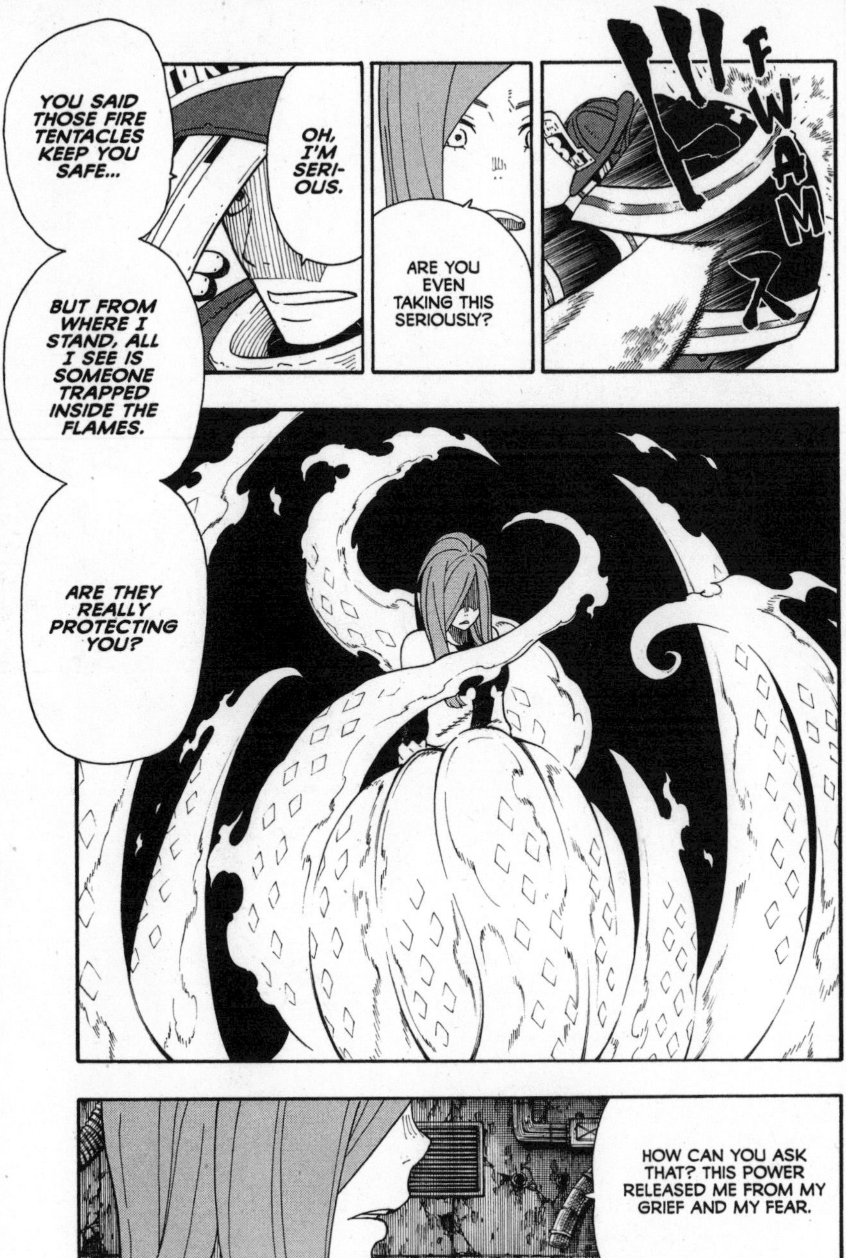
FWAM
ARE YOU EVEN TAKING THIS SERIOUSLY?
OH, I'M SERI-OUS.
YOU SAID THOSE FIRE TENTACLES KEEP YOU SAFE...
BUT FROM WHERE I STAND, ALL I SEE IS SOMEONE TRAPPED INSIDE THE FLAMES.
ARE THEY REALLY PROTECTING YOU?
HOW CAN YOU ASK THAT? THIS POWER RELEASED ME FROM MY GRIEF AND MY FEAR.

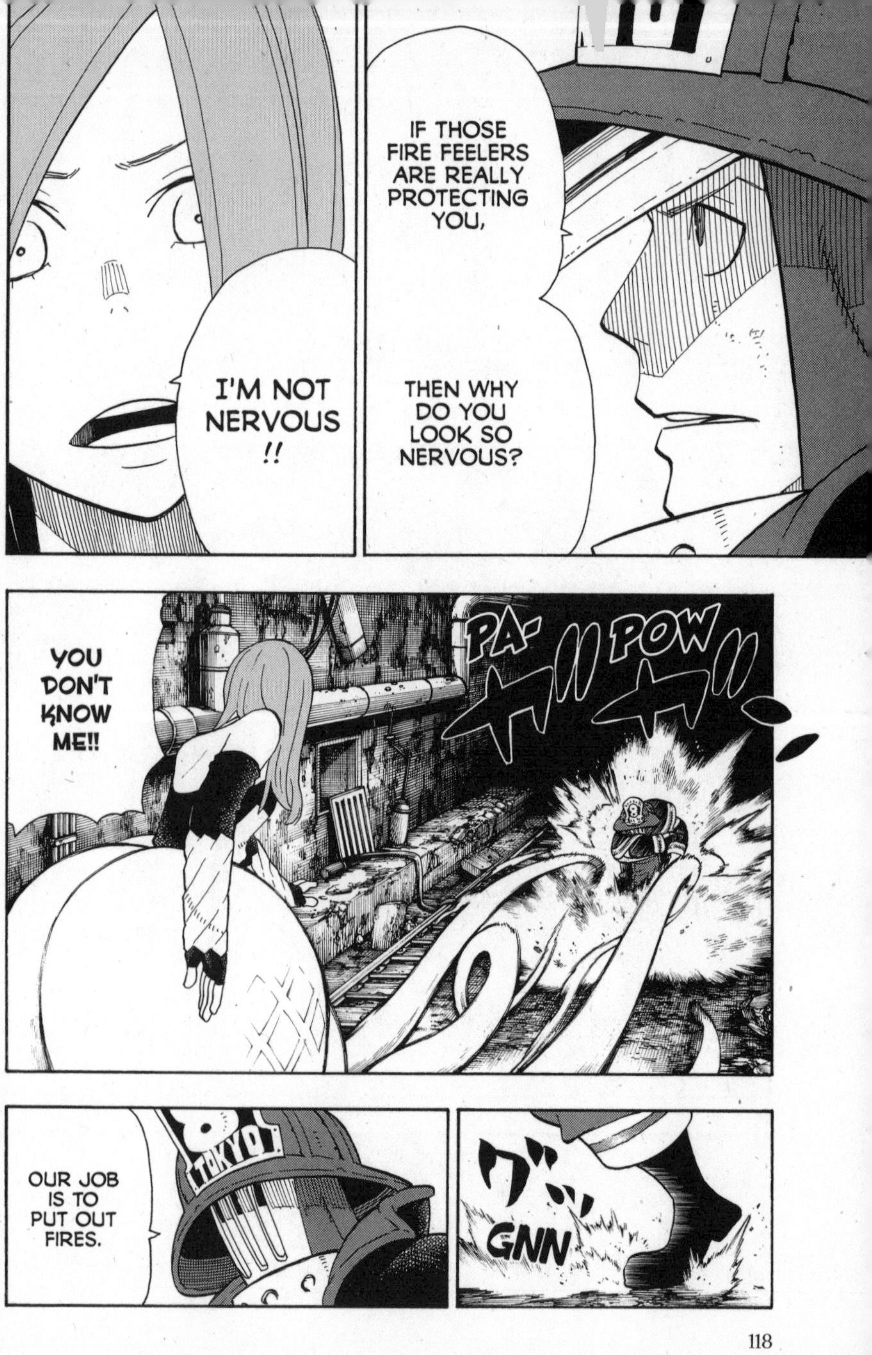
IF THOSE FIRE FEELERS ARE REALLY PROTECTING YOU,
THEN WHY DO YOU LOOK SO NERVOUS?
I'M NOT NERVOUS!!
PA-POW
YOU DON'T KNOW ME!!
GNN
OUR JOB IS TO PUT OUT FIRES.

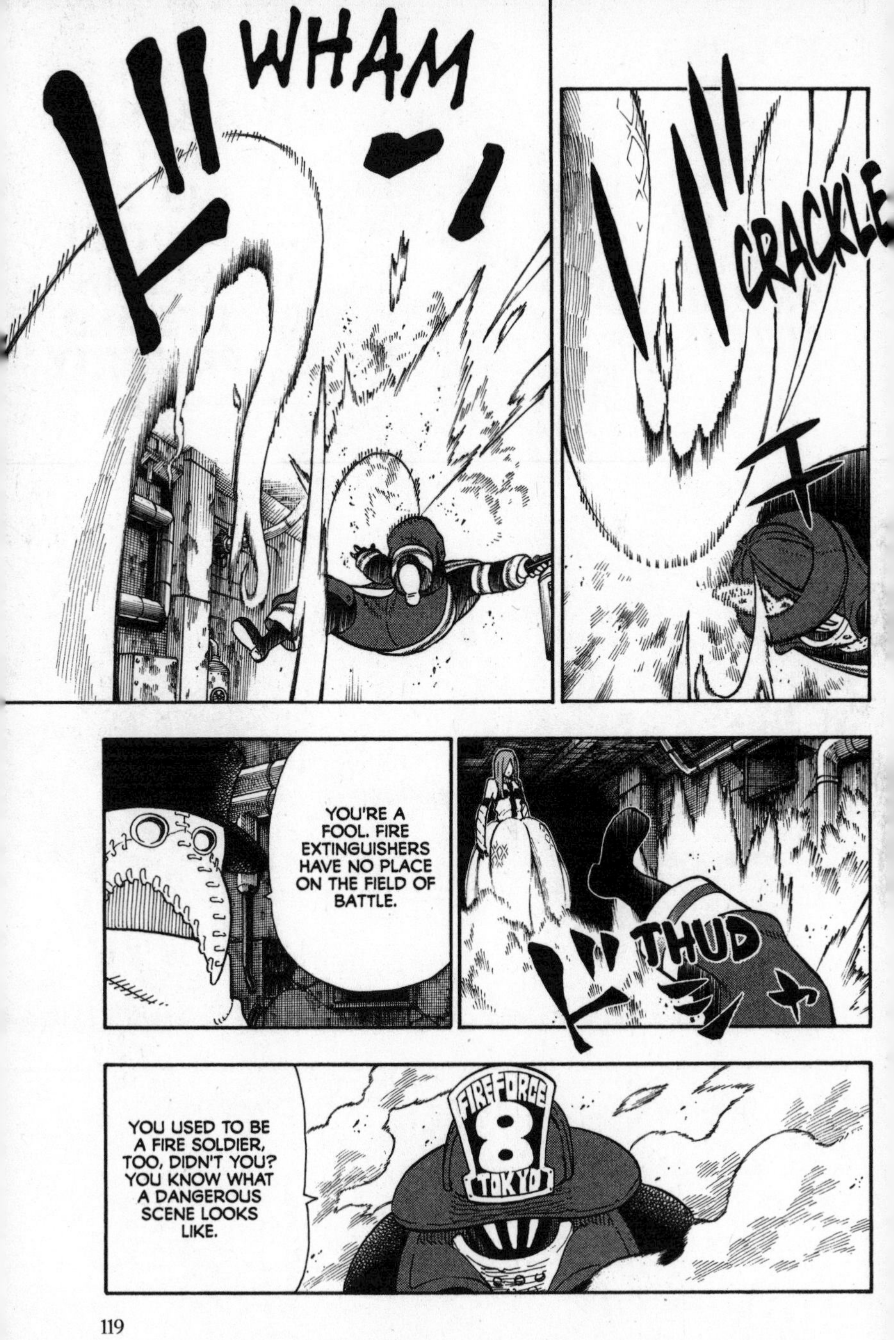
CRACKLE
WHAM
THUD
YOU'RE A FOOL. FIRE EXTINGUISHERS HAVE NO PLACE ON THE FIELD OF BATTLE.
YOU USED TO BE A FIRE SOLDIER, TOO, DIDN'T YOU? YOU KNOW WHAT A DANGEROUS SCENE LOOKS LIKE.
FIRE FORCE 8 TOKYO

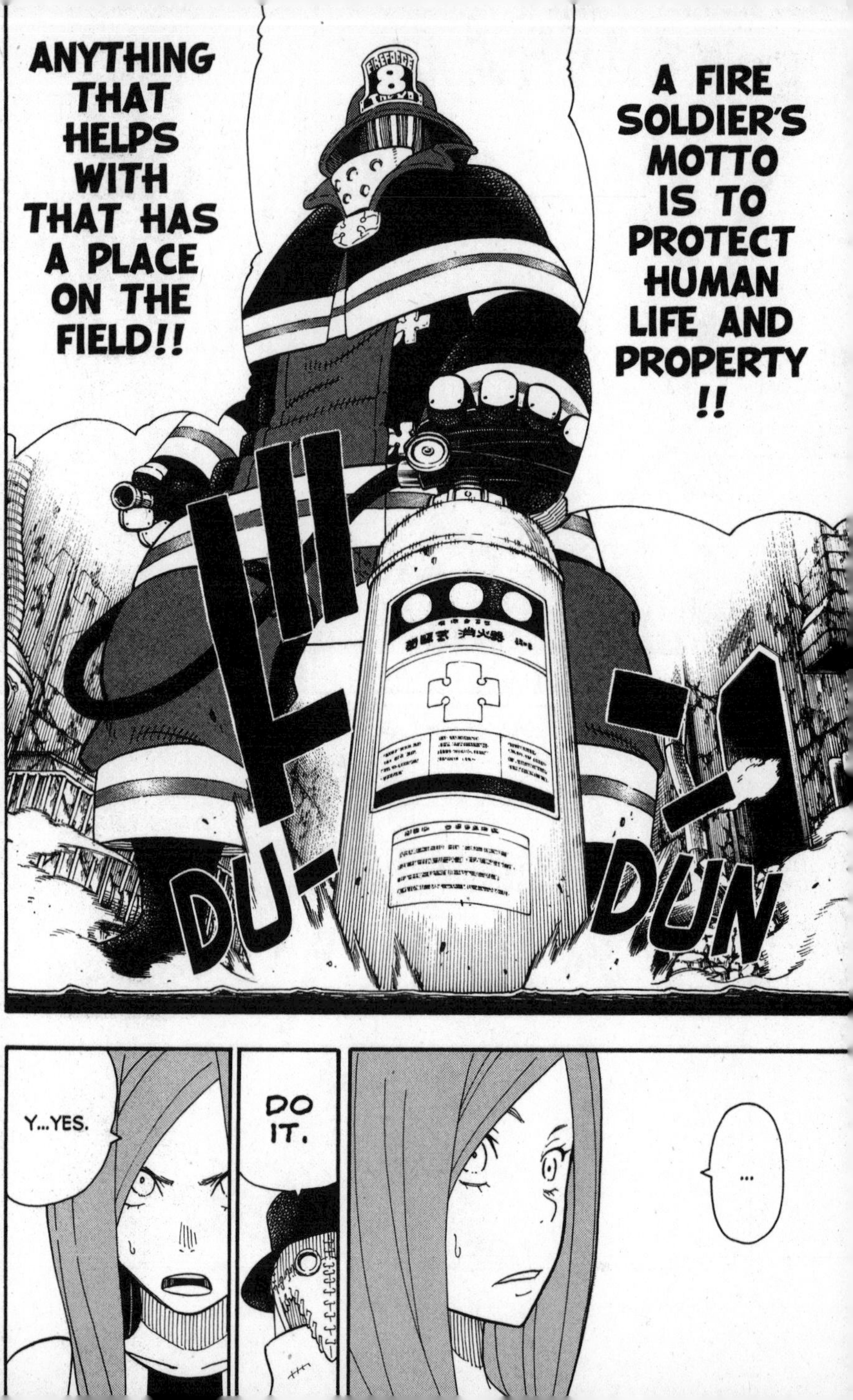
A FIRE SOLDIER'S MOTTO IS TO PROTECT HUMAN LIFE AND PROPERTY !!
ANYTHING THAT HELPS WITH THAT HAS A PLACE ON THE FIELD!!
DU-DUN
FIREFORCE 8
...
DO IT.
Y...YES.

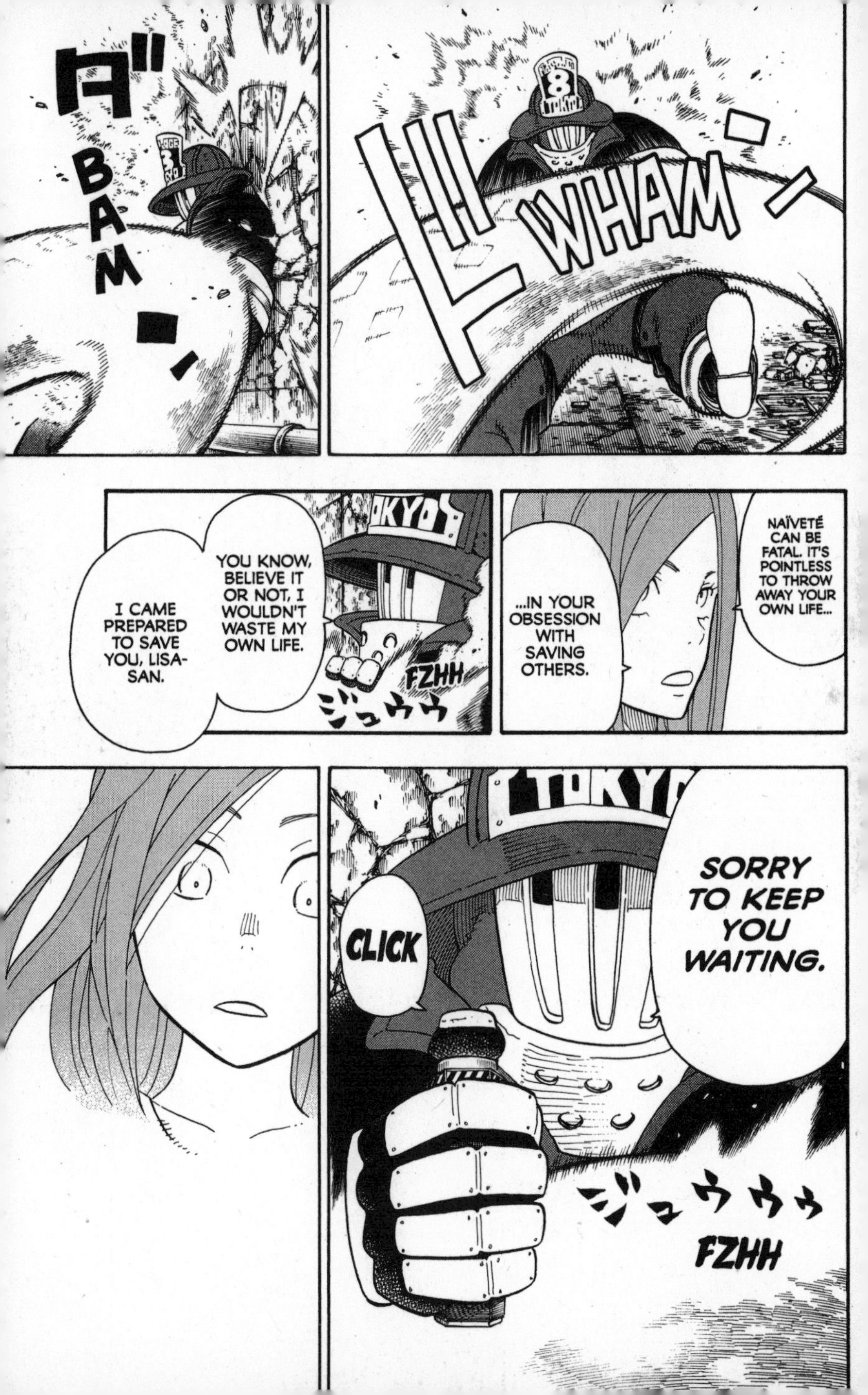
WHAM
BAM
NAÏVETÉ CAN BE FATAL. IT'S POINTLESS TO THROW AWAY YOUR OWN LIFE...
...IN YOUR OBSESSION WITH SAVING OTHERS.
YOU KNOW, BELIEVE IT OR NOT, I WOULDN'T WASTE MY OWN LIFE.
I CAME PREPARED TO SAVE YOU, LISA-SAN.
ジュウウ
FZHH
SORRY TO KEEP YOU WAITING.
CLICK
ジュウウウ
FZHH

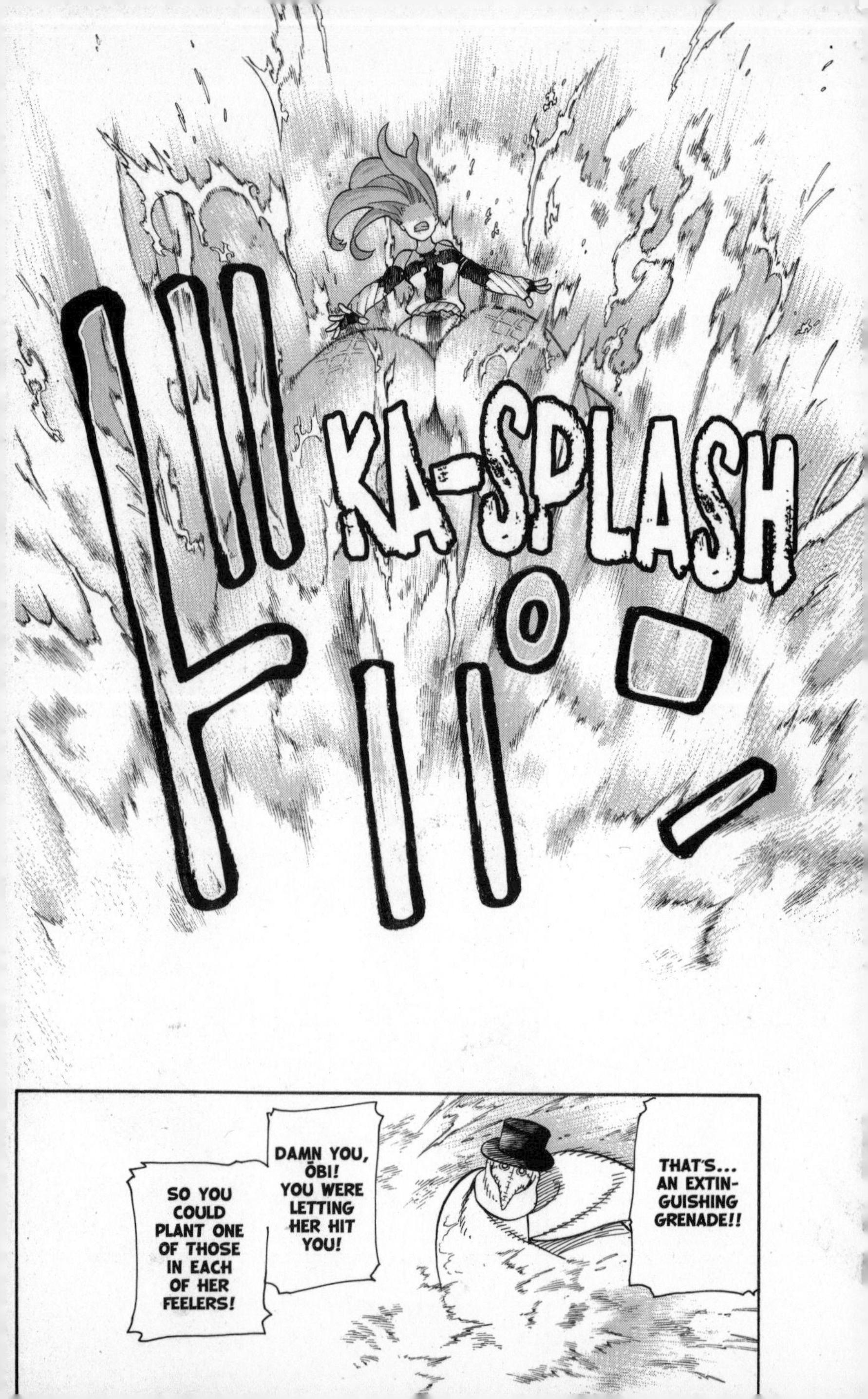
KA-SPLASH
THAT'S... AN EXTIN-GUISHING GRENADE!!
DAMN YOU, ŌBI! YOU WERE LETTING HER HIT YOU!
SO YOU COULD PLANT ONE OF THOSE IN EACH OF HER FEELERS!

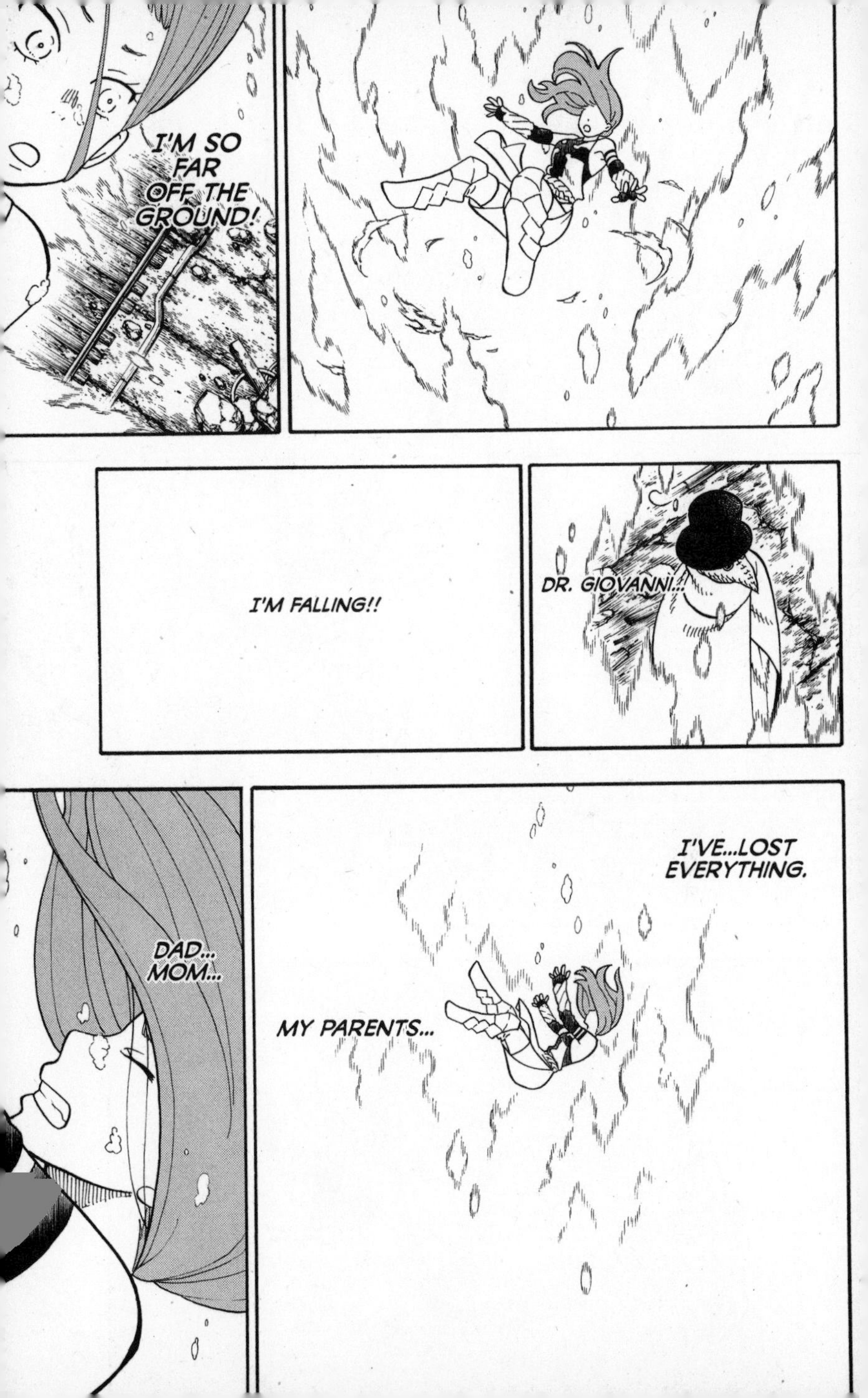
I'M SO FAR OFF THE GROUND!
DR. GIOVANNI...
I'M FALLING!!
I'VE...LOST EVERYTHING.
MY PARENTS...
DAD... MOM...

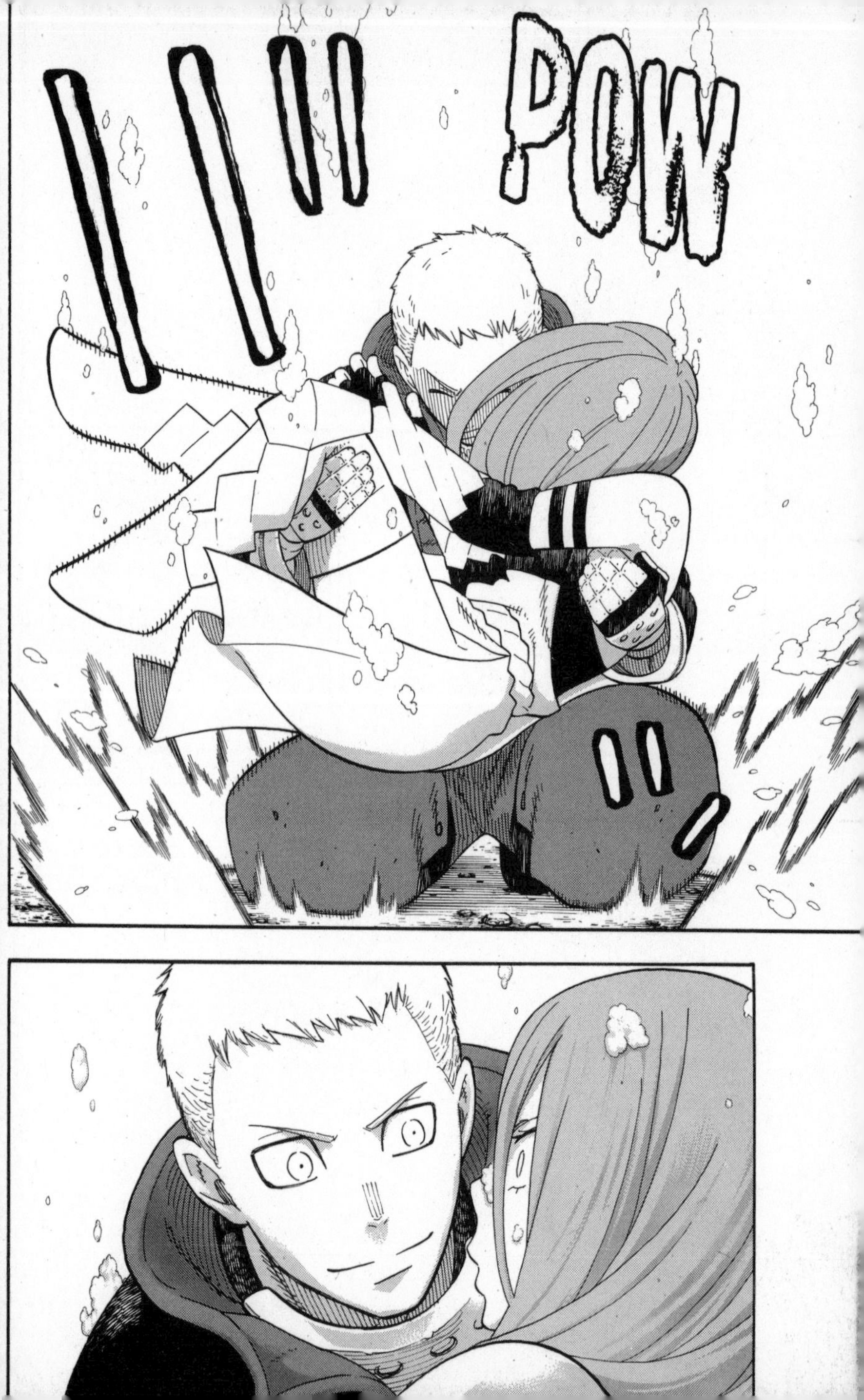
POW

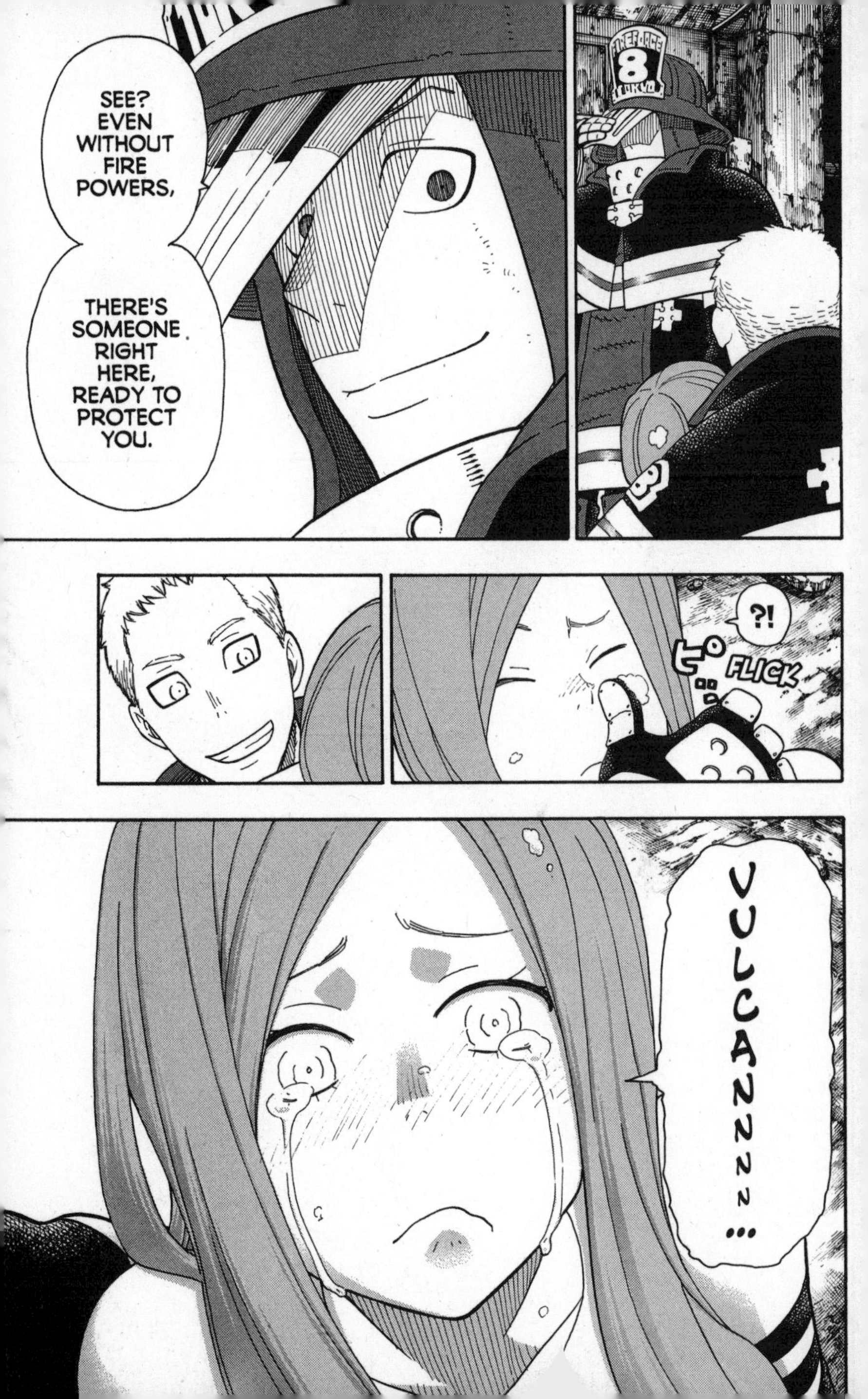
SEE? EVEN WITHOUT FIRE POWERS,
THERE'S SOMEONE RIGHT HERE, READY TO PROTECT YOU.
?!
ピ
FLICK
VULCANNNN..

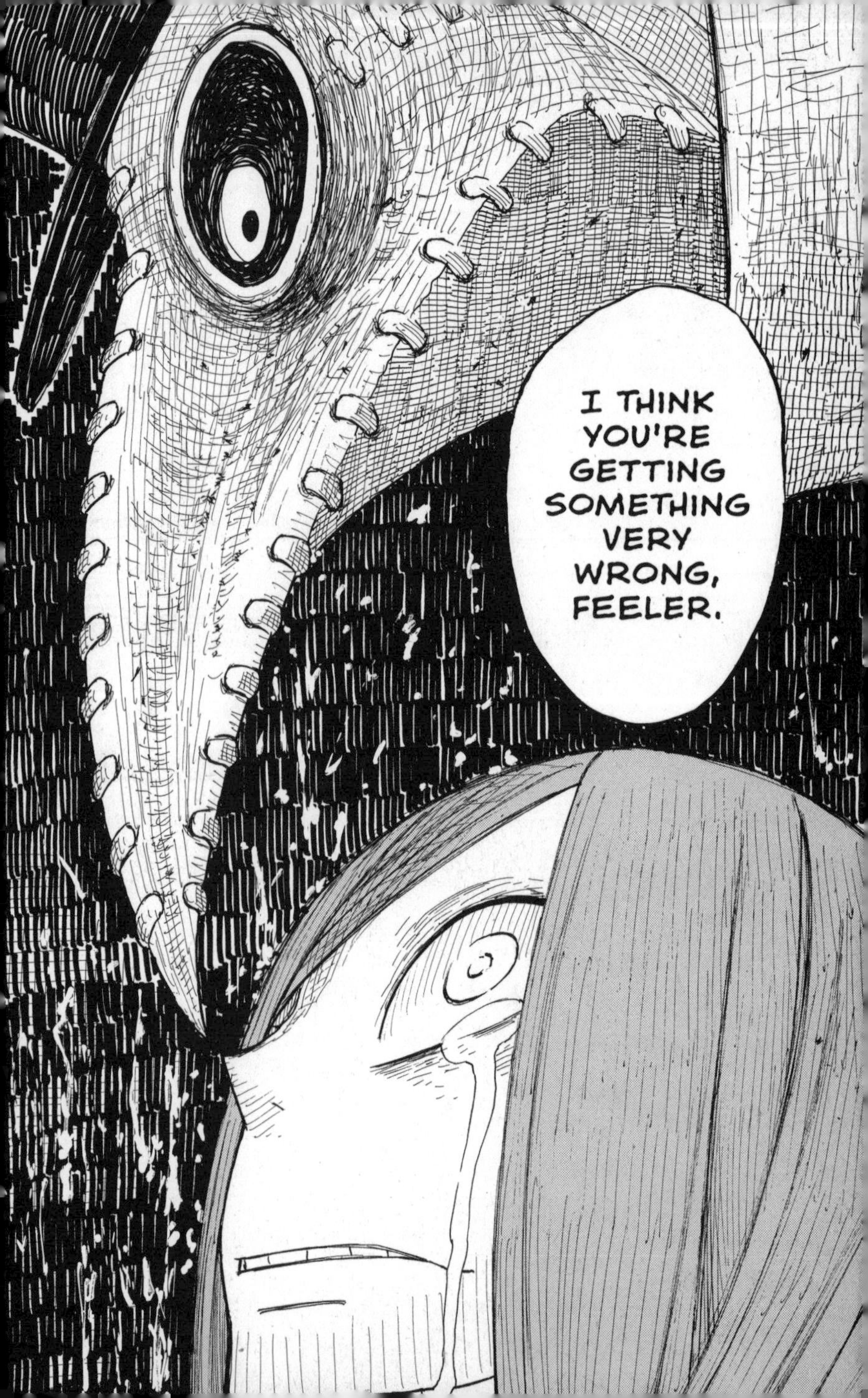
I THINK YOU'RE GETTING SOMETHING VERY WRONG, FEELER.

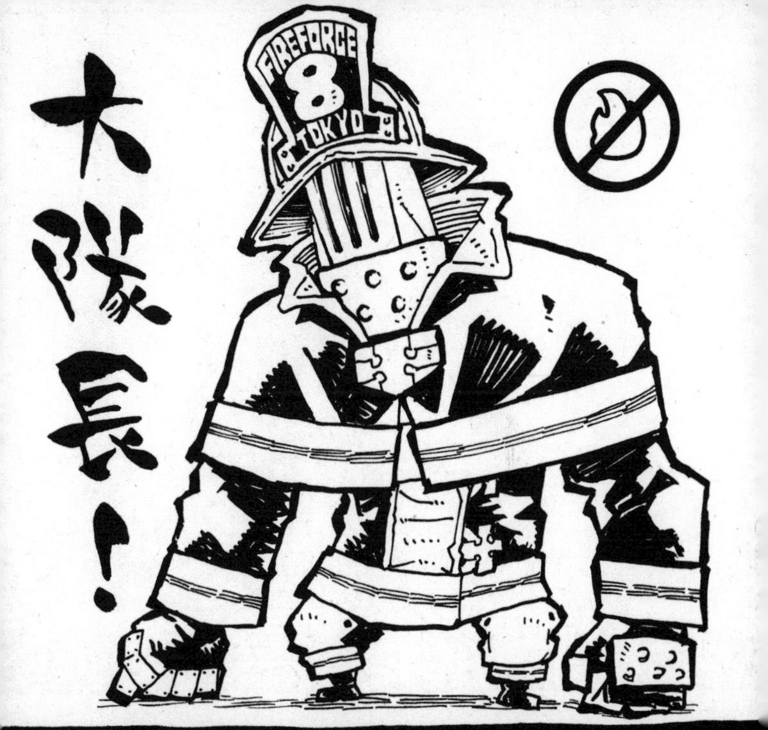
大隊長!
FIREFORCE
8
TOKYO

Text: Captain!

CHAPTER LXXVI: STICKING TO YOUR GUNS

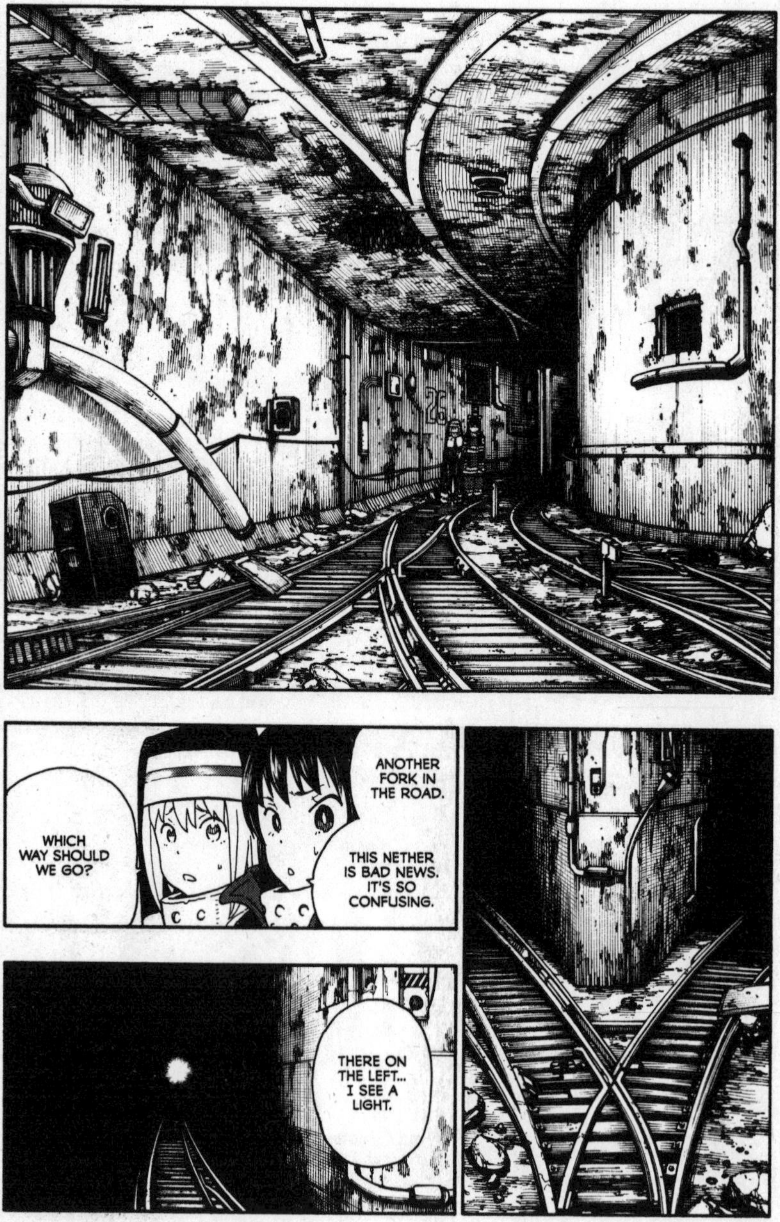
ANOTHER FORK IN THE ROAD.
THIS NETHER IS BAD NEWS. IT'S SO CONFUSING.
WHICH WAY SHOULD WE GO?
THERE ON THE LEFT... I SEE A LIGHT.

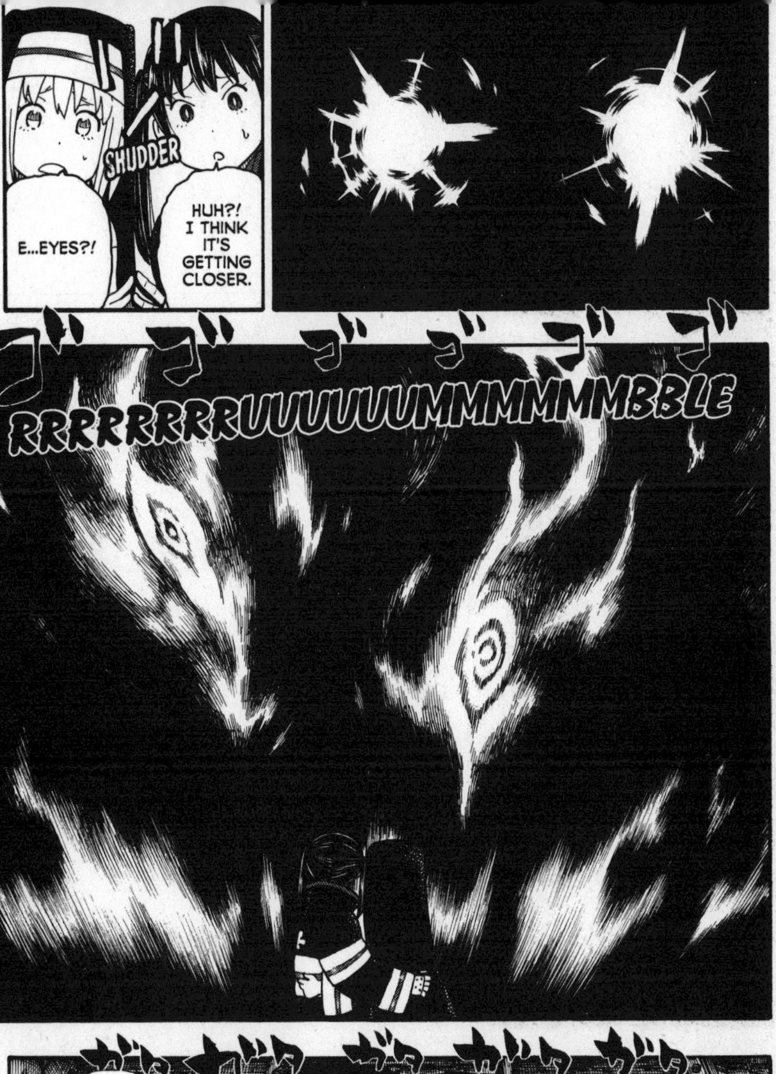
SHUDDER
HUH?! I THINK IT'S GETTING CLOSER.
E...EYES?!
RRRRRRRUUUUUUMMMMMMMBBLE
SSSSSSSHHHHIIIIVVVEEERRR
EEEEK!
DEMON!

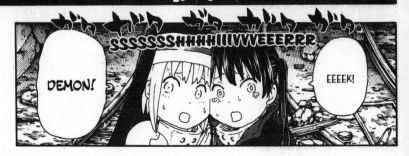

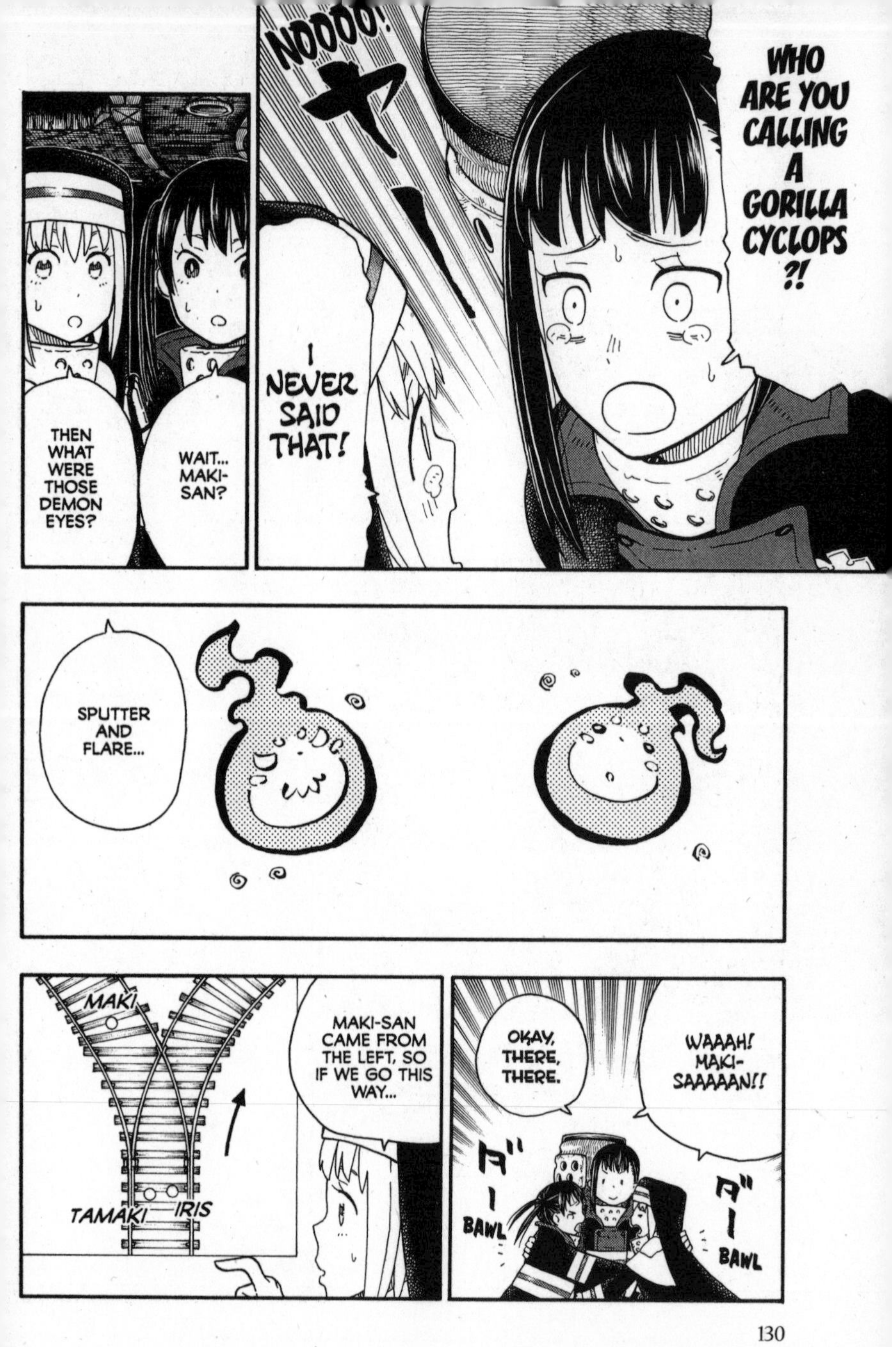
WHO ARE YOU CALLING A GORILLA CYCLOPS?!
NOOOO!
I NEVER SAID THAT!
WAIT... MAKI-SAN?
THEN WHAT WERE THOSE DEMON EYES?
SPUTTER AND FLARE...
WAAAH! MAKI-SAAAAAN!!
OKAY, THERE, THERE.
BAWL
BAWL
MAKI-SAN CAME FROM THE LEFT, SO IF WE GO THIS WAY...
MAKI
TAMAKI
IRIS

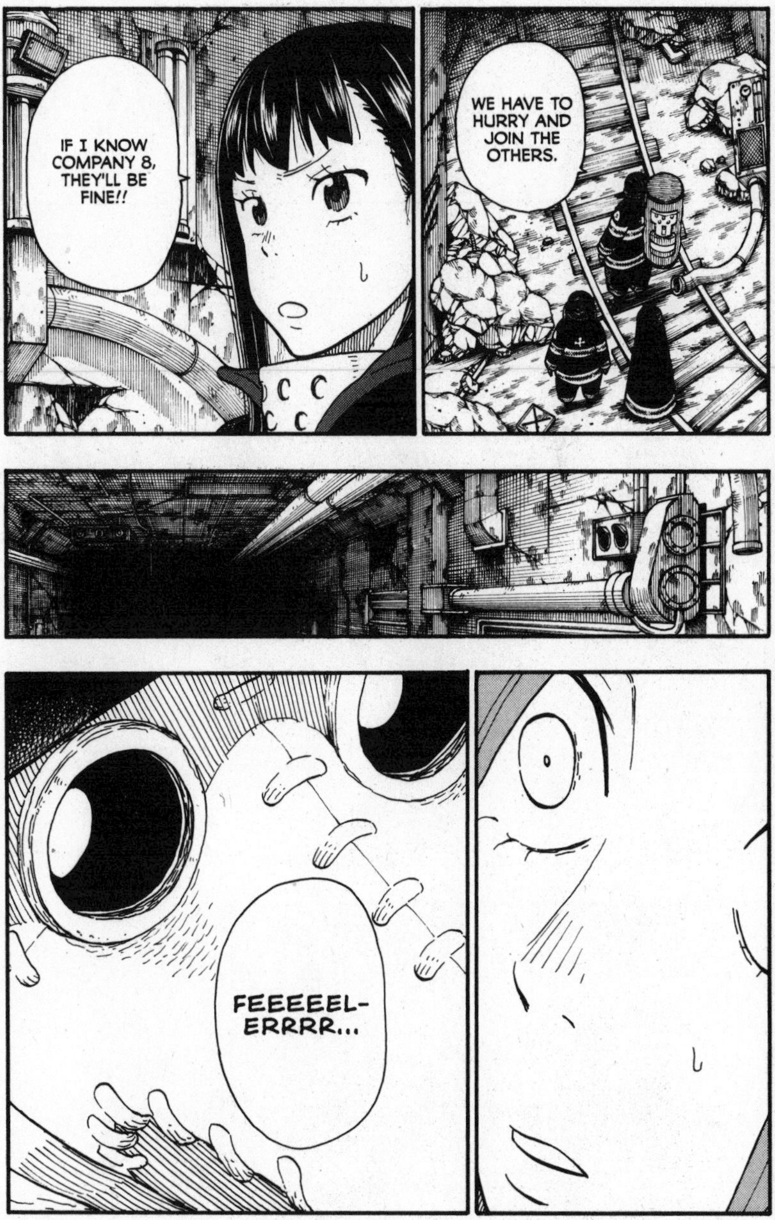
WE HAVE TO HURRY AND JOIN THE OTHERS.
IF I KNOW COMPANY 8, THEY'LL BE FINE!!
FEEEEEL-ERRRR...

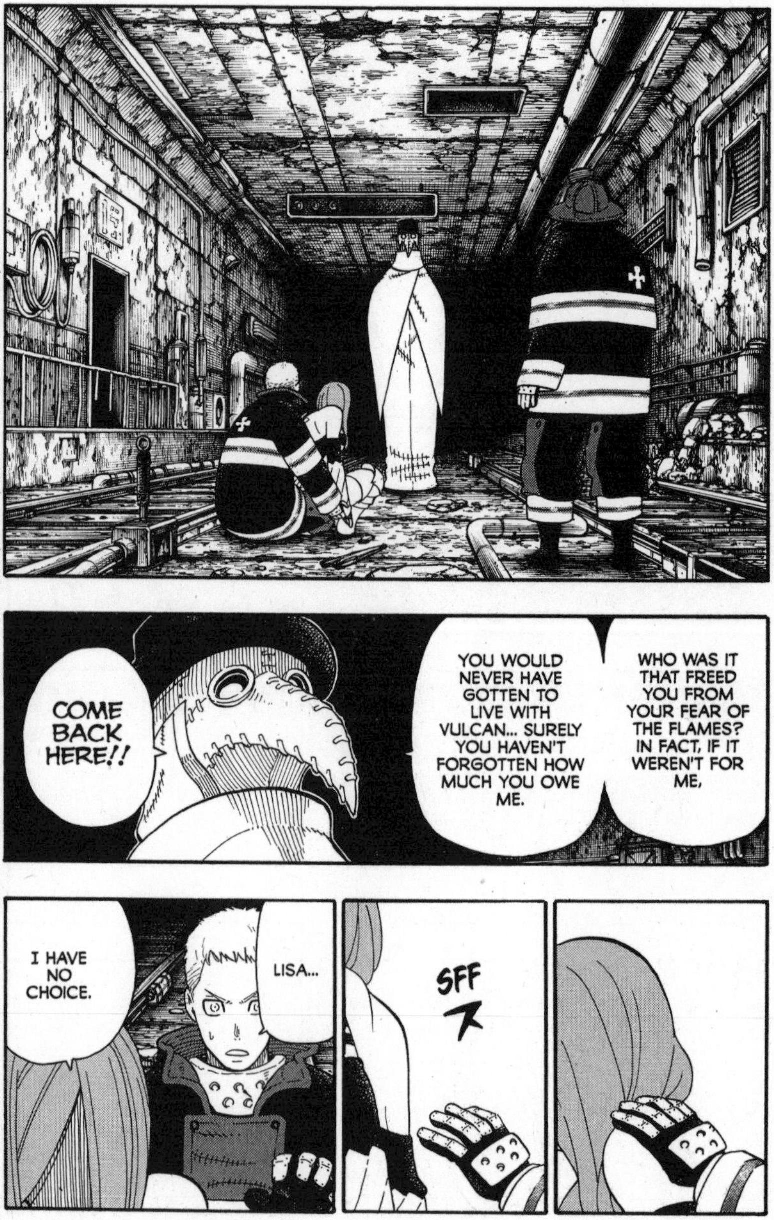
WHO WAS IT THAT FREED YOU FROM YOUR FEAR OF THE FLAMES? IN FACT, IF IT WEREN'T FOR ME,
YOU WOULD NEVER HAVE GOTTEN TO LIVE WITH VULCAN... SURELY YOU HAVEN'T FORGOTTEN HOW MUCH YOU OWE ME.
COME BACK HERE!!
SFF
LISA...
I HAVE NO CHOICE.

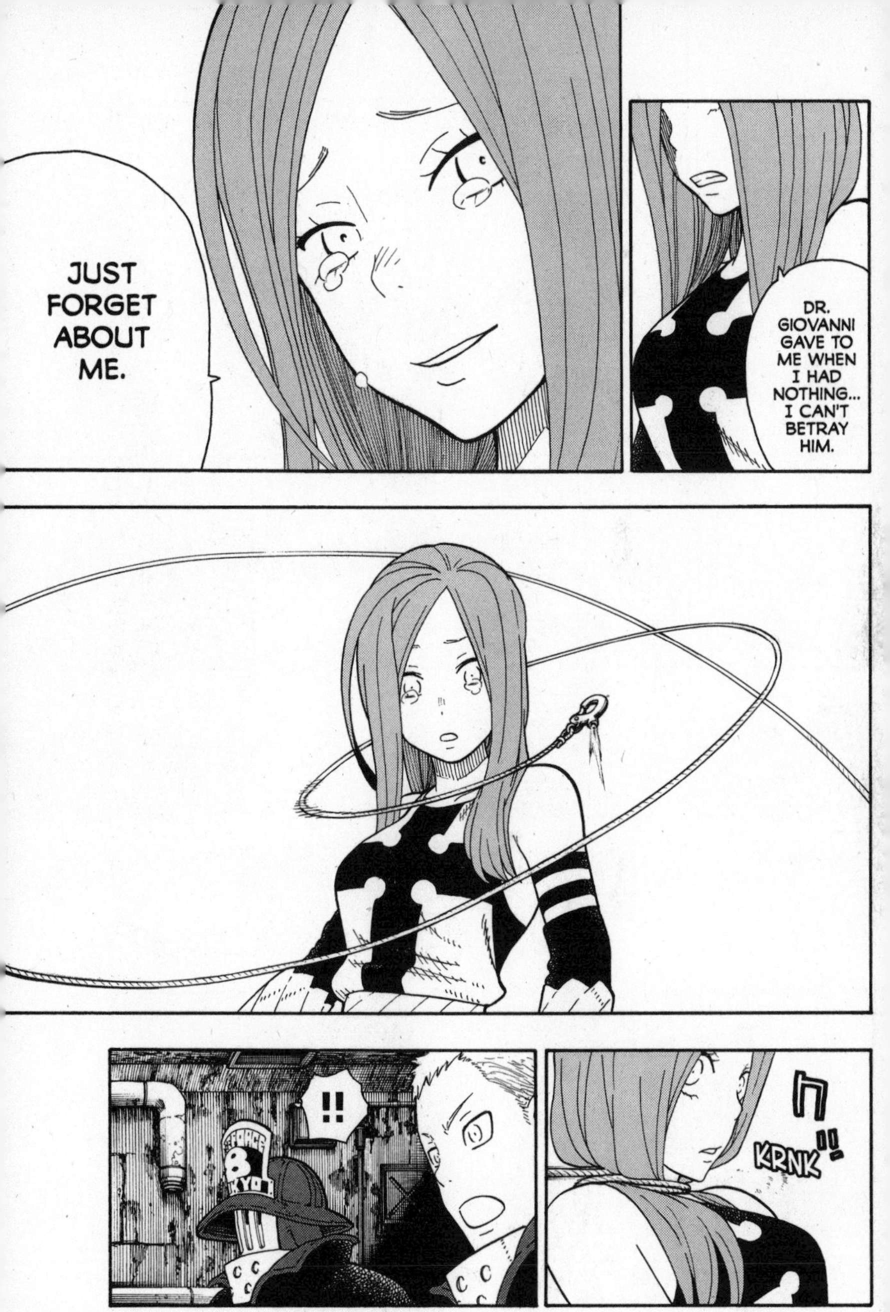
DR. GIOVANNI GAVE TO ME WHEN I HAD NOTHING... I CAN'T BETRAY HIM.
JUST FORGET ABOUT ME.
KRNK!!
!!

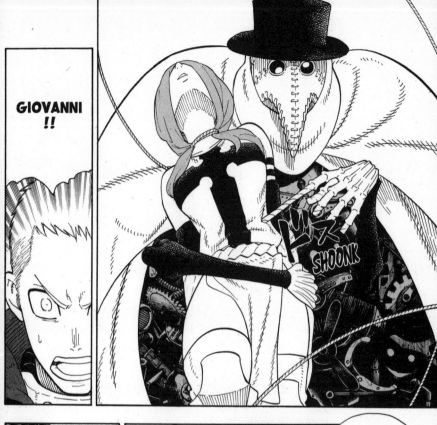

GIOVANNI
!!

SHOONK

NO!!

DON'T MOVE!
OR THESE
HEATED WIRES
WILL BURN
THROUGH HER
NECK.

RUSTLE

RUSTLE

VULCAN. IF YOU WANT TO SAVE HER, YOU'LL DO AS I SAY.

CLATTER
CLATTER

TAKE THAT GUN AND SHOOT ŌBI.

HOW ROTTEN CAN YOU BE?

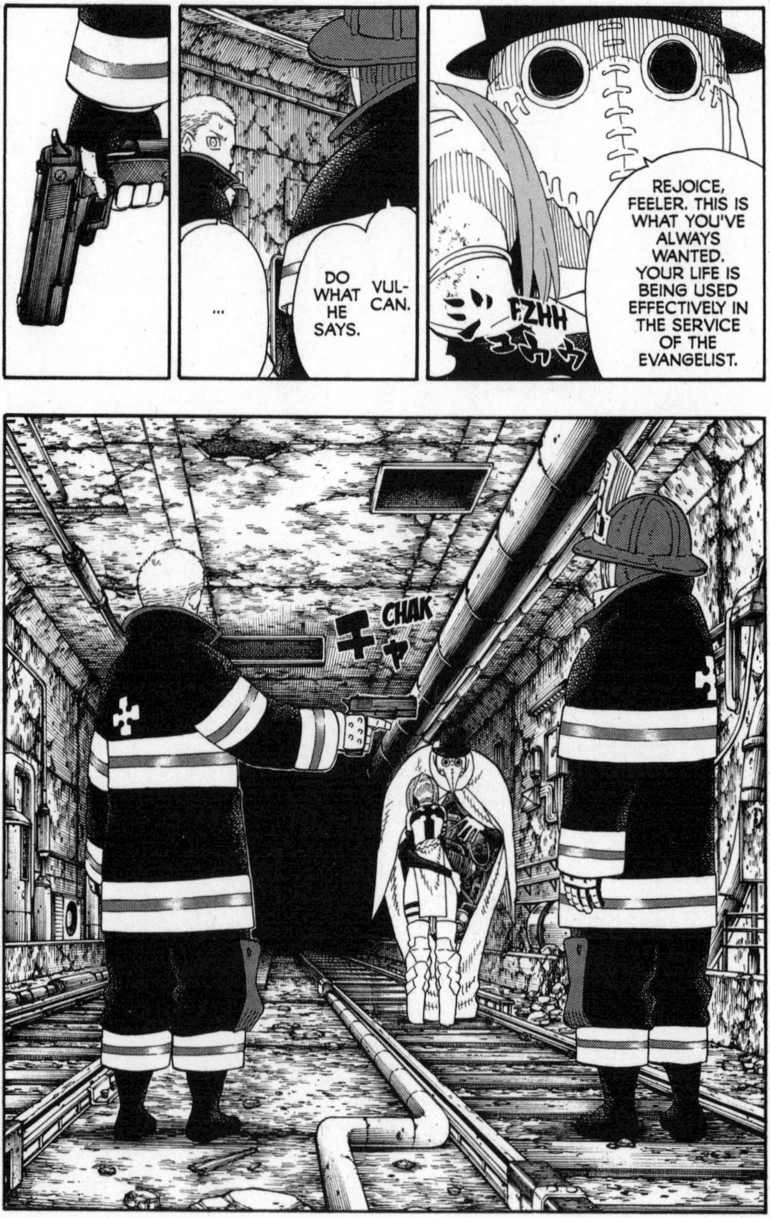
REJOICE, FEELER. THIS IS WHAT YOU'VE ALWAYS WANTED. YOUR LIFE IS BEING USED EFFECTIVELY IN THE SERVICE OF THE EVANGELIST.
FZHH
VUL-CAN.
DO WHAT HE SAYS.
...
CHAK

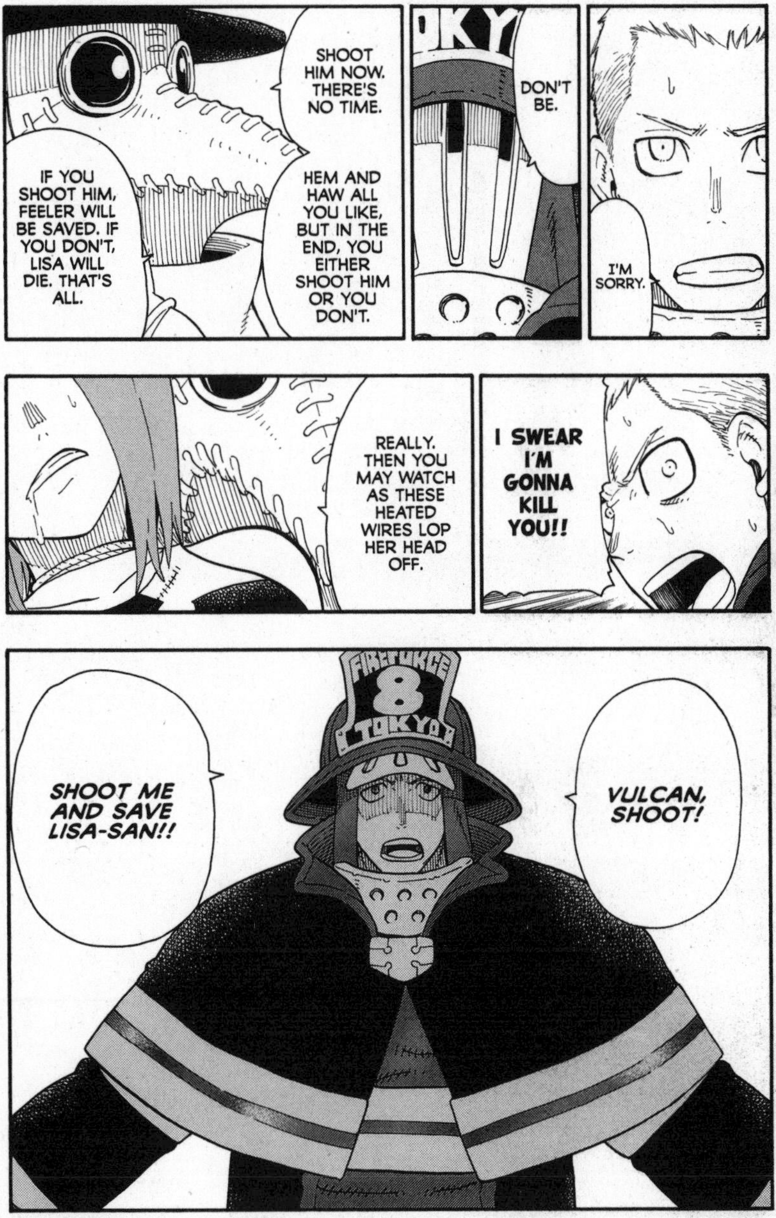
I'M SORRY.
DON'T BE.
SHOOT HIM NOW. THERE'S NO TIME.
HEM AND HAW ALL YOU LIKE, BUT IN THE END, YOU EITHER SHOOT HIM OR YOU DON'T.
IF YOU SHOOT HIM, FEELER WILL BE SAVED. IF YOU DON'T, LISA WILL DIE. THAT'S ALL.
I SWEAR I'M GONNA KILL YOU!!
REALLY. THEN YOU MAY WATCH AS THESE HEATED WIRES LOP HER HEAD OFF.
VULCAN, SHOOT!
SHOOT ME AND SAVE LISA-SAN!!

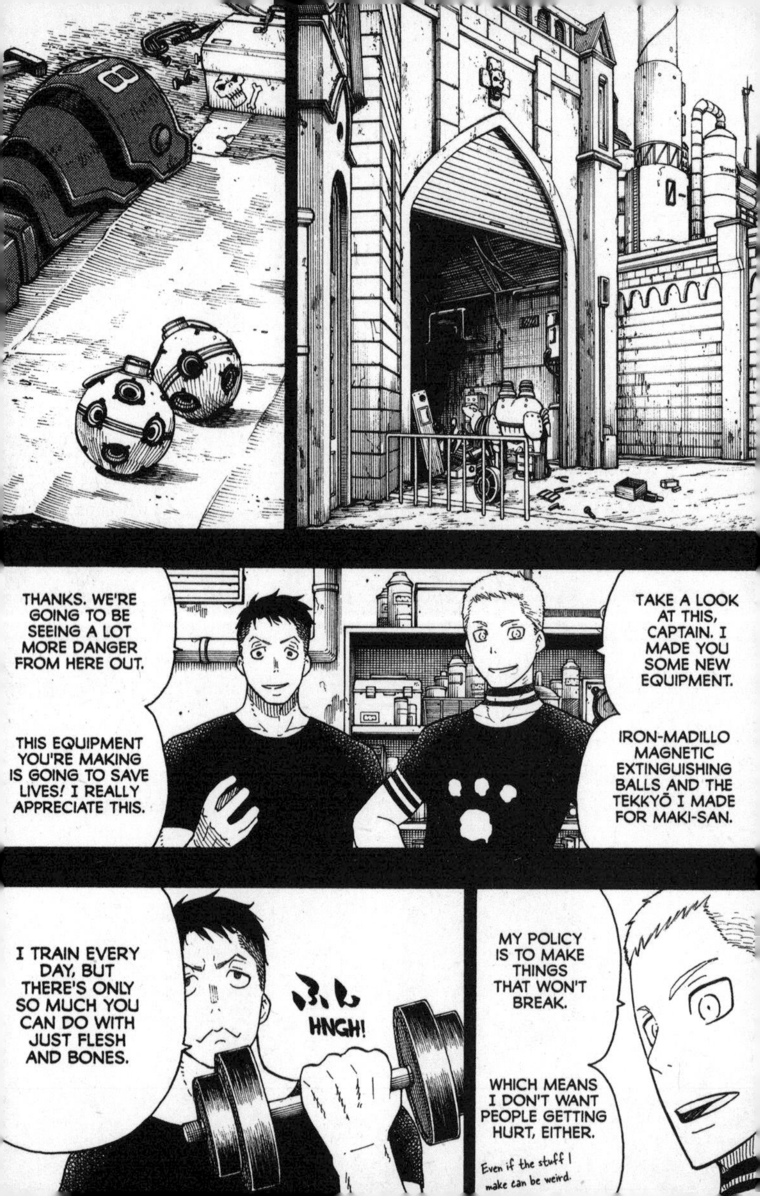
TAKE A LOOK AT THIS, CAPTAIN. I MADE YOU SOME NEW EQUIPMENT.
IRON-MADILLO MAGNETIC EXTINGUISHING BALLS AND THE TEKKYŌ I MADE FOR MAKI-SAN.
THANKS. WE'RE GOING TO BE SEEING A LOT MORE DANGER FROM HERE OUT.
THIS EQUIPMENT YOU'RE MAKING IS GOING TO SAVE LIVES! I REALLY APPRECIATE THIS.
MY POLICY IS TO MAKE THINGS THAT WON'T BREAK.
WHICH MEANS I DON'T WANT PEOPLE GETTING HURT, EITHER.
Even if the stuff I make can be weird.
I TRAIN EVERY DAY, BUT THERE'S ONLY SO MUCH YOU CAN DO WITH JUST FLESH AND BONES.
ふん
HNGH!

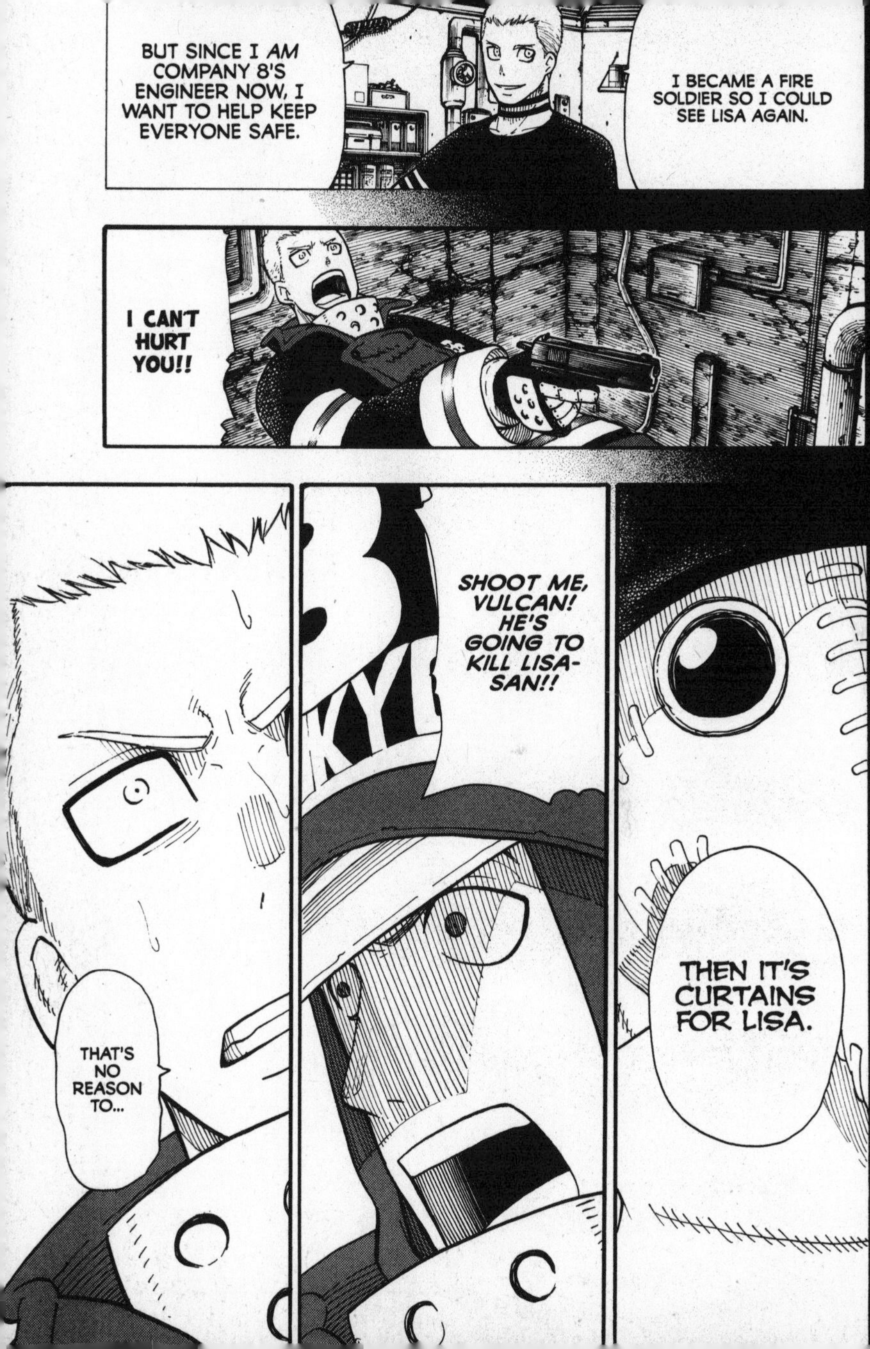
I BECAME A FIRE SOLDIER SO I COULD SEE LISA AGAIN.
BUT SINCE I *AM* COMPANY 8'S ENGINEER NOW, I WANT TO HELP KEEP EVERYONE SAFE.
I CAN'T HURT YOU!!
THEN IT'S CURTAINS FOR LISA.
SHOOT ME, VULCAN! HE'S GOING TO KILL LISA-SAN!!
THAT'S NO REASON TO...

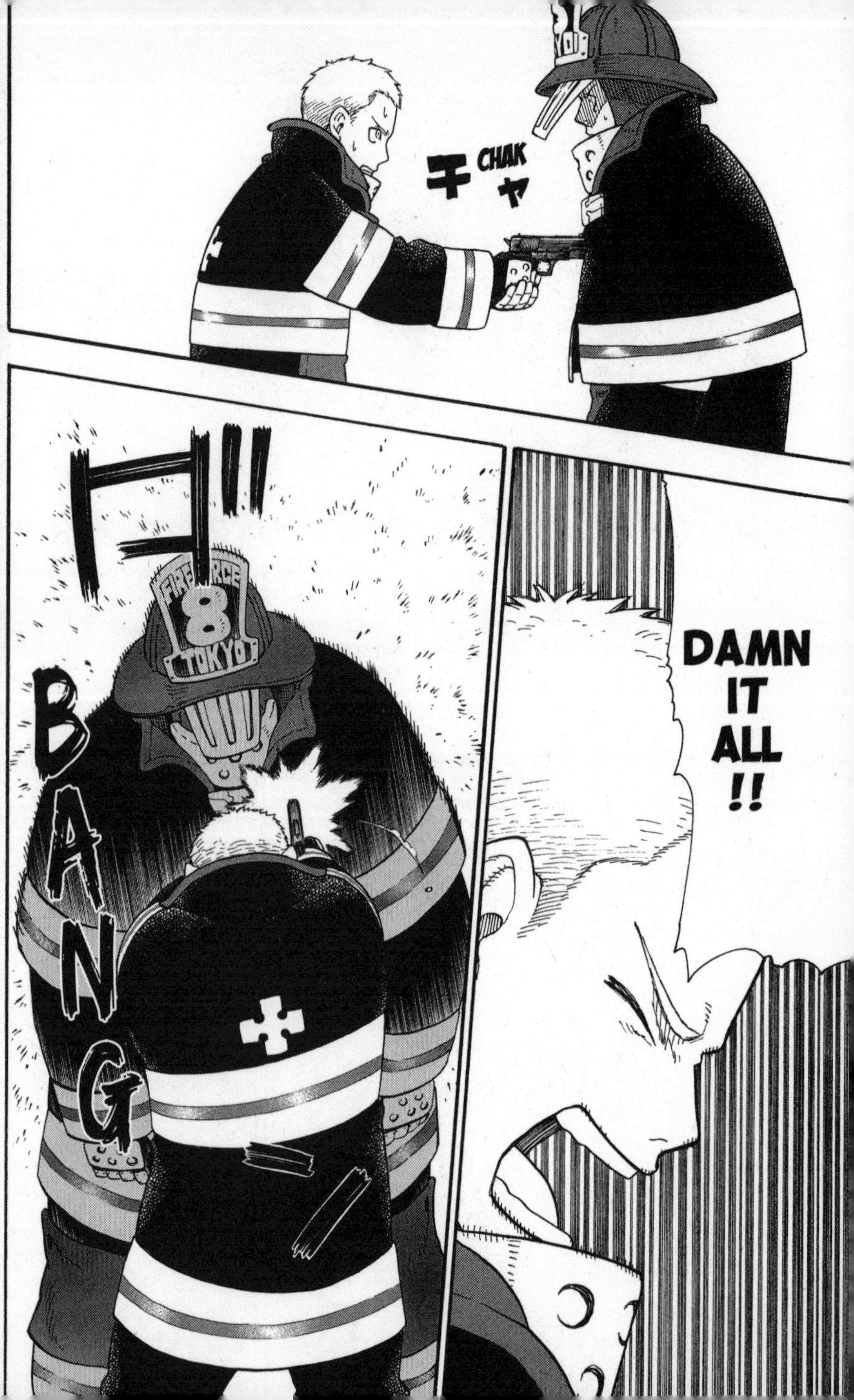
チャ
CHAK
BANG
DAMN IT ALL!!

CAPTAIN...

LISA...

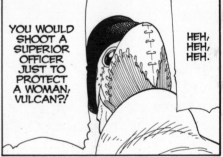

YOU WOULD SHOOT A SUPERIOR OFFICER JUST TO PROTECT A WOMAN, VULCAN?!

HEH, HEH, HEH.

COUGH COUGH!

COUGH!

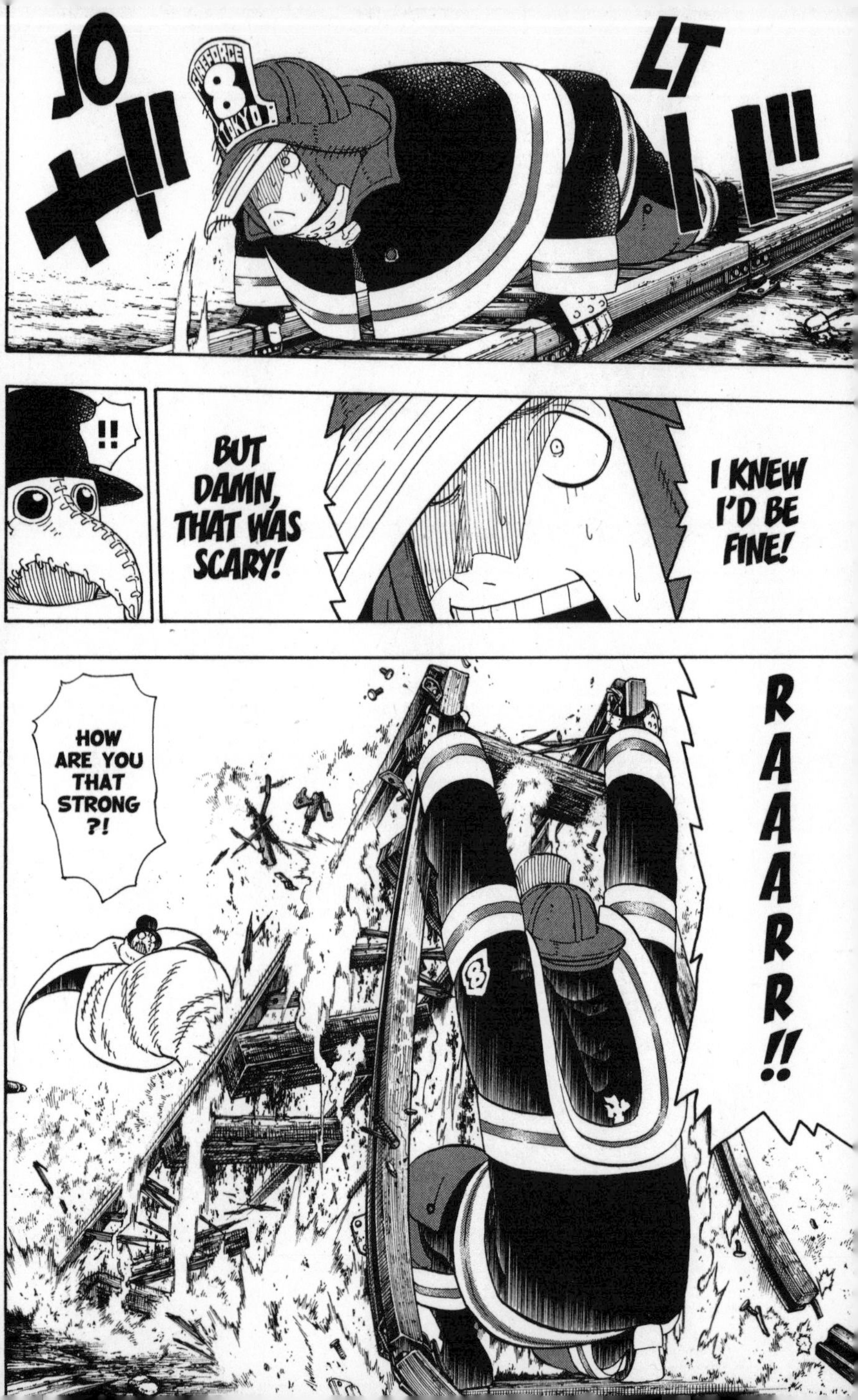
JOLT!!
I KNEW I'D BE FINE!
BUT DAMN, THAT WAS SCARY!
!!
RAAAARR!!
HOW ARE YOU THAT STRONG?!

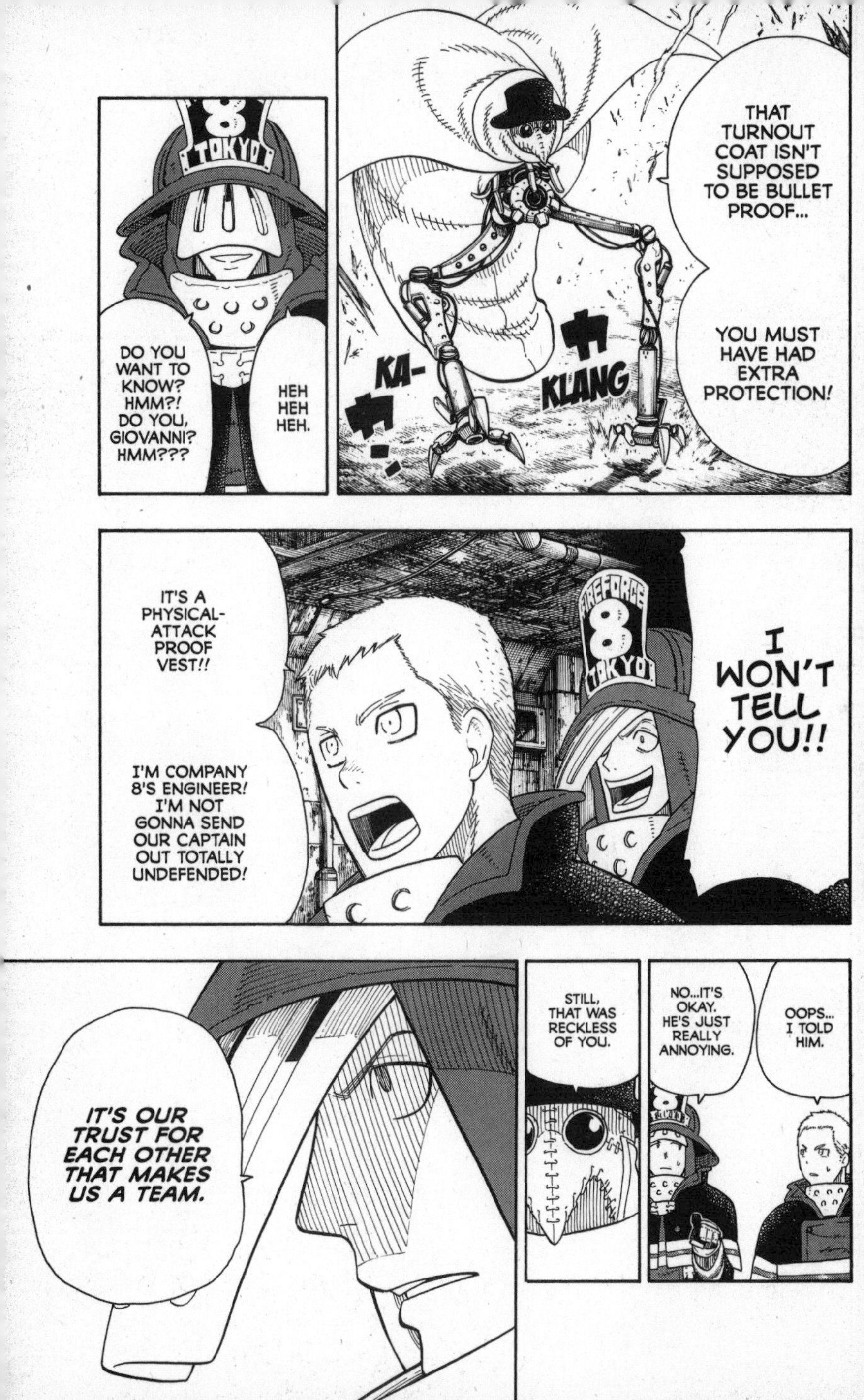
THAT TURNOUT COAT ISN'T SUPPOSED TO BE BULLET PROOF...
YOU MUST HAVE HAD EXTRA PROTECTION!
KA-
KLANG
HEH HEH HEH.
DO YOU WANT TO KNOW? HMM?! DO YOU, GIOVANNI? HMM???
I WON'T TELL YOU!!
IT'S A PHYSICAL-ATTACK PROOF VEST!!
I'M COMPANY 8'S ENGINEER! I'M NOT GONNA SEND OUR CAPTAIN OUT TOTALLY UNDEFENDED!
OOPS... I TOLD HIM.
NO...IT'S OKAY. HE'S JUST REALLY ANNOYING.
STILL, THAT WAS RECKLESS OF YOU.
IT'S OUR TRUST FOR EACH OTHER THAT MAKES US A TEAM.

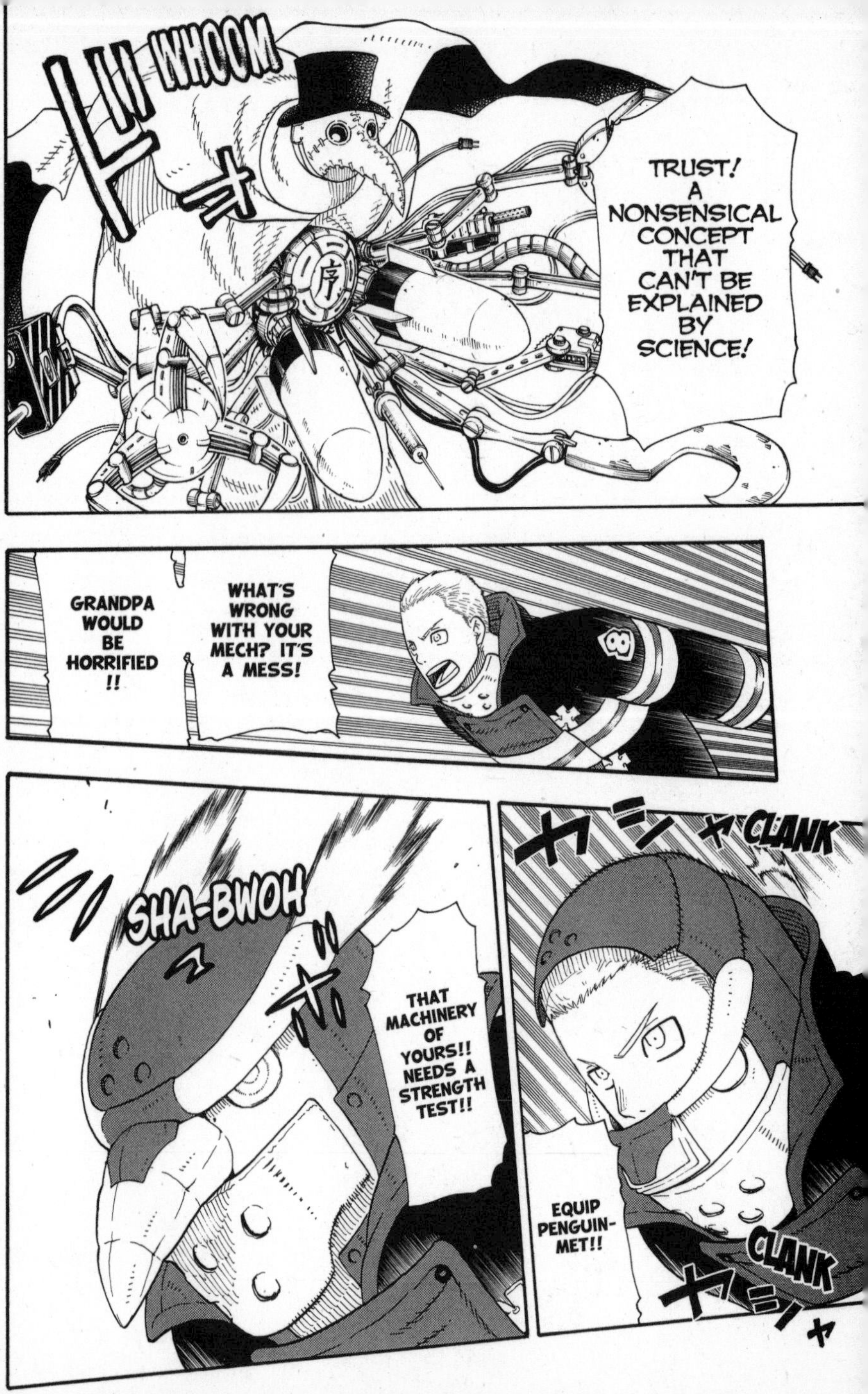
WHOOM
TRUST! A NONSENSICAL CONCEPT THAT CAN'T BE EXPLAINED BY SCIENCE!
WHAT'S WRONG WITH YOUR MECH? IT'S A MESS!
GRANDPA WOULD BE HORRIFIED !!
CLANK
EQUIP PENGUIN-MET!!
CLANK
SHA-BWOH
THAT MACHINERY OF YOURS!! NEEDS A STRENGTH TEST!!

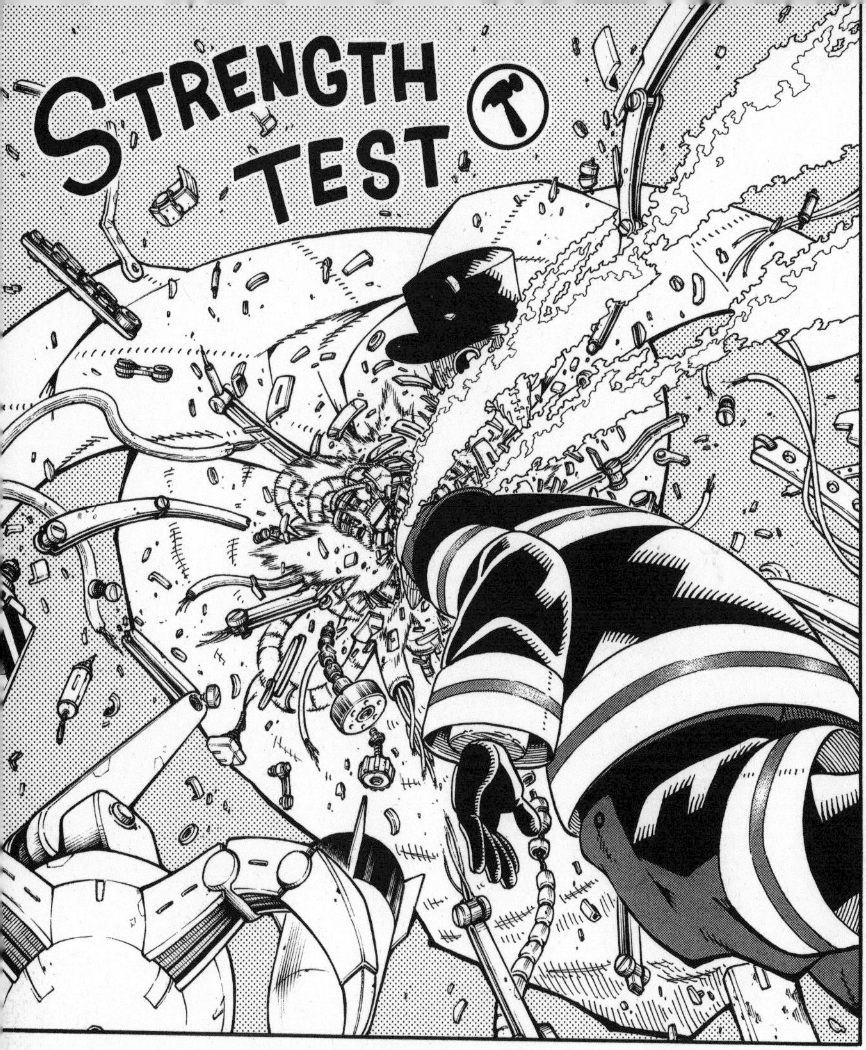
STRENGTH TEST

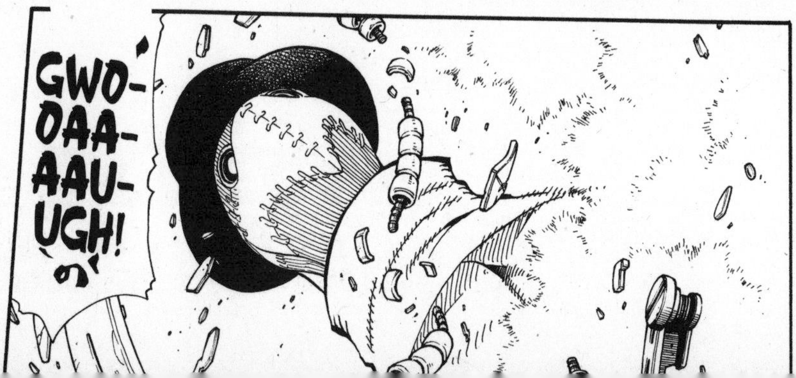
GWO-OAA-AAU-UGH!

FIRE FORCE

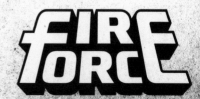

CHAPTER LXXVII: CONNECTION

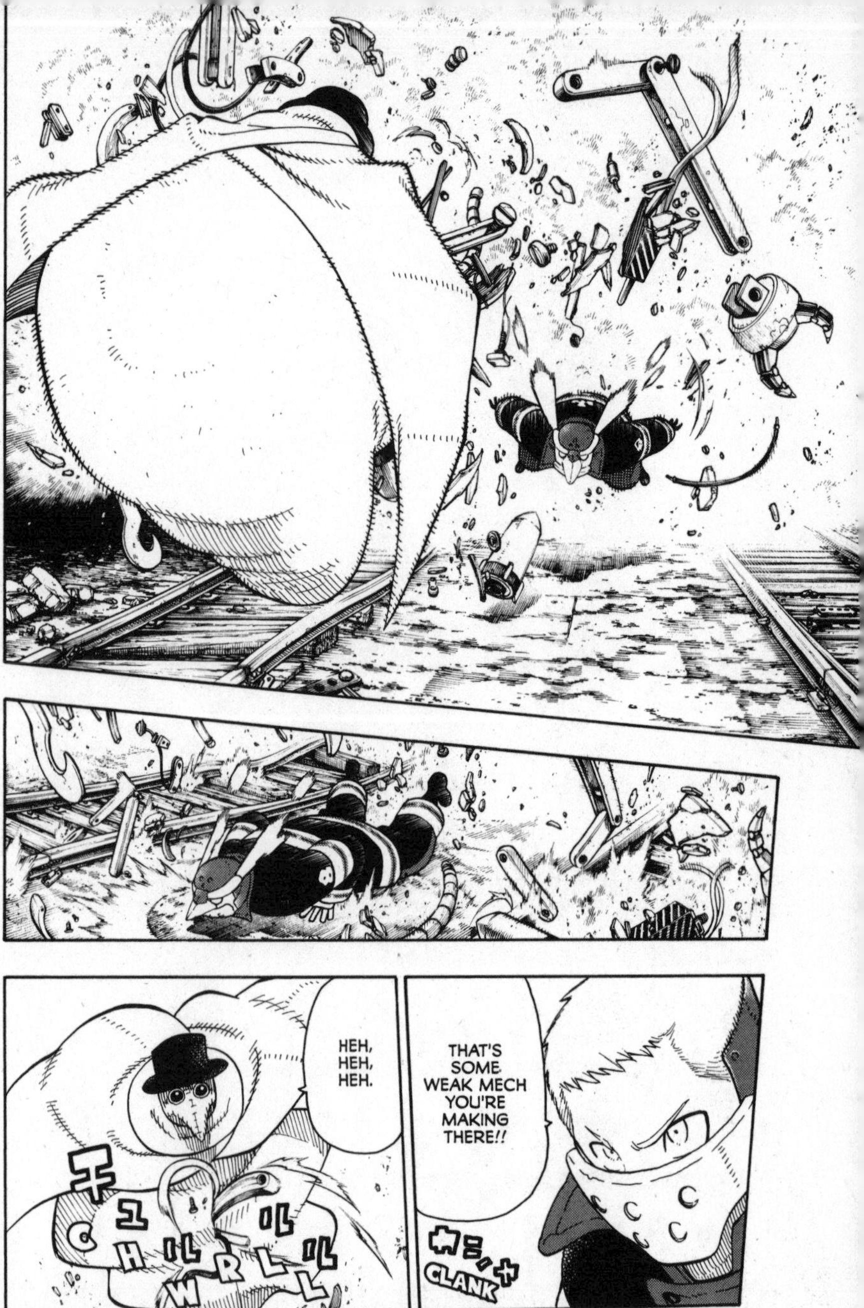
THAT'S SOME WEAK MECH YOU'RE MAKING THERE!!
CLANK
HEH, HEH, HEH.
CHWRLL

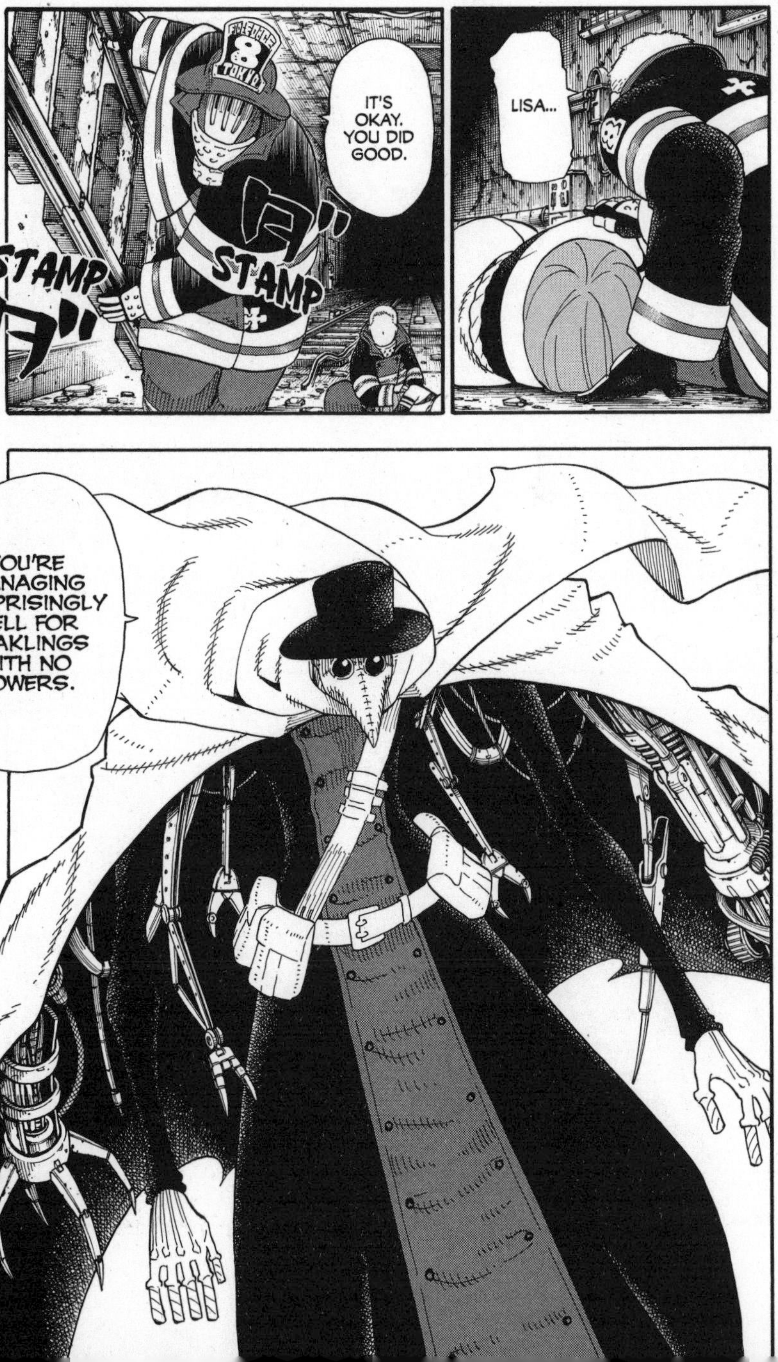
LISA...
IT'S OKAY. YOU DID GOOD.
STAMP
STAMP
YOU'RE MANAGING SURPRISINGLY WELL FOR WEAKLINGS WITH NO POWERS.

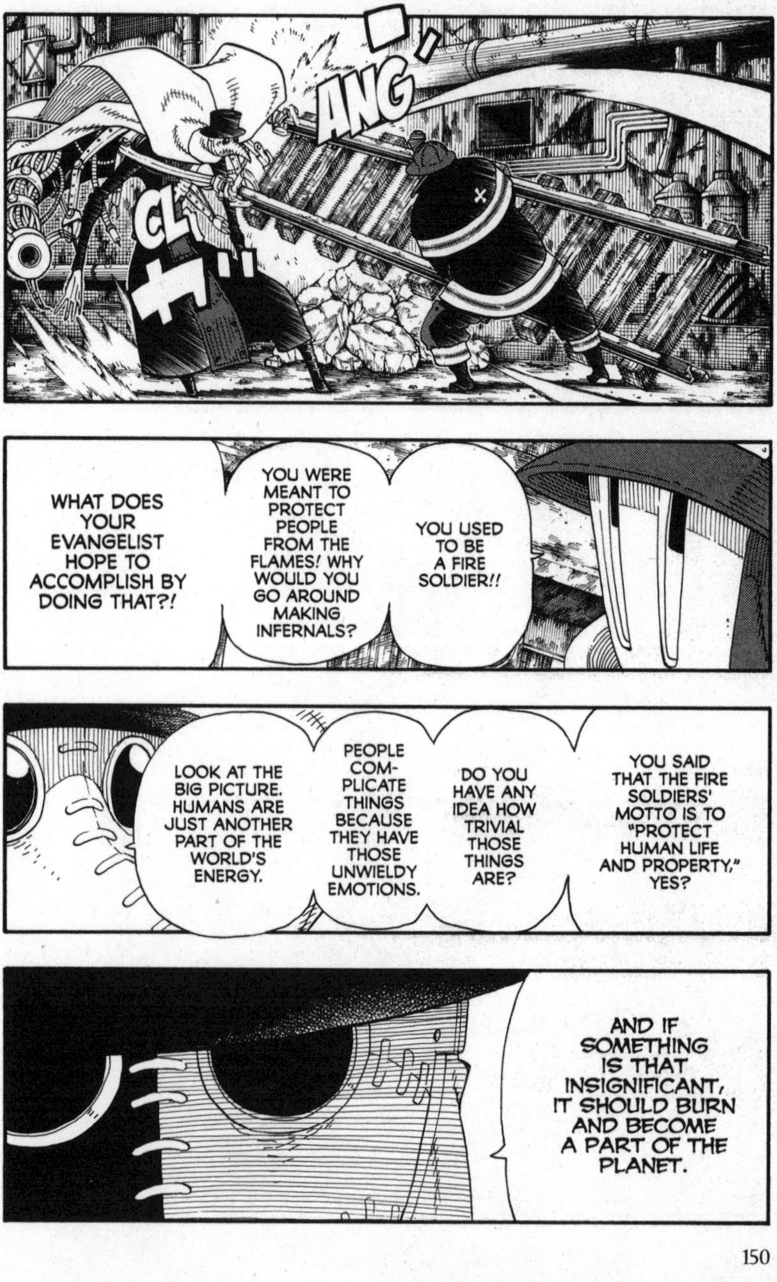
CLANG
YOU USED TO BE A FIRE SOLDIER!!
YOU WERE MEANT TO PROTECT PEOPLE FROM THE FLAMES! WHY WOULD YOU GO AROUND MAKING INFERNALS?
WHAT DOES YOUR EVANGELIST HOPE TO ACCOMPLISH BY DOING THAT?!
YOU SAID THAT THE FIRE SOLDIERS' MOTTO IS TO "PROTECT HUMAN LIFE AND PROPERTY," YES?
DO YOU HAVE ANY IDEA HOW TRIVIAL THOSE THINGS ARE?
PEOPLE COMPLICATE THINGS BECAUSE THEY HAVE THOSE UNWIELDY EMOTIONS.
LOOK AT THE BIG PICTURE. HUMANS ARE JUST ANOTHER PART OF THE WORLD'S ENERGY.
AND IF SOMETHING IS THAT INSIGNIFICANT, IT SHOULD BURN AND BECOME A PART OF THE PLANET.

APPROXI-
MATELY 200
YEARS AGO,
THE GREAT
CATACLYSM
BEFELL THE
EARTH.

IT WAS
CAUSED BY AN
ENORMOUS
ADOLLA BURST
ERUPTION.

WHAM

AND THE
SOURCE OF
THAT ADOLLA
BURST IS A
PLACE IN WHICH
YOU HAVE
ALREADY PUT
YOUR FAITH.

CULTIC
HOOEY
!!

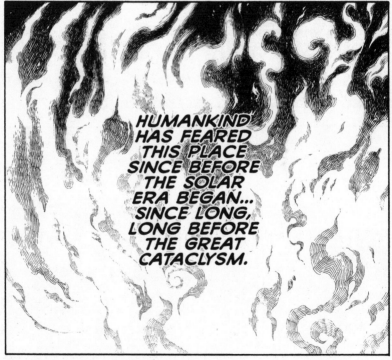

HUMANKIND
HAS FEARED
THIS PLACE
SINCE BEFORE
THE SOLAR
ERA BEGAN...
SINCE LONG,
LONG BEFORE
THE GREAT
CATACLYSM.

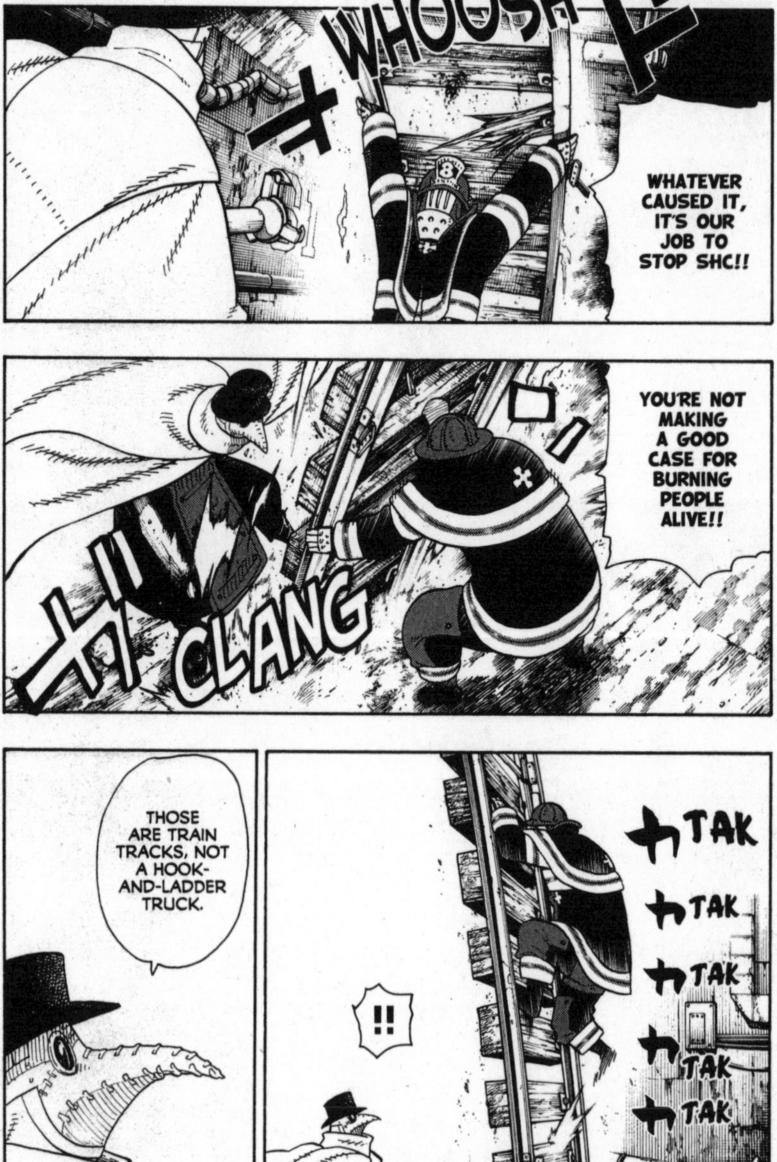
WHOOSH
WHATEVER CAUSED IT, IT'S OUR JOB TO STOP SHC!!
YOU'RE NOT MAKING A GOOD CASE FOR BURNING PEOPLE ALIVE!!
CLANG
TAK
TAK
TAK
TAK
TAK
!!
THOSE ARE TRAIN TRACKS, NOT A HOOK-AND-LADDER TRUCK.

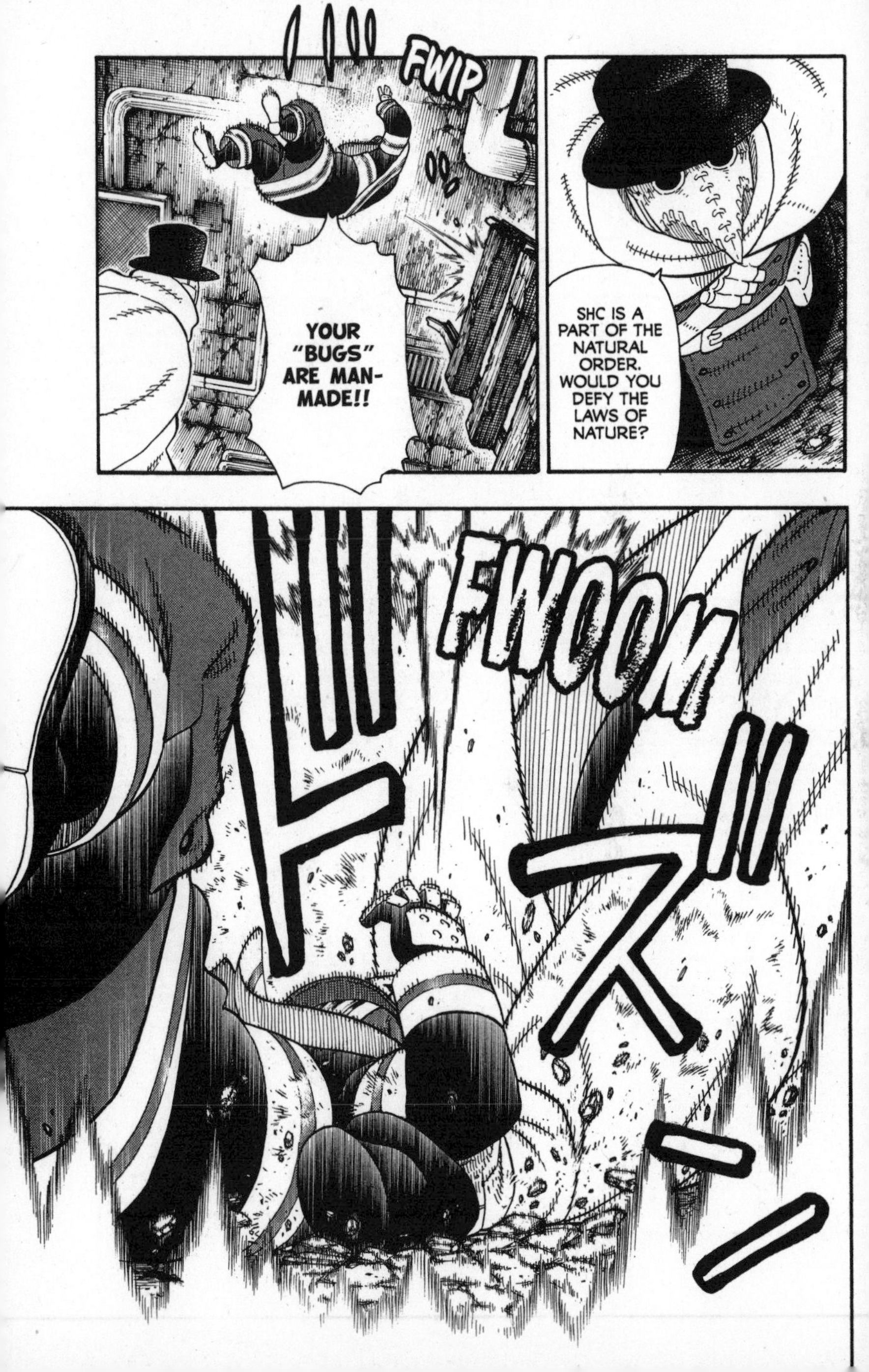
SHC IS A PART OF THE NATURAL ORDER. WOULD YOU DEFY THE LAWS OF NATURE?
FWIP
YOUR "BUGS" ARE MAN-MADE!!
FWOOM

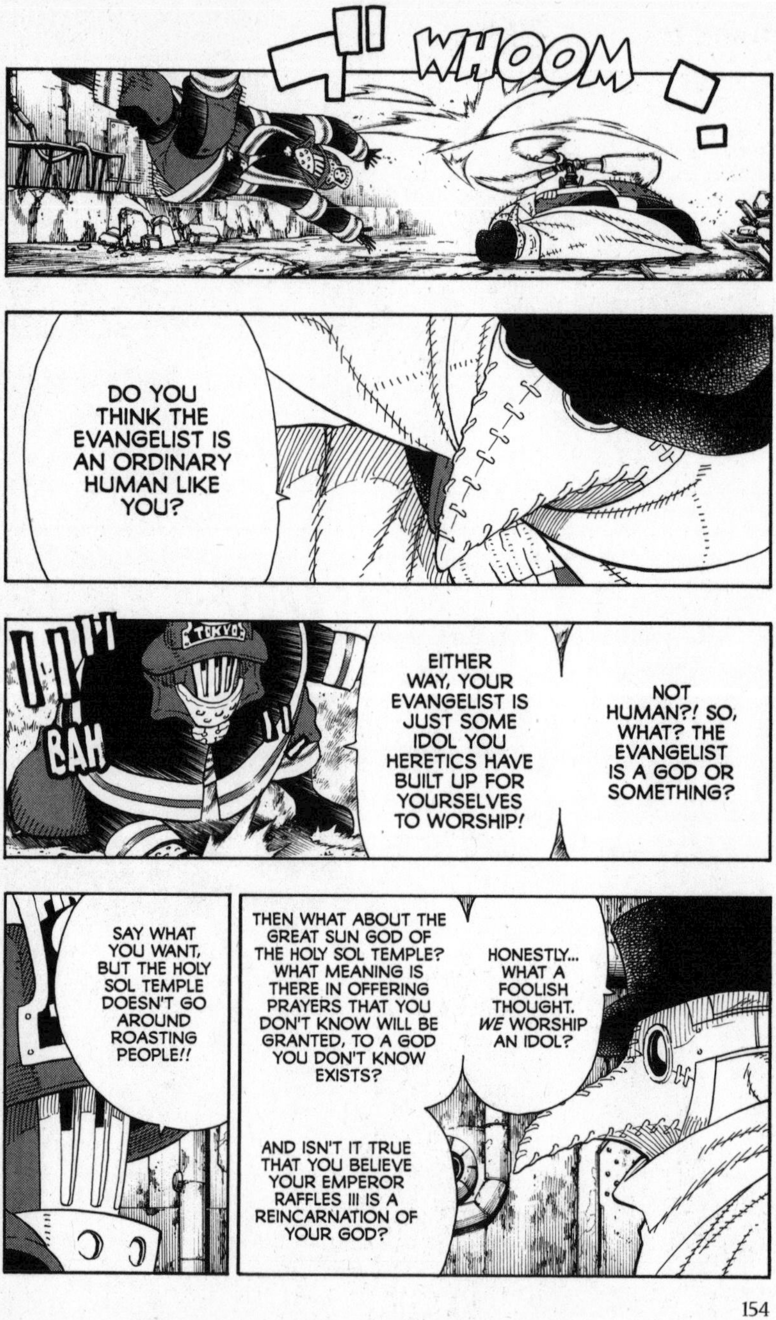
WHOOM
DO YOU THINK THE EVANGELIST IS AN ORDINARY HUMAN LIKE YOU?
NOT HUMAN?! SO, WHAT? THE EVANGELIST IS A GOD OR SOMETHING?
EITHER WAY, YOUR EVANGELIST IS JUST SOME IDOL YOU HERETICS HAVE BUILT UP FOR YOURSELVES TO WORSHIP!
BAH
HONESTLY... WHAT A FOOLISH THOUGHT. *WE* WORSHIP AN IDOL?
THEN WHAT ABOUT THE GREAT SUN GOD OF THE HOLY SOL TEMPLE? WHAT MEANING IS THERE IN OFFERING PRAYERS THAT YOU DON'T KNOW WILL BE GRANTED, TO A GOD YOU DON'T KNOW EXISTS?
AND ISN'T IT TRUE THAT YOU BELIEVE YOUR EMPEROR RAFFLES III IS A REINCARNATION OF YOUR GOD?
SAY WHAT YOU WANT, BUT THE HOLY SOL TEMPLE DOESN'T GO AROUND ROASTING PEOPLE!!

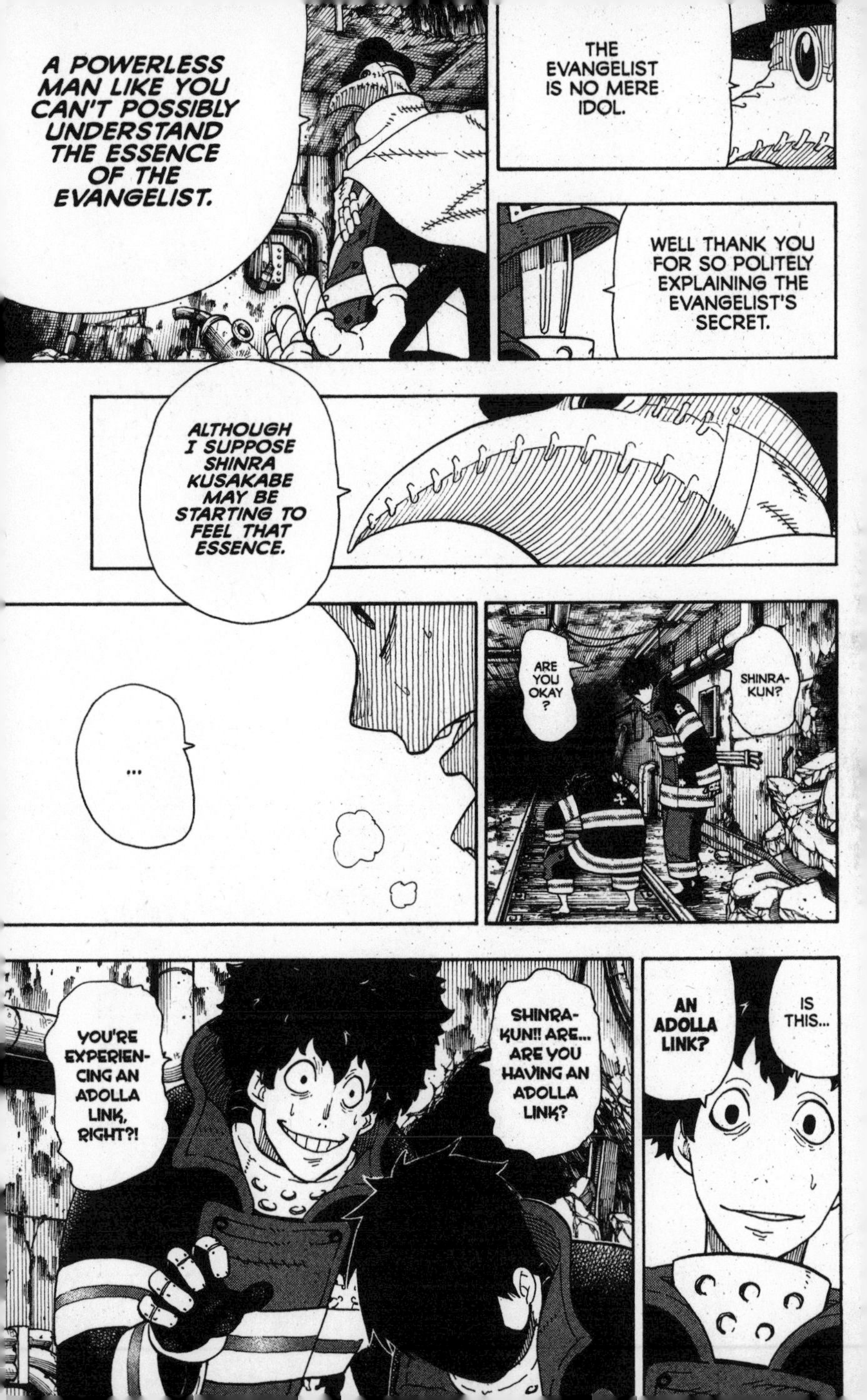
THE EVANGELIST IS NO MERE IDOL.
WELL THANK YOU FOR SO POLITELY EXPLAINING THE EVANGELIST'S SECRET.
A POWERLESS MAN LIKE YOU CAN'T POSSIBLY UNDERSTAND THE ESSENCE OF THE EVANGELIST.
ALTHOUGH I SUPPOSE SHINRA KUSAKABE MAY BE STARTING TO FEEL THAT ESSENCE.
SHINRA-KUN?
ARE YOU OKAY?
...
IS THIS...
AN ADOLLA LINK?
SHINRA-KUN!! ARE... ARE YOU HAVING AN ADOLLA LINK?
YOU'RE EXPERIENCING AN ADOLLA LINK, RIGHT?!

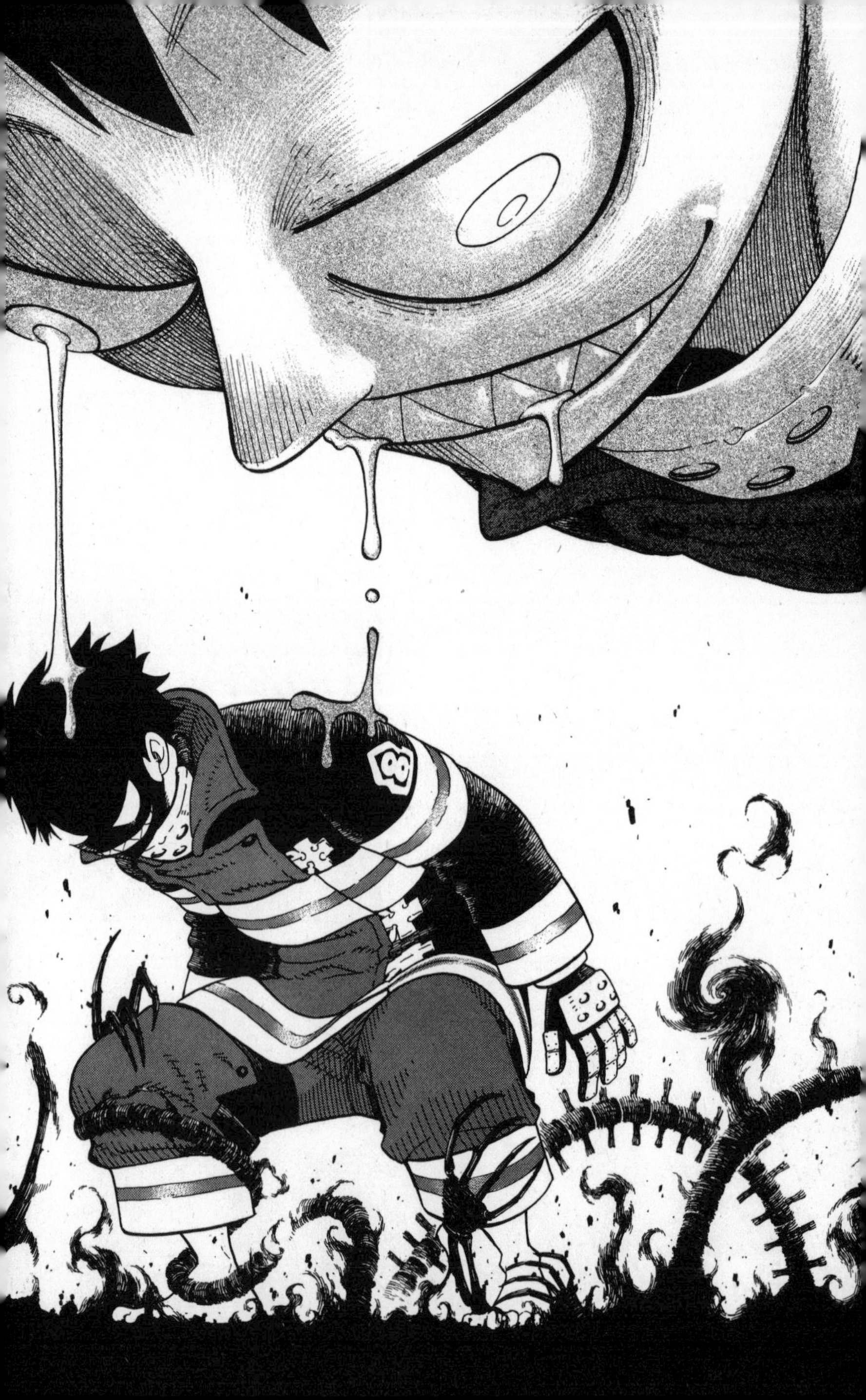

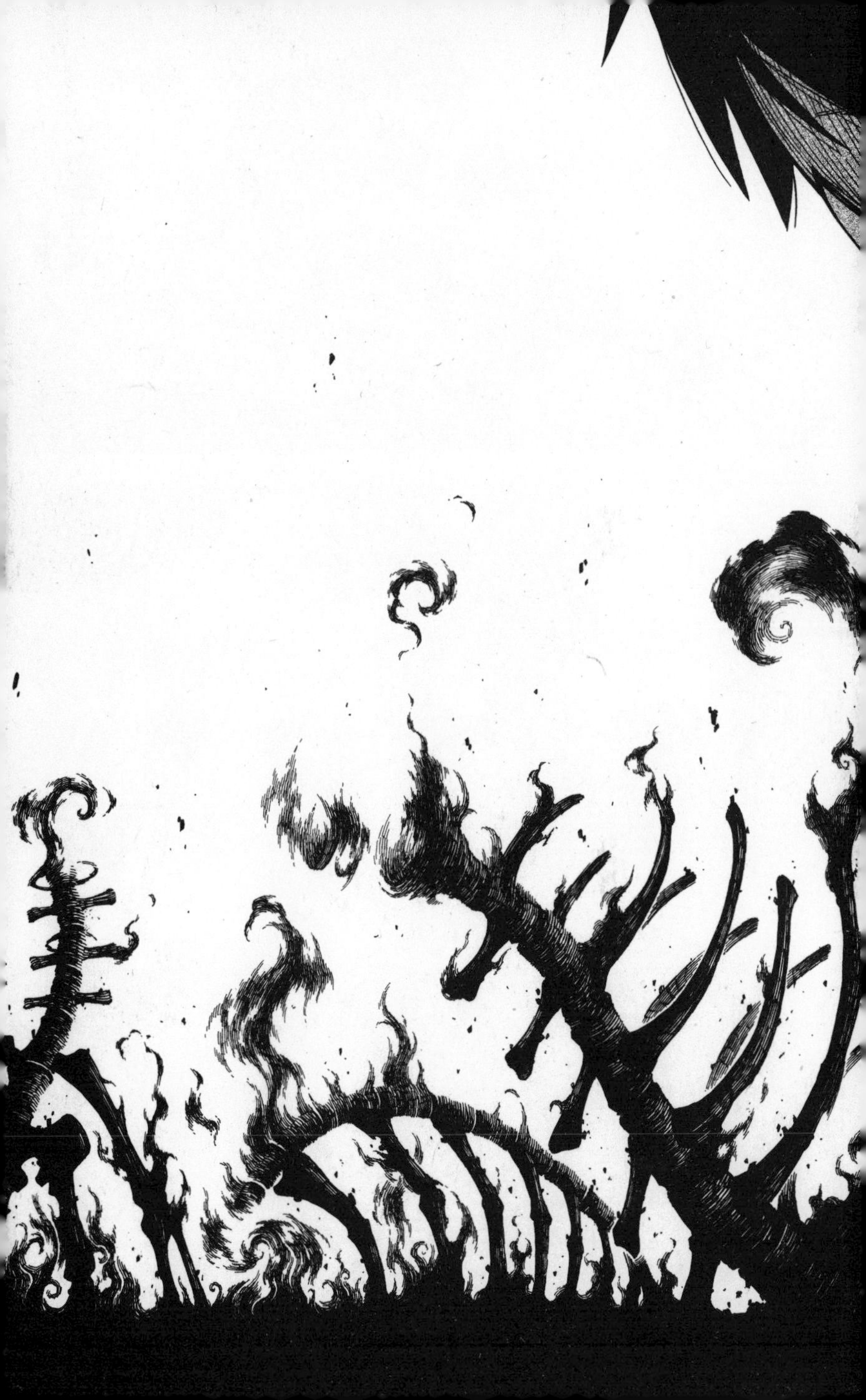

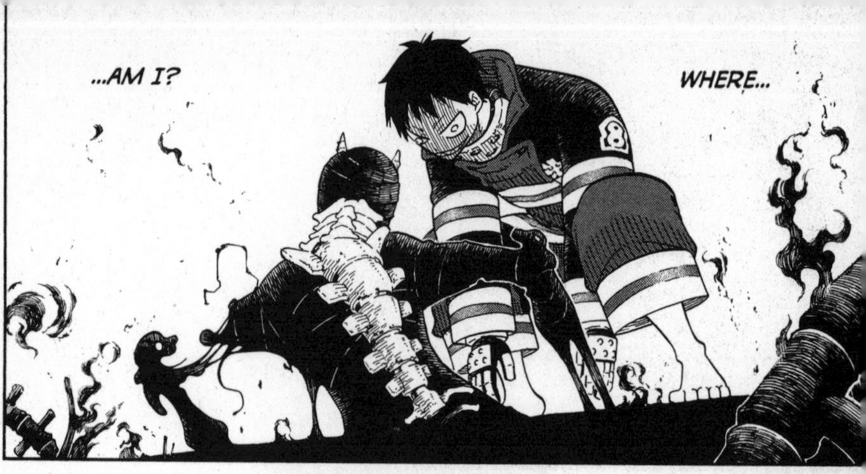
WHERE...
...AM I?
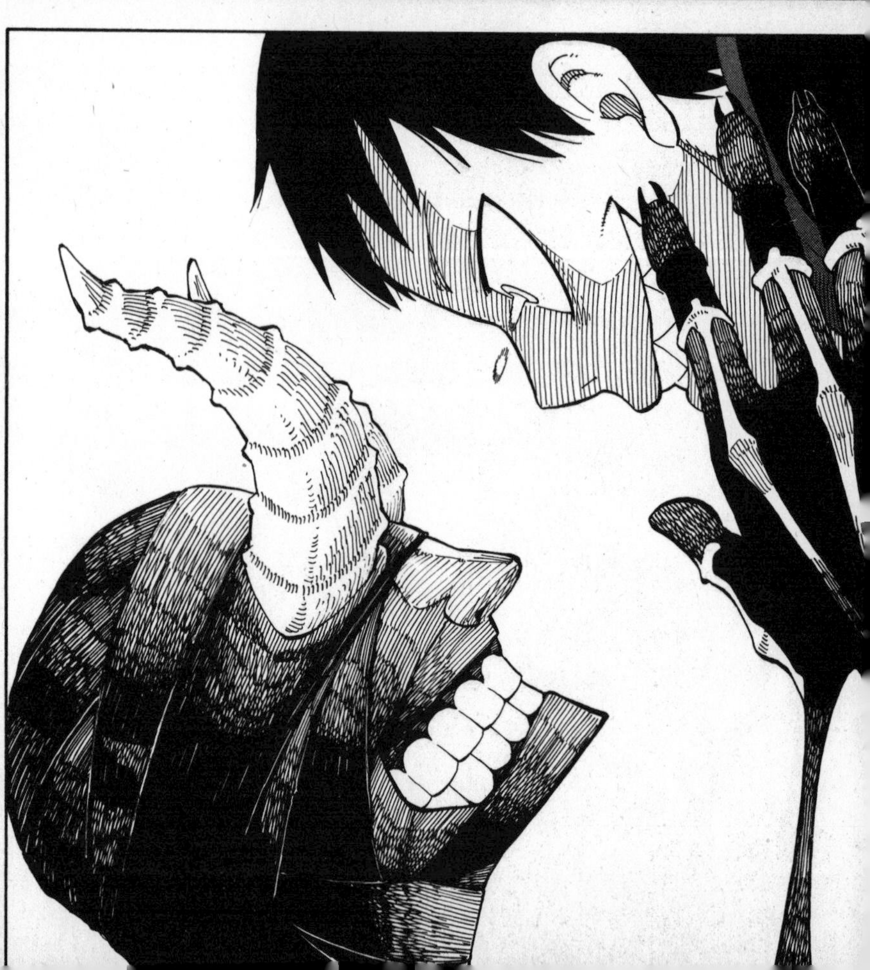

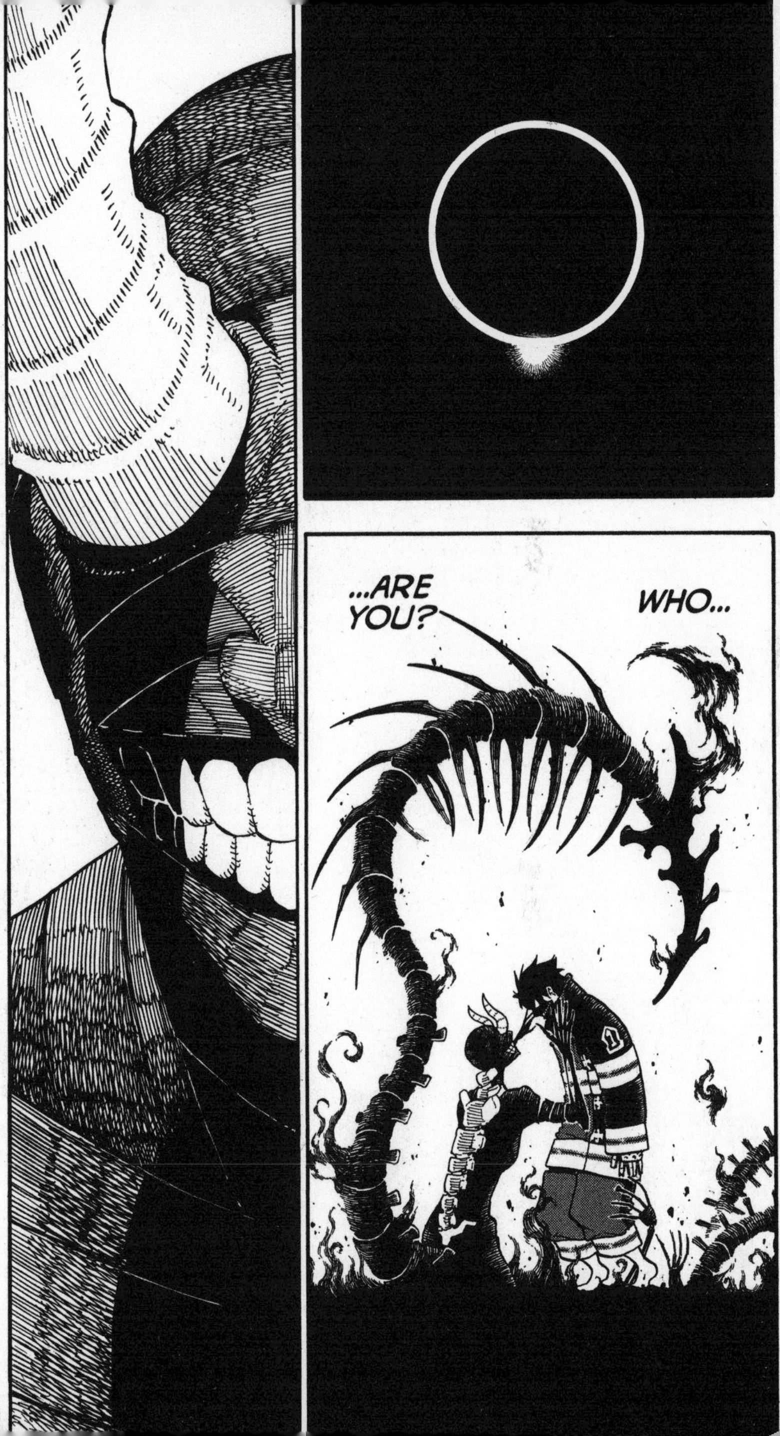
WHO...
...ARE YOU?

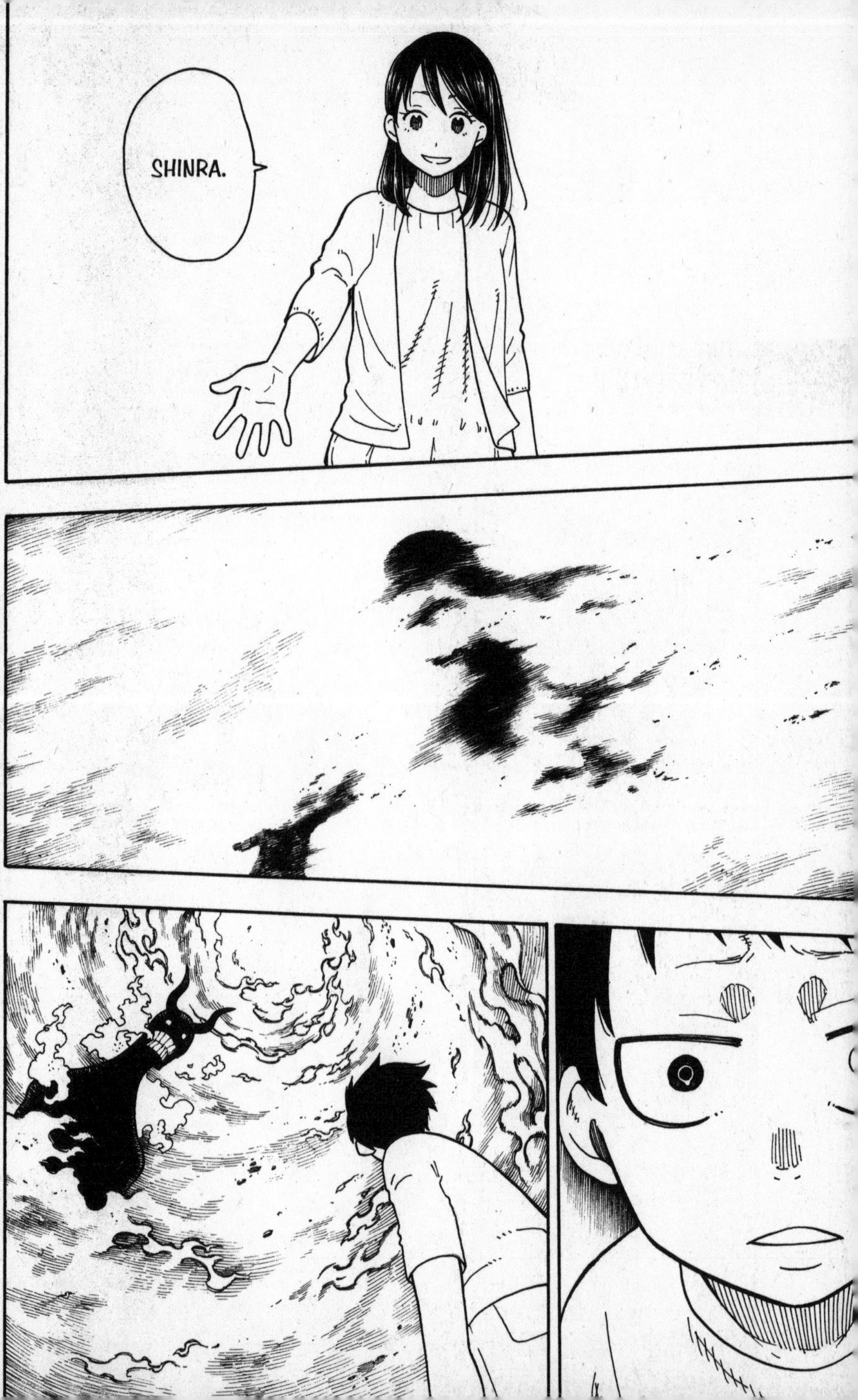
SHINRA.

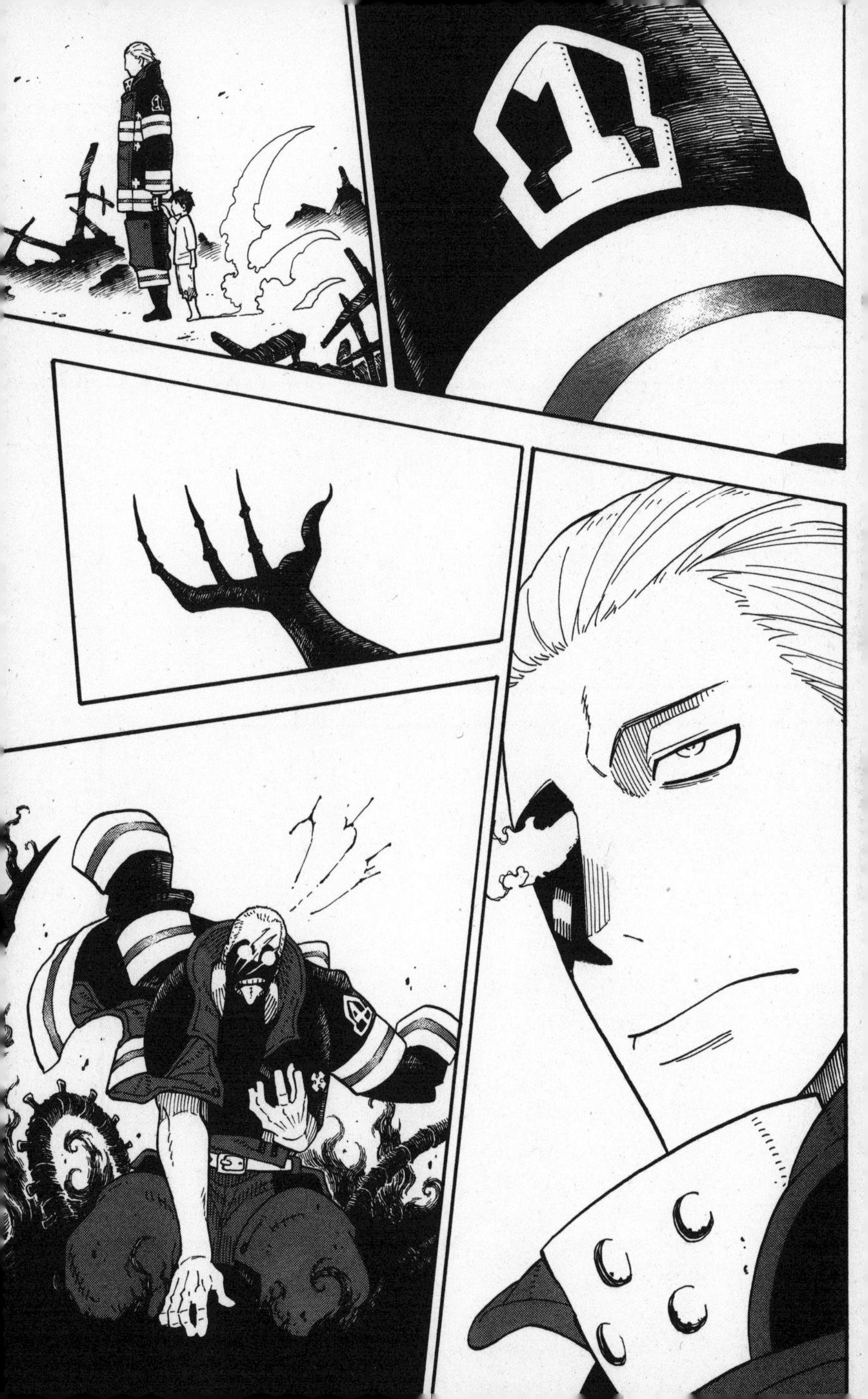

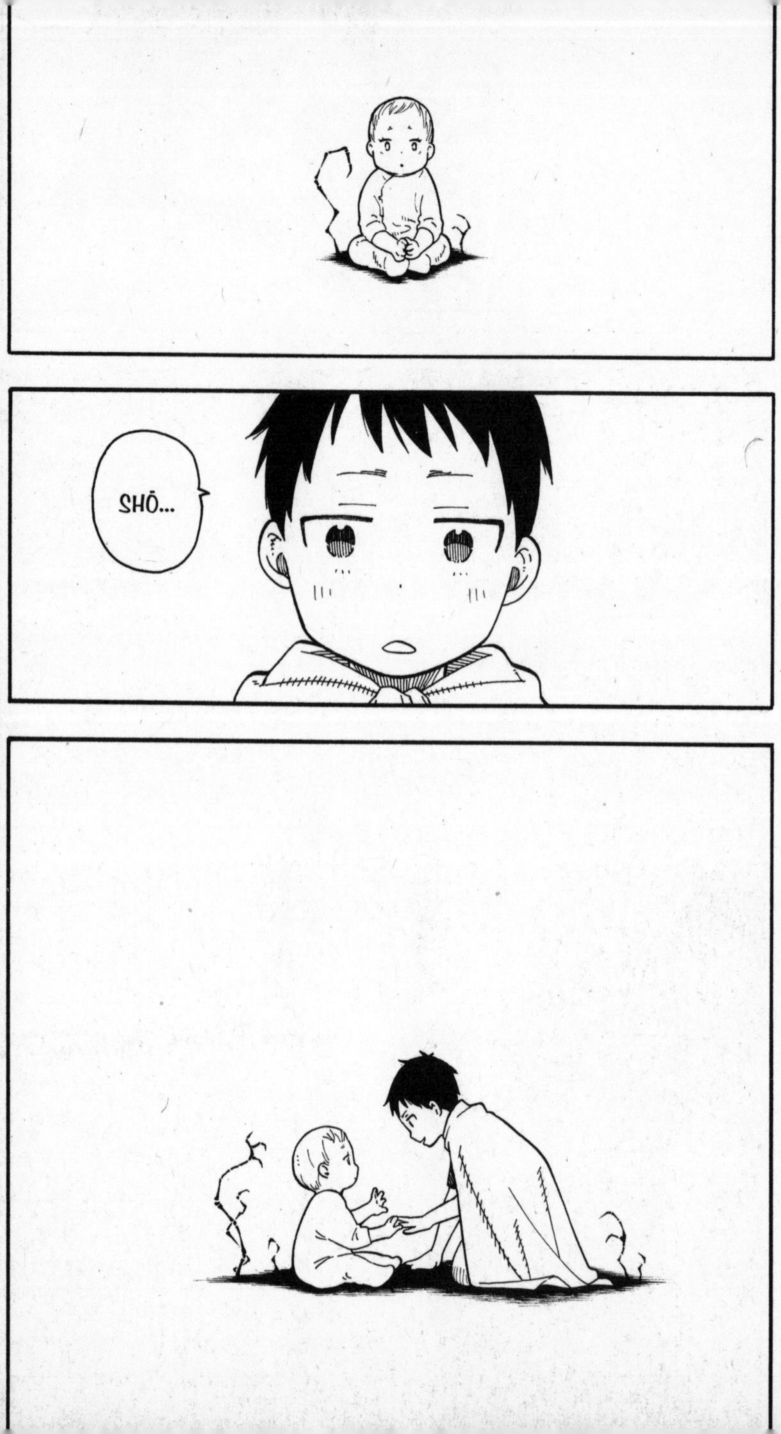
SHŌ...

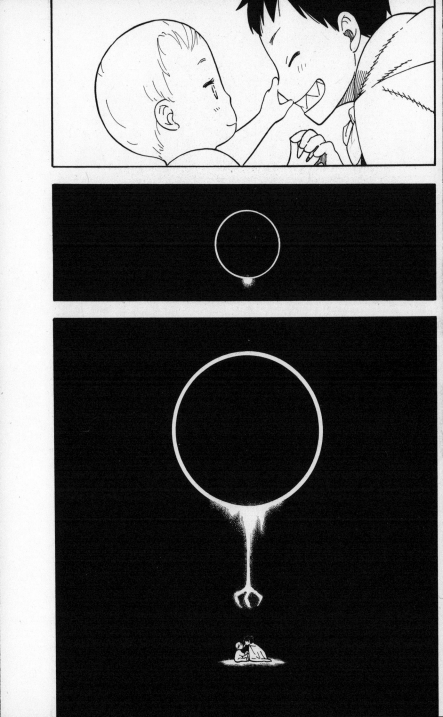

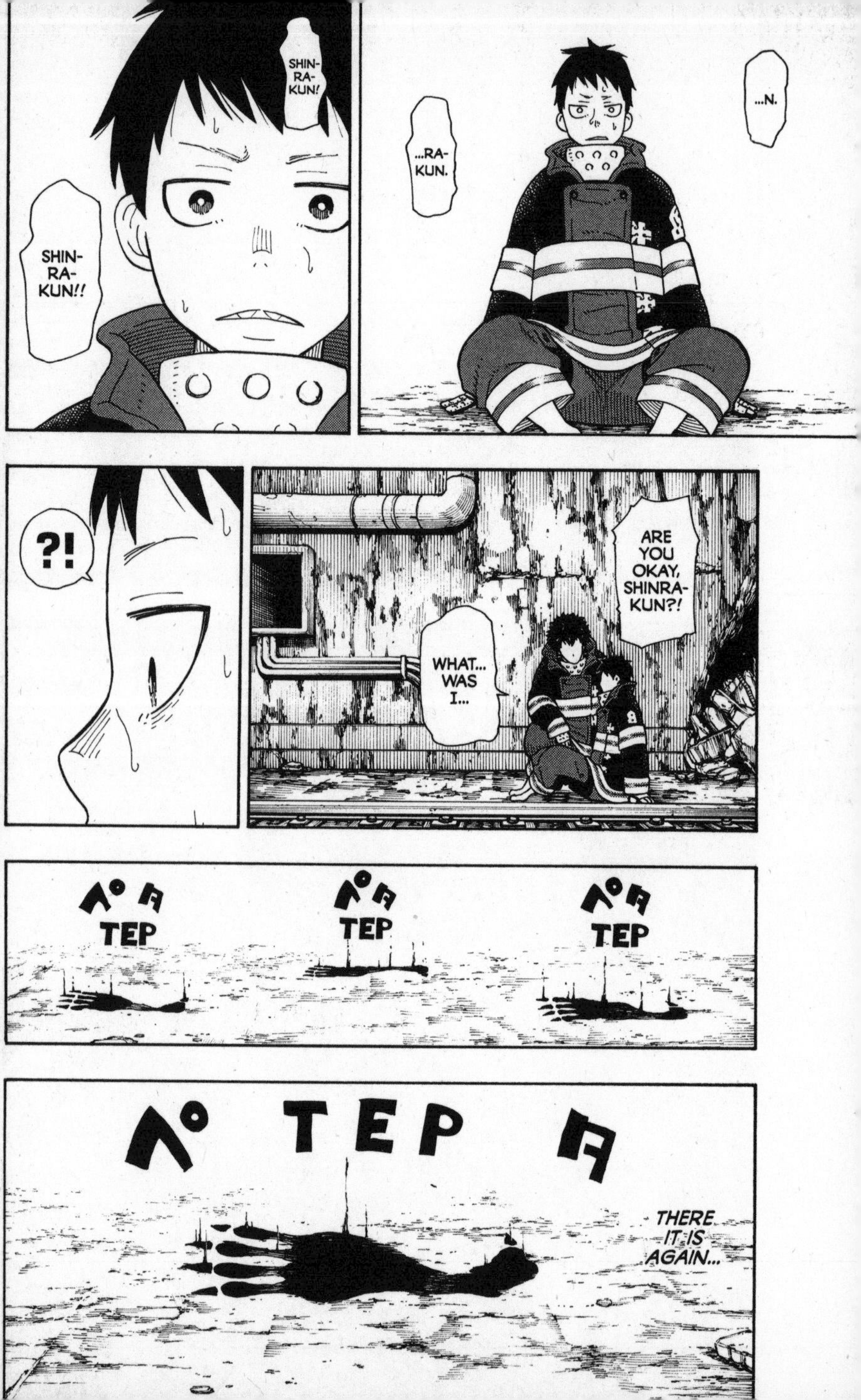
...N.
...RA-KUN.
SHIN-RA-KUN!
SHIN-RA-KUN!!
ARE YOU OKAY, SHINRA-KUN?!
WHAT... WAS I...
?!
ペタ TEP
ペタ TEP
ペタ TEP
ペ TEP タ
THERE IT IS AGAIN...

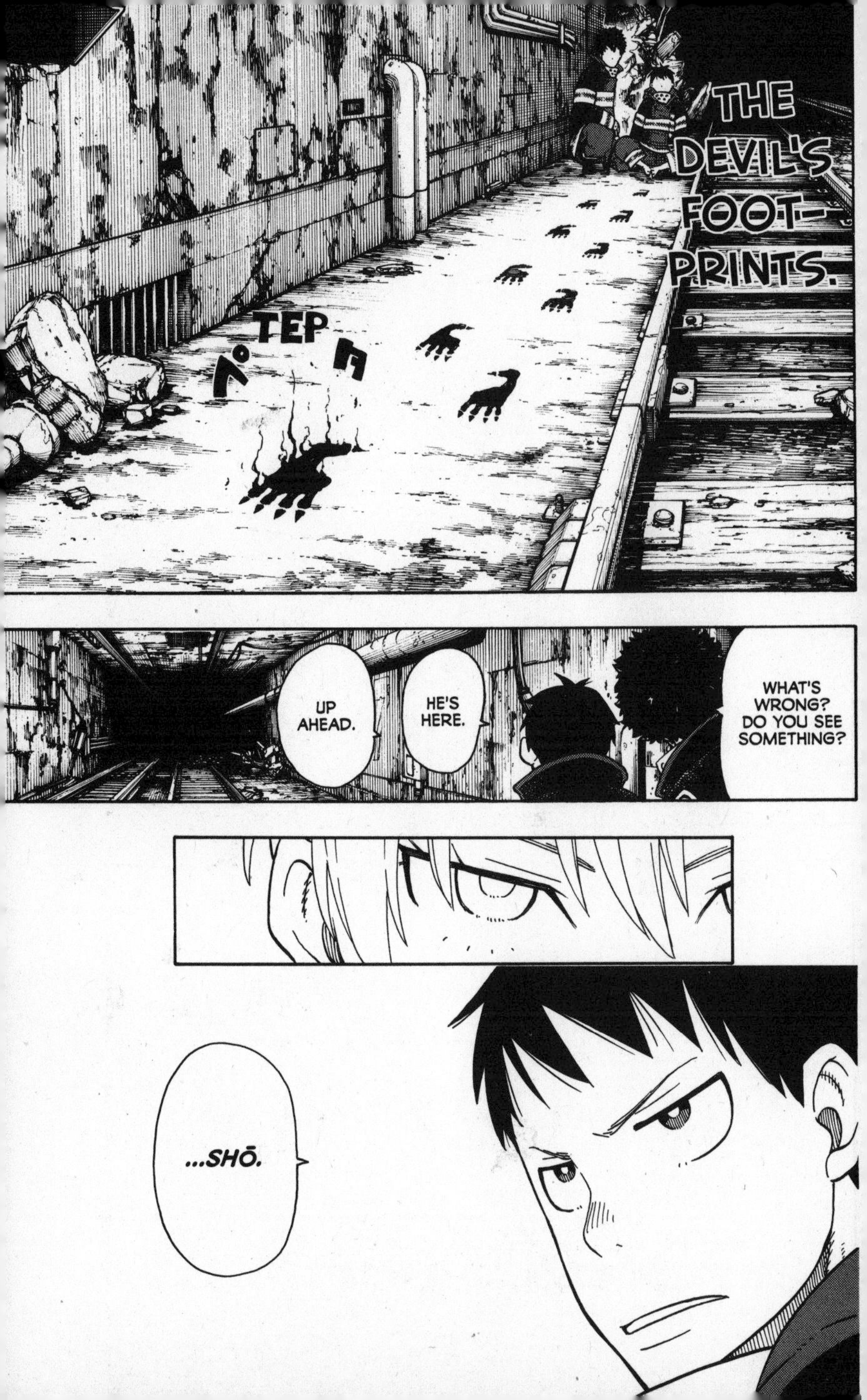
THE DEVIL'S FOOT-PRINTS.
TEP
WHAT'S WRONG? DO YOU SEE SOMETHING?
HE'S HERE.
UP AHEAD.
...SHŌ.

CHAPTER LXXVIII: BROTHER TO BROTHER

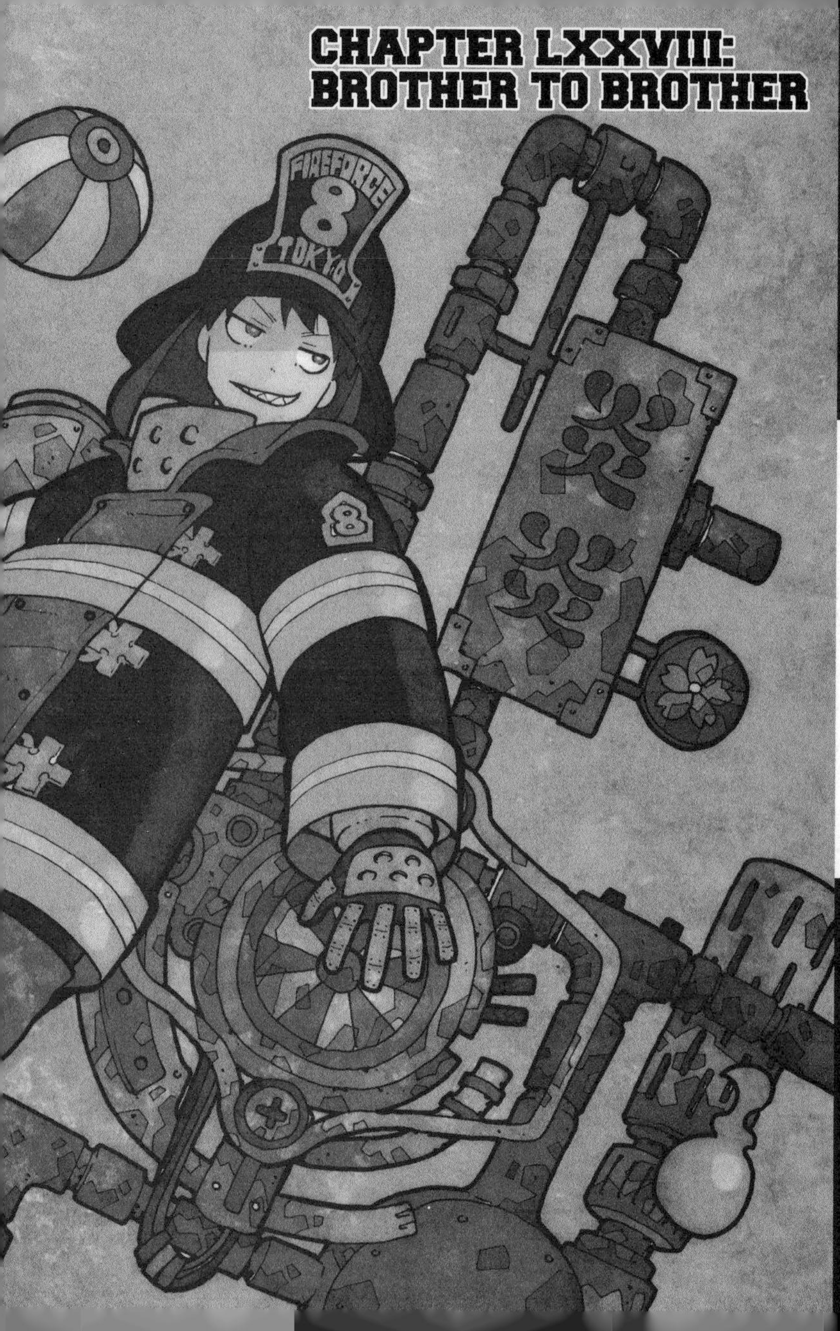
FIREFORCE
8
TOKYO
炎炎

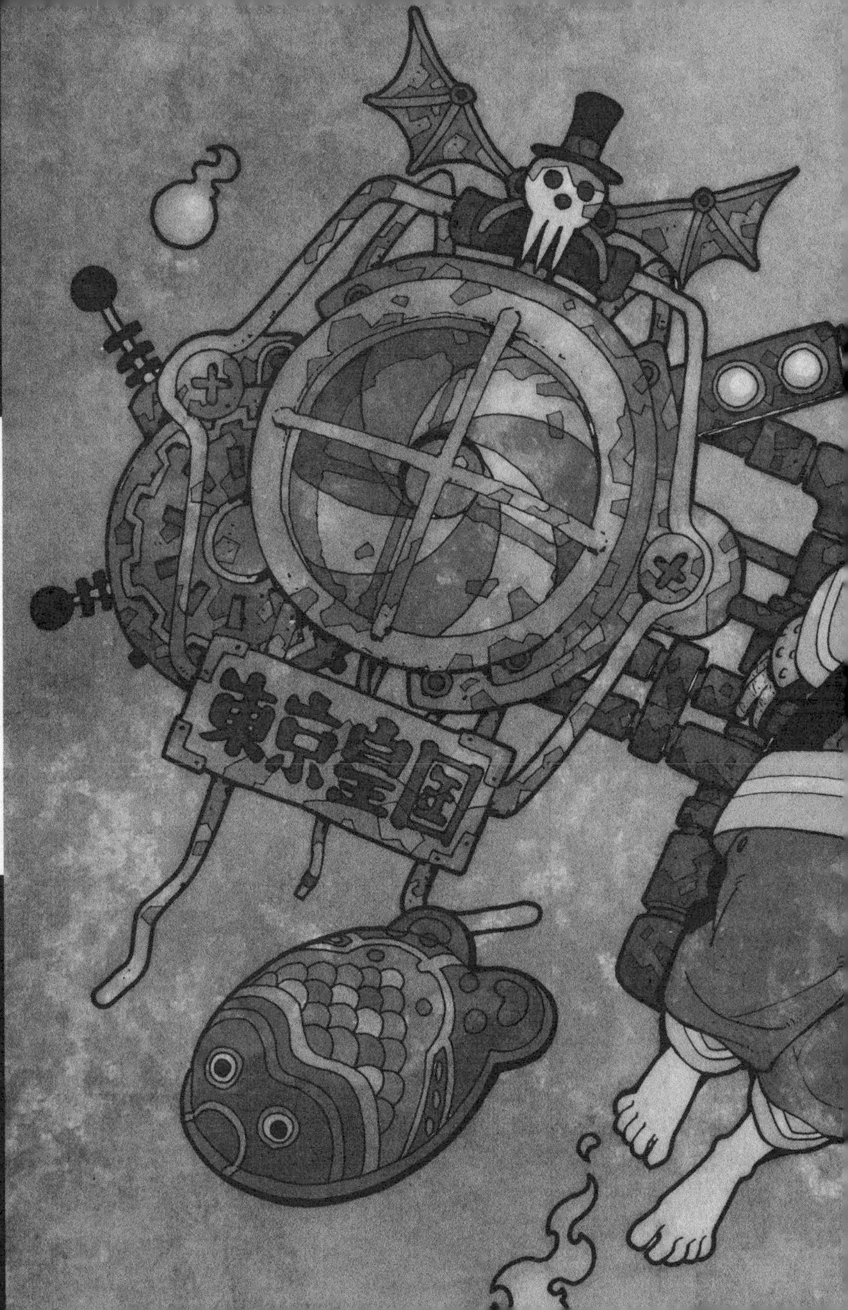
東京皇国

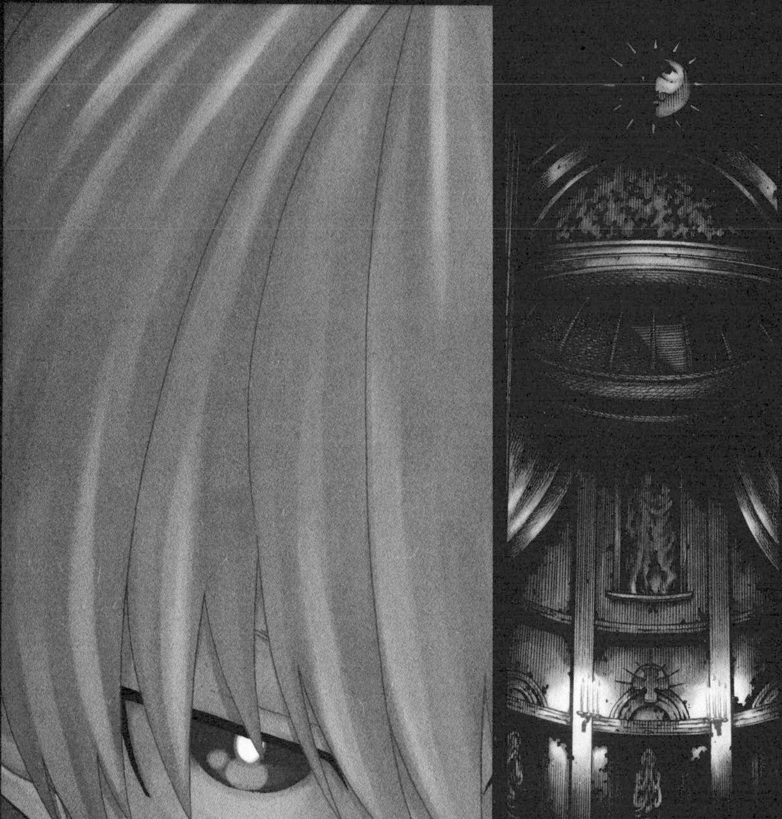

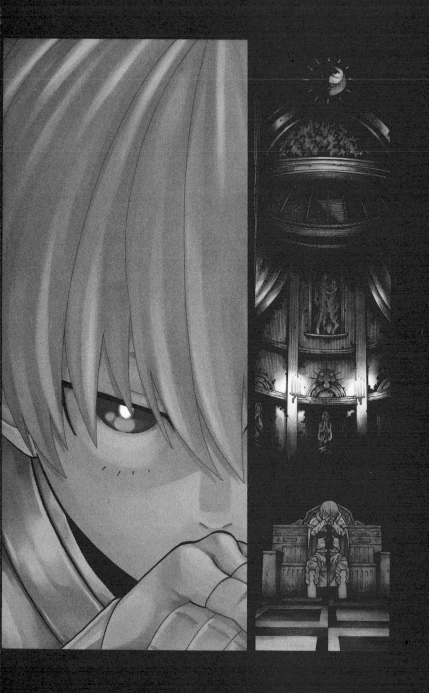

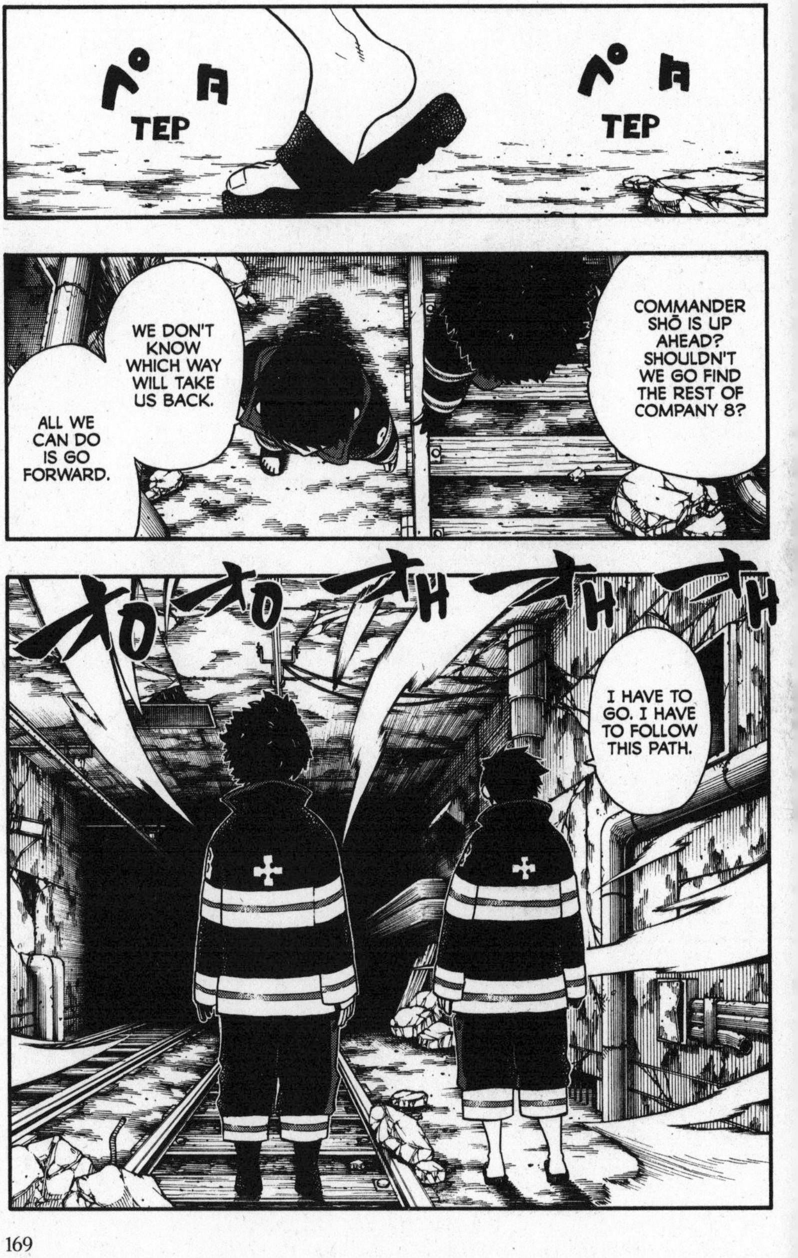
ペタ
TEP
ペタ
TEP
COMMANDER SHŌ IS UP AHEAD? SHOULDN'T WE GO FIND THE REST OF COMPANY 8?
WE DON'T KNOW WHICH WAY WILL TAKE US BACK.
ALL WE CAN DO IS GO FORWARD.
OOHHH
I HAVE TO GO. I HAVE TO FOLLOW THIS PATH.

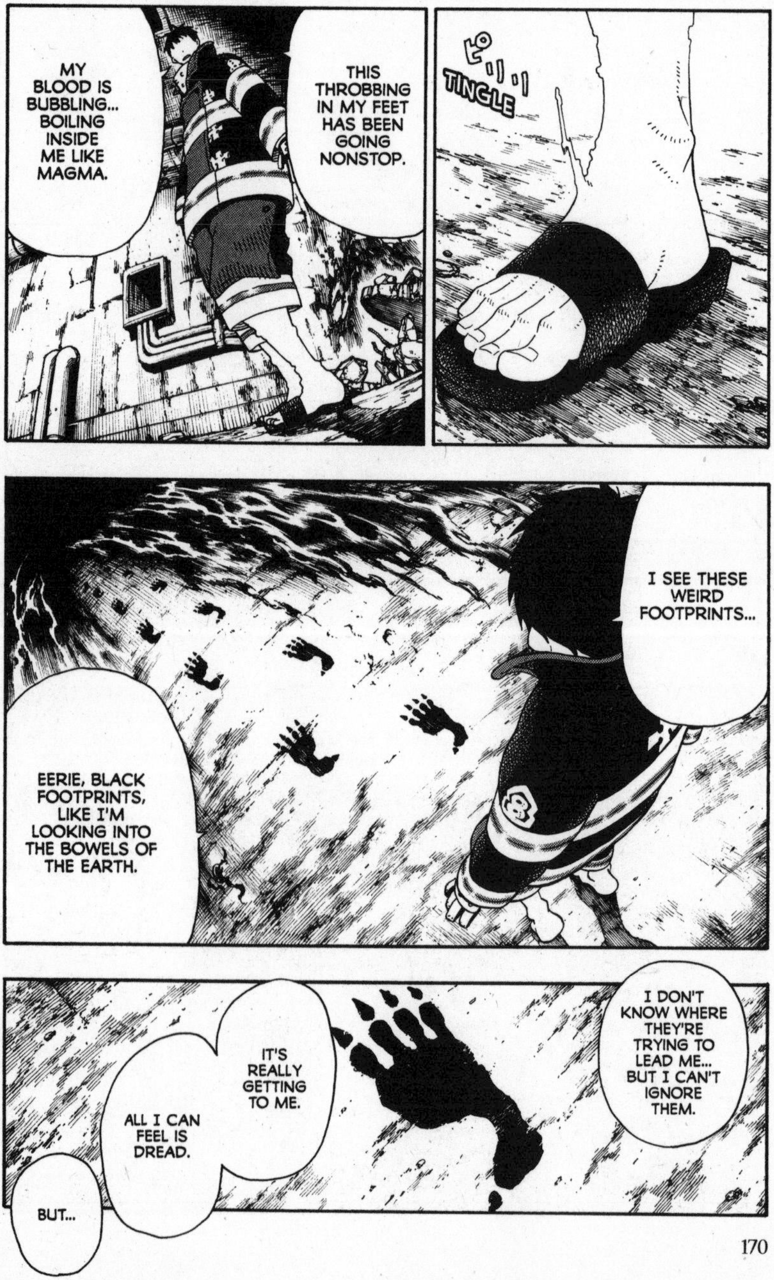
TINGLE
THIS THROBBING IN MY FEET HAS BEEN GOING NONSTOP.
MY BLOOD IS BUBBLING... BOILING INSIDE ME LIKE MAGMA.
I SEE THESE WEIRD FOOTPRINTS...
EERIE, BLACK FOOTPRINTS, LIKE I'M LOOKING INTO THE BOWELS OF THE EARTH.
I DON'T KNOW WHERE THEY'RE TRYING TO LEAD ME... BUT I CAN'T IGNORE THEM.
IT'S REALLY GETTING TO ME.
ALL I CAN FEEL IS DREAD.
BUT...

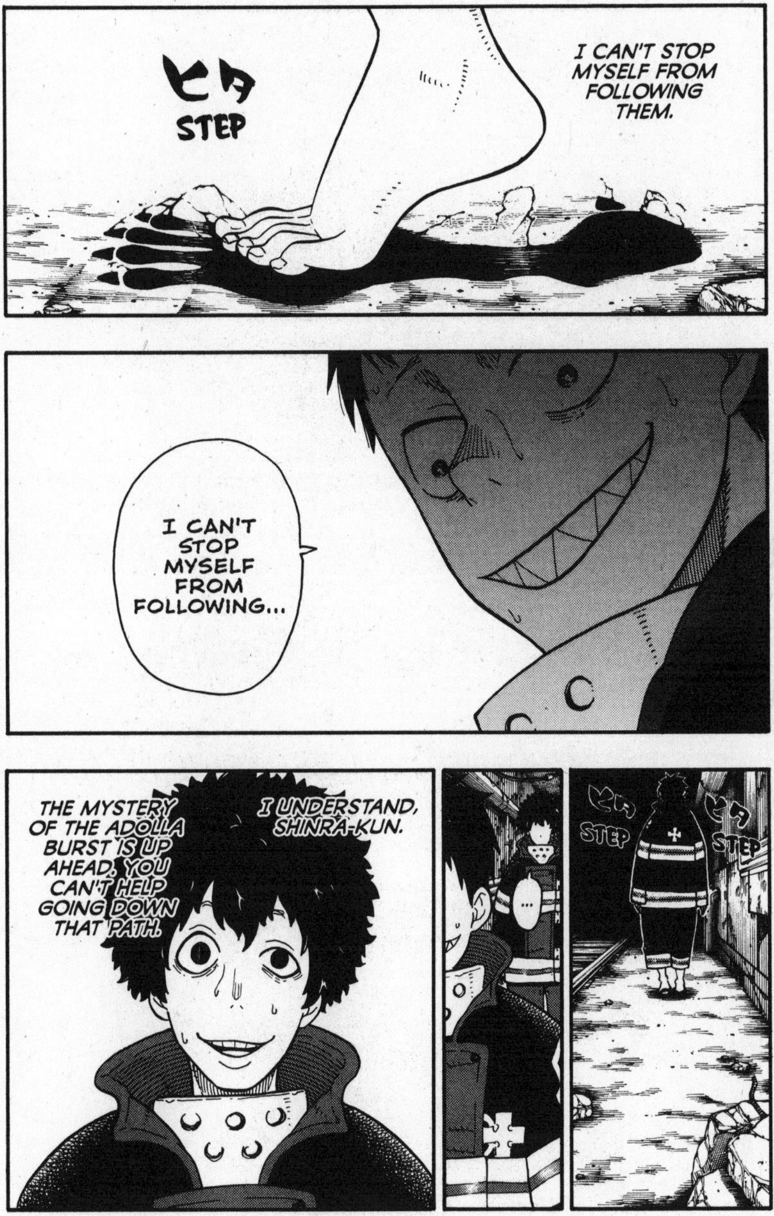
ヒタ
STEP
I CAN'T STOP MYSELF FROM FOLLOWING THEM.
I CAN'T STOP MYSELF FROM FOLLOWING...
ヒタ
STEP
ヒタ
STEP
...
I UNDERSTAND, SHINRA-KUN.
THE MYSTERY OF THE ADOLLA BURST IS UP AHEAD. YOU CAN'T HELP GOING DOWN THAT PATH.

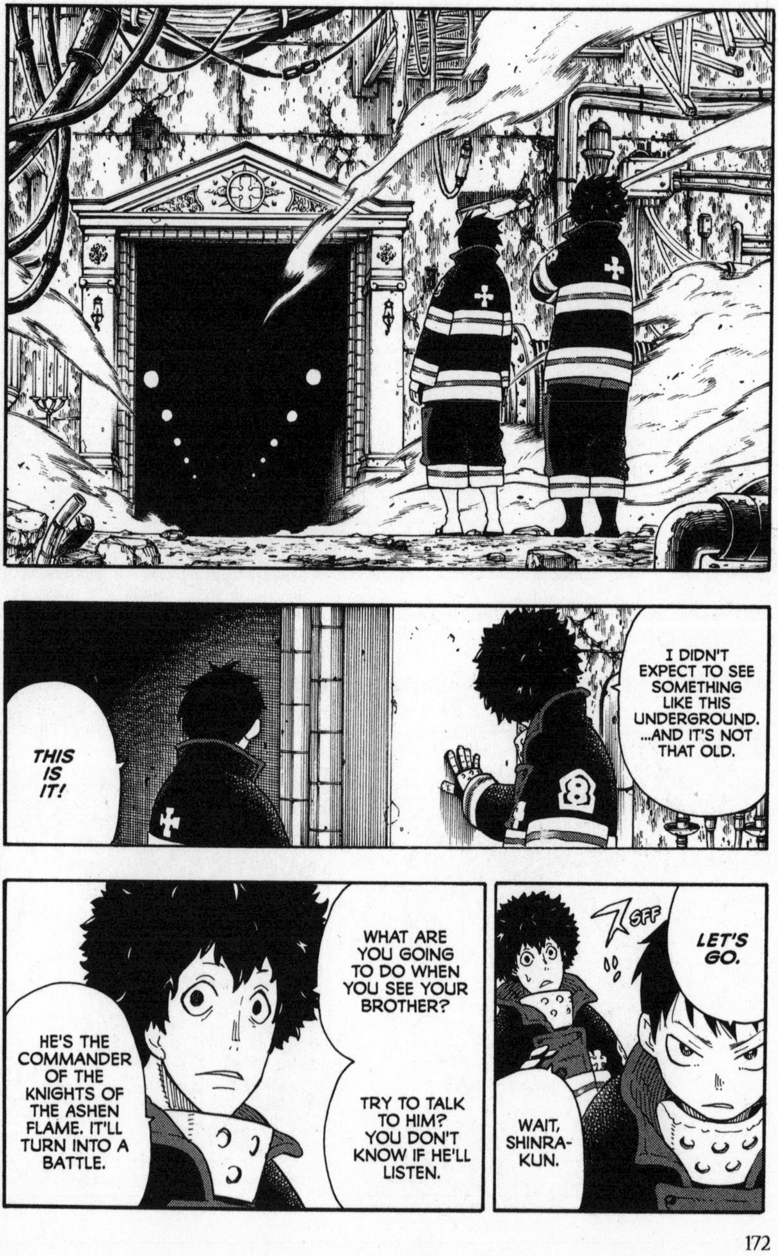
I DIDN'T EXPECT TO SEE SOMETHING LIKE THIS UNDERGROUND. ...AND IT'S NOT THAT OLD.
THIS IS IT!
LET'S GO.
SFF
WAIT, SHINRA-KUN.
WHAT ARE YOU GOING TO DO WHEN YOU SEE YOUR BROTHER?
TRY TO TALK TO HIM? YOU DON'T KNOW IF HE'LL LISTEN.
HE'S THE COMMANDER OF THE KNIGHTS OF THE ASHEN FLAME. IT'LL TURN INTO A BATTLE.

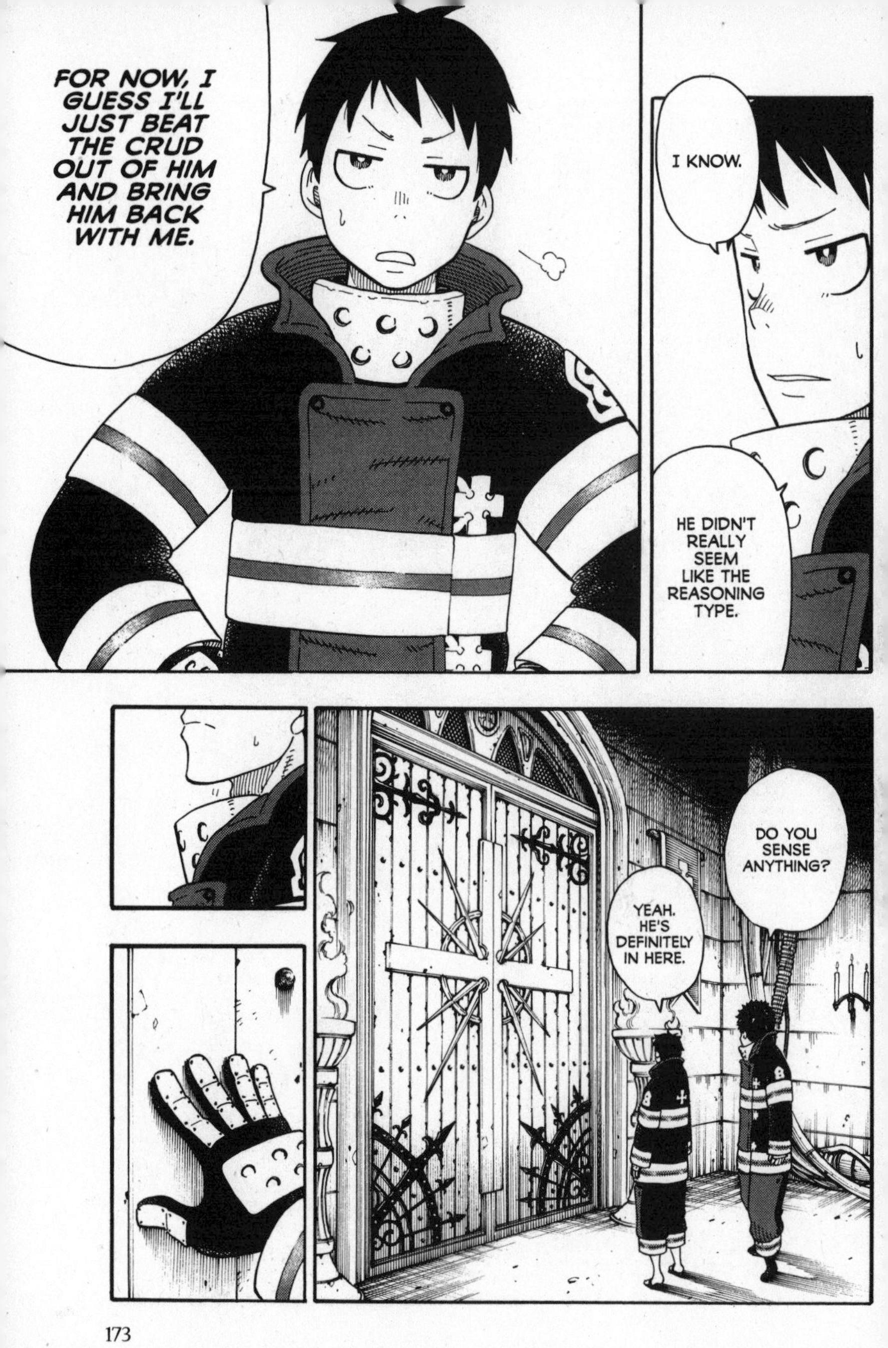
I KNOW.
HE DIDN'T REALLY SEEM LIKE THE REASONING TYPE.
FOR NOW, I GUESS I'LL JUST BEAT THE CRUD OUT OF HIM AND BRING HIM BACK WITH ME.
DO YOU SENSE ANYTHING?
YEAH. HE'S DEFINITELY IN HERE.

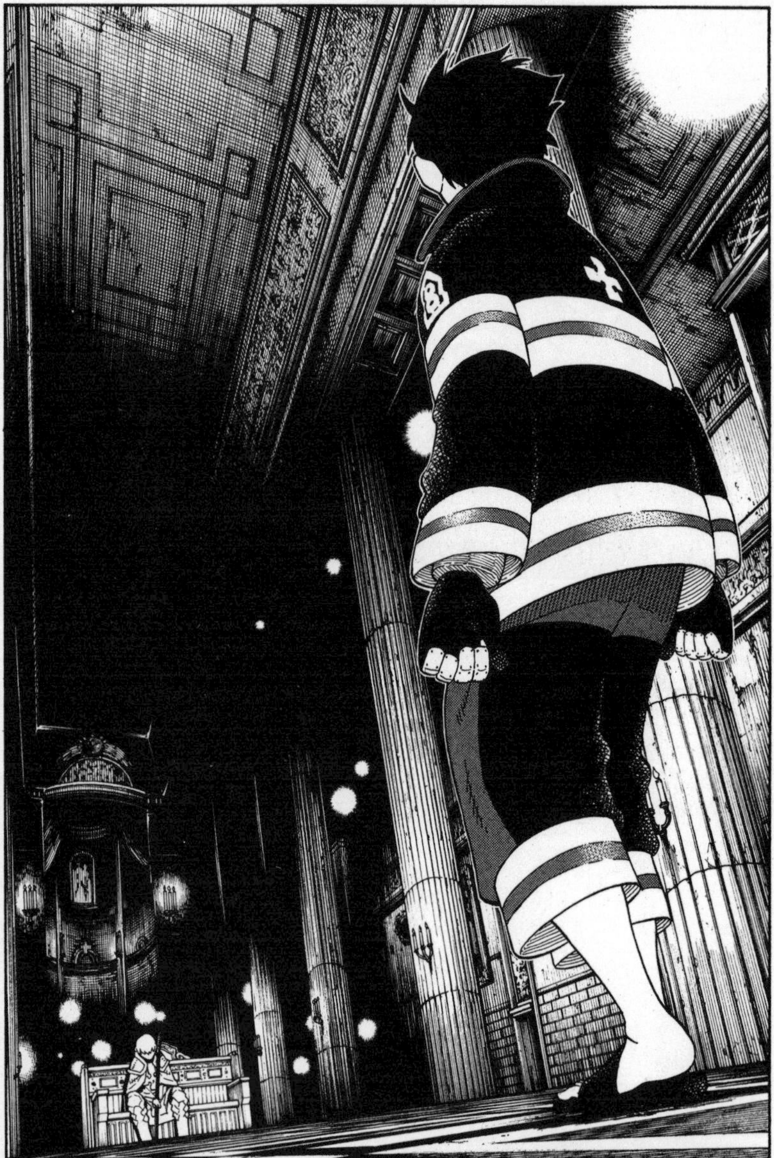

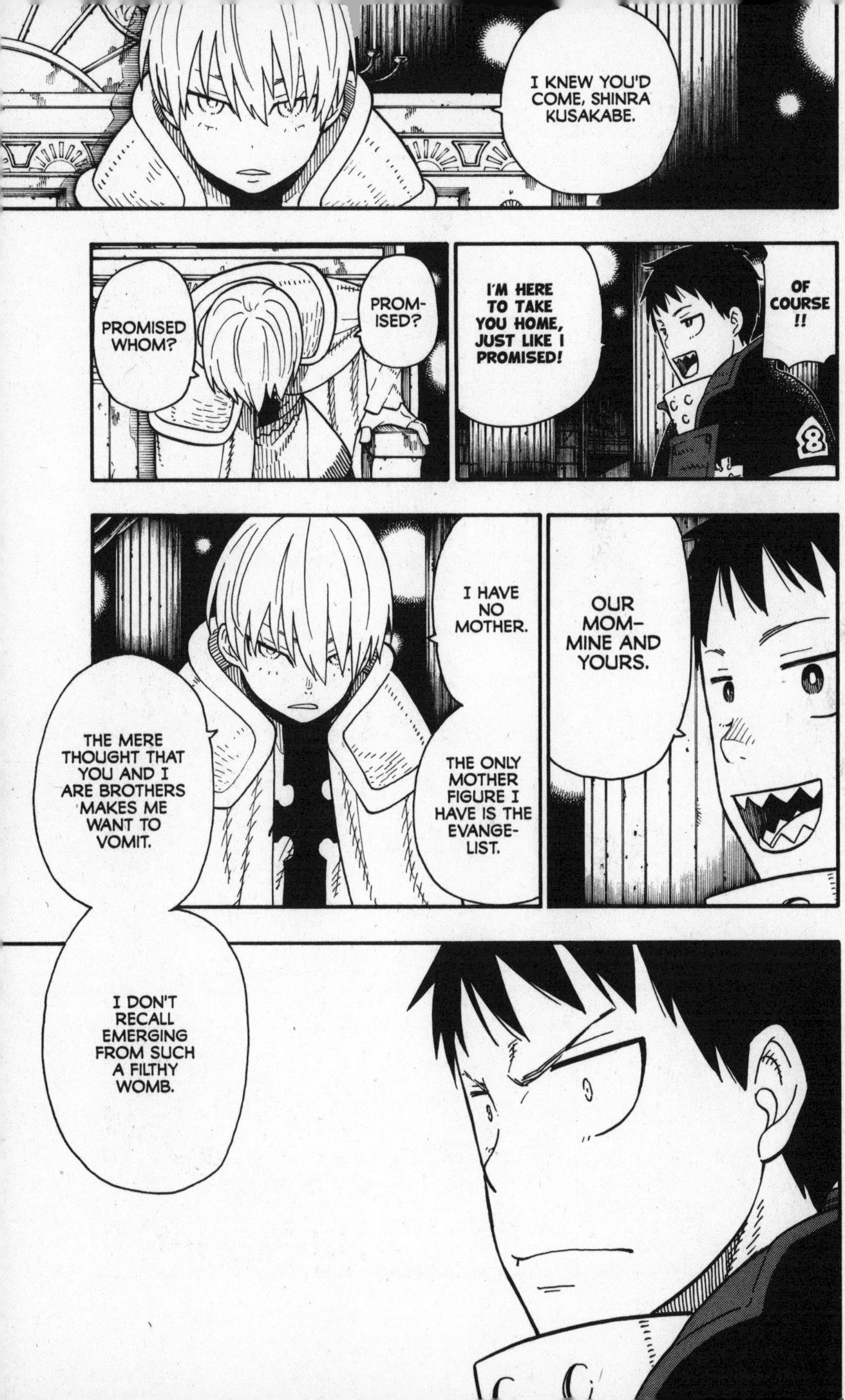
I KNEW YOU'D COME, SHINRA KUSAKABE.
OF COURSE !!
I'M HERE TO TAKE YOU HOME, JUST LIKE I PROMISED!
PROM-ISED?
PROMISED WHOM?
OUR MOM-MINE AND YOURS.
I HAVE NO MOTHER.
THE ONLY MOTHER FIGURE I HAVE IS THE EVANGE-LIST.
THE MERE THOUGHT THAT YOU AND I ARE BROTHERS MAKES ME WANT TO VOMIT.
I DON'T RECALL EMERGING FROM SUCH A FILTHY WOMB.

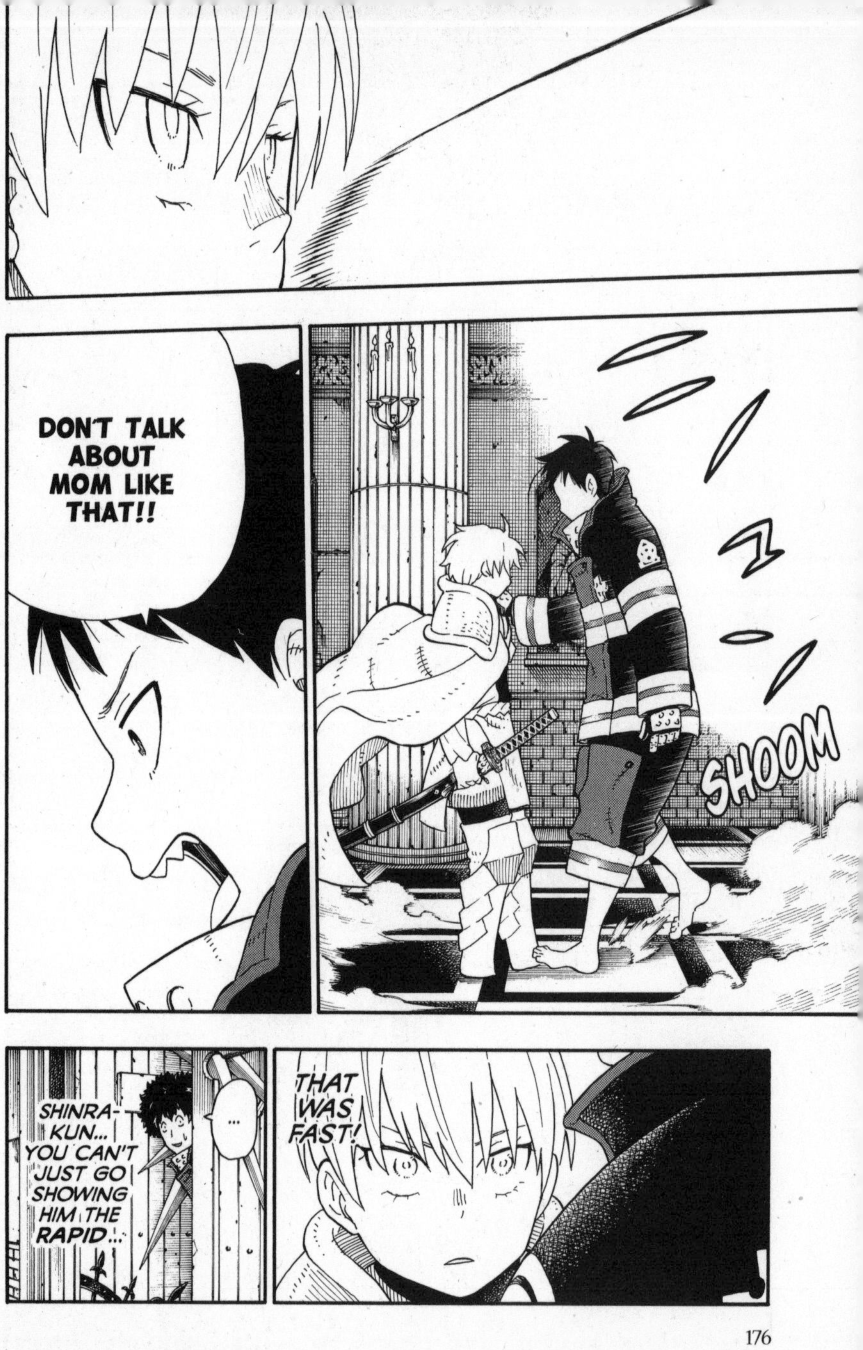
SHOOM
DON'T TALK ABOUT MOM LIKE THAT!!
THAT WAS FAST!
...
SHINRA-KUN... YOU CAN'T JUST GO SHOWING HIM THE RAPID...

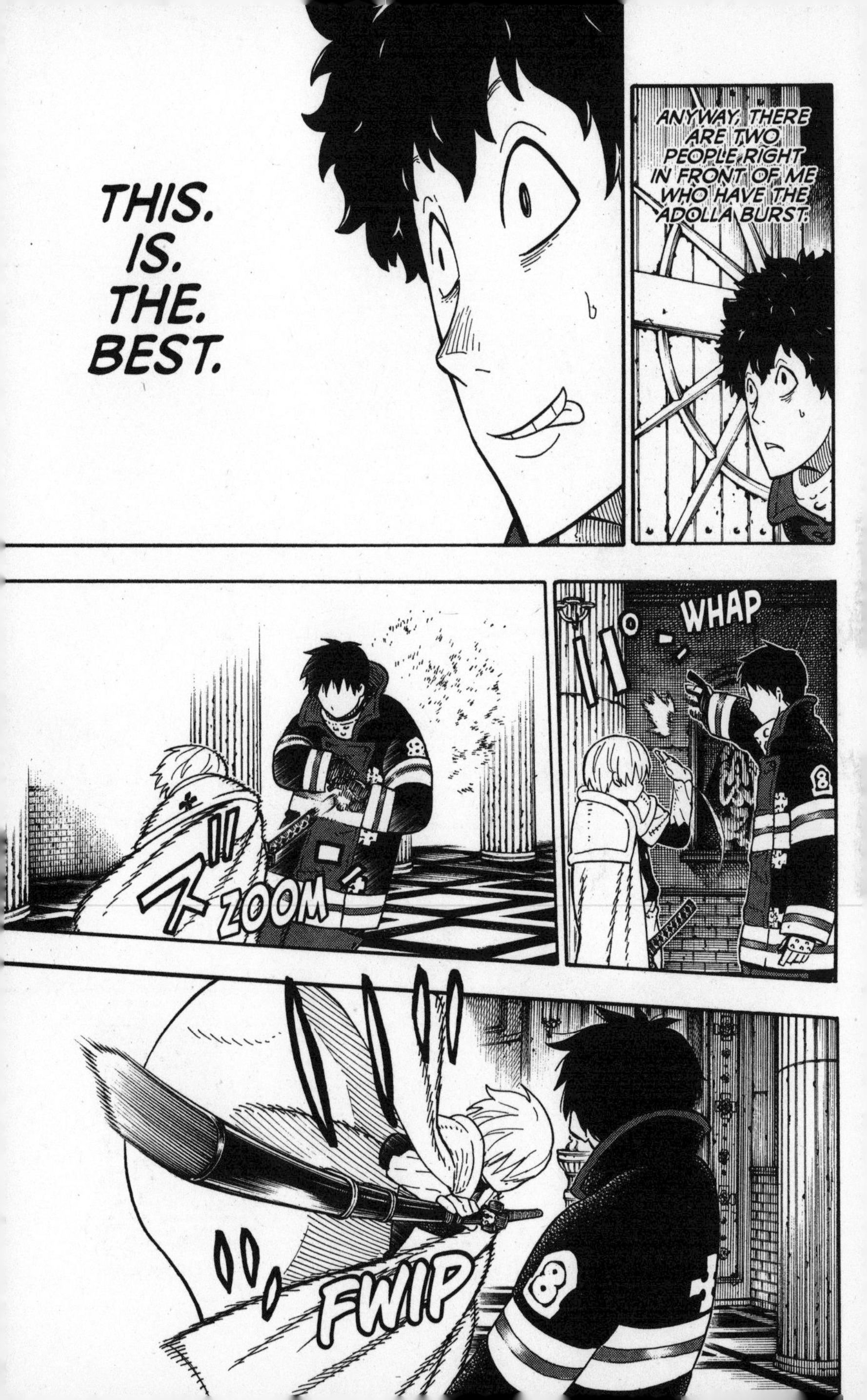
ANYWAY, THERE ARE TWO PEOPLE RIGHT IN FRONT OF ME WHO HAVE THE ADOLLA BURST.
THIS. IS. THE. BEST.
WHAP
ZOOM
FWIP

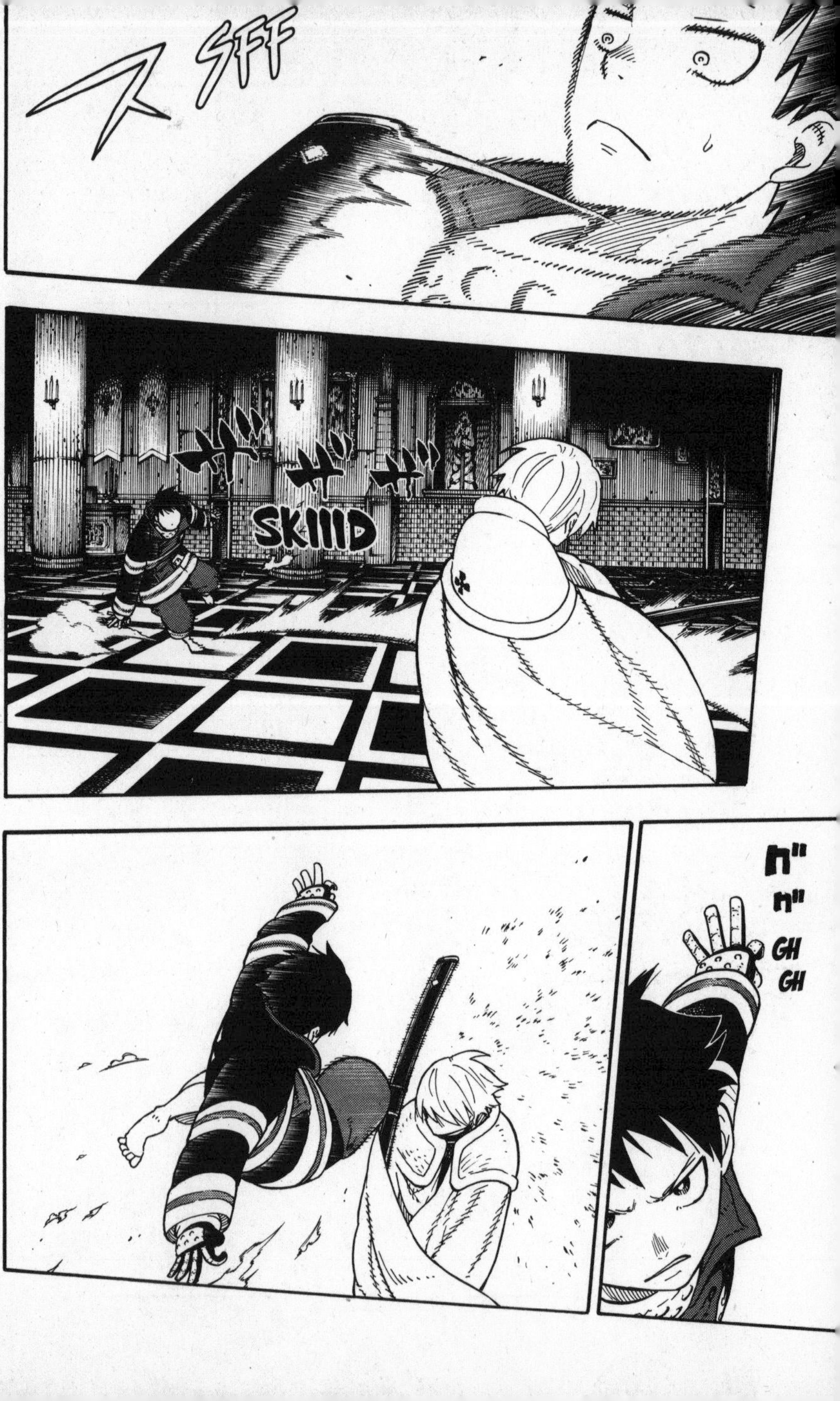
ス SFF
ザザザ
SKIIID
ガガ
GH
GH

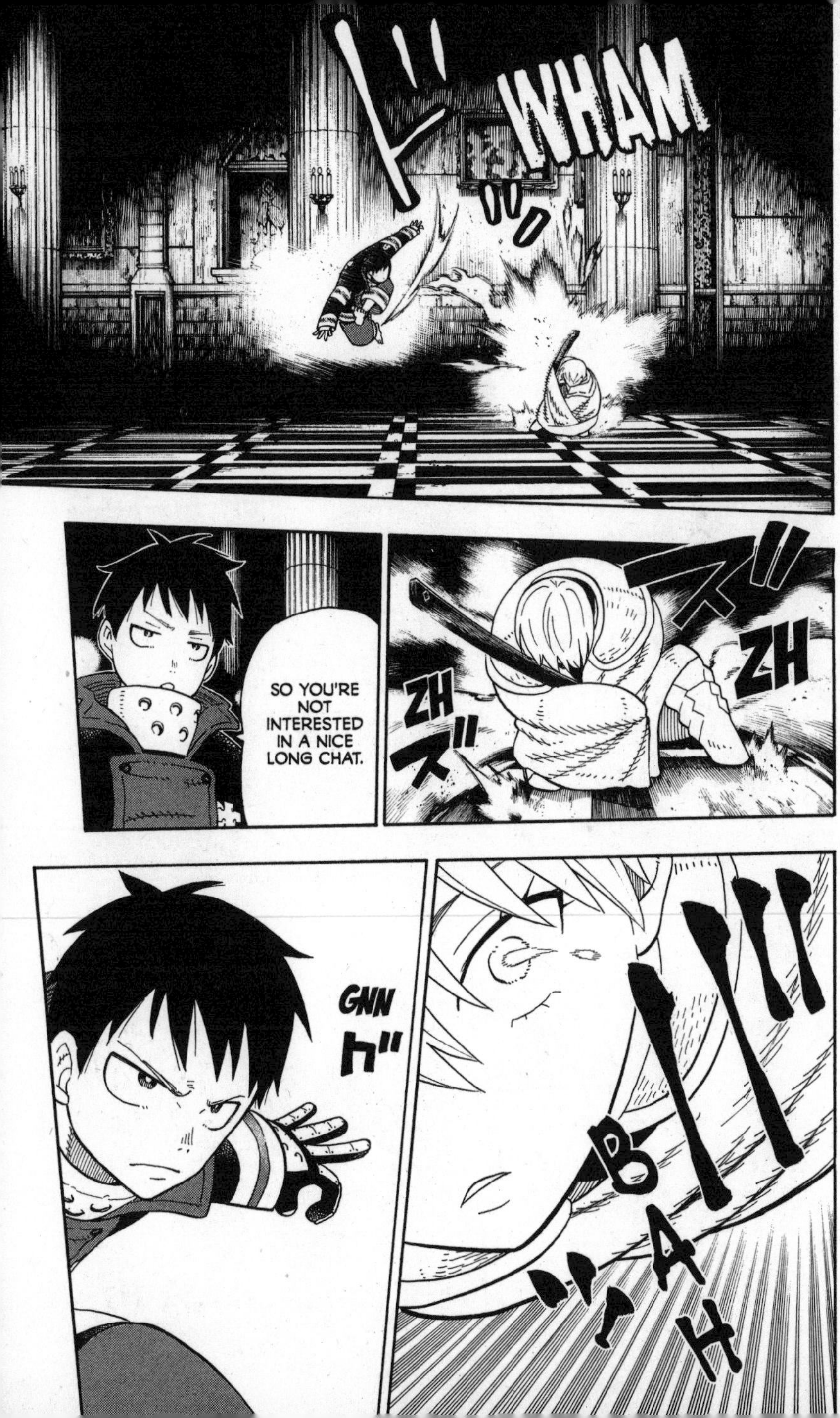
WHAM
ZH
ZH
SO YOU'RE NOT INTERESTED IN A NICE LONG CHAT.
BAH
GNN

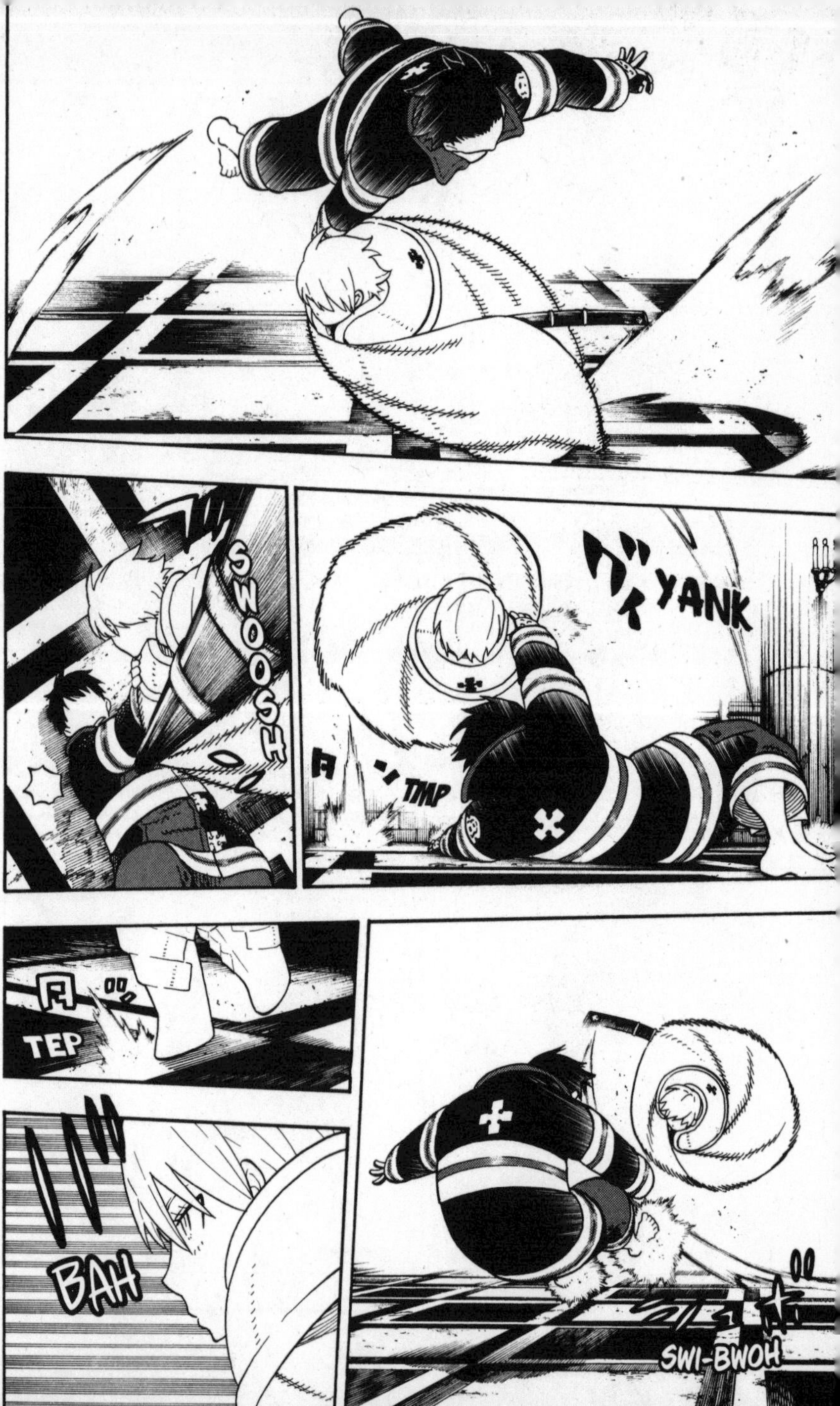
YANK
TMP
SWOOSH
SWI-BWOH
TEP
BAH

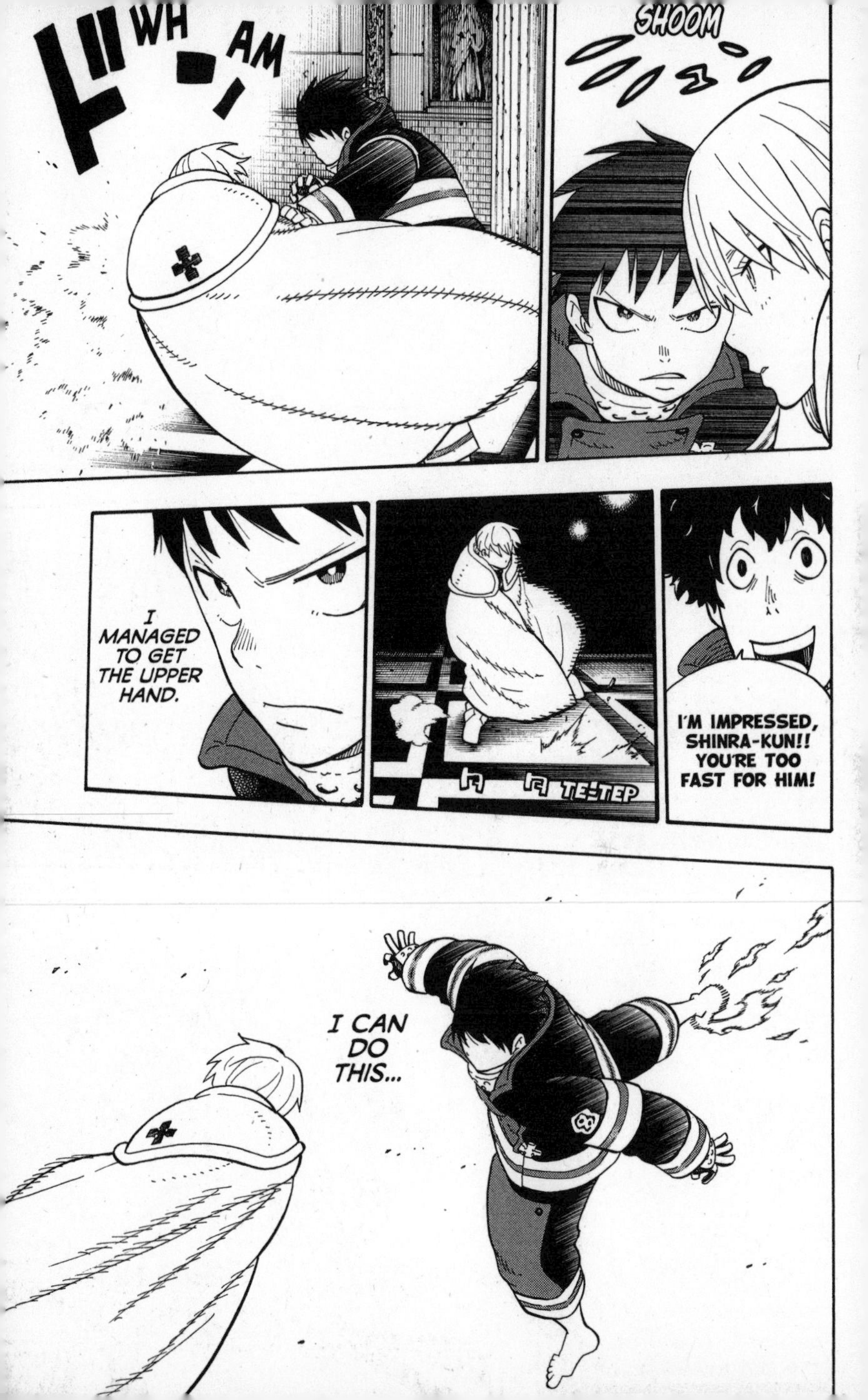
SHOOM
WHAM
I'M IMPRESSED, SHINRA-KUN!! YOU'RE TOO FAST FOR HIM!
TE-TEP
I MANAGED TO GET THE UPPER HAND.
I CAN DO THIS...

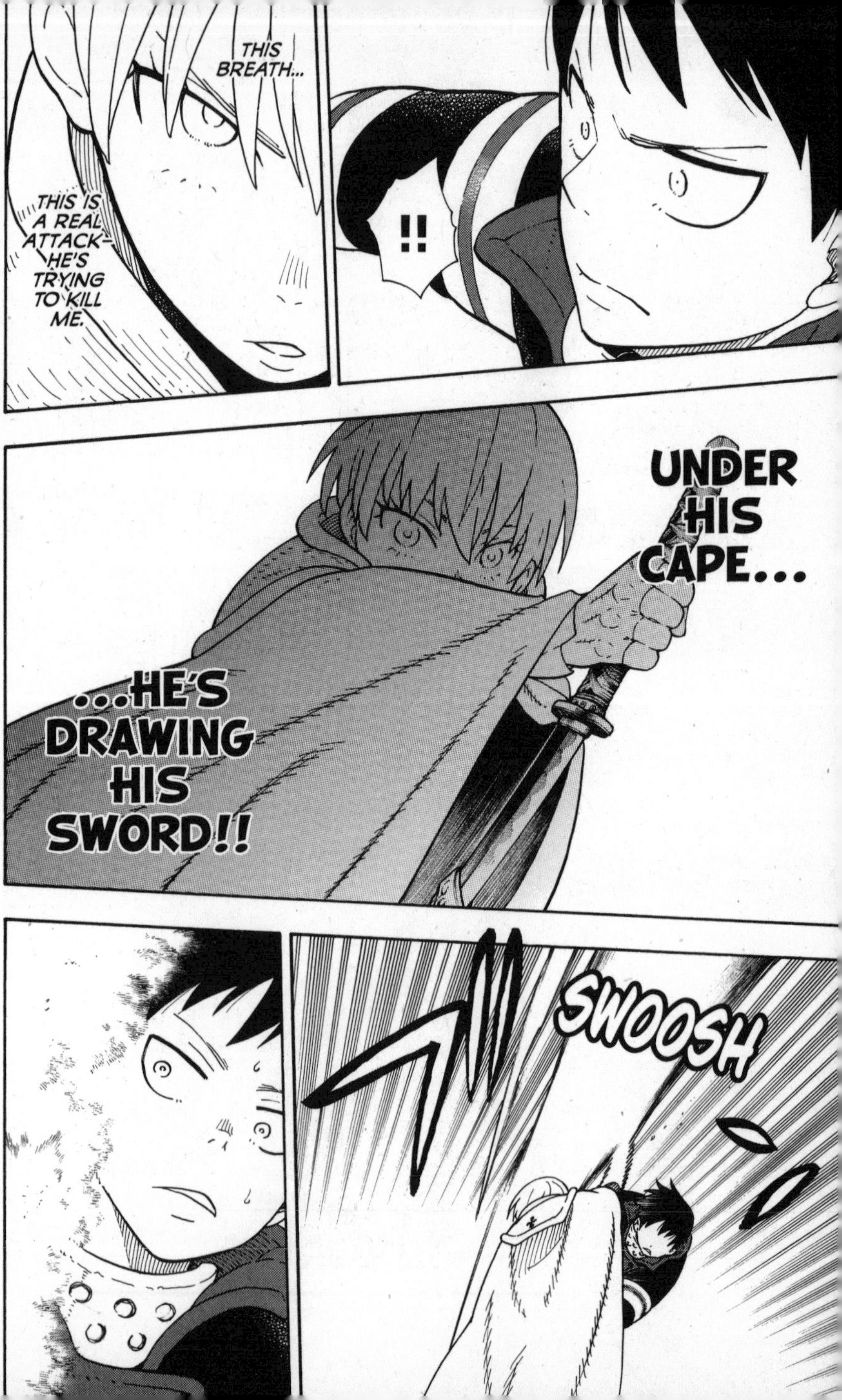
!!
THIS BREATH...
THIS IS A REAL ATTACK- HE'S TRYING TO KILL ME.
UNDER HIS CAPE...
...HE'S DRAWING HIS SWORD!!
SWOOSH

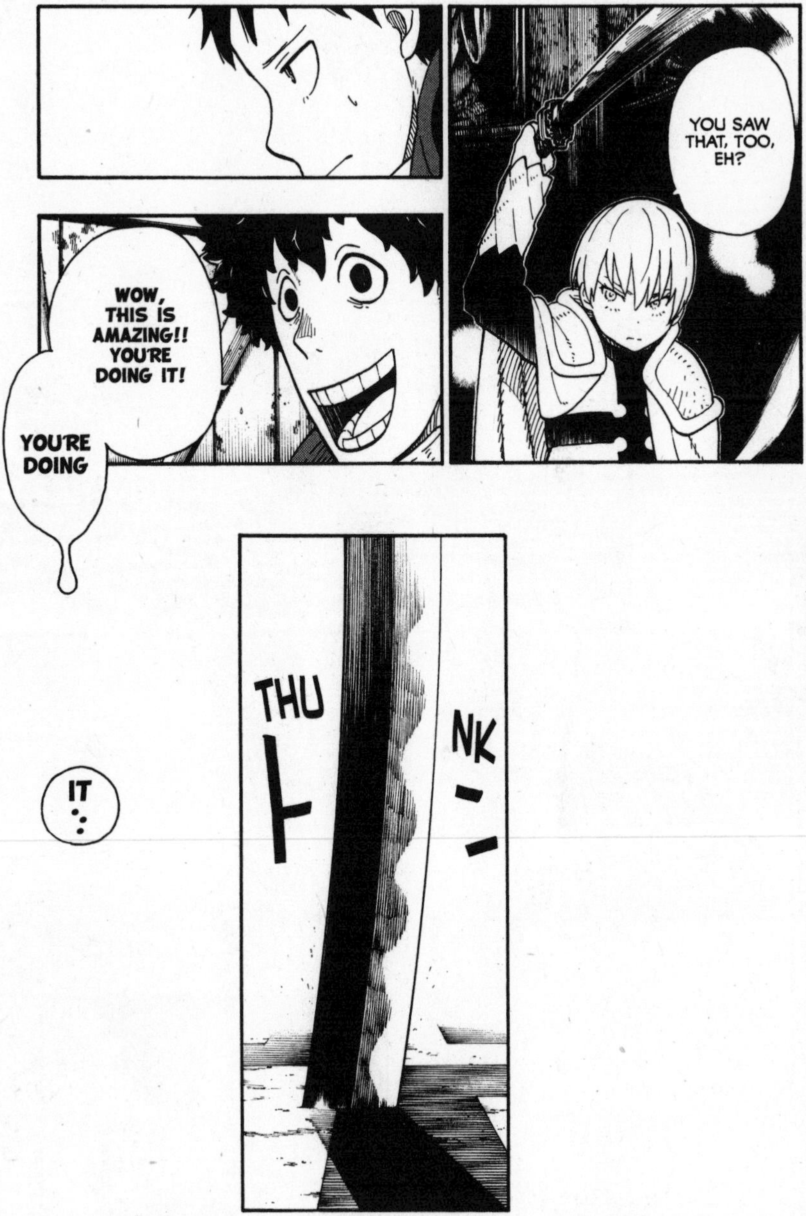
YOU SAW THAT, TOO, EH?
WOW, THIS IS AMAZING!! YOU'RE DOING IT!
YOU'RE DOING
IT..
THU
NK
トン

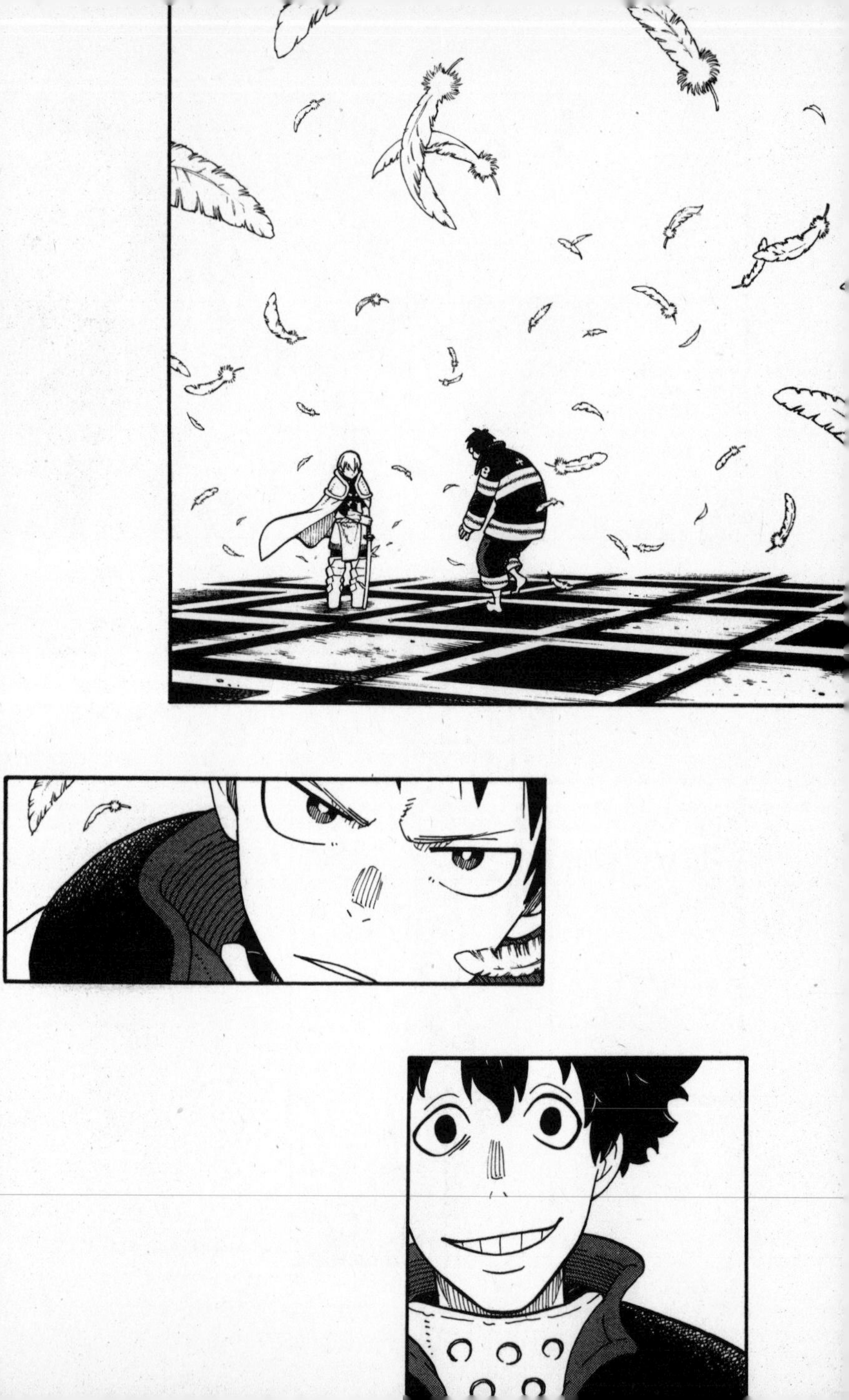

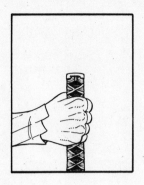
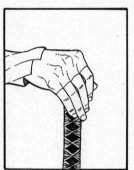

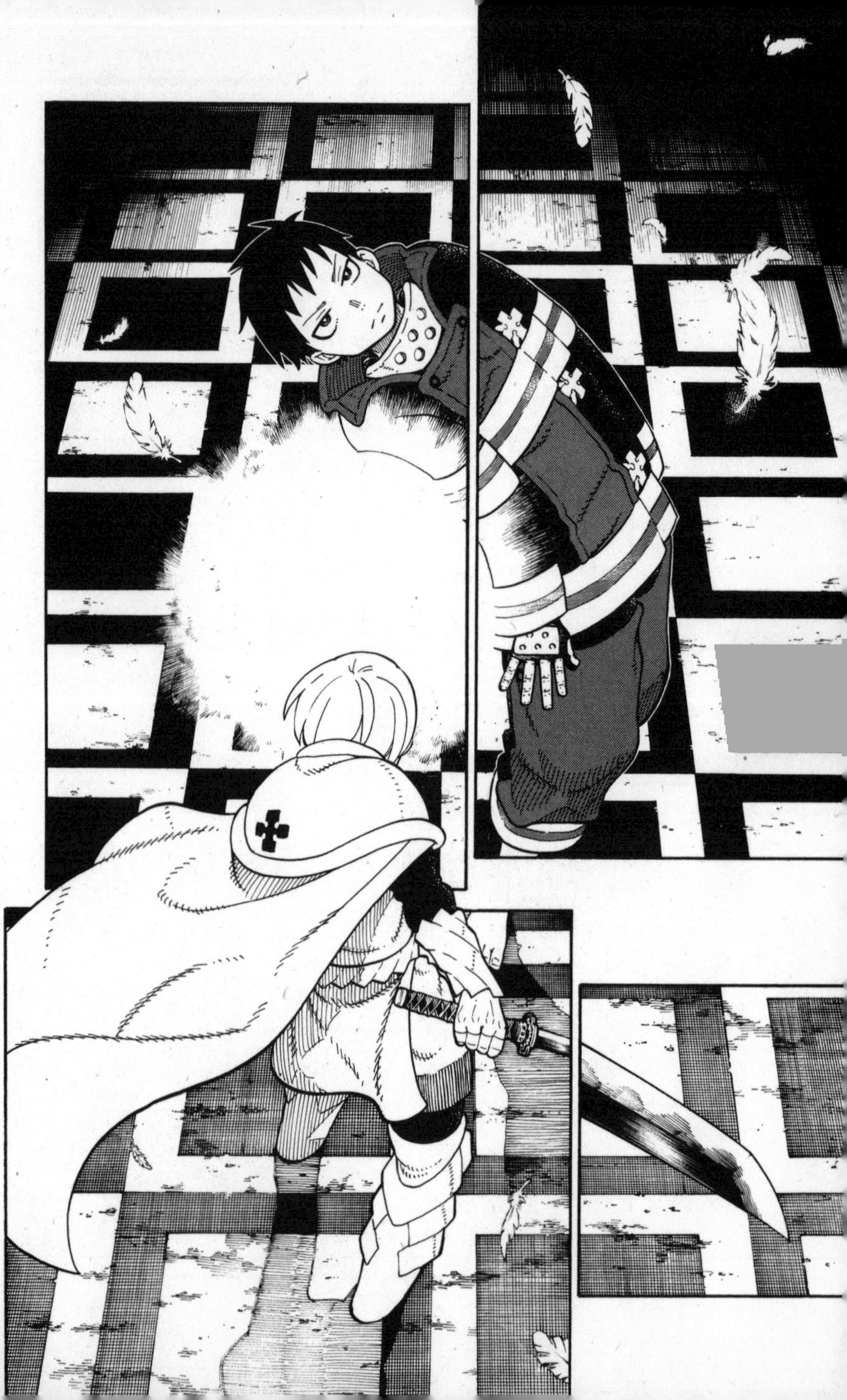

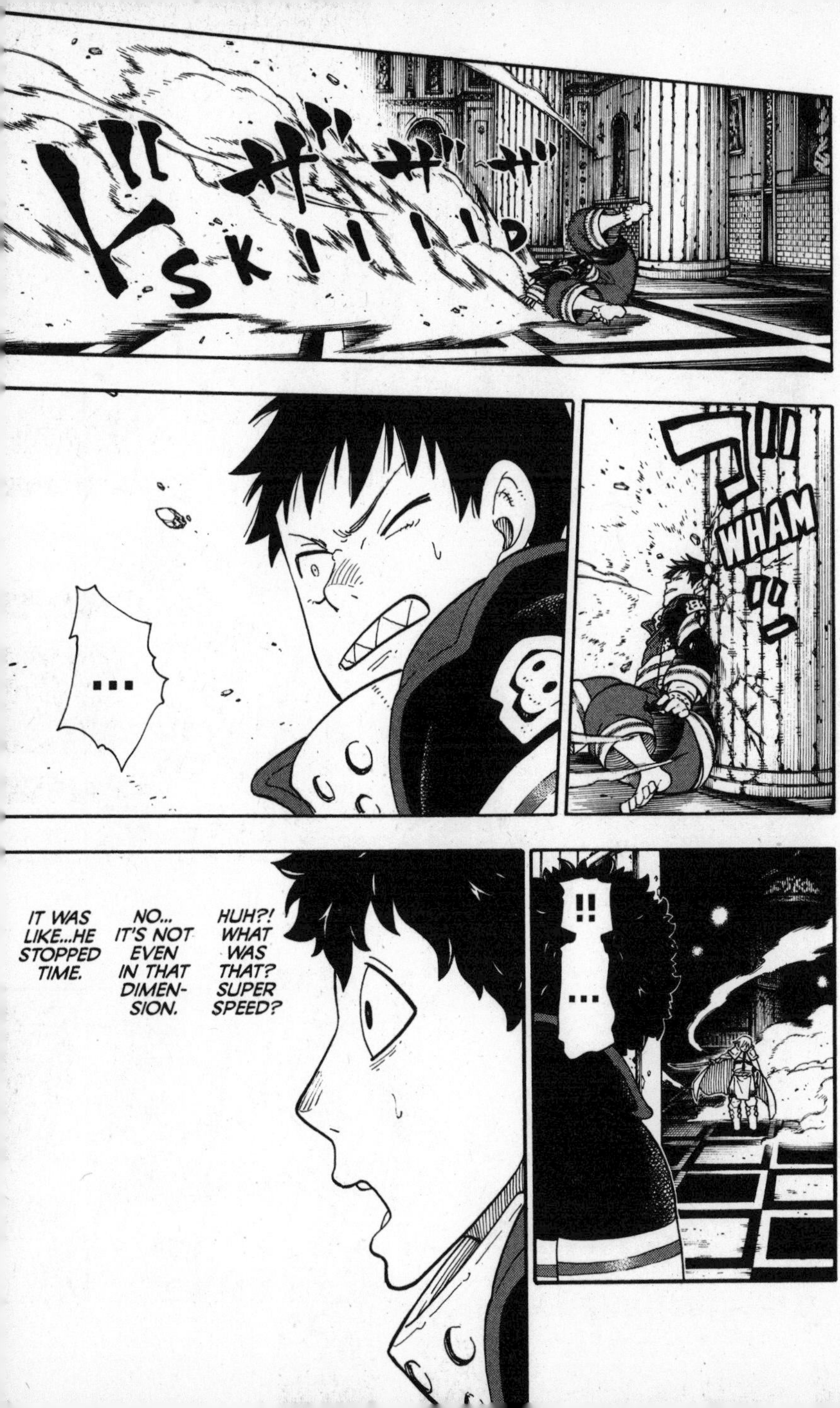
SKIIIID
WHAM
...
!!
...
HUH?! WHAT WAS THAT? SUPER SPEED?
NO... IT'S NOT EVEN IN THAT DIMENSION.
IT WAS LIKE...HE STOPPED TIME.

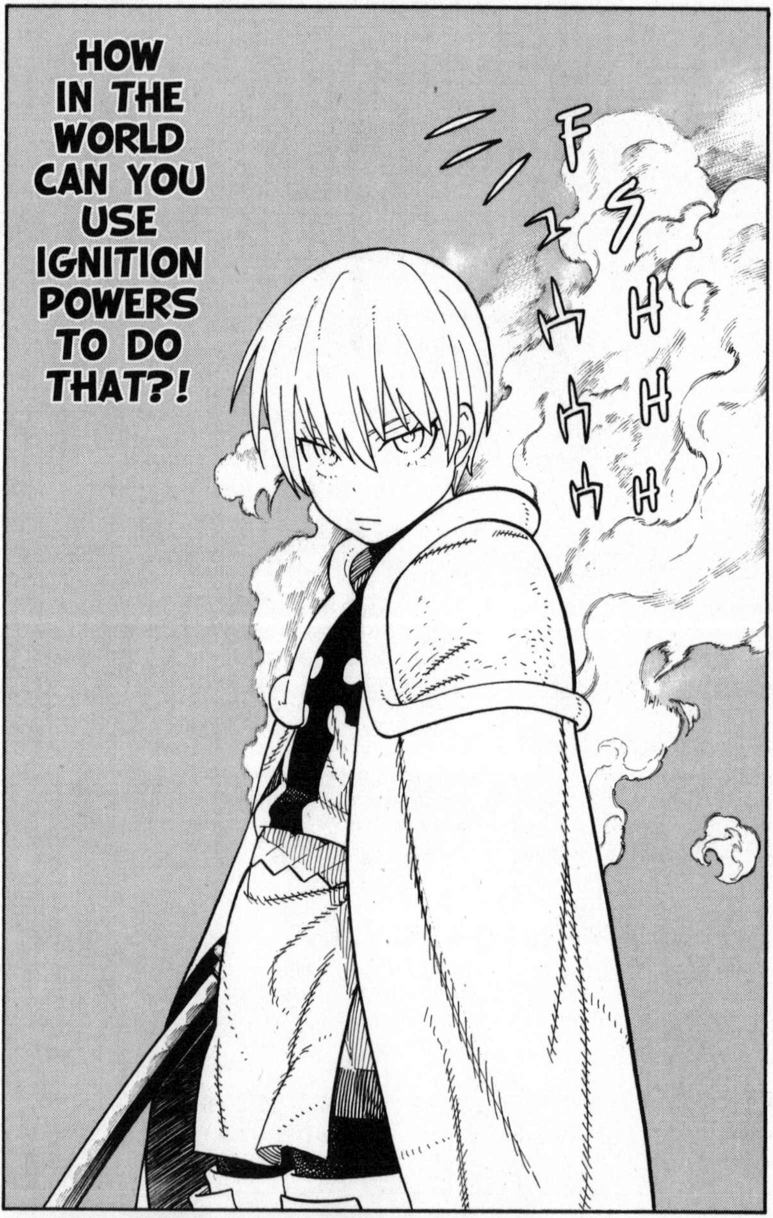
HOW IN THE WORLD CAN YOU USE IGNITION POWERS TO DO THAT?!
FSSHHHHHHH

TO BE CONTINUED IN VOLUME 10!!

Translation Notes:

Canaries in the coal mine, page 9

COMPANY 8 ARE CANARIES IN THE NETHER COAL MINE... BE CAREFUL DOWN THERE, ŌBI.

More literally, Hibana says that Company 8 has been turned into food tasters—servants whose job it is to taste food before an important leader eats it, to make sure it hasn't been poisoned. Because the Nether is underground, the translators felt it would be appropriate to make an allusion to the old practice (ancient by Hibana's time) of taking caged birds into a mine to test for safety. If the mine was filled with poison gas, the canary, as a small creature, would be more sensitive to the poison and die first, thus alerting the miners to the danger.

Horse and deer, page 87

As the reader can see, both of these helmets are marked with the name of a noble animal. As it would happen, in Japanese, when the characters for "horse" and "deer" are put together (in that order), they represent the word *baka*, meaning "stupid." This may come from a Chinese tale about an infamous eunuch who tested people's loyalty to him by pointing at a deer and calling it a horse—those who disagreed and said it was a deer were punished. Or it may simply mean that a fool cannot tell the difference between a horse and a deer. Regardless of the etymology, these two helmets together were clearly meant for Arthur.

Iai-calibur, page 100

Again, Arthur is combining his newfound training with his first love, knights. *Iaidō* is a Japanese martial art that is the study of conscious, aware swordsmanship, that especially has to do with the act of pulling the sword from the scabbard. Here, Arthur is combining the tactic with his plasma sword, Excalibur, and so also folds the name into the attack.

Kyū kyū nyoritsuryō, page 190

This is a phrase asking to quickly obey an order. It originated in China, where it was attached to official documents, but later came to be used to be used by exorcists in dispelling evil spirits. It is most particularly associated with Taoist spiritualists known as *onmyōji*.

Wriggle wriggle Wrigley Field, page 190

The place referenced in the original Japanese is not quite so close to Wrigley Field. The Japanese sound for wriggling is *kone-kone*, and so the sound effect became *kone-kone* Connecticut.

AFTERWORD MANGA: ATSUSHIYA

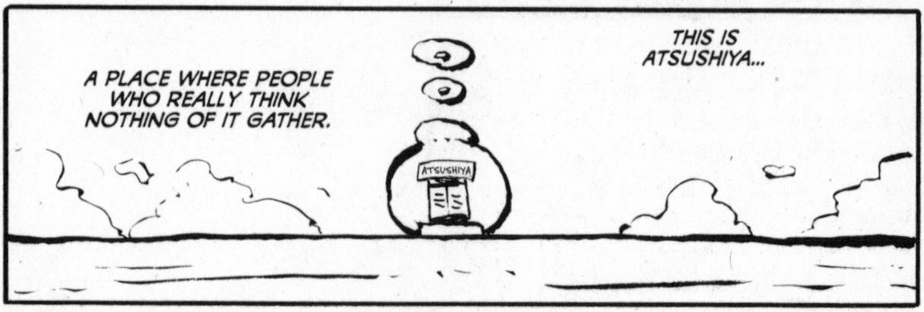
THIS IS ATSUSHIYA...
A PLACE WHERE PEOPLE WHO REALLY THINK NOTHING OF IT GATHER.
ATSUSHIYA

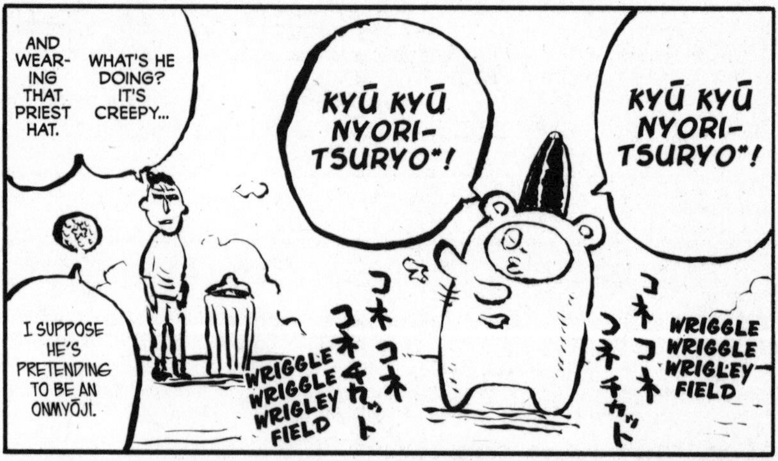
KYŪ KYŪ NYORI-TSURYO*!
コネコネコネチカット
WRIGGLE WRIGGLE WRIGLEY FIELD
KYŪ KYŪ NYORI-TSURYO*!
コネコネコネチカット
WRIGGLE WRIGGLE WRIGLEY FIELD
WHAT'S HE DOING? IT'S CREEPY...
AND WEARING THAT PRIEST HAT.
I SUPPOSE HE'S PRETENDING TO BE AN ONMYŌJI.

*"Make it so"

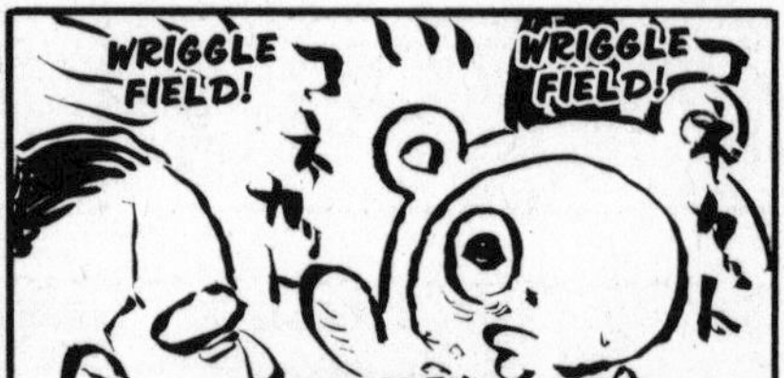
コネチカット
WRIGGLE FIELD!
コネチカット
WRIGGLE FIELD!
WRIGGLEY FIELD!
コネチカット
KYŪ KYŪ NYORI-TSURYO!! KYŪ KYŪ NYORI-TSURYO!!
WAAAAAHH!

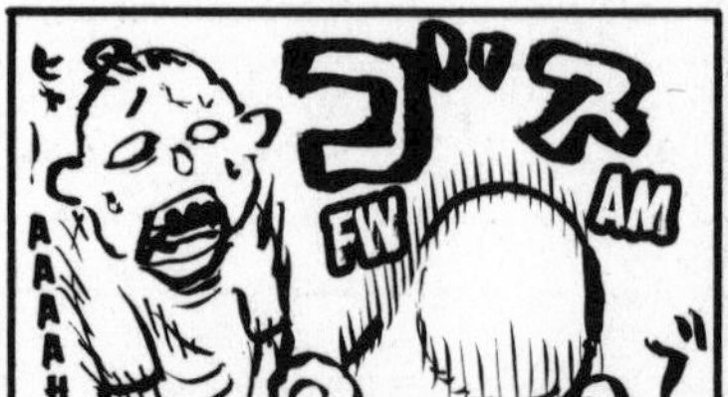
ゴス
FWAM
PFFT
P-PFFFT
PFFT
AAAAHH!!

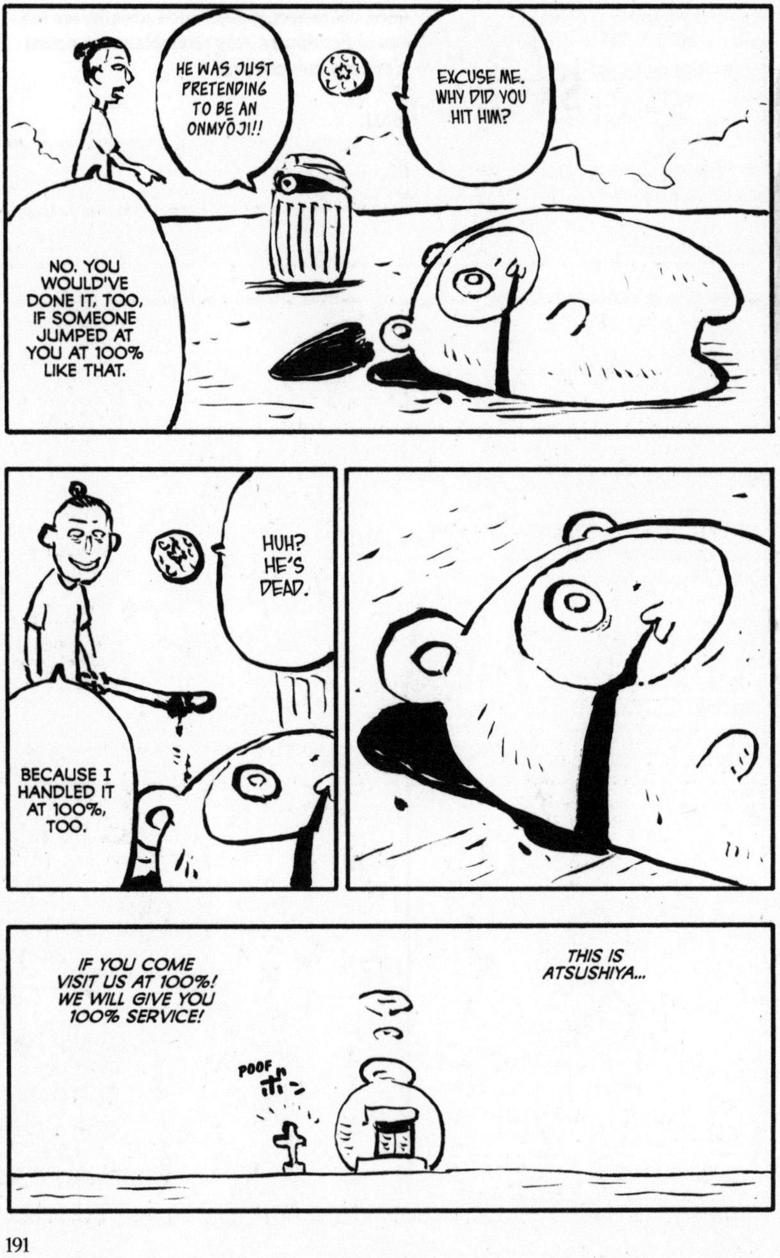
EXCUSE ME. WHY DID YOU HIT HIM?
HE WAS JUST PRETENDING TO BE AN ONMYŌJI!!
NO. YOU WOULD'VE DONE IT, TOO, IF SOMEONE JUMPED AT YOU AT 100% LIKE THAT.
HUH? HE'S DEAD.
BECAUSE I HANDLED IT AT 100%, TOO.
THIS IS ATSUSHIYA...
POOF
ポン
IF YOU COME VISIT US AT 100%! WE WILL GIVE YOU 100% SERVICE!

Fire Force volume 9 is a work of fiction. Na
products of the author's imagination or are
events, locales, or persons, living or dead, is

A Kodansha Comics Trade Paperback Orig

Published in the United States by Kodansha Comics, an imprint of Kodansha USA Publishing, LLC, New York.

Publication rights for this English edition arranged through Kodansha Ltd., Tokyo.

First published in Japan in 2017 by Kodansha Ltd., Tokyo.

ISBN 978-1-63236-548-4

Printed in the United States of America.

www.kodanshacomics.com

9 8 7 6 5 4 3 2 1

Translation: Alethea Nibley & Athena Nibley
Lettering: AndWorld Design
Editing: Lauren Scanlan
Kodansha Comics edition cover design: Phil Balsman